nal · Danbi Original · Danbi Original · Danbi Original · D

Cynical Orange

vol.3

Yun JiUn

ice
Kunion

About the Creator

Cynical Orange

Ji-Un Yun

Ji-Un Yun made her professional debut in 2000 by placing second in a Manhwa competition with her short story <Are you? I am!>. However, she was already famous among the amateur Manhwa clubs in Korea for her delicate drawings, unique heroines, and distinctive plots. Her special style of combining artistic creativity with beautiful composition has led to an enormous fan base in Asia.

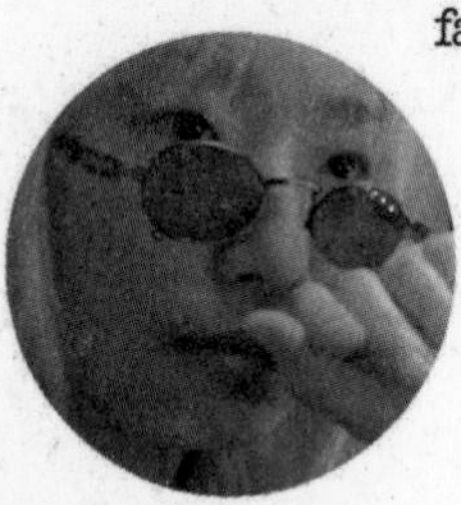

Other major works
<Are you? I am!>, <The Doll's Request>, <Happy End>, <Hush>, <Excel>

Words from the Creator

When
I was young, almost all the
comic books I read were about robots.
Some of the titles I remember are *Ironman
28* (which was super popular), the *Mazinga*
series, *Geta*, *Grandizer*, *Voltex V*, *Dancougar*, *Gold
Lion*, *Psycho-Armor Gobarian*, *Titan*, etc., to name a
few. I read so many of them, I don't even remember
all the titles. As I got older, I got into realistic
robot series like *Gundam*. I also rented
Flashman and *Bioman*. The era of
mechanical robots seems to be over, ending
with *Evangelion*, but my thought process is still
very much influenced by the memory of the robot
comics I read. For example, I tend to punish
wrongdoings in my comics the same way they did in
those comics. Sigh...*Genesis Climber Mospeada*
was such a wonderful series...

- Ji-Un Yun

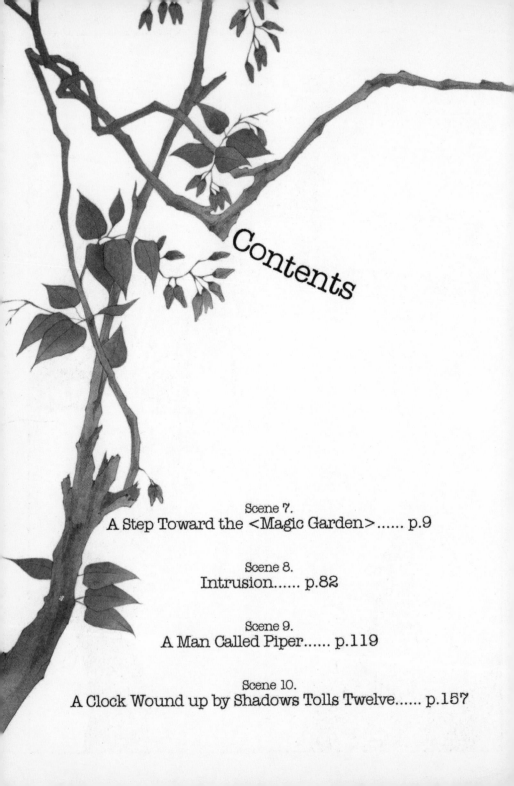

Contents

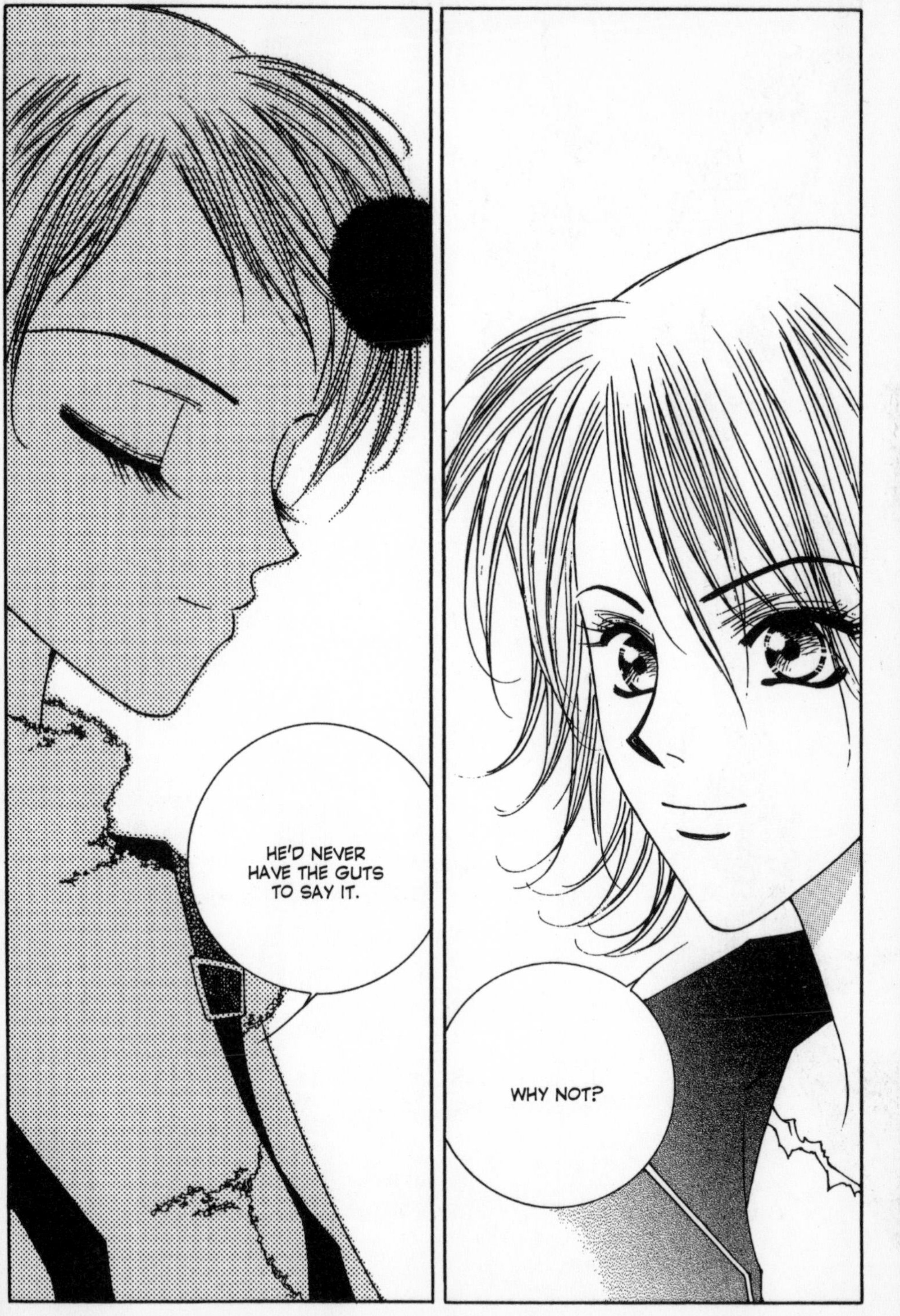
HE'D NEVER HAVE THE GUTS TO SAY IT.
WHY NOT?

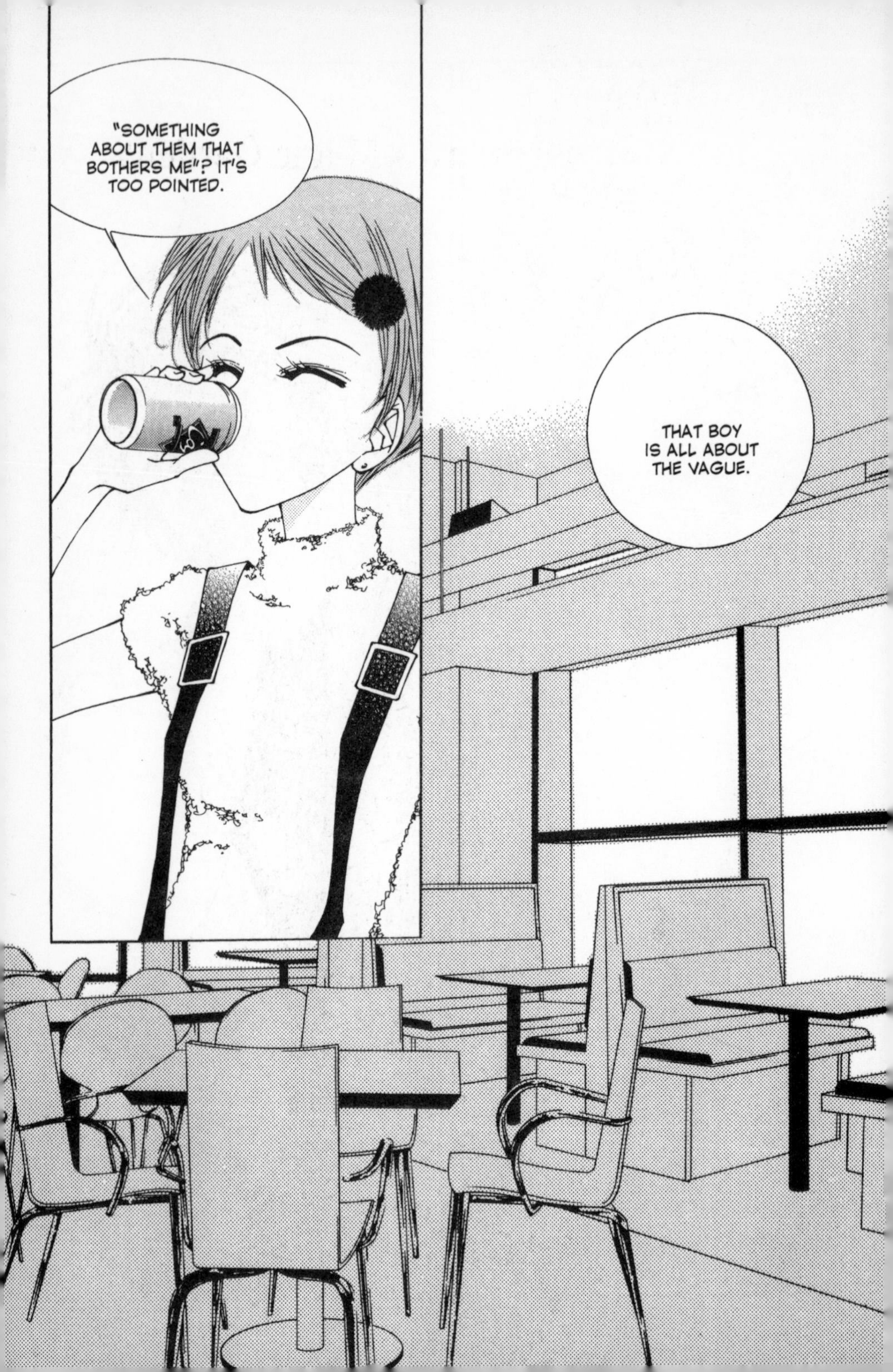
"SOMETHING ABOUT THEM THAT BOTHERS ME"? IT'S TOO POINTED.
THAT BOY IS ALL ABOUT THE VAGUE.

Scene. 7

A Step Toward <Magic Garden>

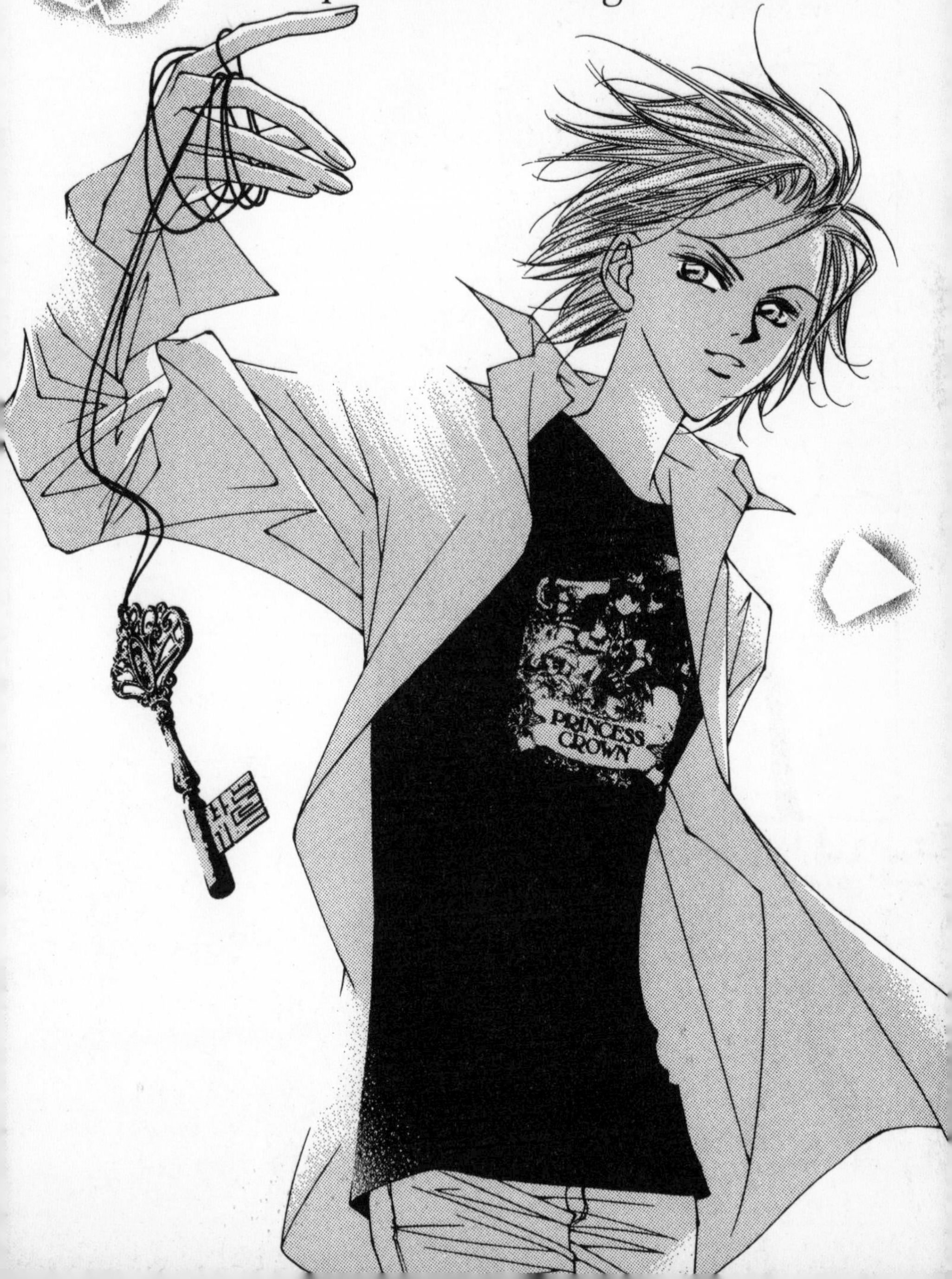
PRINCESS
CROWN

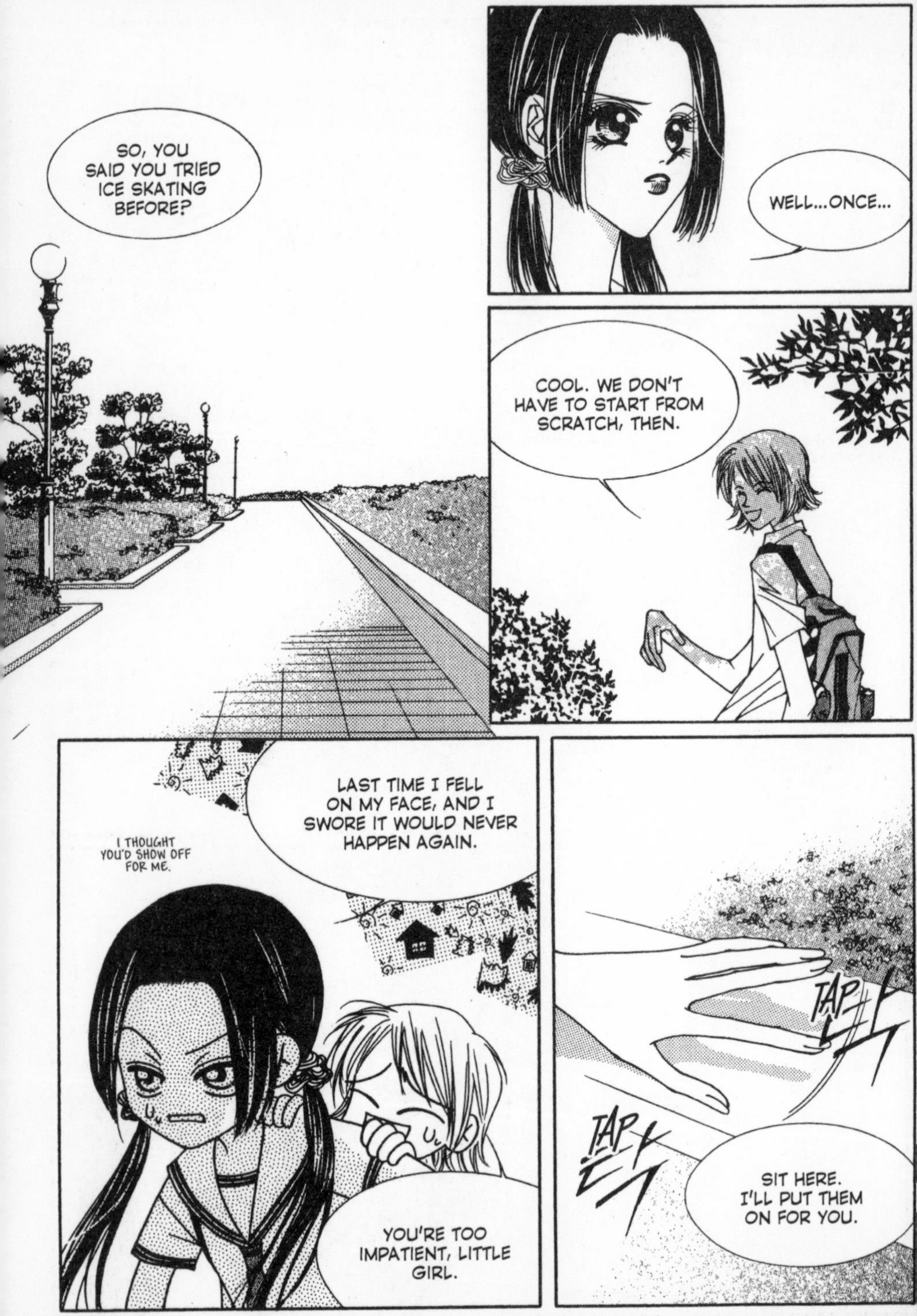
SO, YOU SAID YOU TRIED ICE SKATING BEFORE?
WELL...ONCE...
COOL. WE DON'T HAVE TO START FROM SCRATCH, THEN.
LAST TIME I FELL ON MY FACE, AND I SWORE IT WOULD NEVER HAPPEN AGAIN.
I THOUGHT YOU'D SHOW OFF FOR ME.
YOU'RE TOO IMPATIENT, LITTLE GIRL.
TAP
TAP
SIT HERE. I'LL PUT THEM ON FOR YOU.

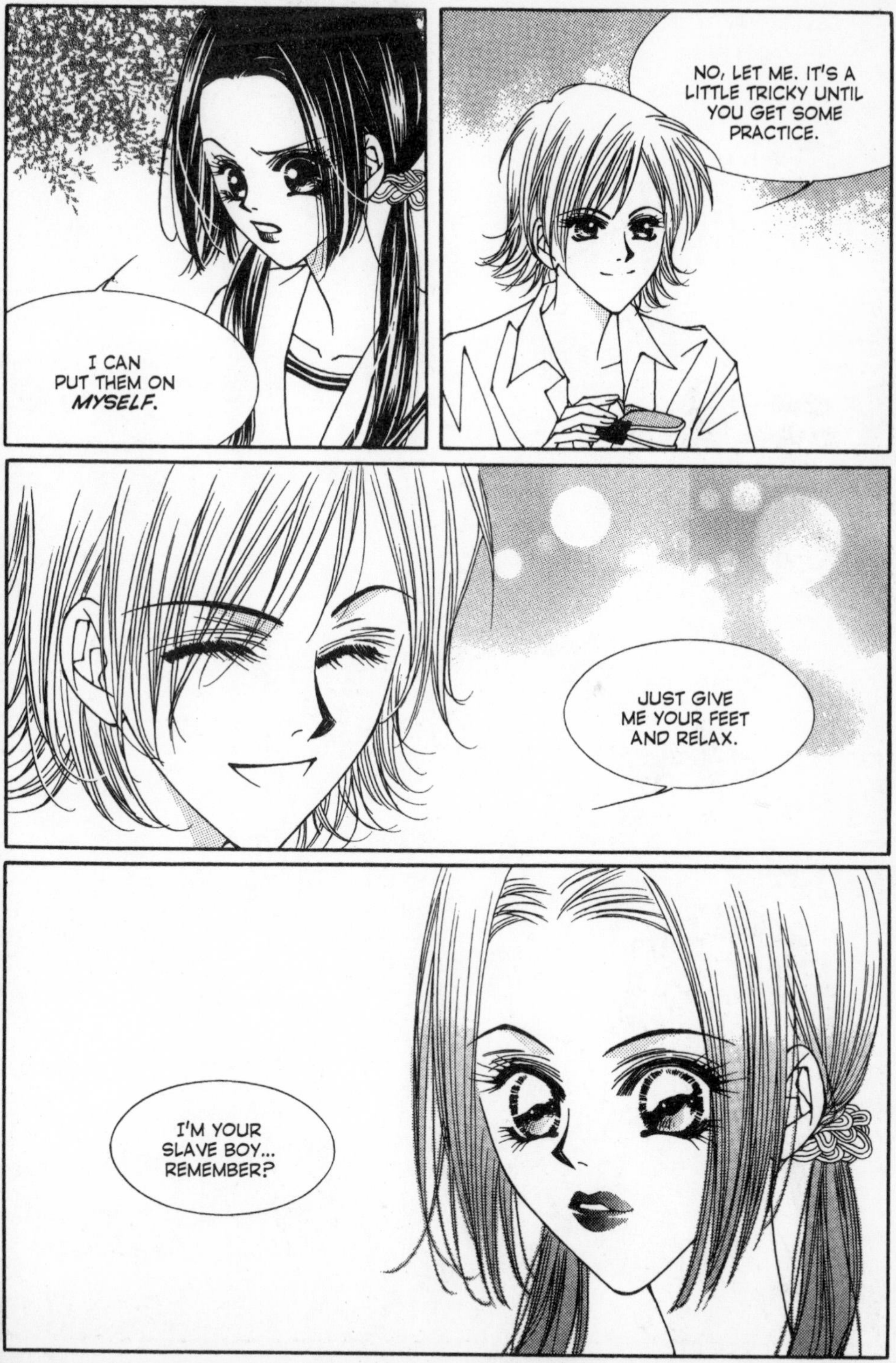
I CAN PUT THEM ON *MYSELF*.
NO, LET ME. IT'S A LITTLE TRICKY UNTIL YOU GET SOME PRACTICE.
JUST GIVE ME YOUR FEET AND RELAX.
I'M YOUR SLAVE BOY... REMEMBER?

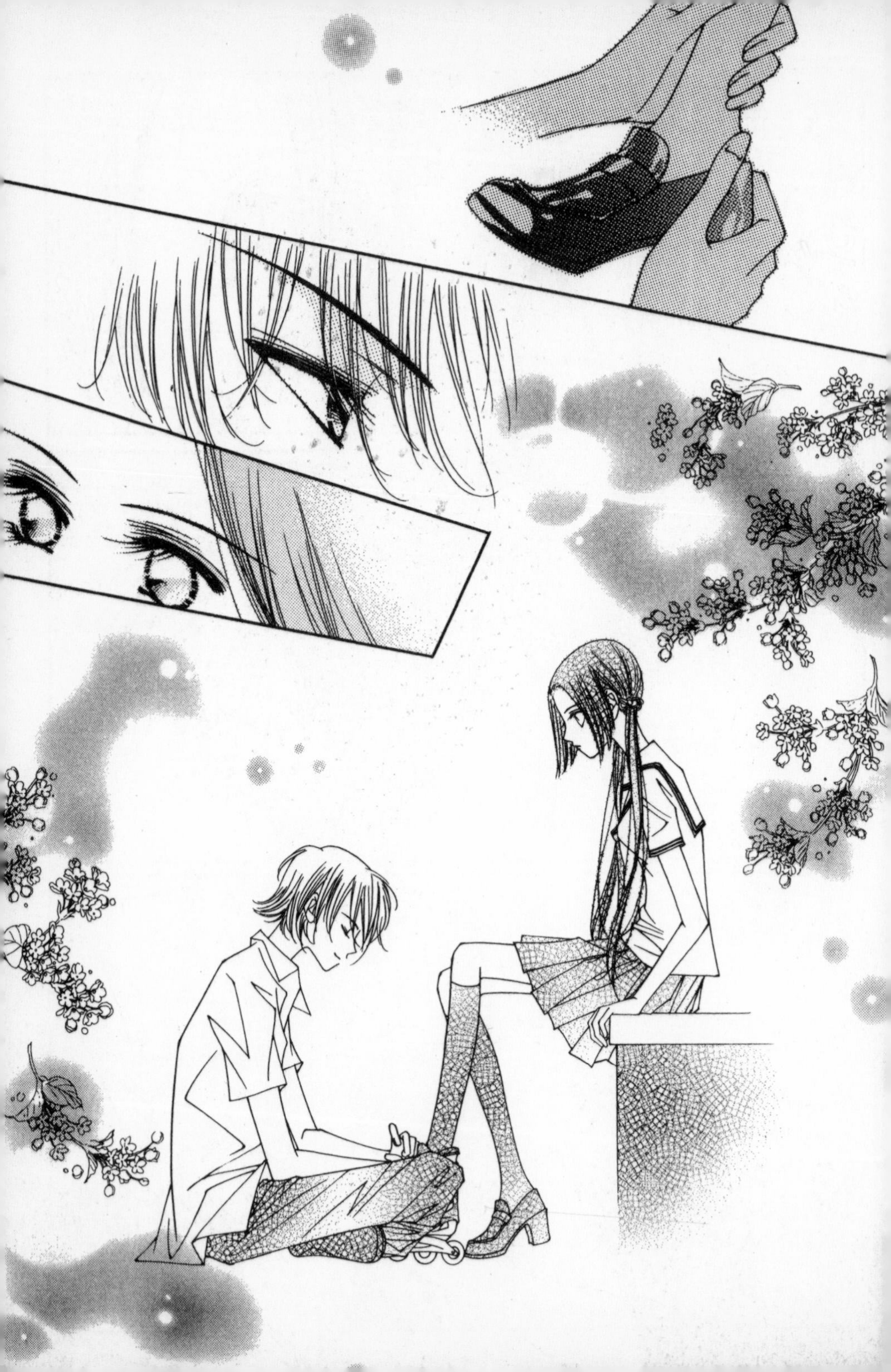

* "COME ON" BY EVE

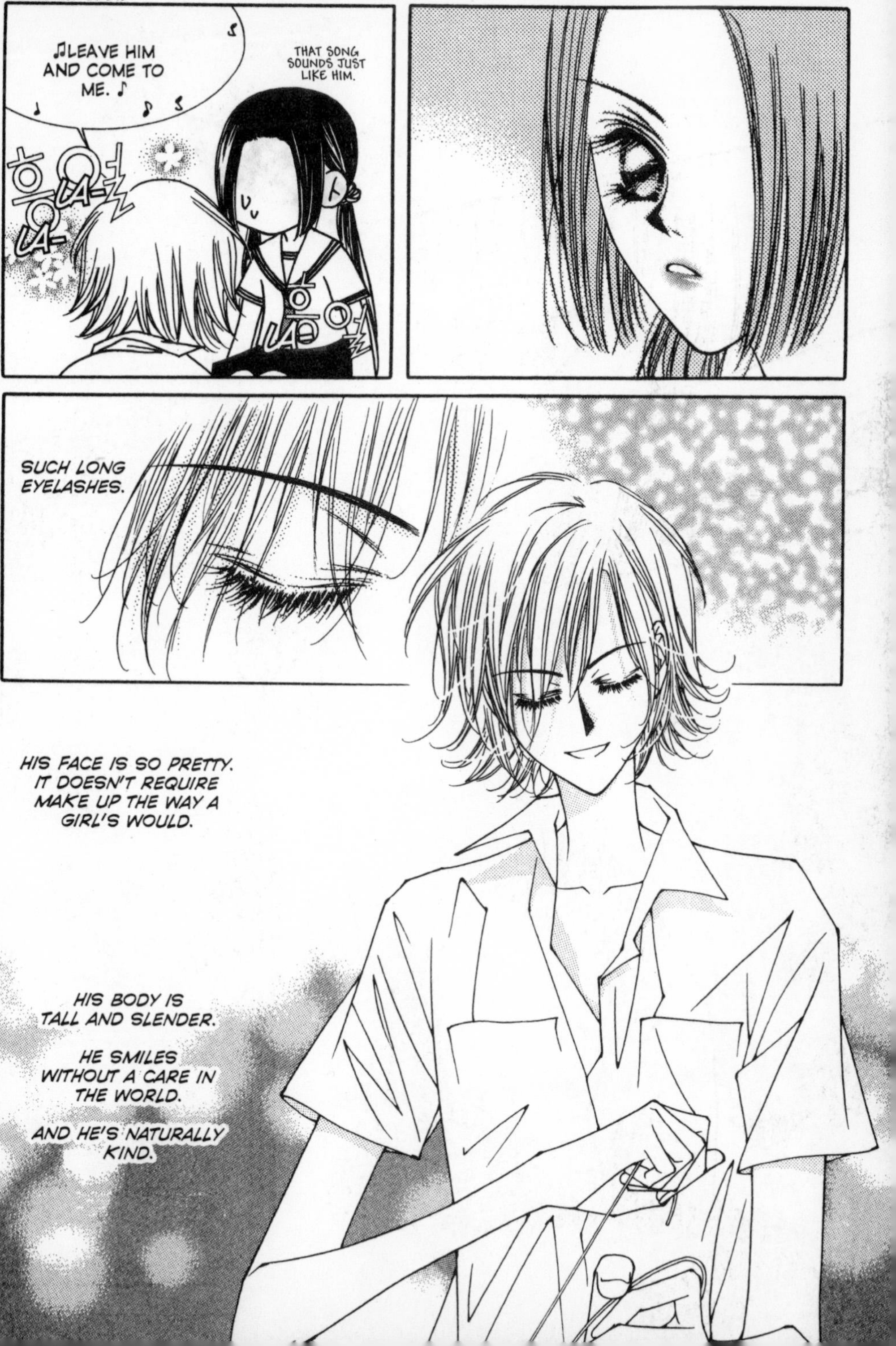

♫LEAVE HIM AND COME TO ME. ♪
흥얼 LA- LA-
THAT SONG SOUNDS JUST LIKE HIM.
흥얼 LA-
SUCH LONG EYELASHES.
HIS FACE IS SO PRETTY. IT DOESN'T REQUIRE MAKE UP THE WAY A GIRL'S WOULD.
HIS BODY IS TALL AND SLENDER.
HE SMILES WITHOUT A CARE IN THE WORLD.
AND HE'S NATURALLY KIND.

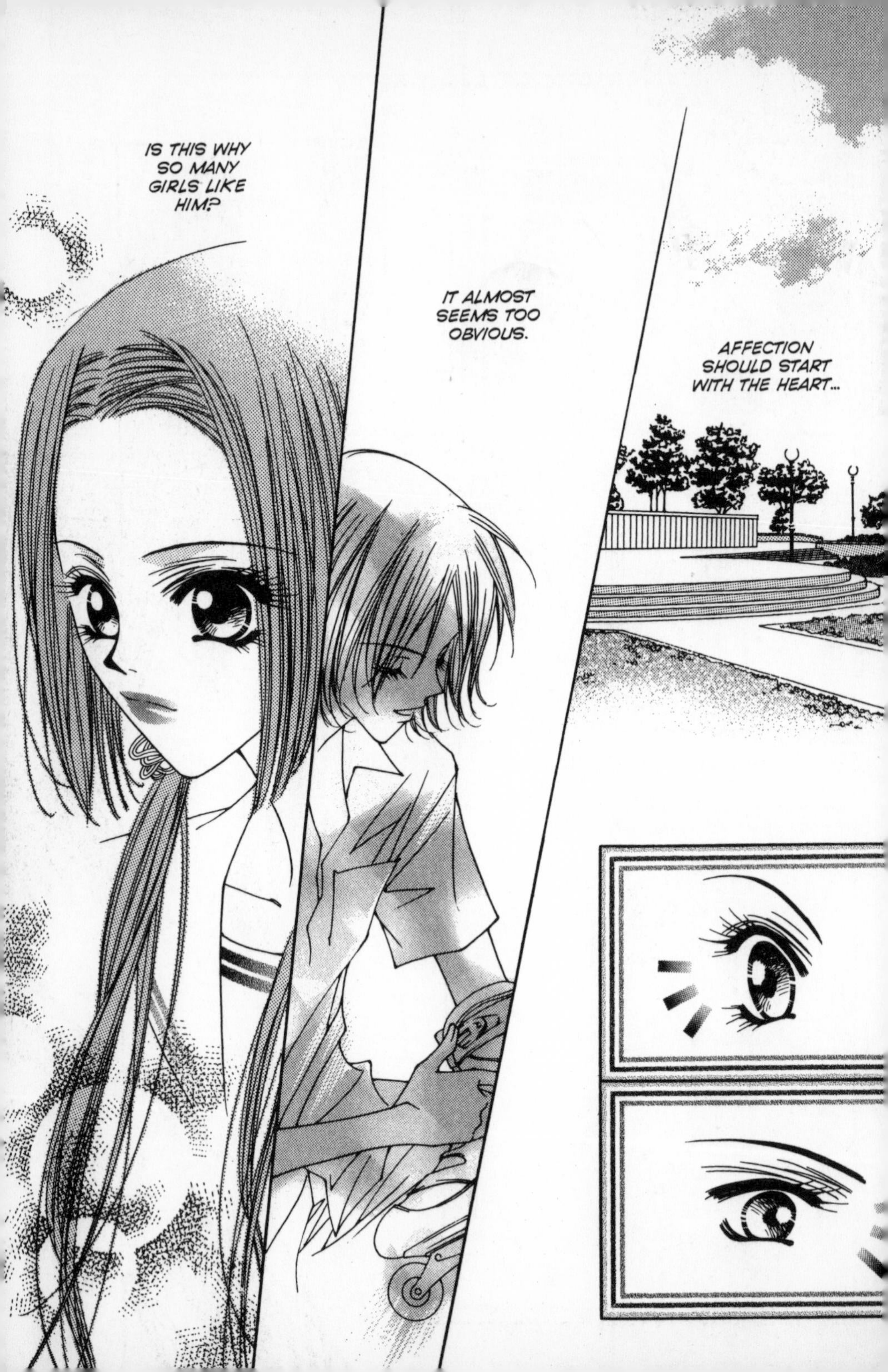
IS THIS WHY SO MANY GIRLS LIKE HIM?
IT ALMOST SEEMS TOO OBVIOUS.
AFFECTION SHOULD START WITH THE HEART...

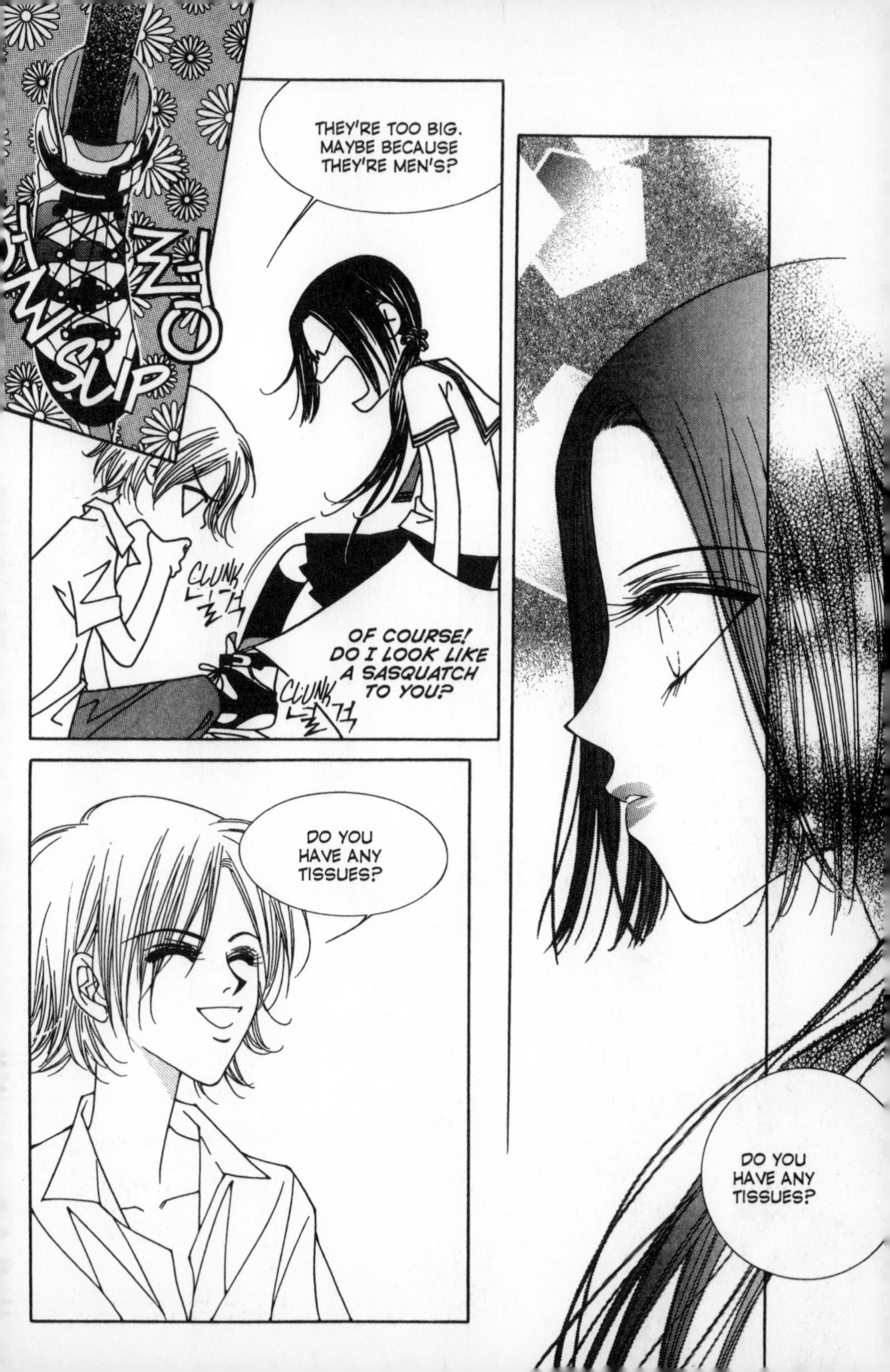
SLIP
THEY'RE TOO BIG. MAYBE BECAUSE THEY'RE MEN'S?
CLUNK
OF COURSE! DO I LOOK LIKE A SASQUATCH TO YOU?
CLUNK
DO YOU HAVE ANY TISSUES?
DO YOU HAVE ANY TISSUES?

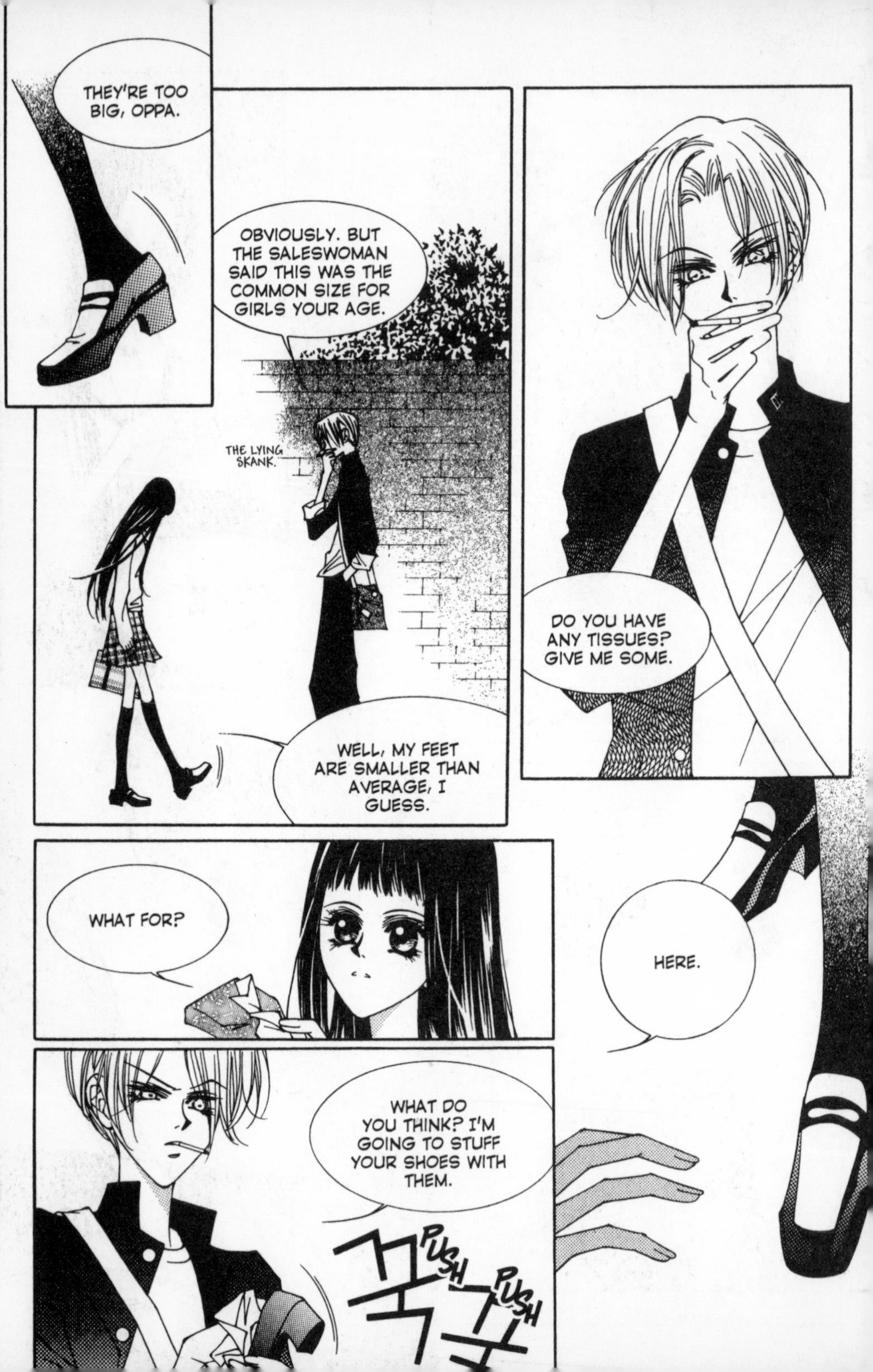
THEY'RE TOO BIG, OPPA.
OBVIOUSLY. BUT THE SALESWOMAN SAID THIS WAS THE COMMON SIZE FOR GIRLS YOUR AGE.
THE LYING SKANK.
WELL, MY FEET ARE SMALLER THAN AVERAGE, I GUESS.
DO YOU HAVE ANY TISSUES? GIVE ME SOME.
WHAT FOR?
HERE.
WHAT DO YOU THINK? I'M GOING TO STUFF YOUR SHOES WITH THEM.
PUSH
PUSH

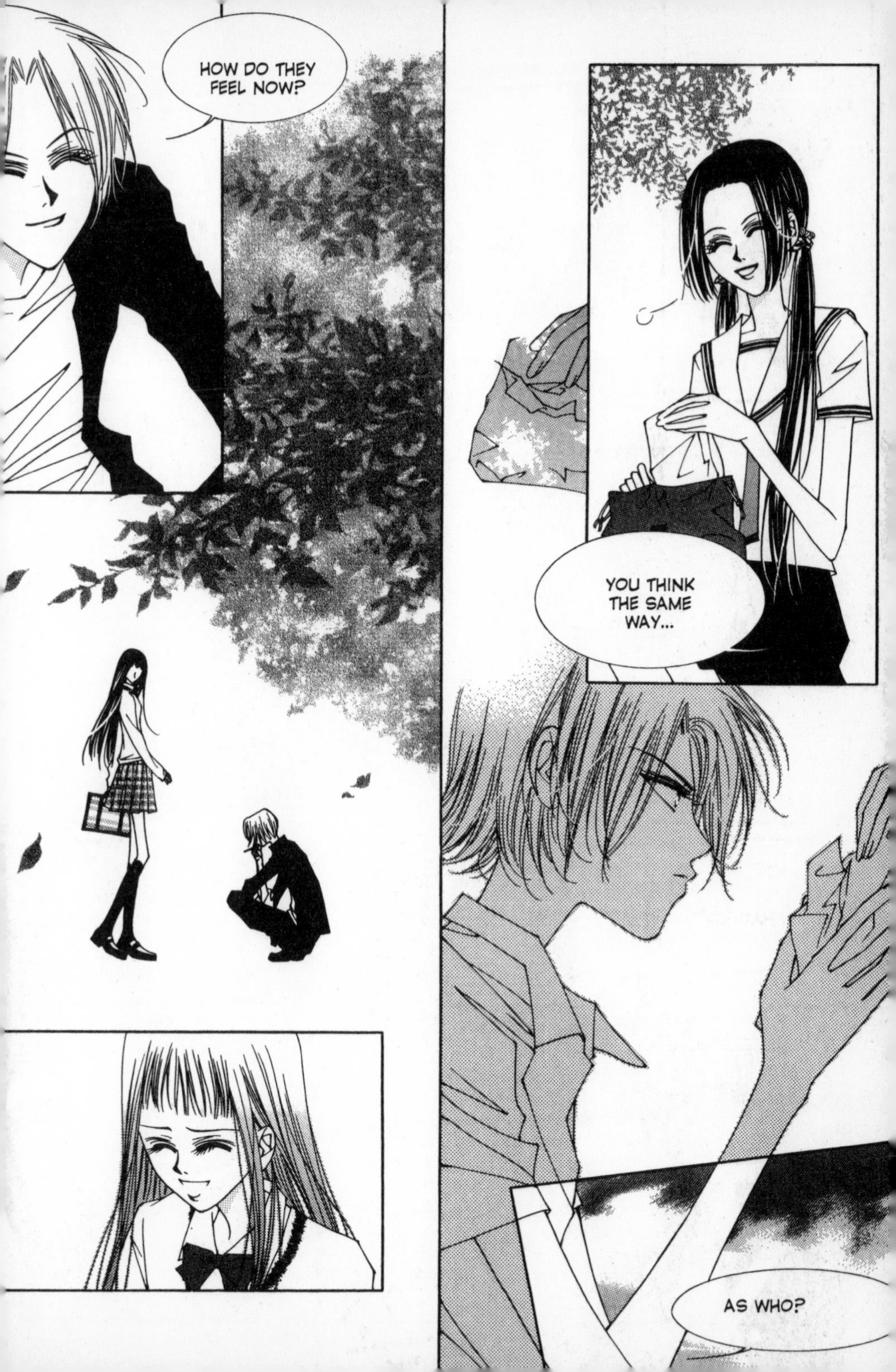
HOW DO THEY FEEL NOW?
YOU THINK THE SAME WAY...
AS WHO?

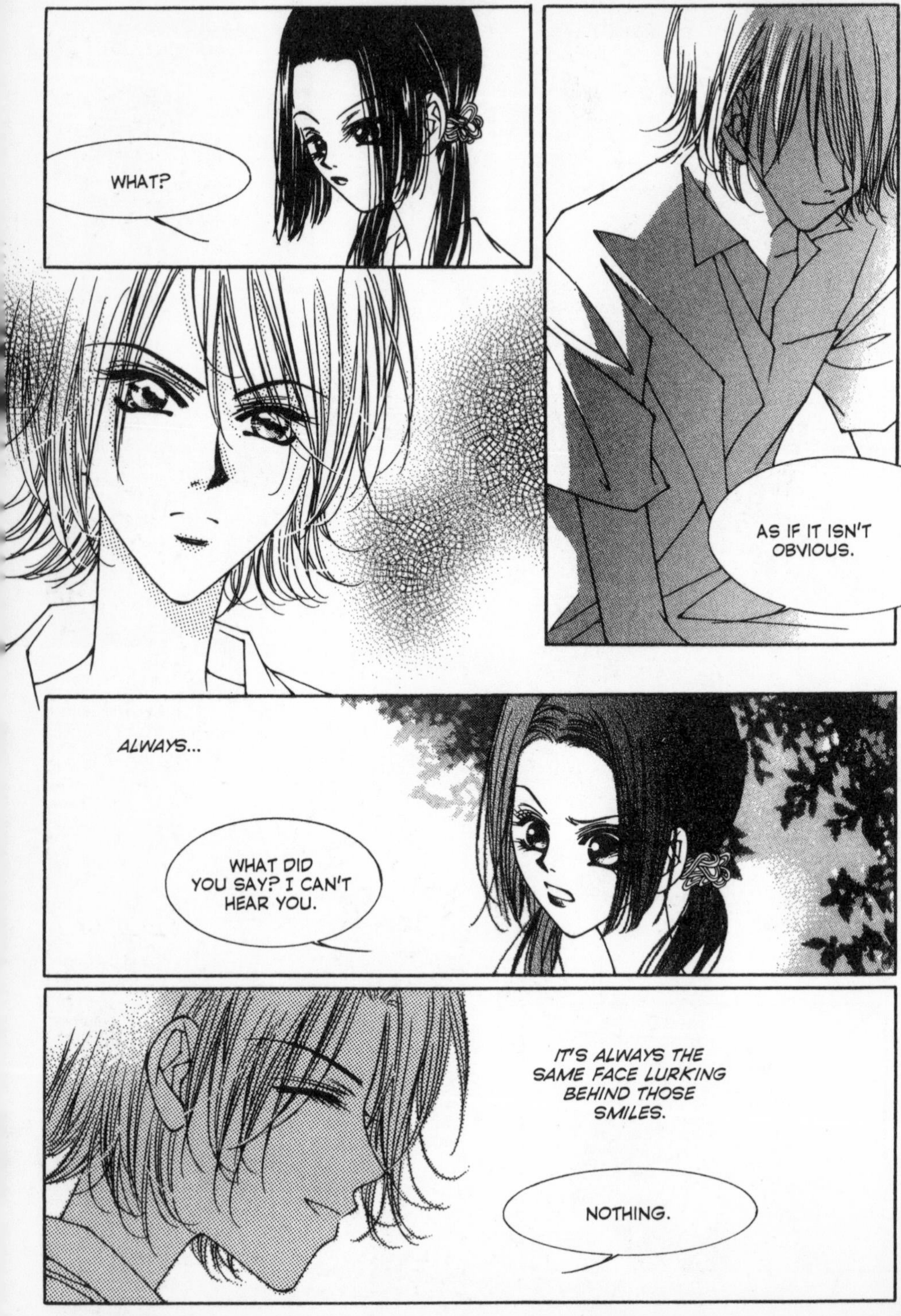
WHAT?
AS IF IT ISN'T OBVIOUS.
ALWAYS...
WHAT DID YOU SAY? I CAN'T HEAR YOU.
IT'S ALWAYS THE SAME FACE LURKING BEHIND THOSE SMILES.
NOTHING.

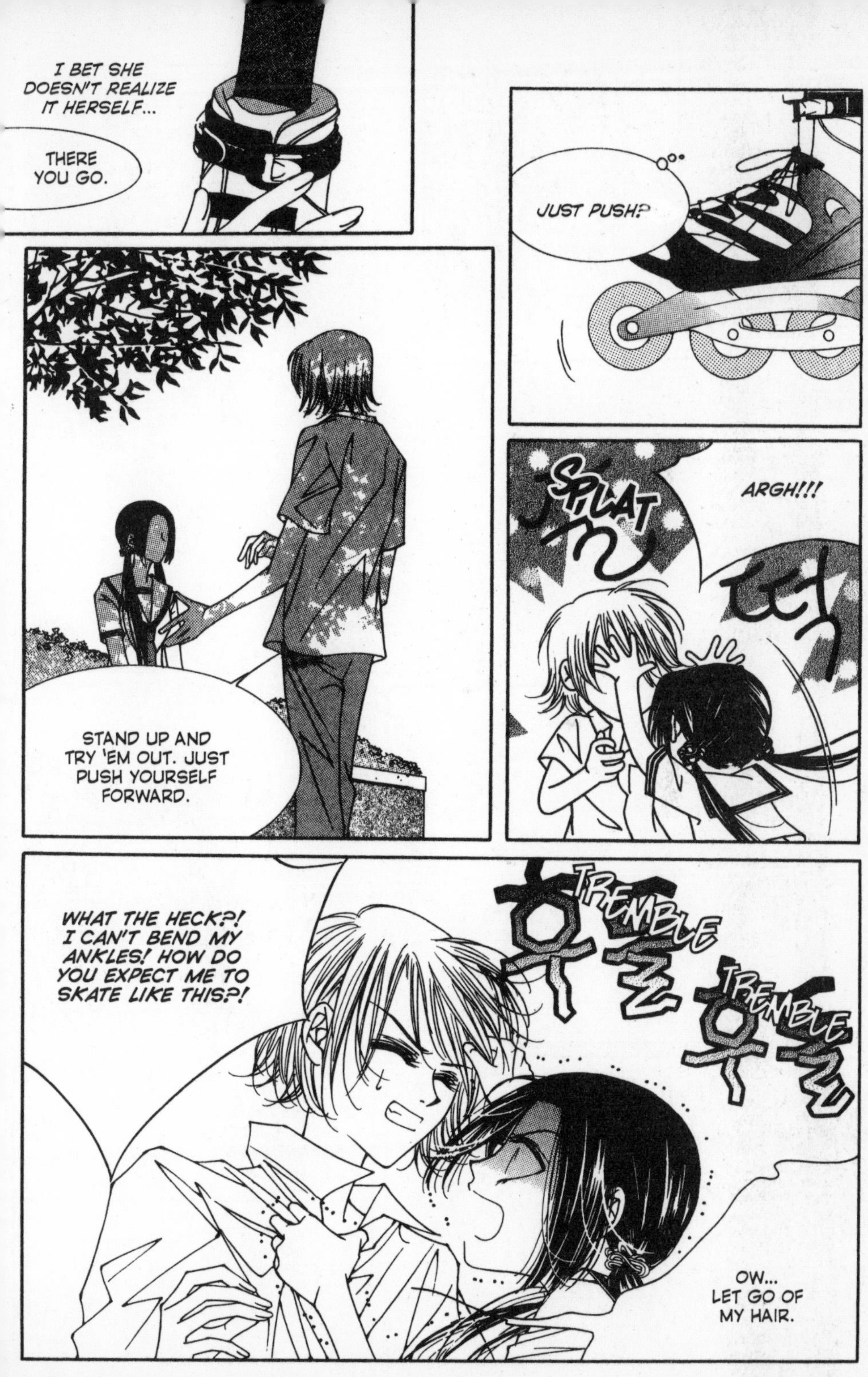
I BET SHE DOESN'T REALIZE IT HERSELF...
THERE YOU GO.
JUST PUSH?
STAND UP AND TRY 'EM OUT. JUST PUSH YOURSELF FORWARD.
SPLAT
ARGH!!!
떡
WHAT THE HECK?! I CAN'T BEND MY ANKLES! HOW DO YOU EXPECT ME TO SKATE LIKE THIS?!
후들 TREMBLE
후들 TREMBLE
OW... LET GO OF MY HAIR.

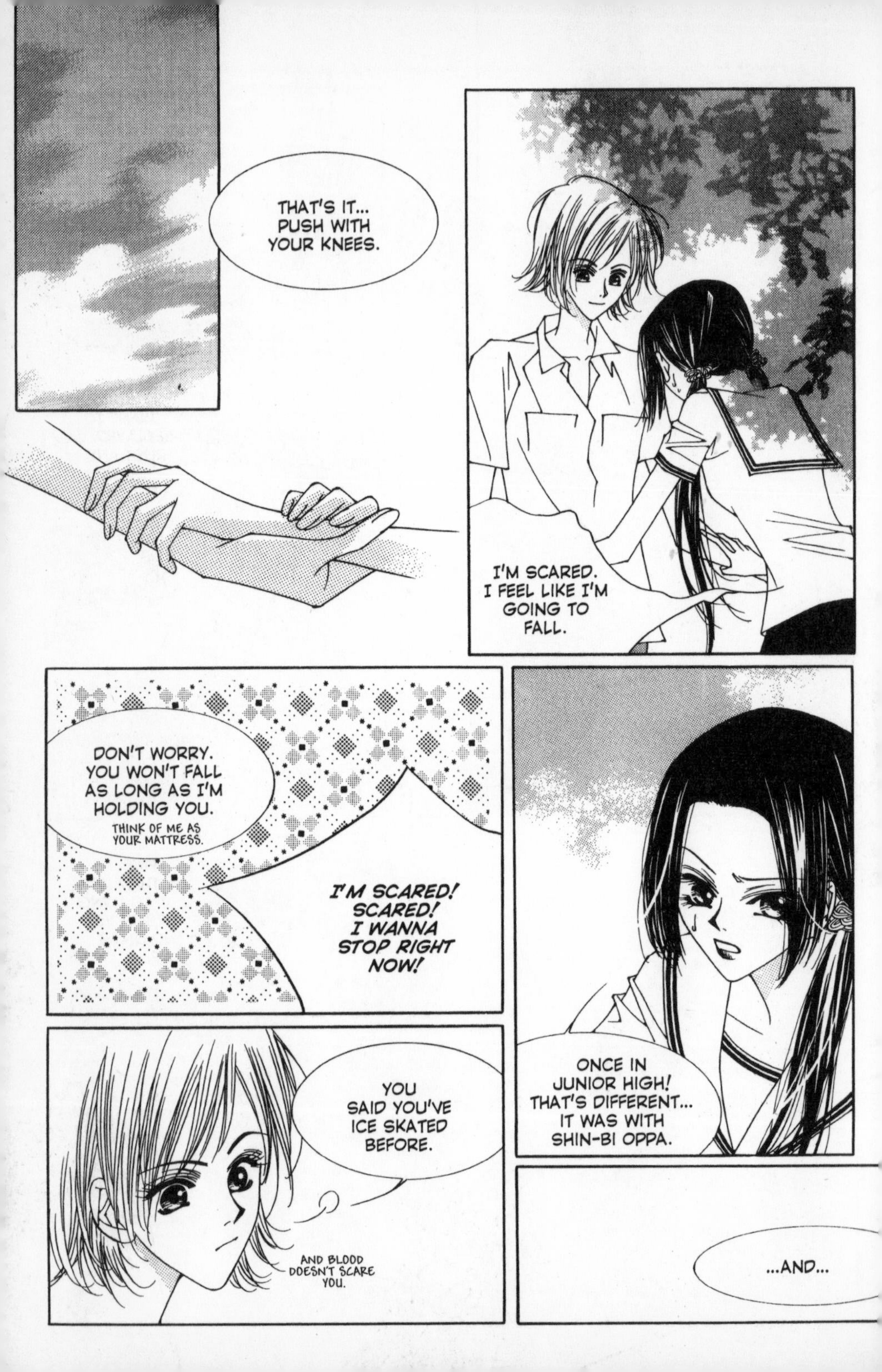
THAT'S IT... PUSH WITH YOUR KNEES.
I'M SCARED. I FEEL LIKE I'M GOING TO FALL.
DON'T WORRY. YOU WON'T FALL AS LONG AS I'M HOLDING YOU.
THINK OF ME AS YOUR MATTRESS.
I'M SCARED! SCARED! I WANNA STOP RIGHT NOW!
YOU SAID YOU'VE ICE SKATED BEFORE.
AND BLOOD DOESN'T SCARE YOU.
ONCE IN JUNIOR HIGH! THAT'S DIFFERENT... IT WAS WITH SHIN-BI OPPA.
...AND...

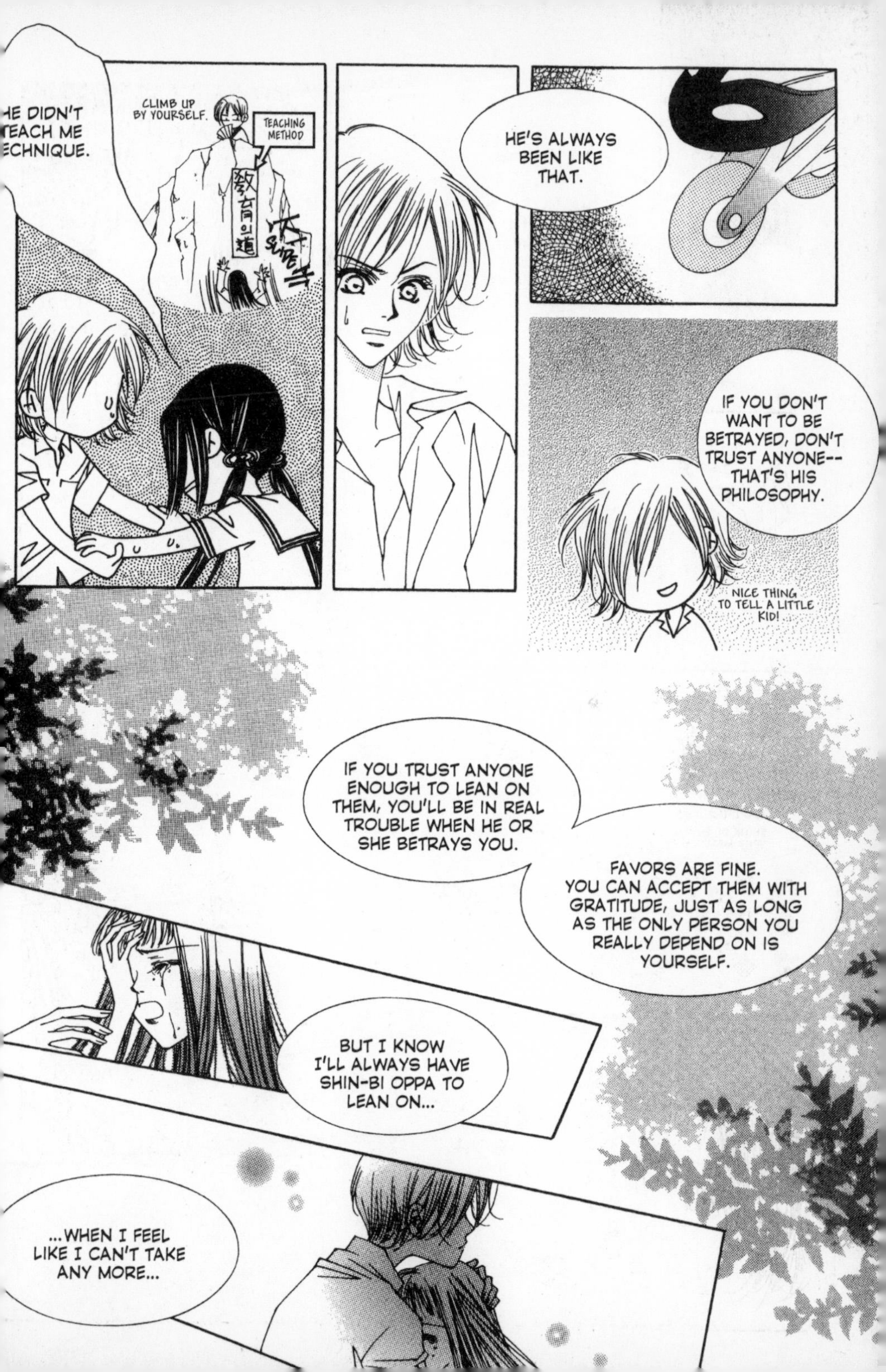
HE DIDN'T TEACH ME ECHNIQUE.
CLIMB UP BY YOURSELF.
TEACHING METHOD
敎育의道
HE'S ALWAYS BEEN LIKE THAT.
IF YOU DON'T WANT TO BE BETRAYED, DON'T TRUST ANYONE-- THAT'S HIS PHILOSOPHY.
NICE THING TO TELL A LITTLE KID!
IF YOU TRUST ANYONE ENOUGH TO LEAN ON THEM, YOU'LL BE IN REAL TROUBLE WHEN HE OR SHE BETRAYS YOU.
FAVORS ARE FINE. YOU CAN ACCEPT THEM WITH GRATITUDE, JUST AS LONG AS THE ONLY PERSON YOU REALLY DEPEND ON IS YOURSELF.
BUT I KNOW I'LL ALWAYS HAVE SHIN-BI OPPA TO LEAN ON...
...WHEN I FEEL LIKE I CAN'T TAKE ANY MORE...

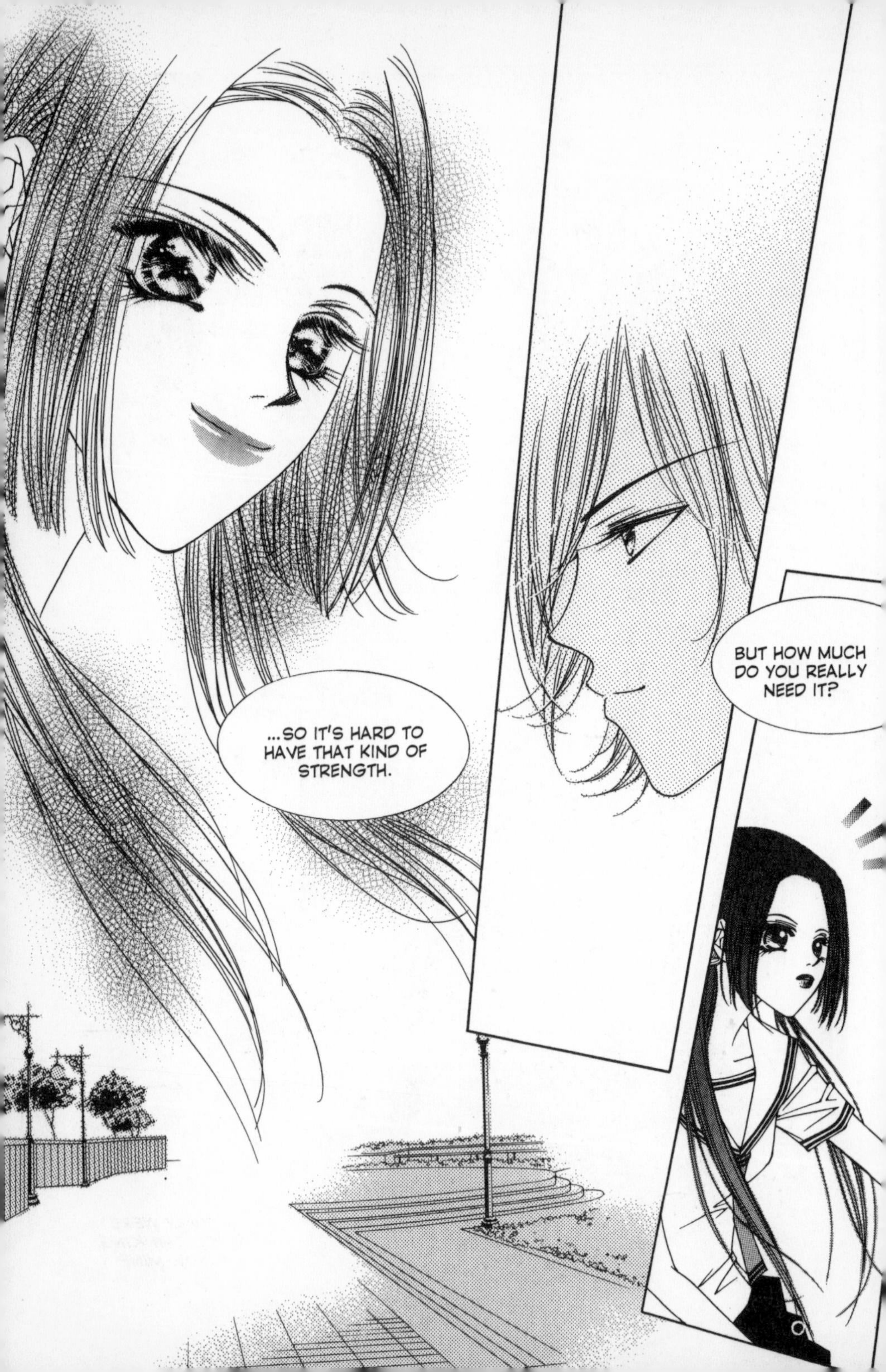
...SO IT'S HARD TO HAVE THAT KIND OF STRENGTH.
BUT HOW MUCH DO YOU REALLY NEED IT?

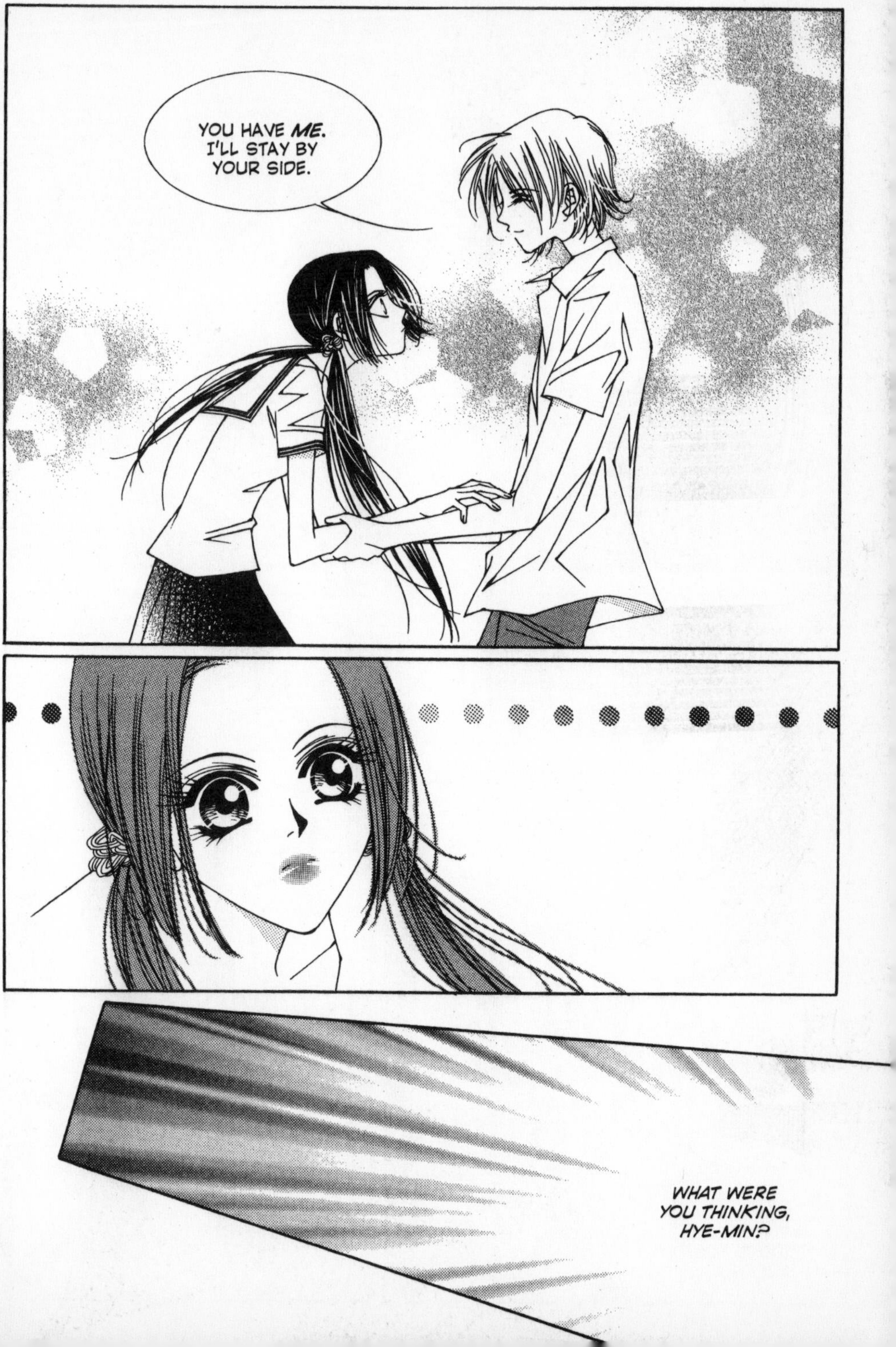
YOU HAVE ME. I'LL STAY BY YOUR SIDE.
WHAT WERE YOU THINKING, HYE-MIN?

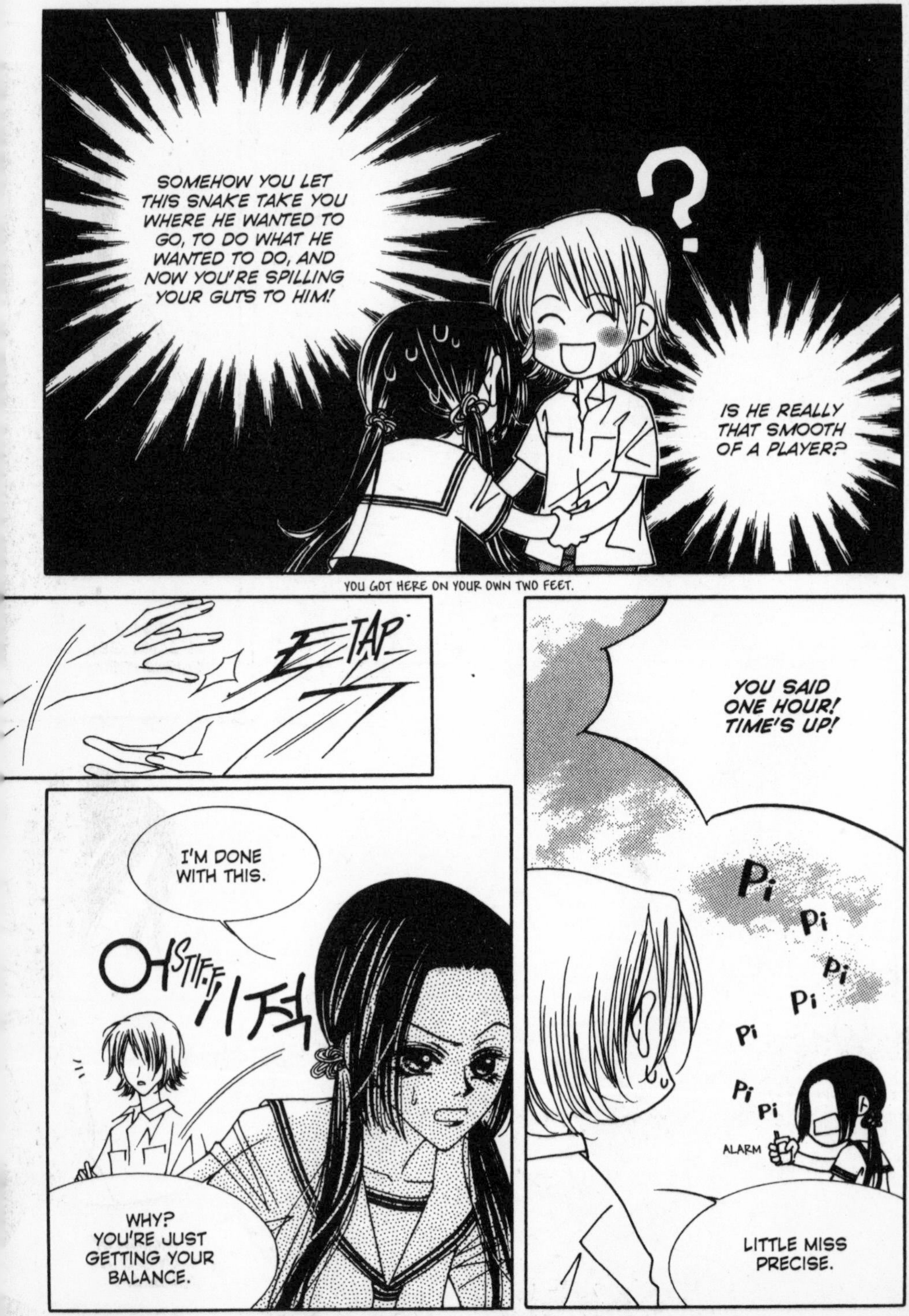
SOMEHOW YOU LET THIS SNAKE TAKE YOU WHERE HE WANTED TO GO, TO DO WHAT HE WANTED TO DO, AND NOW YOU'RE SPILLING YOUR GUTS TO HIM!
?
IS HE REALLY THAT SMOOTH OF A PLAYER?
YOU GOT HERE ON YOUR OWN TWO FEET.
TAP
I'M DONE WITH THIS.
STIFF
WHY? YOU'RE JUST GETTING YOUR BALANCE.
YOU SAID ONE HOUR! TIME'S UP!
Pi
Pi
Pi
Pi
Pi
Pi
Pi
ALARM
LITTLE MISS PRECISE.

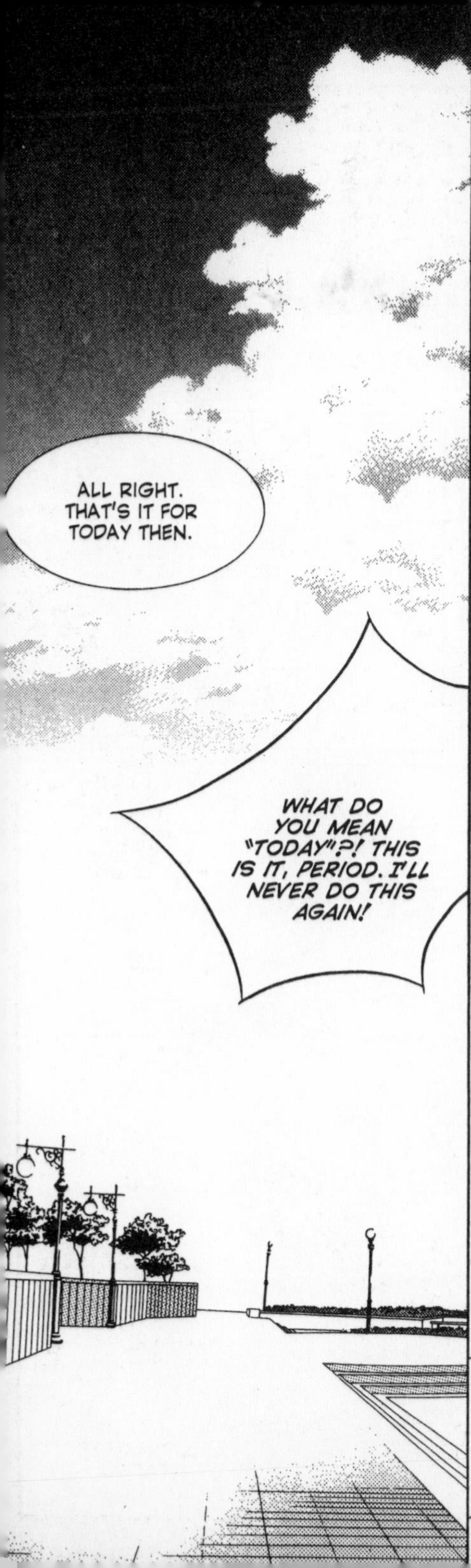
ALL RIGHT. THAT'S IT FOR TODAY THEN.
WHAT DO YOU MEAN "TODAY"?! THIS IS IT, PERIOD. I'LL NEVER DO THIS AGAIN!

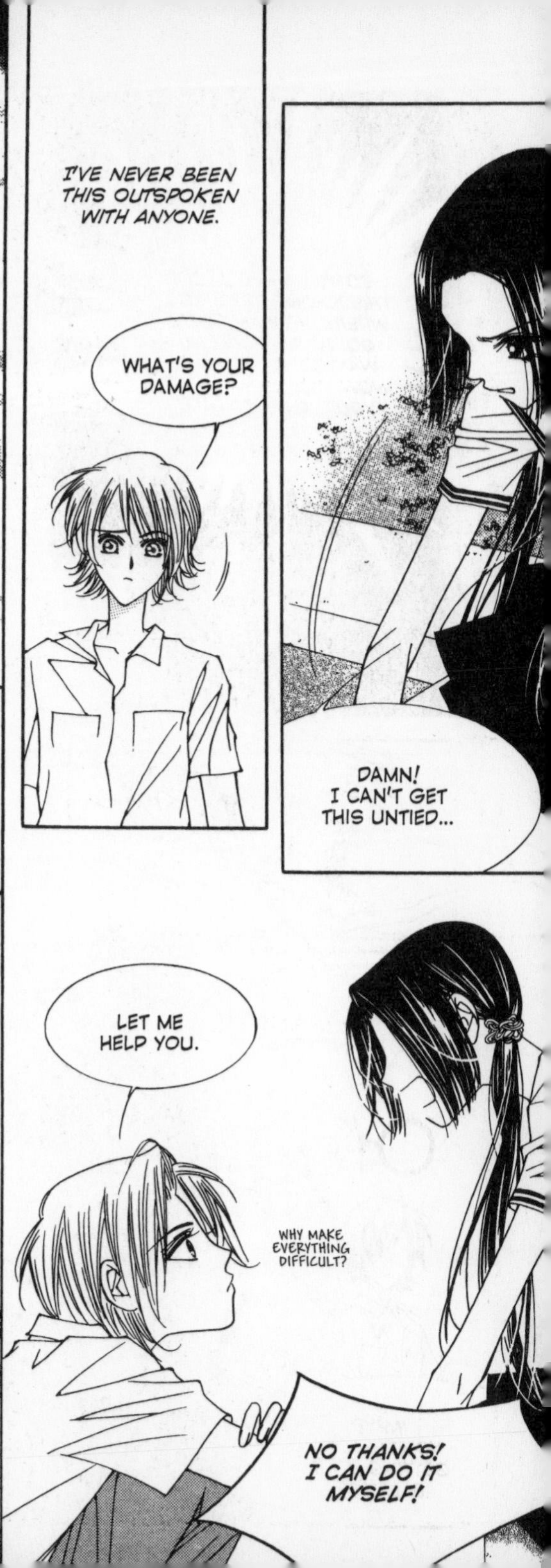
I'VE NEVER BEEN THIS OUTSPOKEN WITH ANYONE.
WHAT'S YOUR DAMAGE?
DAMN! I CAN'T GET THIS UNTIED...
LET ME HELP YOU.
WHY MAKE EVERYTHING DIFFICULT?
NO THANKS! I CAN DO IT MYSELF!

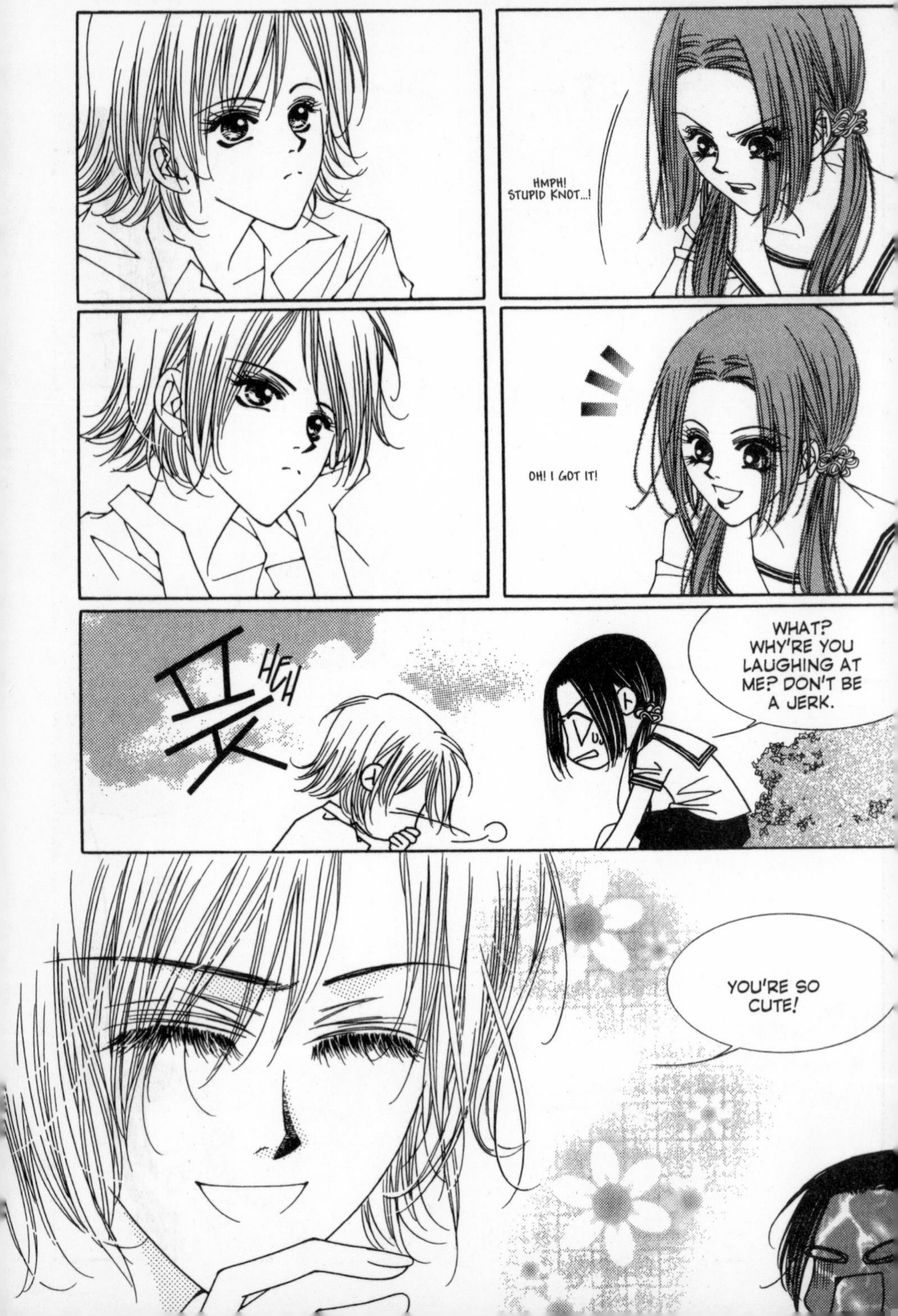
HMPH! STUPID KNOT...!
OH! I GOT IT!
HEH
WHAT? WHY'RE YOU LAUGHING AT ME? DON'T BE A JERK.
YOU'RE SO CUTE!

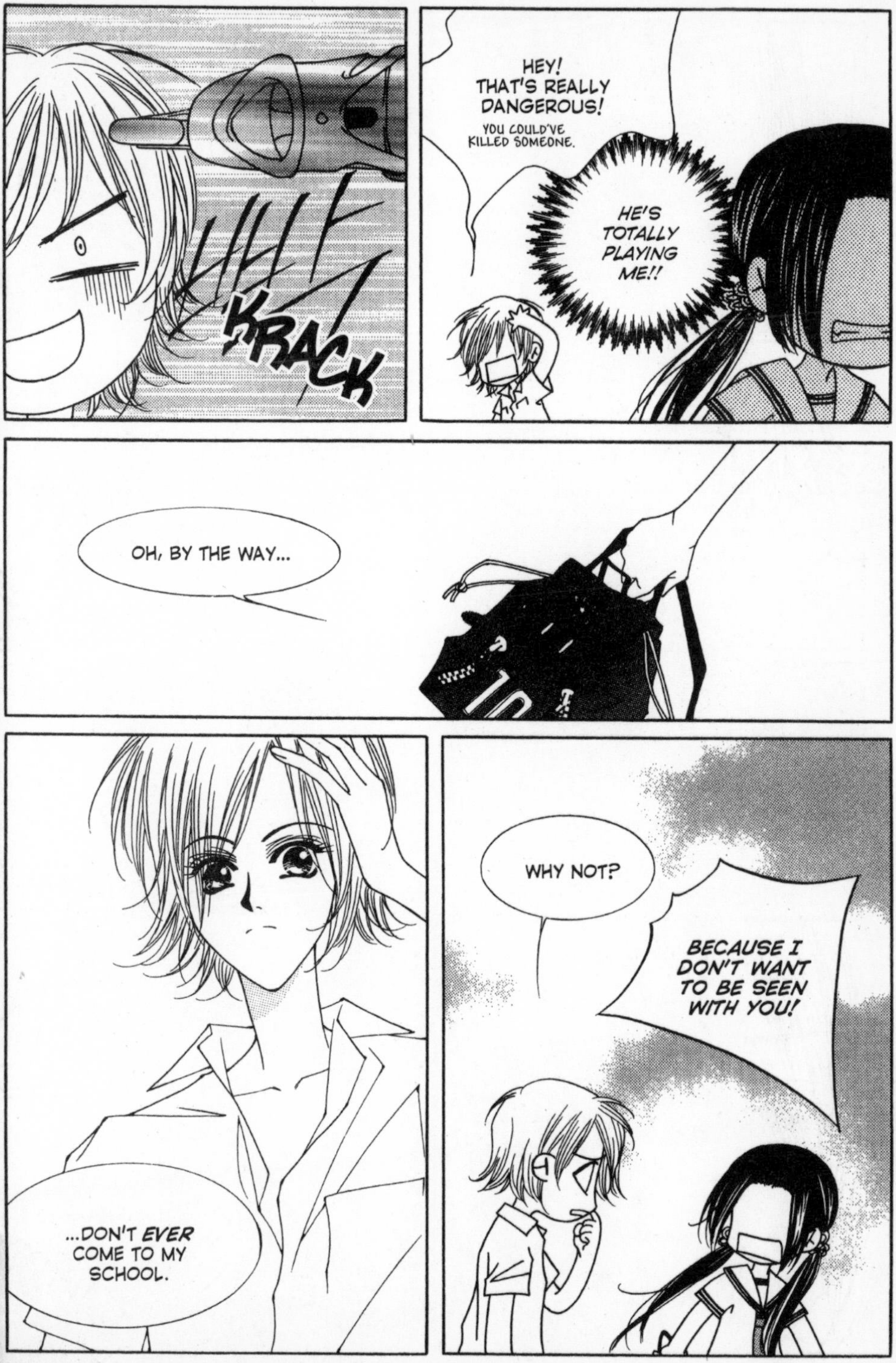

KRACK
HEY! THAT'S REALLY DANGEROUS!
YOU COULD'VE KILLED SOMEONE.
HE'S TOTALLY PLAYING ME!!
OH, BY THE WAY...
...DON'T EVER COME TO MY SCHOOL.
WHY NOT?
BECAUSE I DON'T WANT TO BE SEEN WITH YOU!

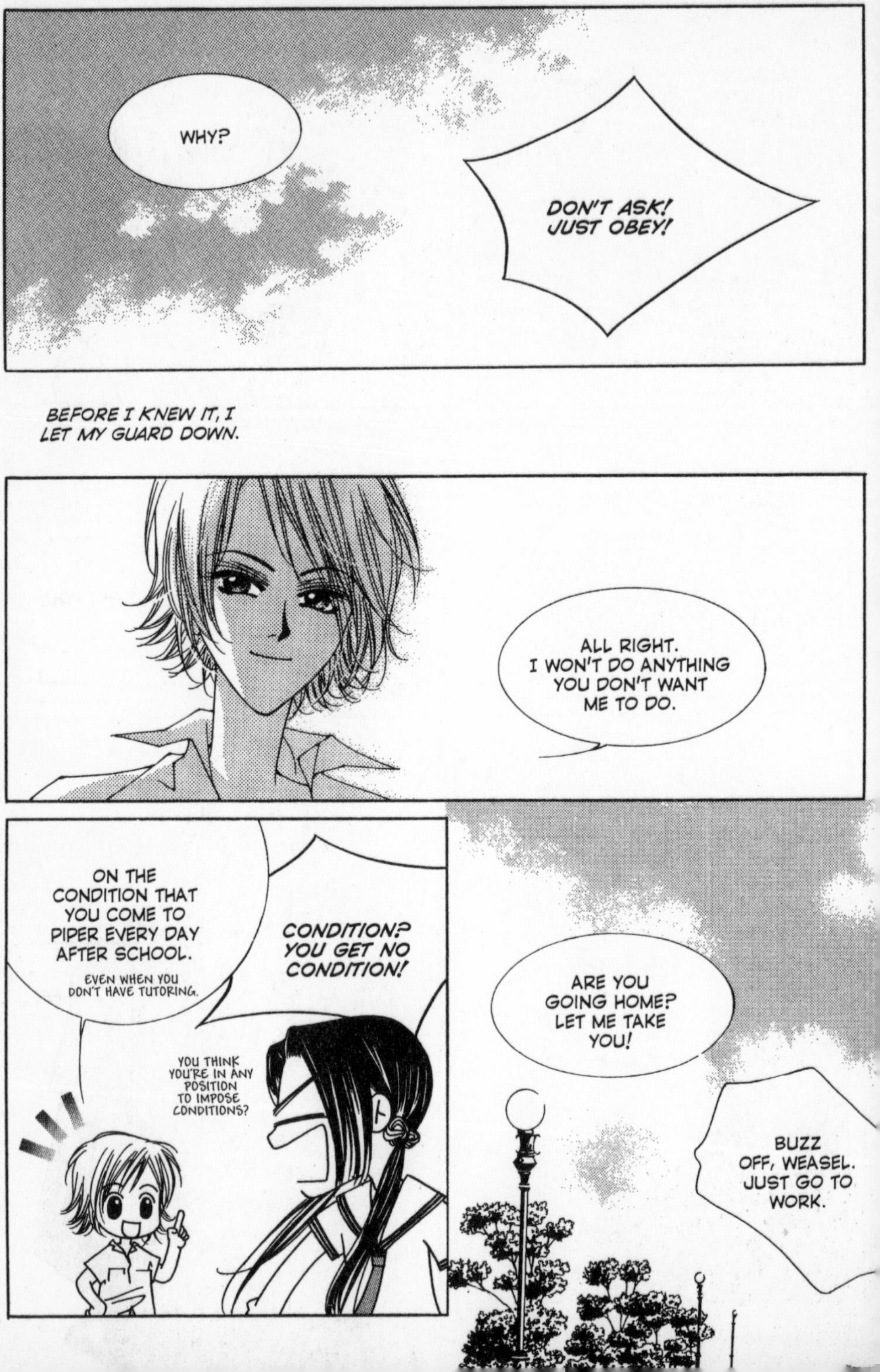
WHY?
DON'T ASK! JUST OBEY!
BEFORE I KNEW IT, I LET MY GUARD DOWN.
ALL RIGHT. I WON'T DO ANYTHING YOU DON'T WANT ME TO DO.
ON THE CONDITION THAT YOU COME TO PIPER EVERY DAY AFTER SCHOOL.
EVEN WHEN YOU DON'T HAVE TUTORING.
CONDITION? YOU GET NO CONDITION!
YOU THINK YOU'RE IN ANY POSITION TO IMPOSE CONDITIONS?
ARE YOU GOING HOME? LET ME TAKE YOU!
BUZZ OFF, WEASEL. JUST GO TO WORK.

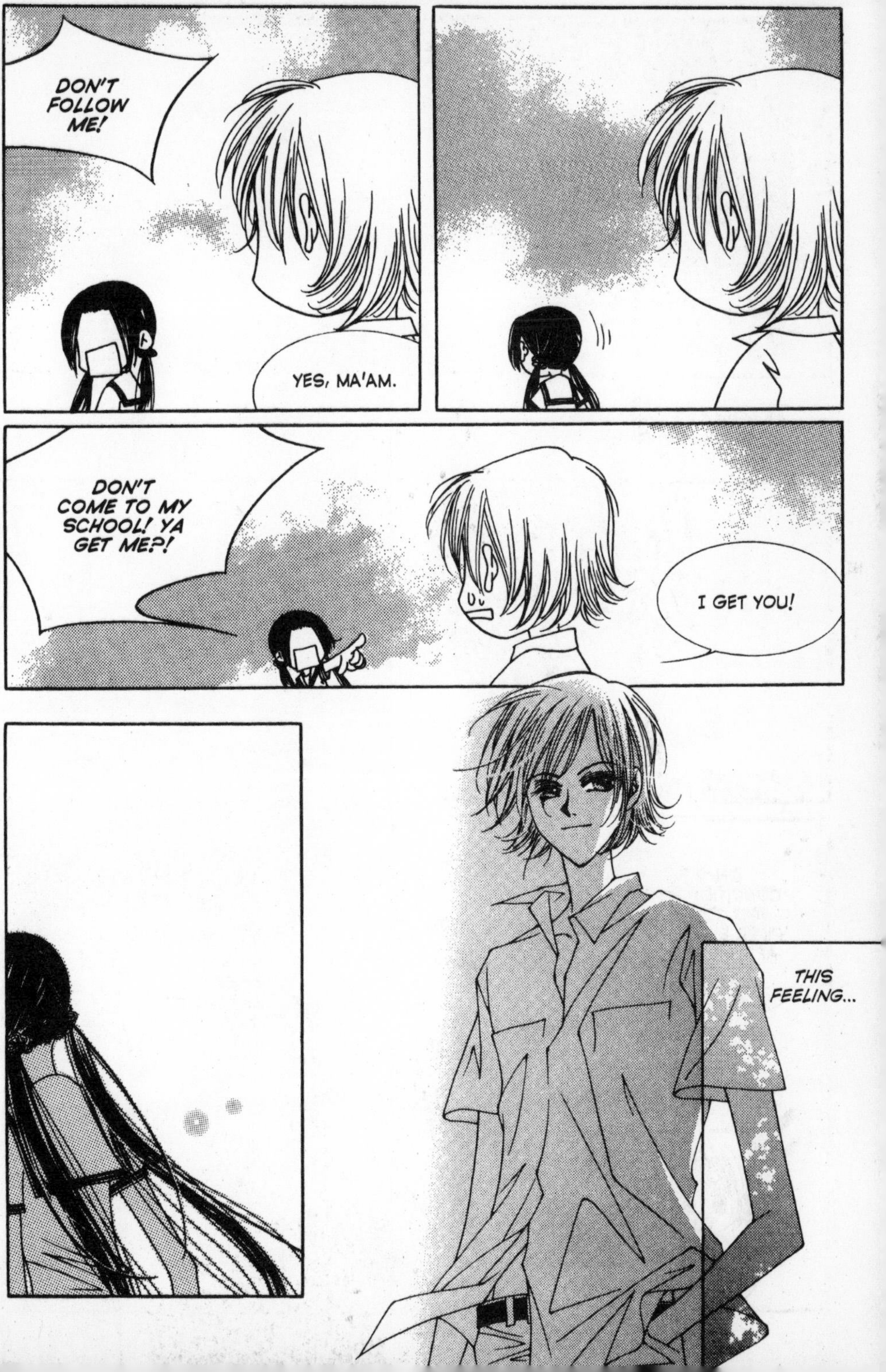
DON'T FOLLOW ME!
YES, MA'AM.
DON'T COME TO MY SCHOOL! YA GET ME?!
I GET YOU!
THIS FEELING...

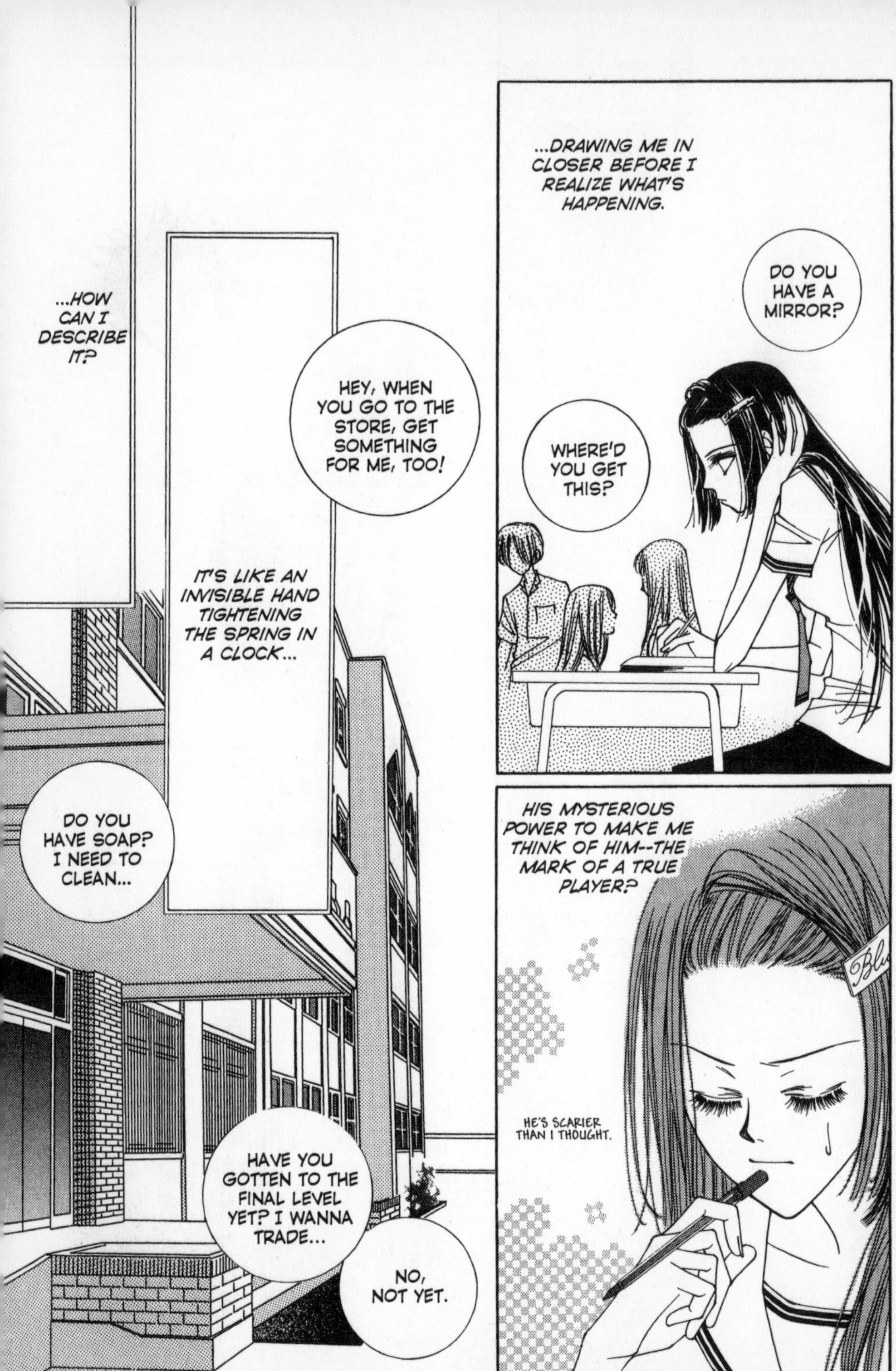
...HOW CAN I DESCRIBE IT?
HEY, WHEN YOU GO TO THE STORE, GET SOMETHING FOR ME, TOO!
IT'S LIKE AN INVISIBLE HAND TIGHTENING THE SPRING IN A CLOCK...
DO YOU HAVE SOAP? I NEED TO CLEAN...
HAVE YOU GOTTEN TO THE FINAL LEVEL YET? I WANNA TRADE...
NO, NOT YET.
...DRAWING ME IN CLOSER BEFORE I REALIZE WHAT'S HAPPENING.
DO YOU HAVE A MIRROR?
WHERE'D YOU GET THIS?
HIS MYSTERIOUS POWER TO MAKE ME THINK OF HIM--THE MARK OF A TRUE PLAYER?
HE'S SCARIER THAN I THOUGHT.

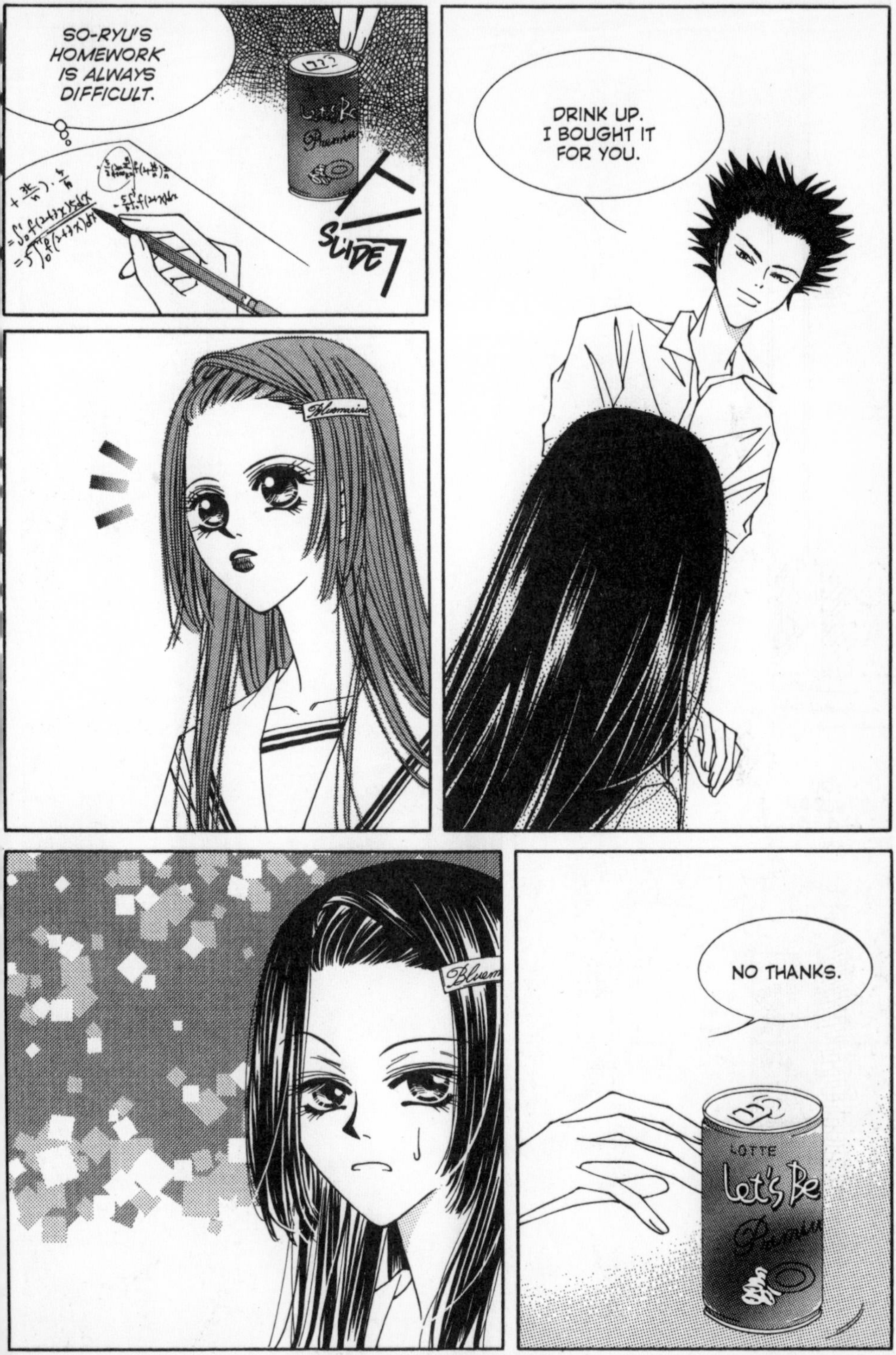
SO-RYU'S HOMEWORK IS ALWAYS DIFFICULT.
SLIDE
DRINK UP. I BOUGHT IT FOR YOU.
NO THANKS.
LOTTE
Let's Be

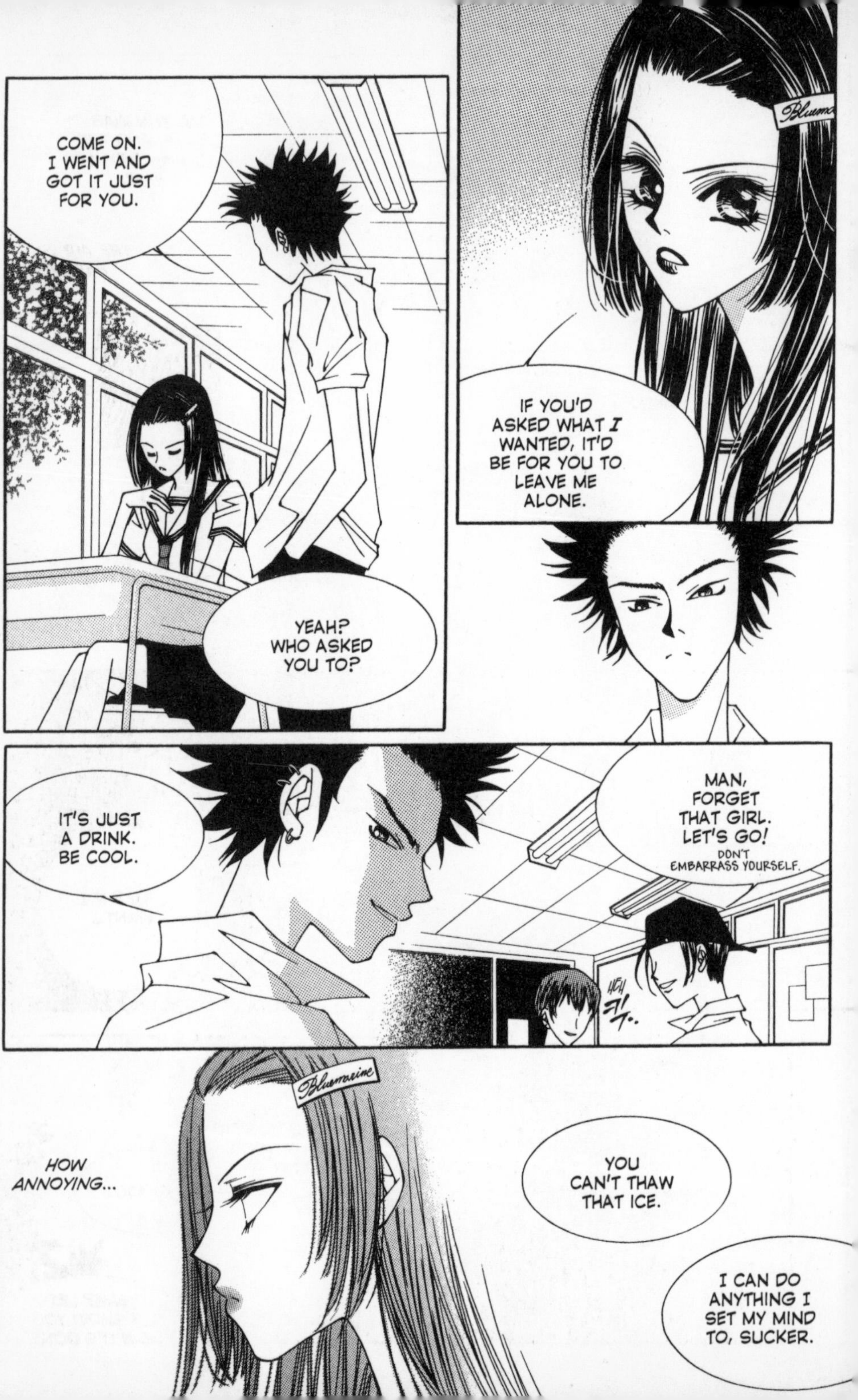
COME ON. I WENT AND GOT IT JUST FOR YOU.
YEAH? WHO ASKED YOU TO?
IF YOU'D ASKED WHAT *I* WANTED, IT'D BE FOR YOU TO LEAVE ME ALONE.
IT'S JUST A DRINK. BE COOL.
MAN, FORGET THAT GIRL. LET'S GO!
DON'T EMBARRASS YOURSELF.
HEH
HOW ANNOYING...
YOU CAN'T THAW THAT ICE.
I CAN DO ANYTHING I SET MY MIND TO, SUCKER.

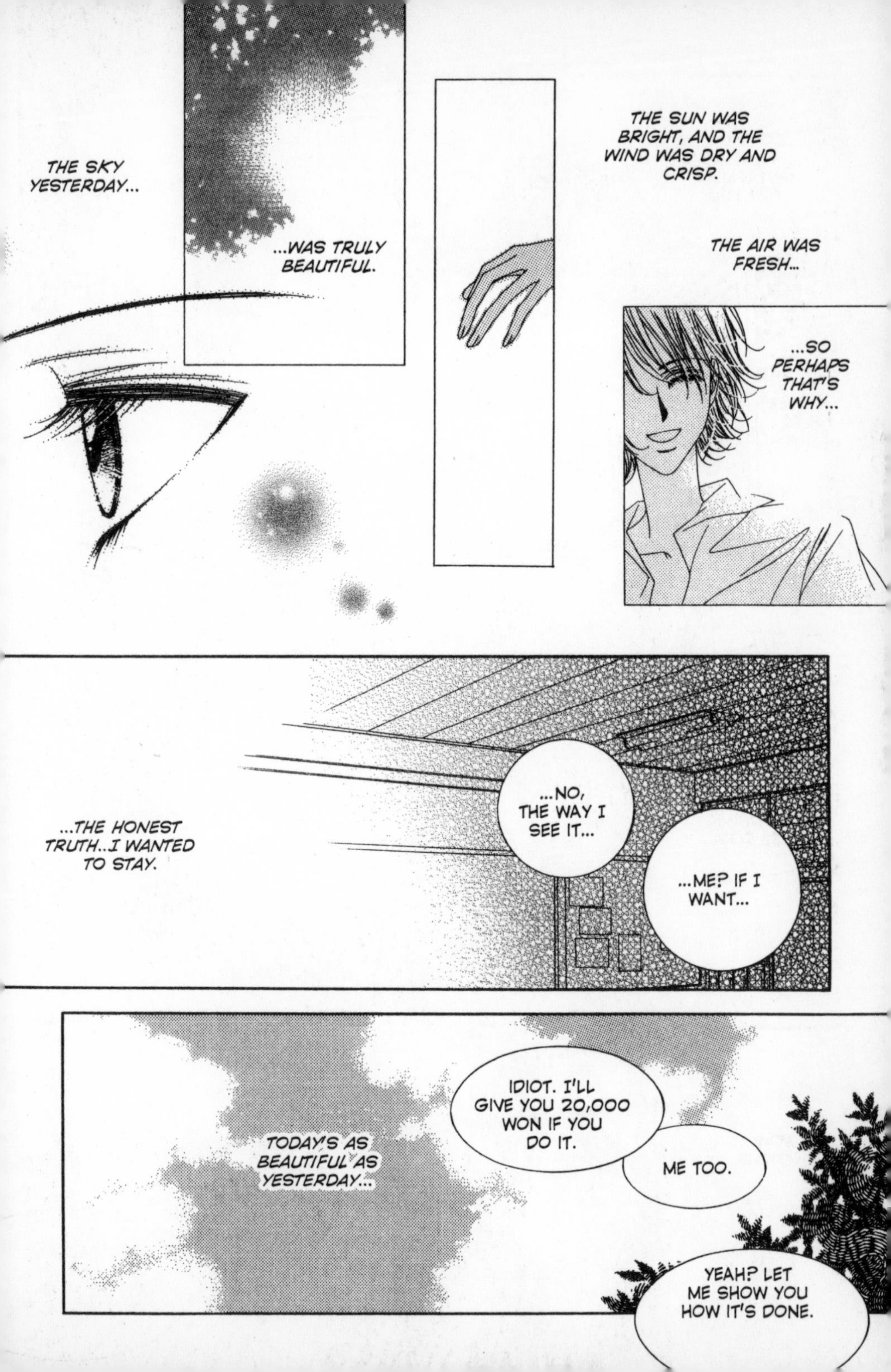
THE SKY YESTERDAY...
...WAS TRULY BEAUTIFUL.
THE SUN WAS BRIGHT, AND THE WIND WAS DRY AND CRISP.
THE AIR WAS FRESH...
...SO PERHAPS THAT'S WHY...
...THE HONEST TRUTH..I WANTED TO STAY.
...NO, THE WAY I SEE IT...
...ME? IF I WANT...
TODAY'S AS BEAUTIFUL AS YESTERDAY...
IDIOT. I'LL GIVE YOU 20,000 WON IF YOU DO IT.
ME TOO.
YEAH? LET ME SHOW YOU HOW IT'S DONE.

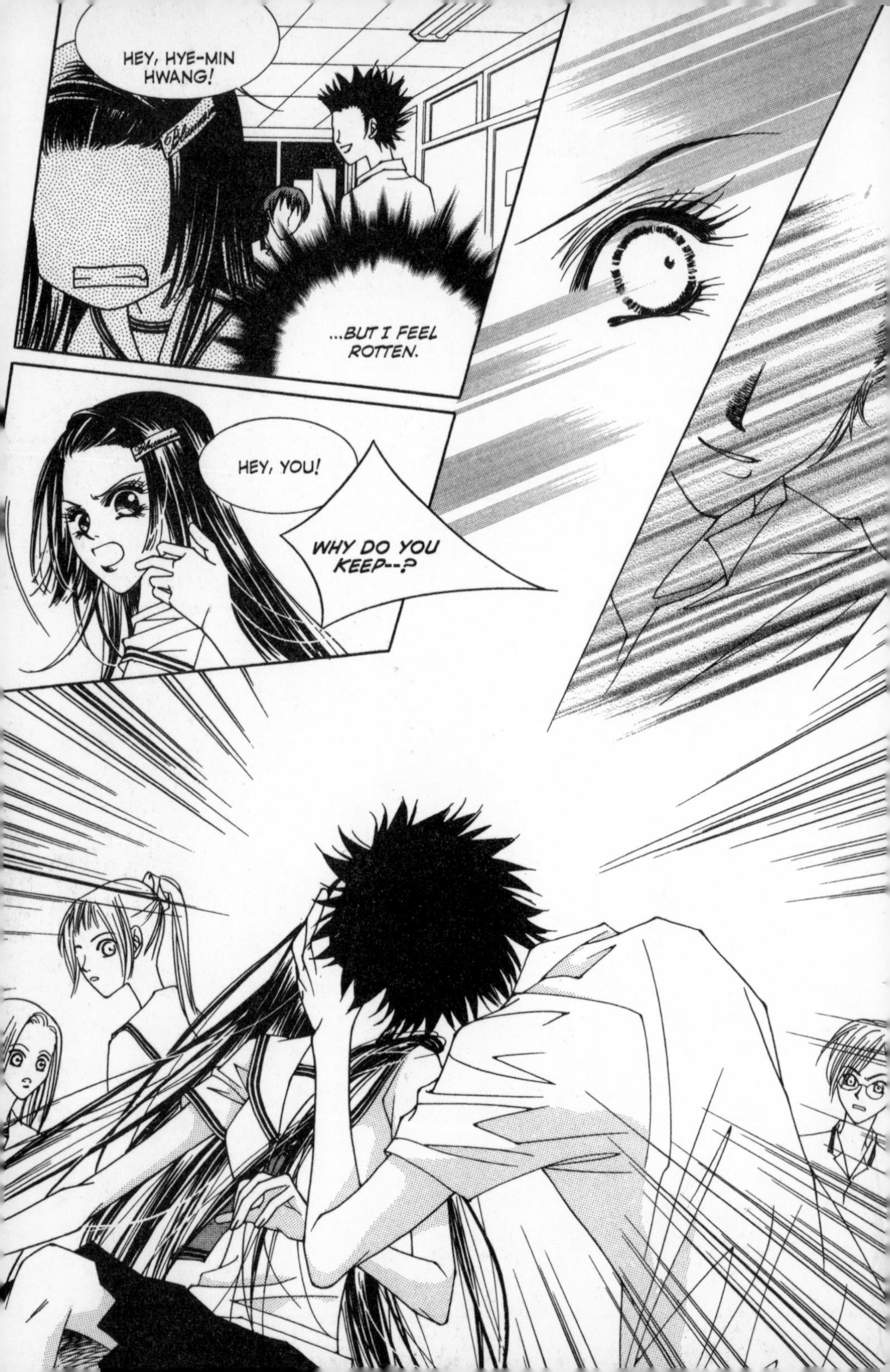
HEY, HYE-MIN HWANG!
...BUT I FEEL ROTTEN.
HEY, YOU!
WHY DO YOU KEEP--?

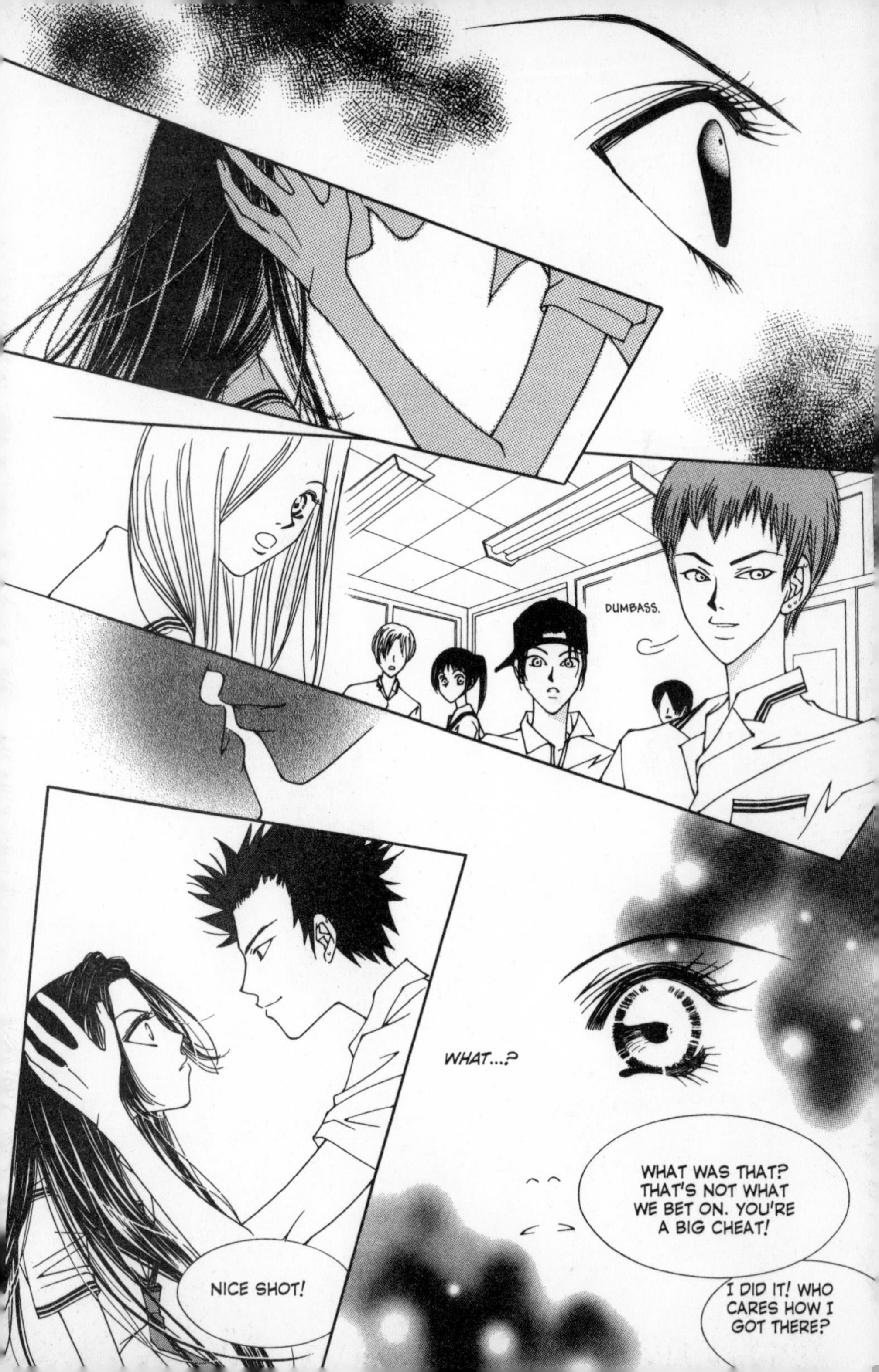
DUMBASS.
WHAT...?
WHAT WAS THAT? THAT'S NOT WHAT WE BET ON. YOU'RE A BIG CHEAT!
NICE SHOT!
I DID IT! WHO CARES HOW I GOT THERE?

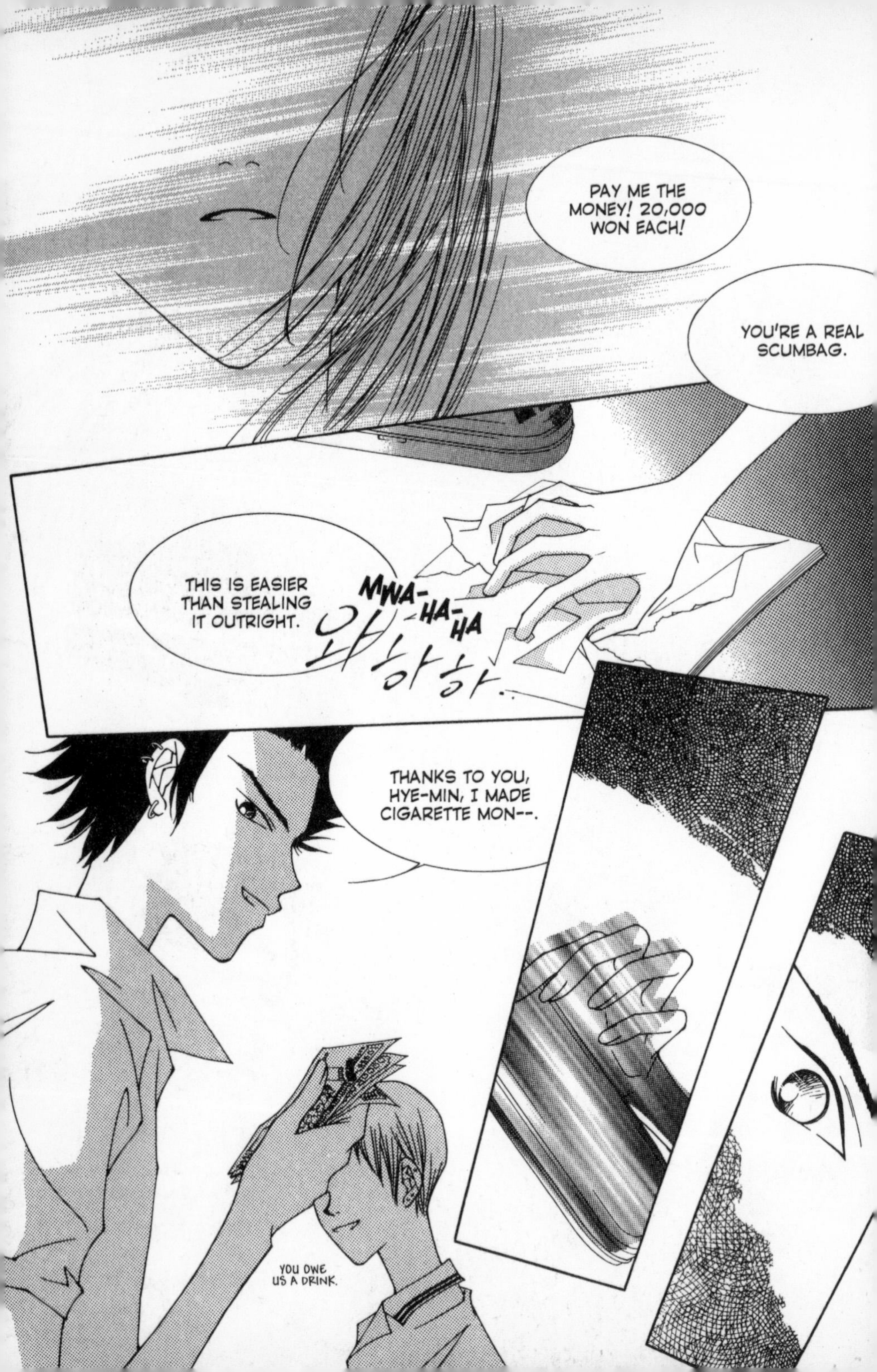
PAY ME THE MONEY! 20,000 WON EACH!
YOU'RE A REAL SCUMBAG.
THIS IS EASIER THAN STEALING IT OUTRIGHT.
MWA-HA-HA
와하하..
THANKS TO YOU, HYE-MIN, I MADE CIGARETTE MON--.
YOU OWE US A DRINK.

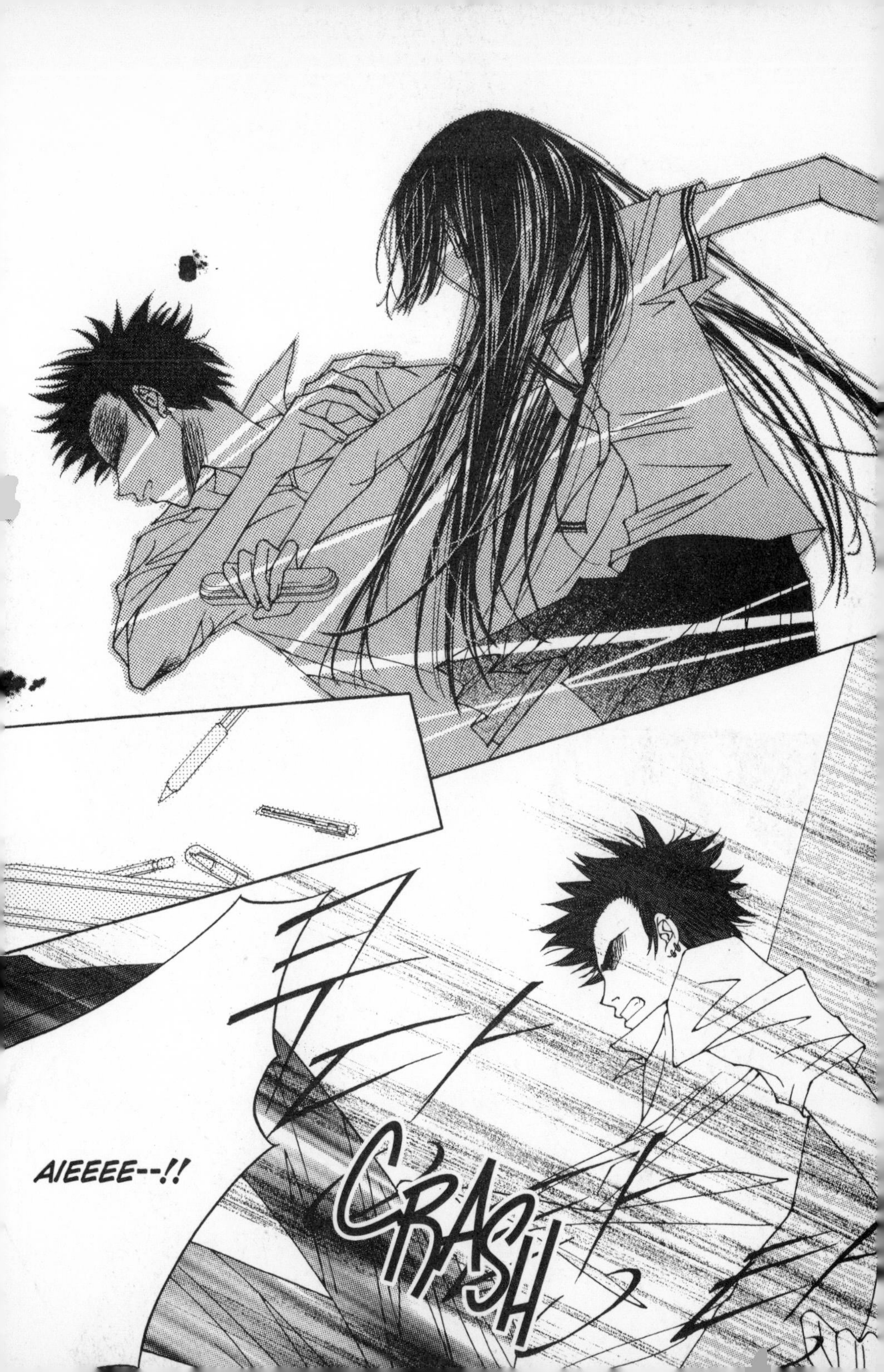
AIEEEE--!!
CRASH

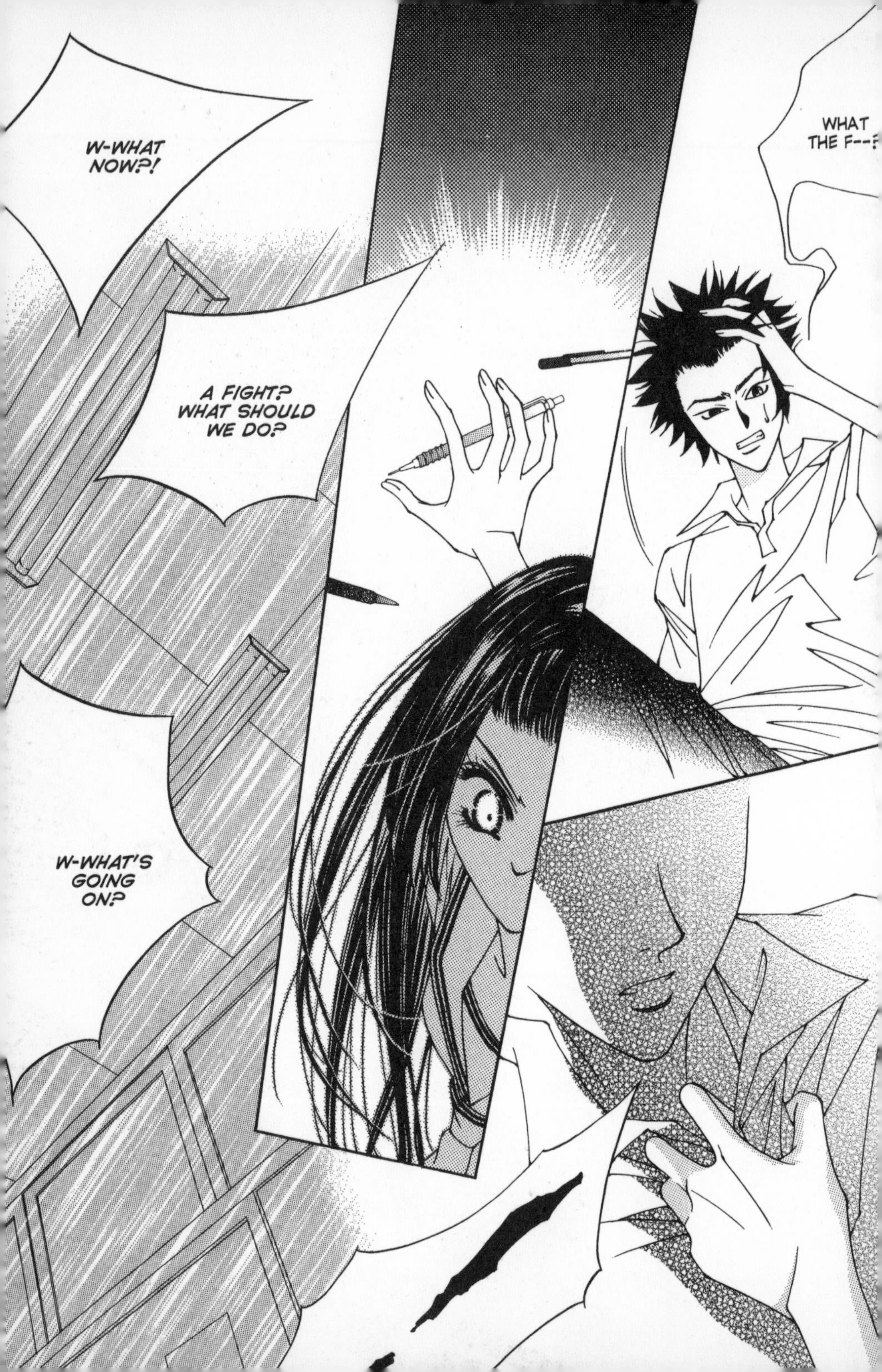
W-WHAT NOW?!
A FIGHT? WHAT SHOULD WE DO?
W-WHAT'S GOING ON?
WHAT THE F--?

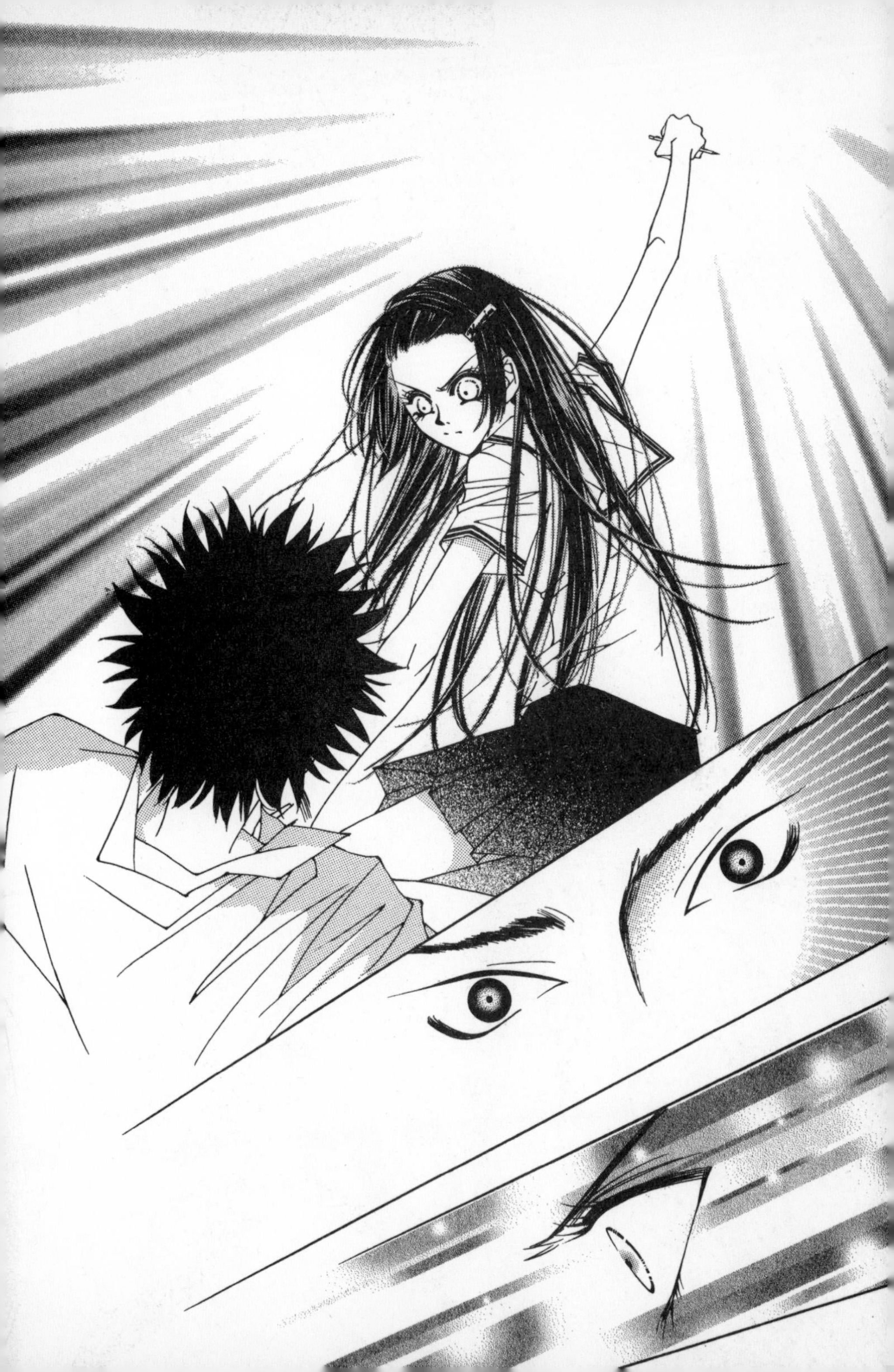

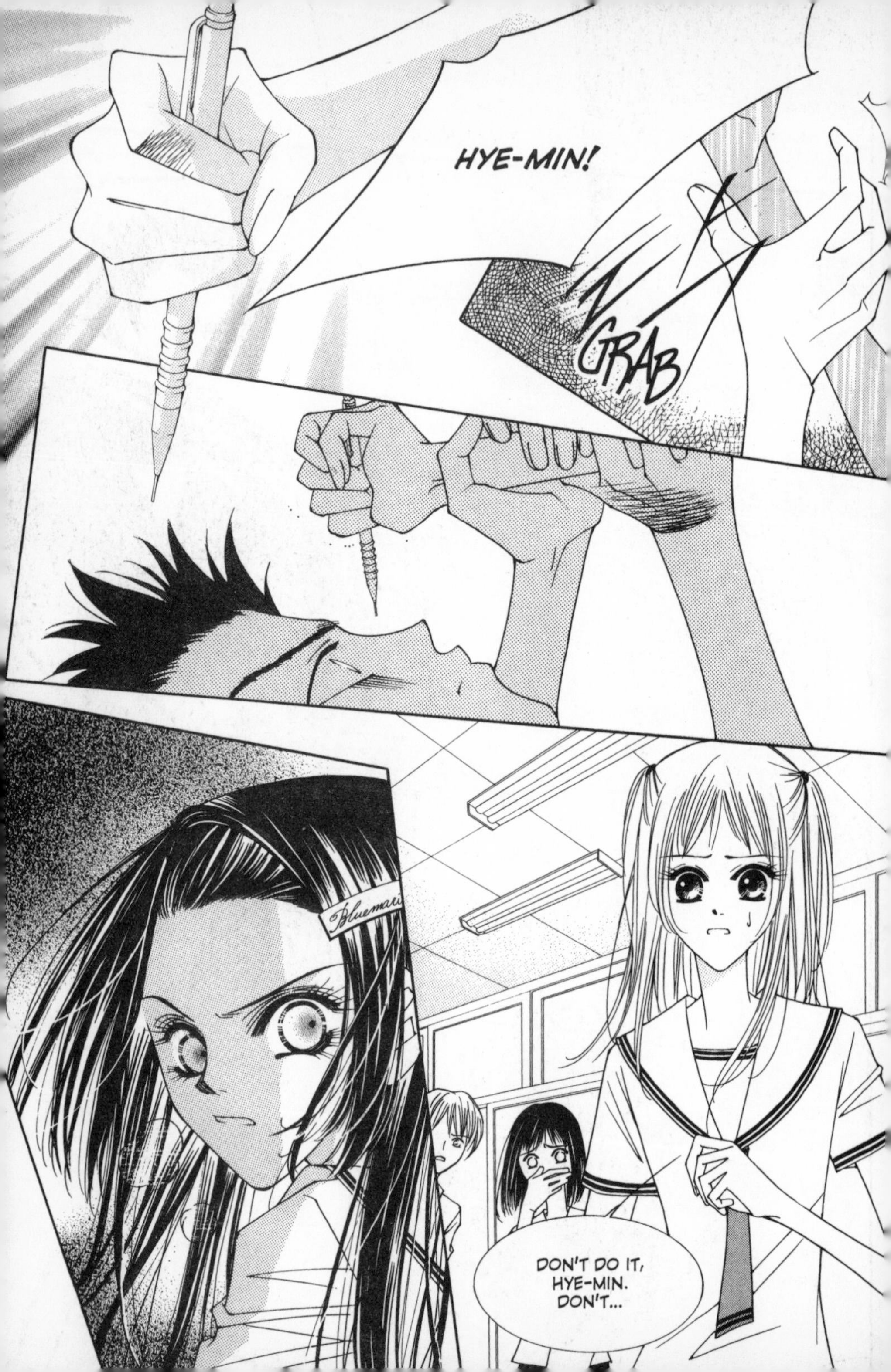
HYE-MIN!
GRAB
DON'T DO IT, HYE-MIN. DON'T...

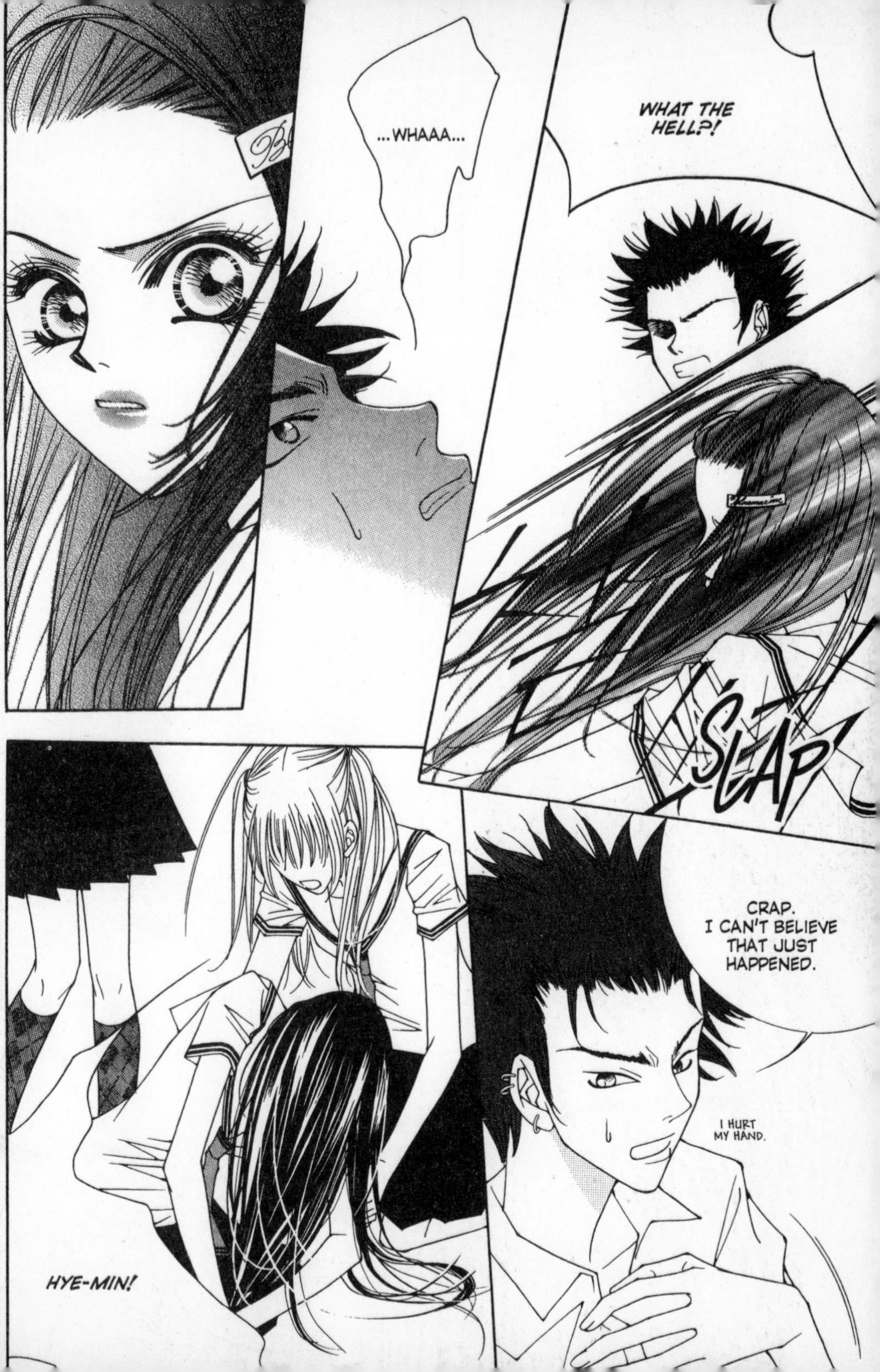
...WHAAA...
WHAT THE HELL?!
SLAP
HYE-MIN!
CRAP. I CAN'T BELIEVE THAT JUST HAPPENED.
I HURT MY HAND.

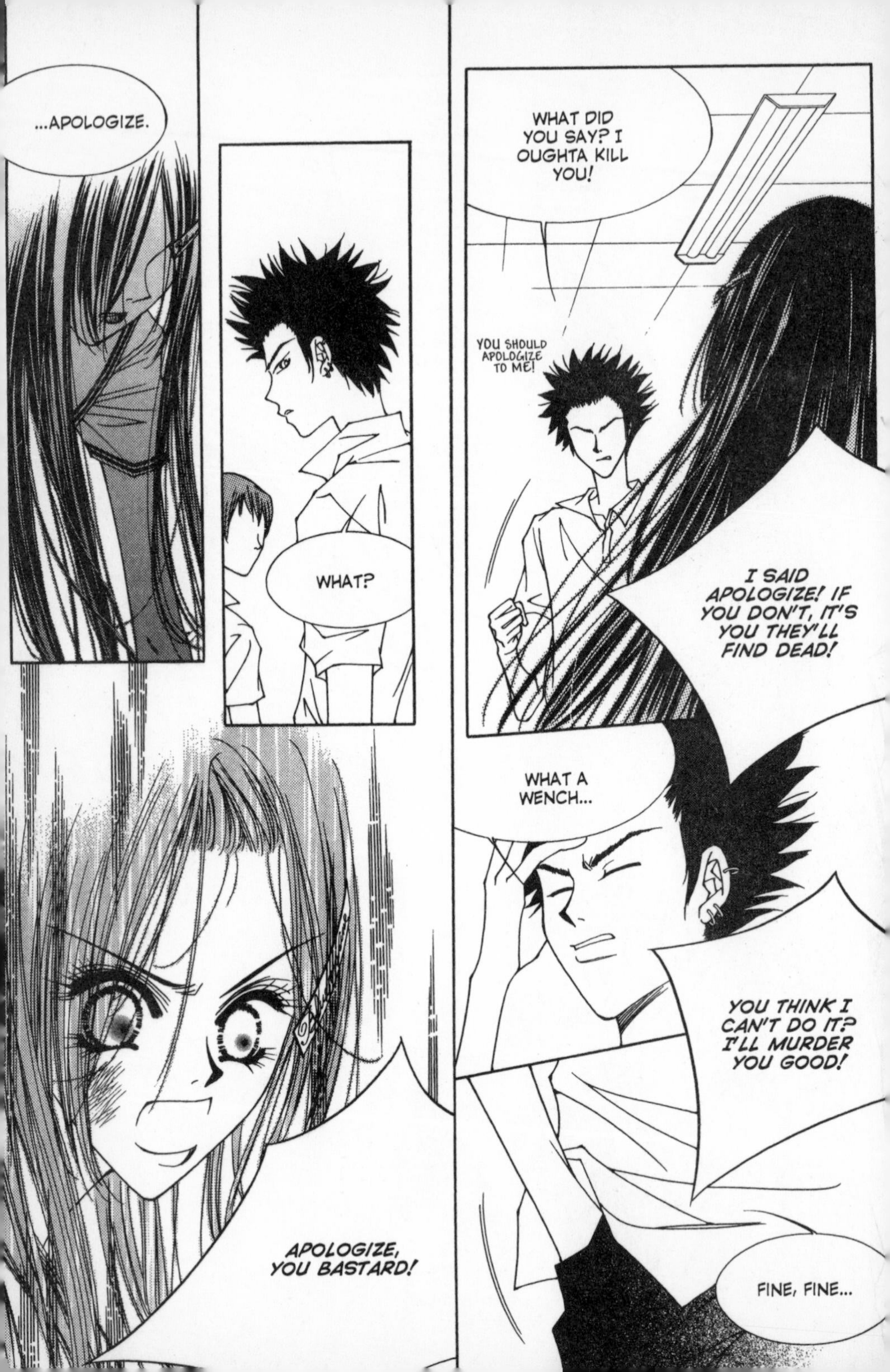
...APOLOGIZE.
WHAT?
APOLOGIZE, YOU BASTARD!
WHAT DID YOU SAY? I OUGHTA KILL YOU!
YOU SHOULD APOLOGIZE TO ME!
I SAID APOLOGIZE! IF YOU DON'T, IT'S YOU THEY'LL FIND DEAD!
WHAT A WENCH...
YOU THINK I CAN'T DO IT? I'LL MURDER YOU GOOD!
FINE, FINE...

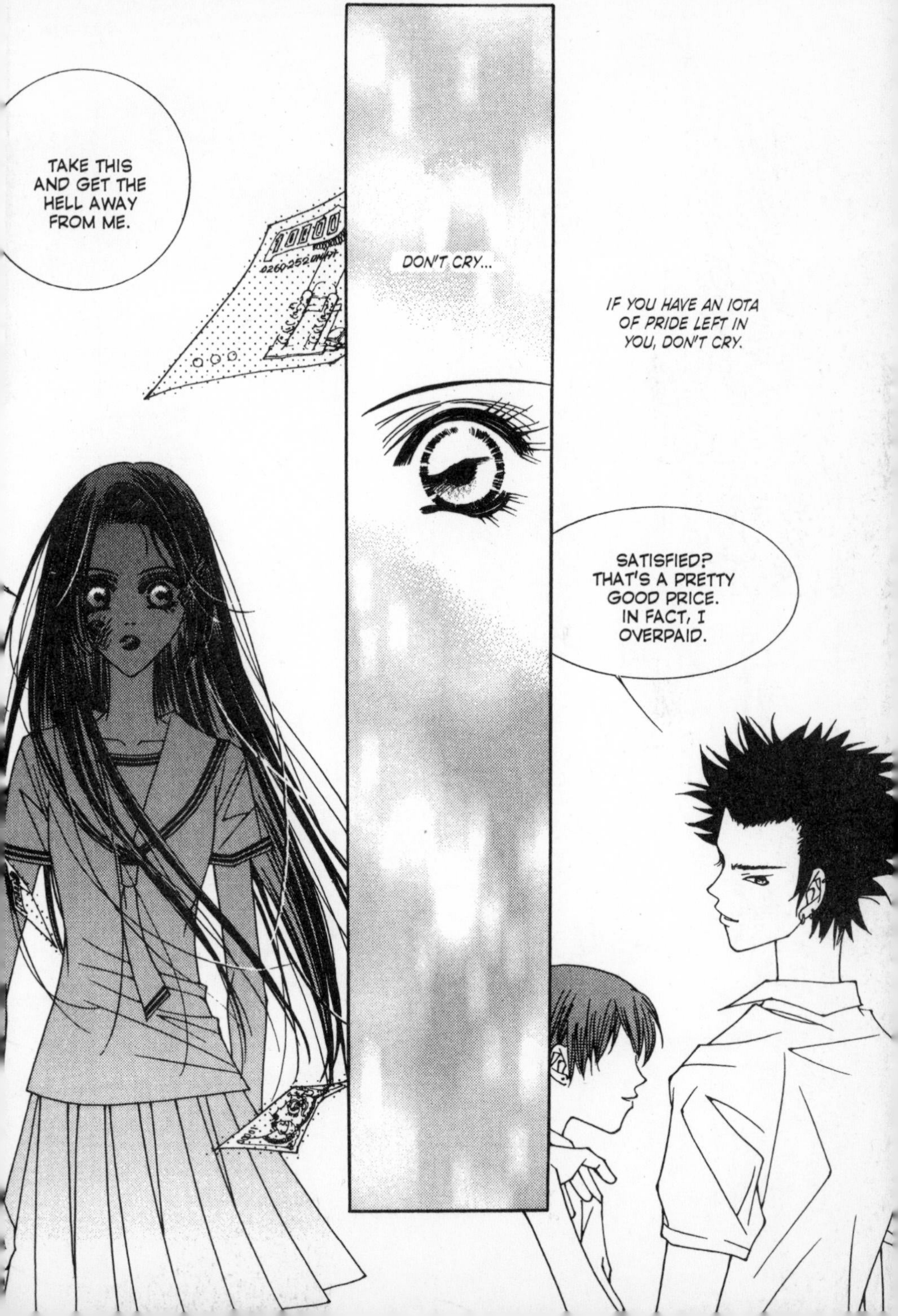
TAKE THIS AND GET THE HELL AWAY FROM ME.
DON'T CRY...
IF YOU HAVE AN IOTA OF PRIDE LEFT IN YOU, DON'T CRY.
SATISFIED? THAT'S A PRETTY GOOD PRICE. IN FACT, I OVERPAID.

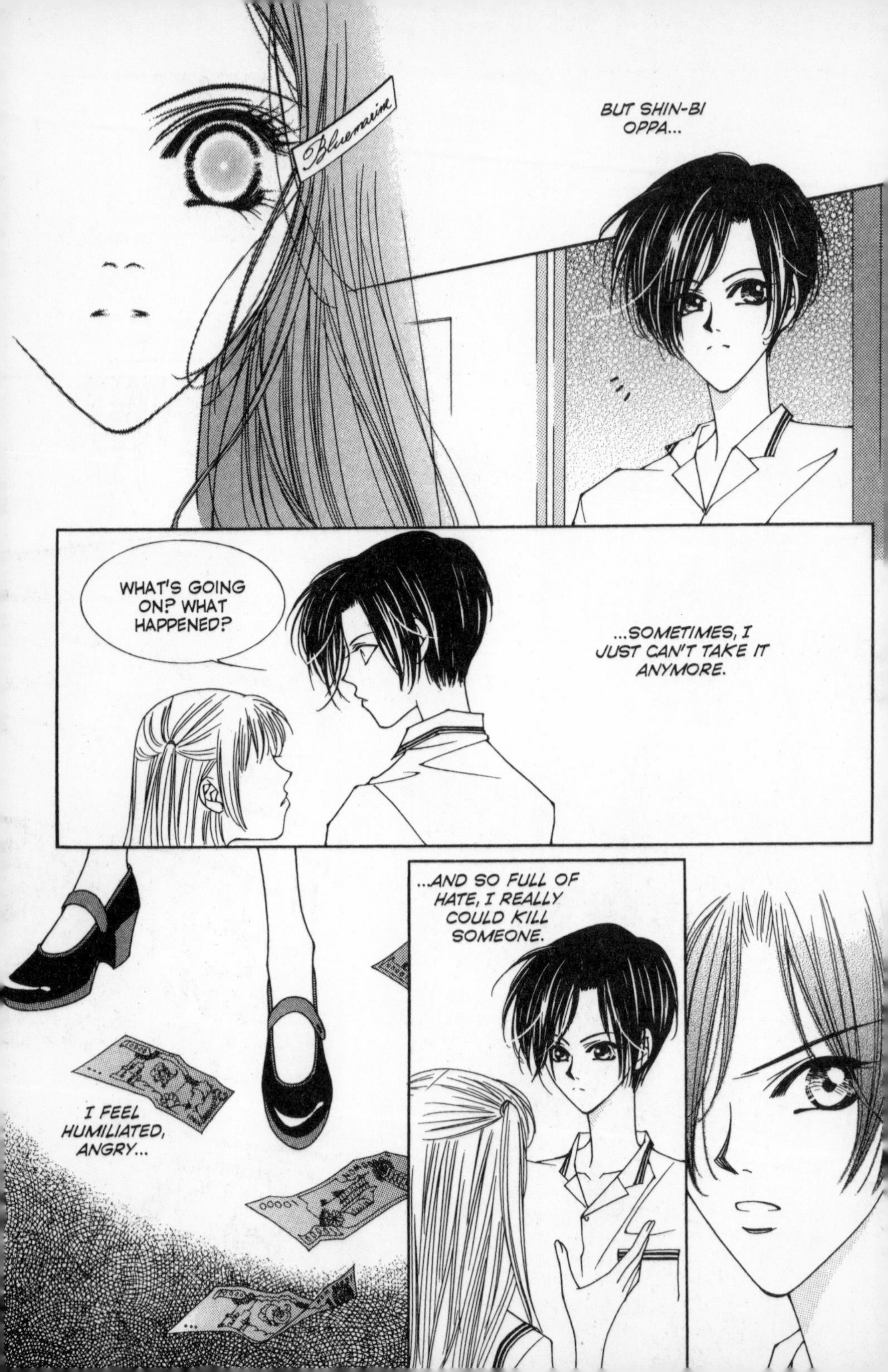
Bluemarine
BUT SHIN-BI OPPA...
WHAT'S GOING ON? WHAT HAPPENED?
...SOMETIMES, I JUST CAN'T TAKE IT ANYMORE.
I FEEL HUMILIATED, ANGRY...
...AND SO FULL OF HATE, I REALLY COULD KILL SOMEONE.

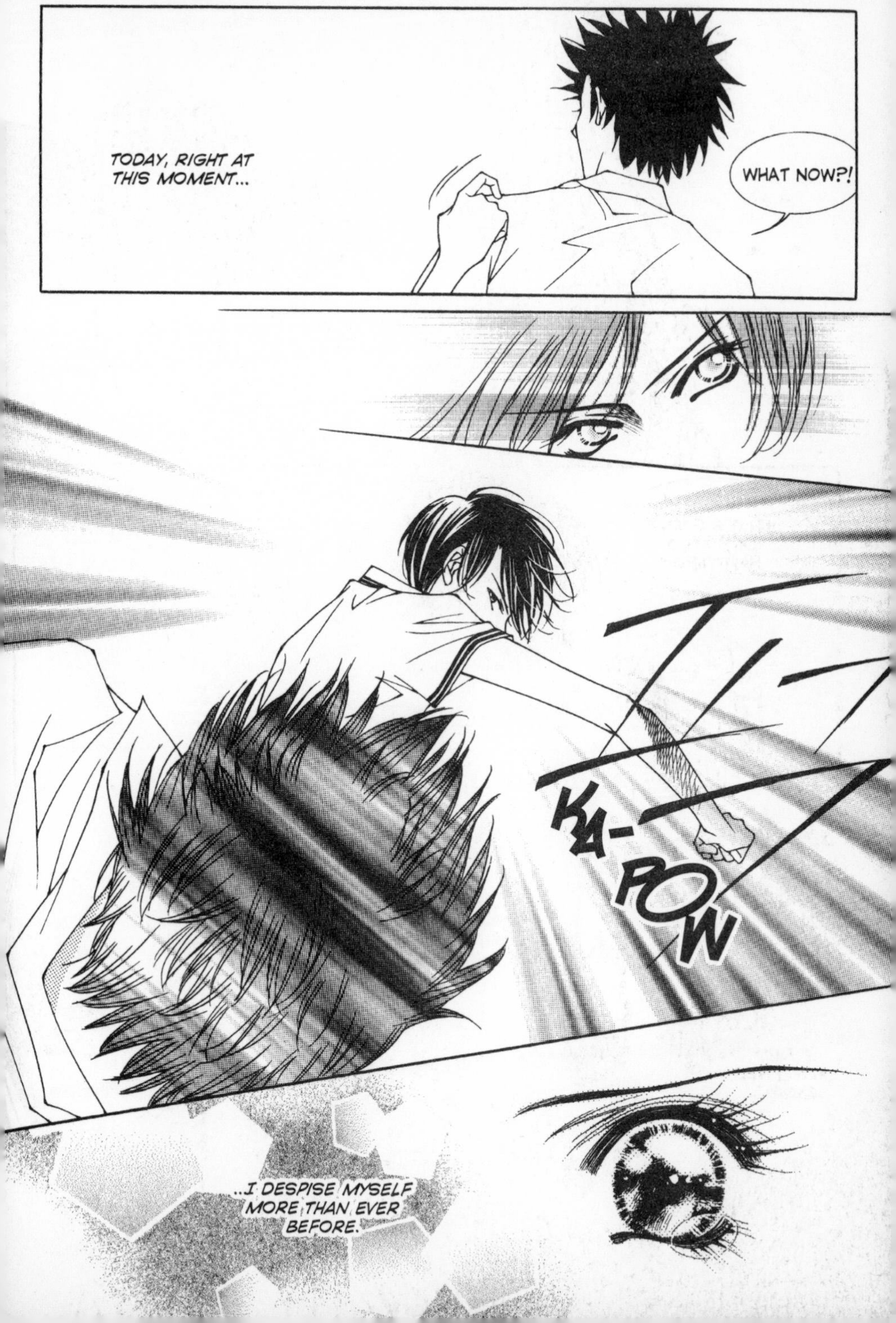
TODAY, RIGHT AT THIS MOMENT...
WHAT NOW?!
KA-POW
...I DESPISE MYSELF MORE THAN EVER BEFORE.

OH, NO! SOMEBODY STOP THEM!!

JUNG-YUN, DON'T--!

CALL THE TEACHER, HURRY!

OPPA...

..I'M NOT STRONG THE WAY YOU ARE.

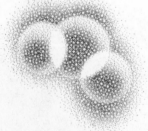

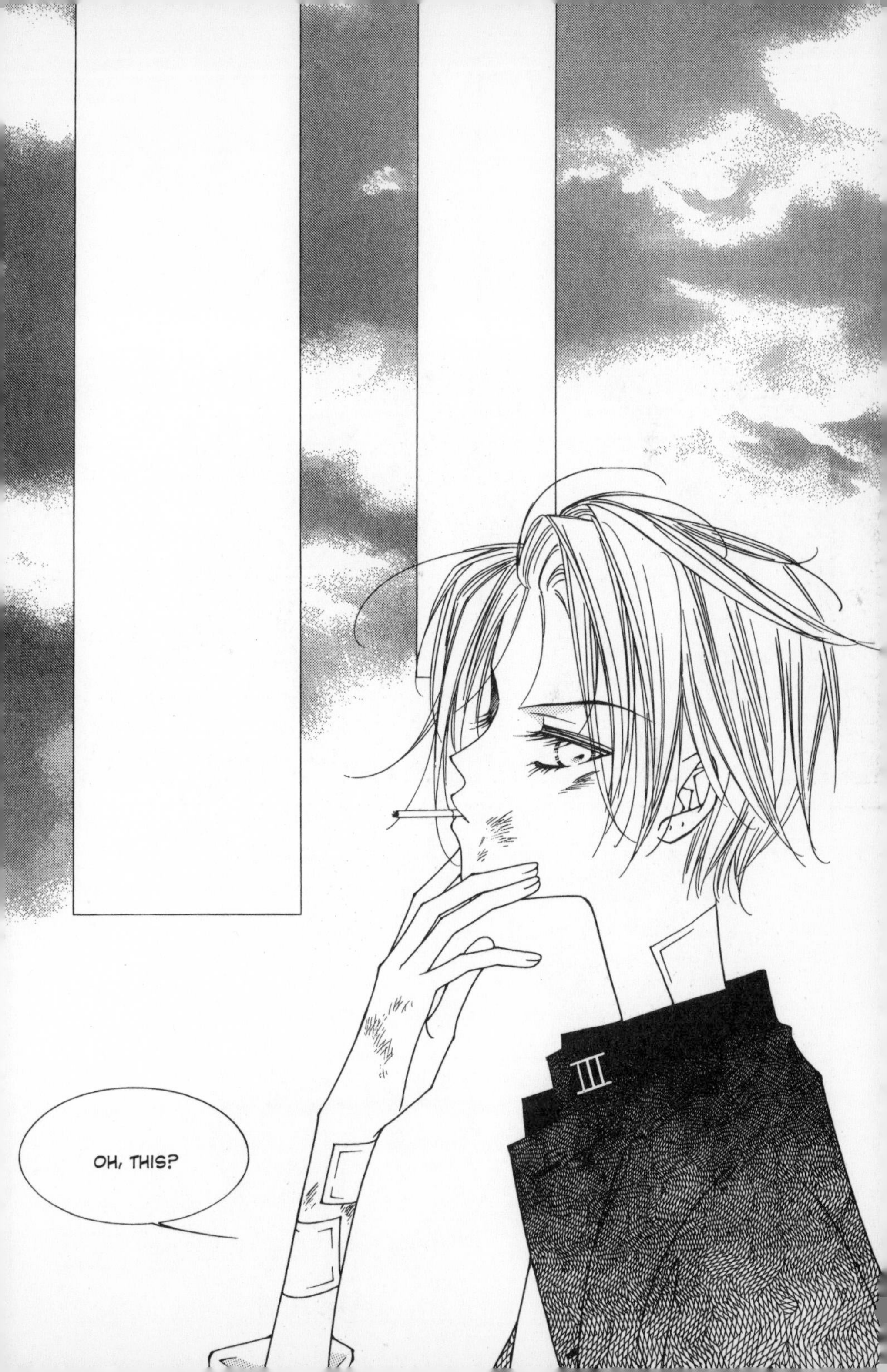
OH, THIS?

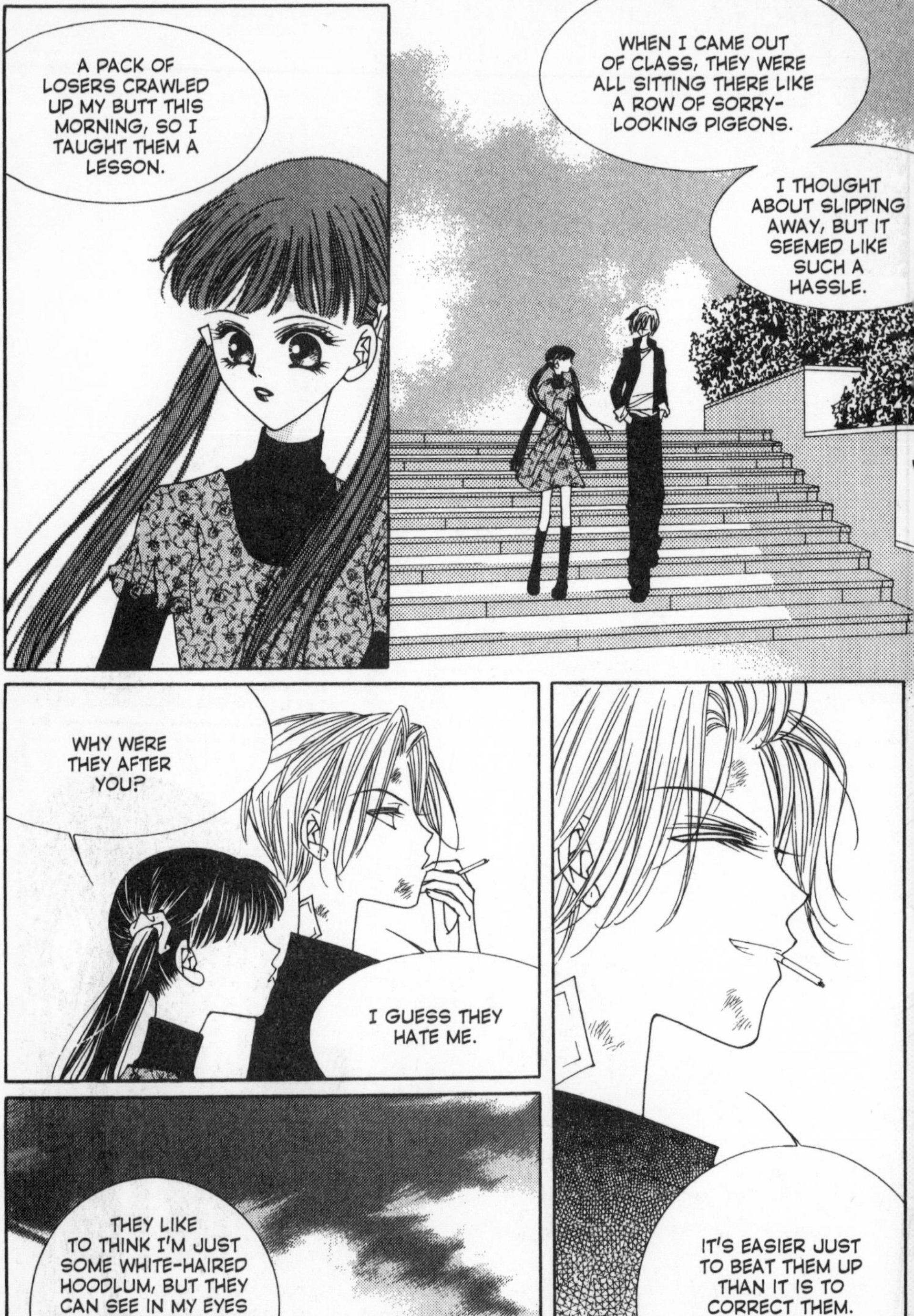
A PACK OF LOSERS CRAWLED UP MY BUTT THIS MORNING, SO I TAUGHT THEM A LESSON.
WHEN I CAME OUT OF CLASS, THEY WERE ALL SITTING THERE LIKE A ROW OF SORRY-LOOKING PIGEONS.
I THOUGHT ABOUT SLIPPING AWAY, BUT IT SEEMED LIKE SUCH A HASSLE.
WHY WERE THEY AFTER YOU?
I GUESS THEY HATE ME.
THEY LIKE TO THINK I'M JUST SOME WHITE-HAIRED HOODLUM, BUT THEY CAN SEE IN MY EYES THAT I'M BETTER THAN THEY ARE.
IT'S EASIER JUST TO BEAT THEM UP THAN IT IS TO CORRECT THEM.

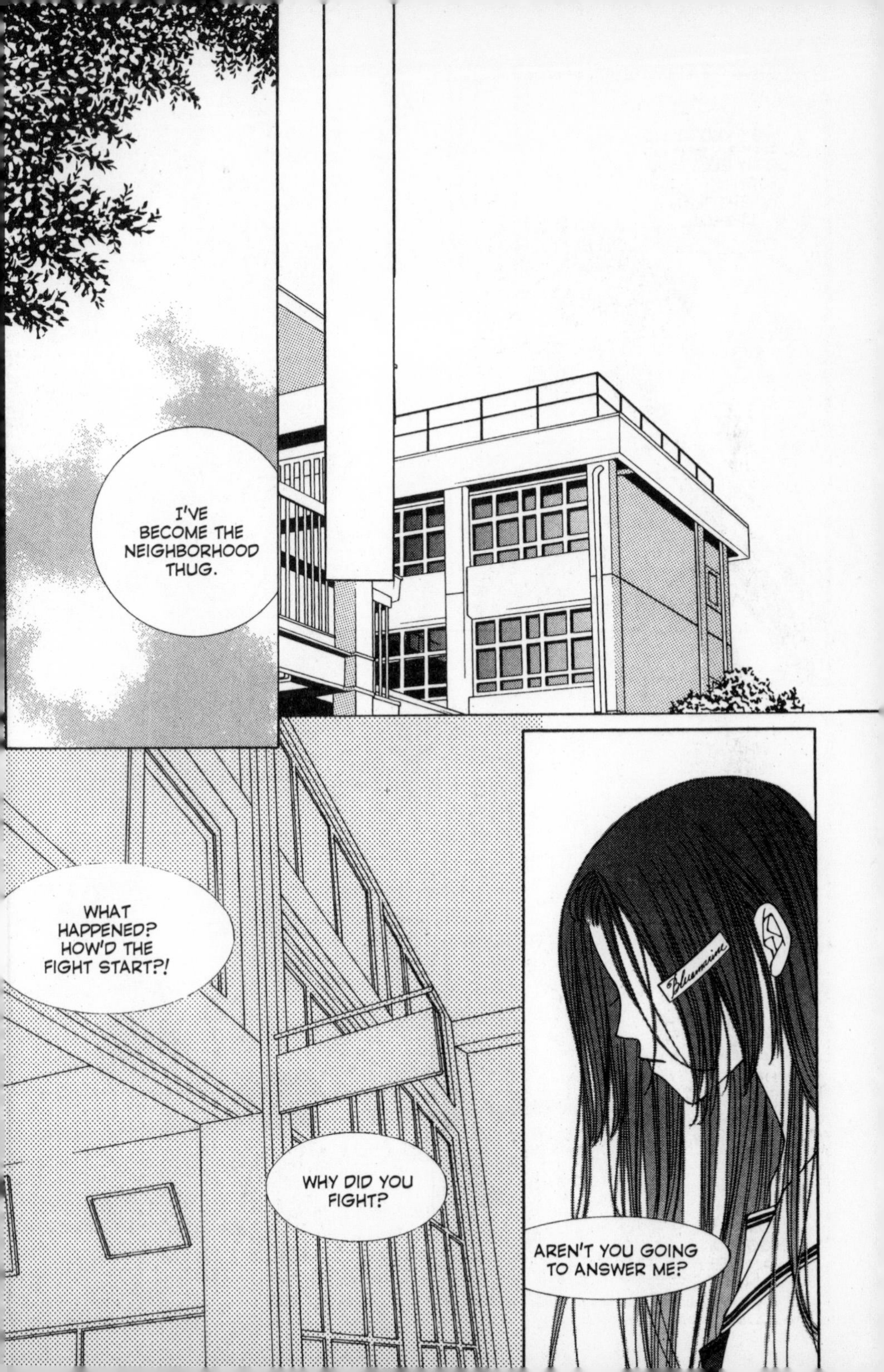
I'VE BECOME THE NEIGHBORHOOD THUG.
WHAT HAPPENED? HOW'D THE FIGHT START?!
WHY DID YOU FIGHT?
AREN'T YOU GOING TO ANSWER ME?

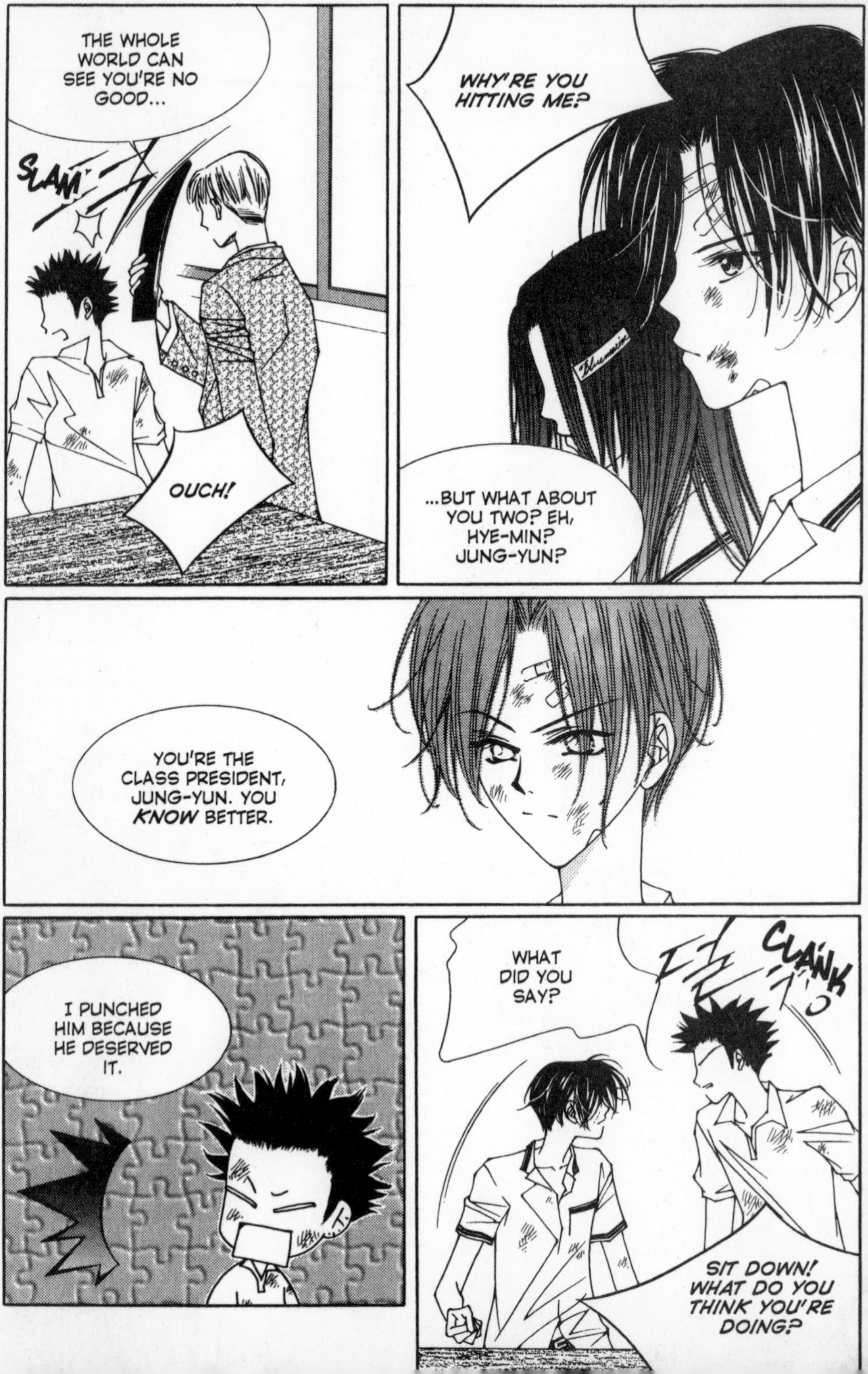
THE WHOLE WORLD CAN SEE YOU'RE NO GOOD...
SLAM
OUCH!
WHY'RE YOU HITTING ME?
...BUT WHAT ABOUT YOU TWO? EH, HYE-MIN? JUNG-YUN?
YOU'RE THE CLASS PRESIDENT, JUNG-YUN. YOU *KNOW* BETTER.
I PUNCHED HIM BECAUSE HE DESERVED IT.
WHAT DID YOU SAY?
CLANK
SIT DOWN! WHAT DO YOU THINK YOU'RE DOING?

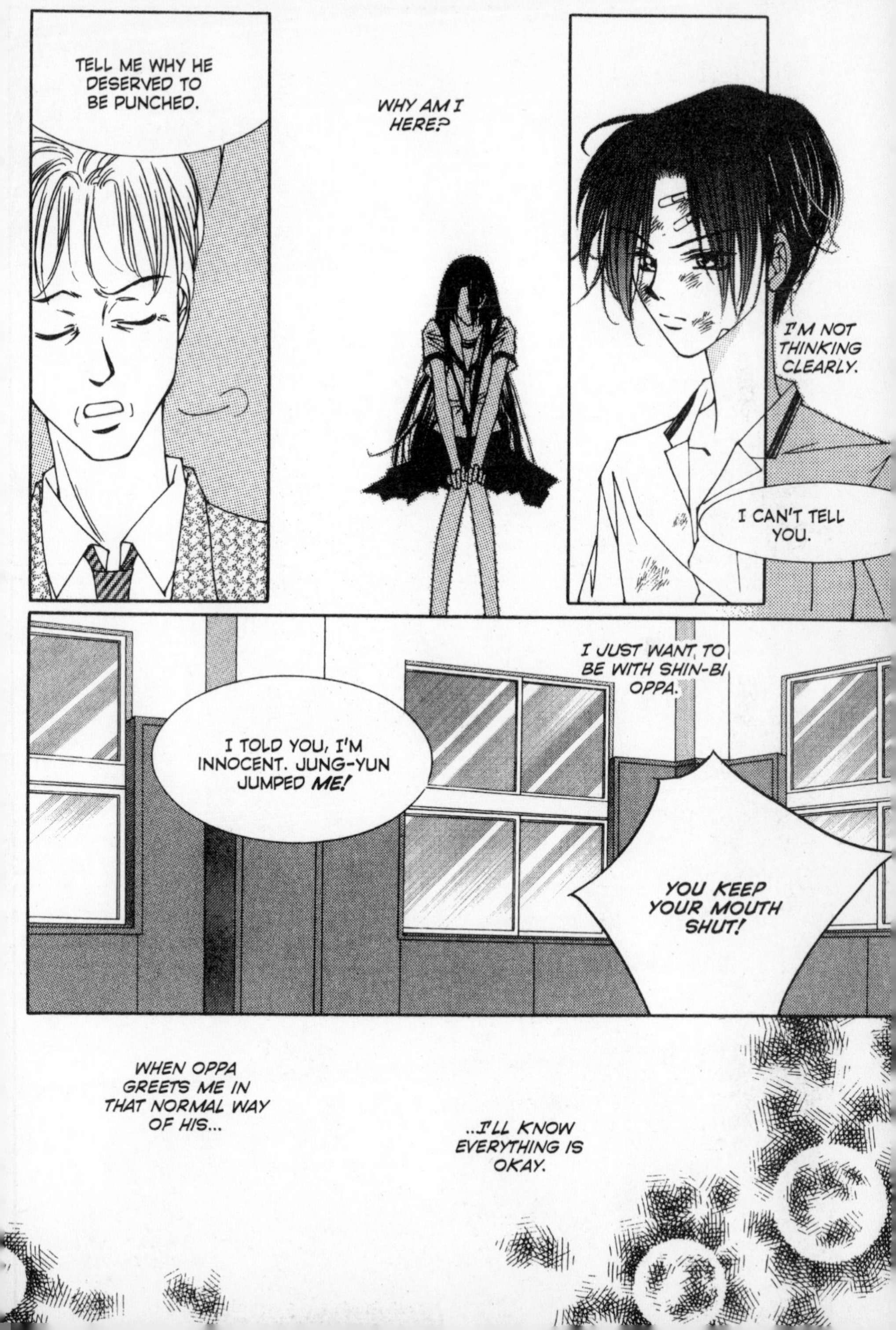
TELL ME WHY HE DESERVED TO BE PUNCHED.
WHY AM I HERE?
I'M NOT THINKING CLEARLY.
I CAN'T TELL YOU.
I TOLD YOU, I'M INNOCENT. JUNG-YUN JUMPED ME!
I JUST WANT TO BE WITH SHIN-BI OPPA.
YOU KEEP YOUR MOUTH SHUT!
WHEN OPPA GREETS ME IN THAT NORMAL WAY OF HIS...
...I'LL KNOW EVERYTHING IS OKAY.

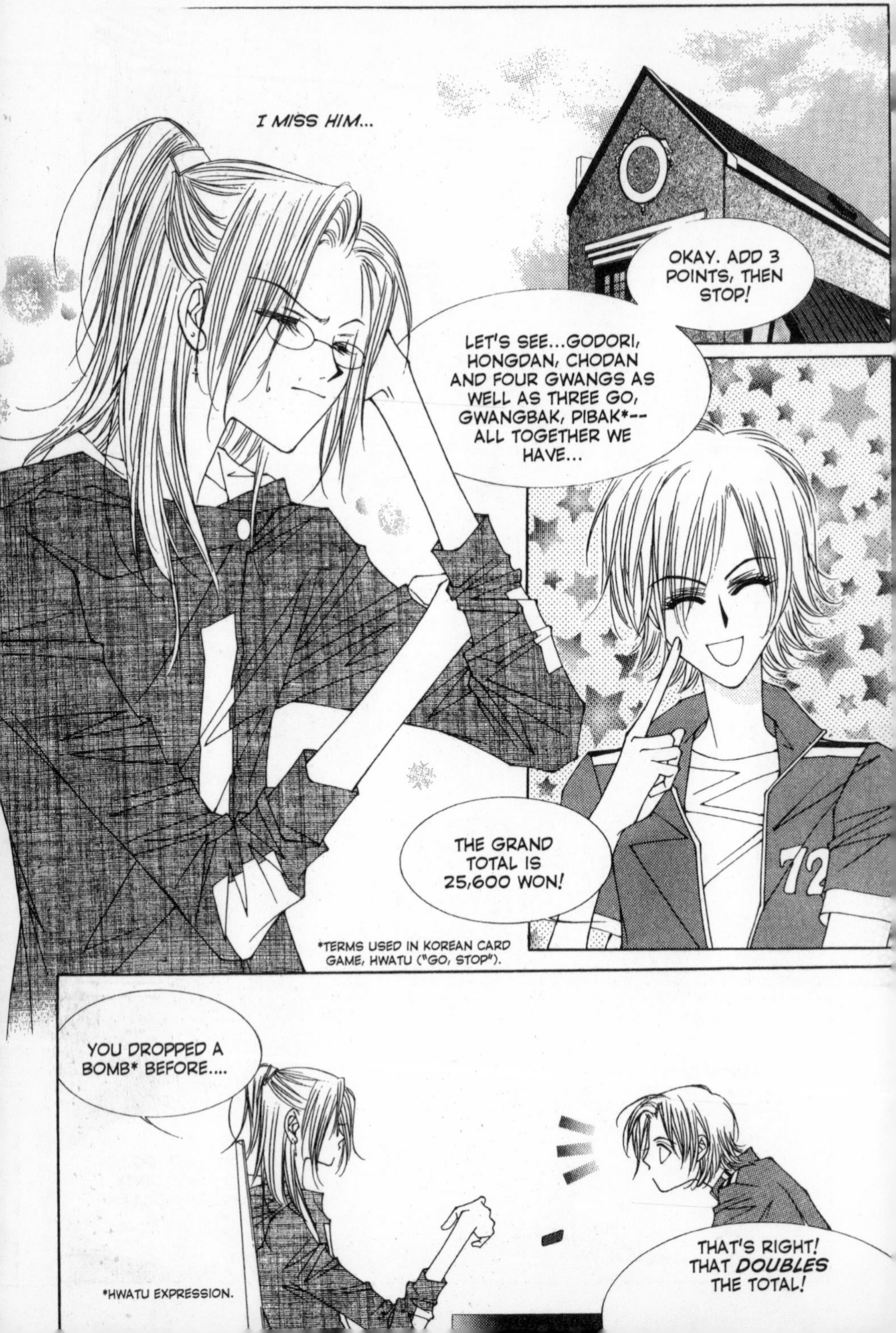
I MISS HIM...
OKAY. ADD 3 POINTS, THEN STOP!
LET'S SEE...GODORI, HONGDAN, CHODAN AND FOUR GWANGS AS WELL AS THREE GO, GWANGBAK, PIBAK*-- ALL TOGETHER WE HAVE...
THE GRAND TOTAL IS 25,600 WON!
*TERMS USED IN KOREAN CARD GAME, HWATU ("GO, STOP").
YOU DROPPED A BOMB* BEFORE....
*HWATU EXPRESSION.
THAT'S RIGHT! THAT DOUBLES THE TOTAL!

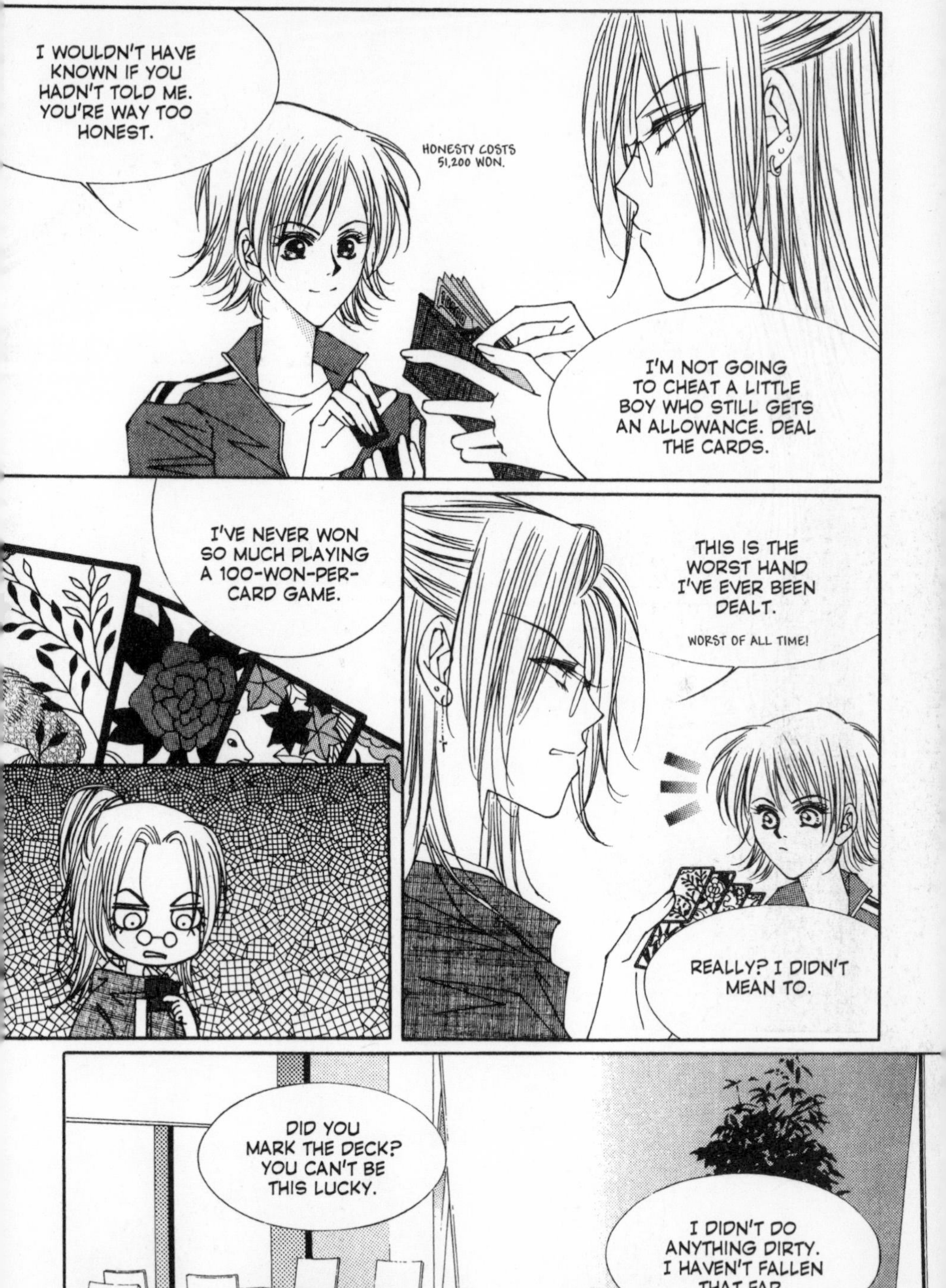
I WOULDN'T HAVE KNOWN IF YOU HADN'T TOLD ME. YOU'RE WAY TOO HONEST.
HONESTY COSTS 51,200 WON.
I'M NOT GOING TO CHEAT A LITTLE BOY WHO STILL GETS AN ALLOWANCE. DEAL THE CARDS.
I'VE NEVER WON SO MUCH PLAYING A 100-WON-PER-CARD GAME.
THIS IS THE WORST HAND I'VE EVER BEEN DEALT.
WORST OF ALL TIME!
REALLY? I DIDN'T MEAN TO.
DID YOU MARK THE DECK? YOU CAN'T BE THIS LUCKY.
I DIDN'T DO ANYTHING DIRTY. I HAVEN'T FALLEN THAT FAR.

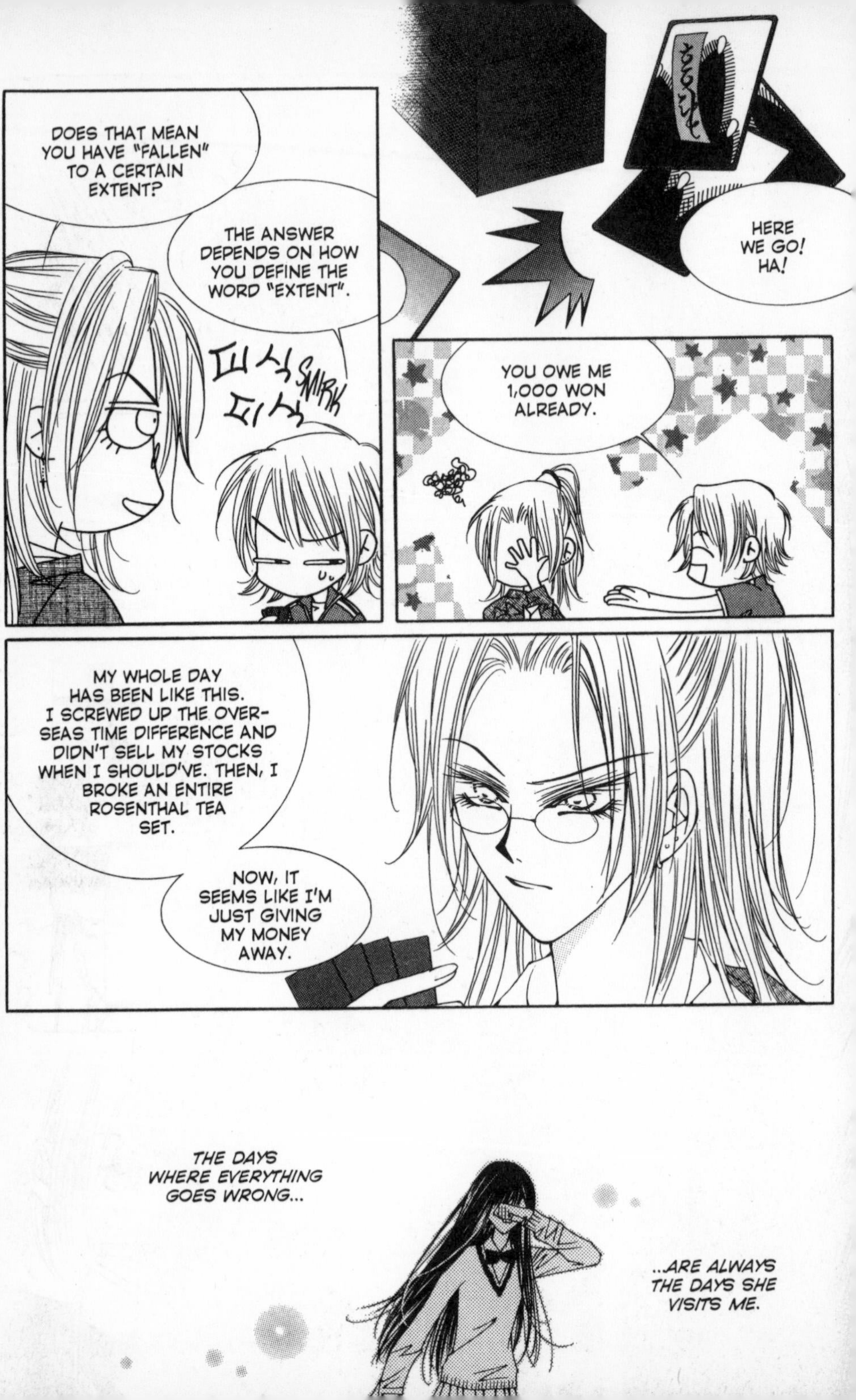
DOES THAT MEAN YOU HAVE "FALLEN" TO A CERTAIN EXTENT?
THE ANSWER DEPENDS ON HOW YOU DEFINE THE WORD "EXTENT".
SMIRK
HERE WE GO! HA!
YOU OWE ME 1,000 WON ALREADY.
MY WHOLE DAY HAS BEEN LIKE THIS. I SCREWED UP THE OVER-SEAS TIME DIFFERENCE AND DIDN'T SELL MY STOCKS WHEN I SHOULD'VE. THEN, I BROKE AN ENTIRE ROSENTHAL TEA SET.
NOW, IT SEEMS LIKE I'M JUST GIVING MY MONEY AWAY.
THE DAYS WHERE EVERYTHING GOES WRONG...
...ARE ALWAYS THE DAYS SHE VISITS ME.

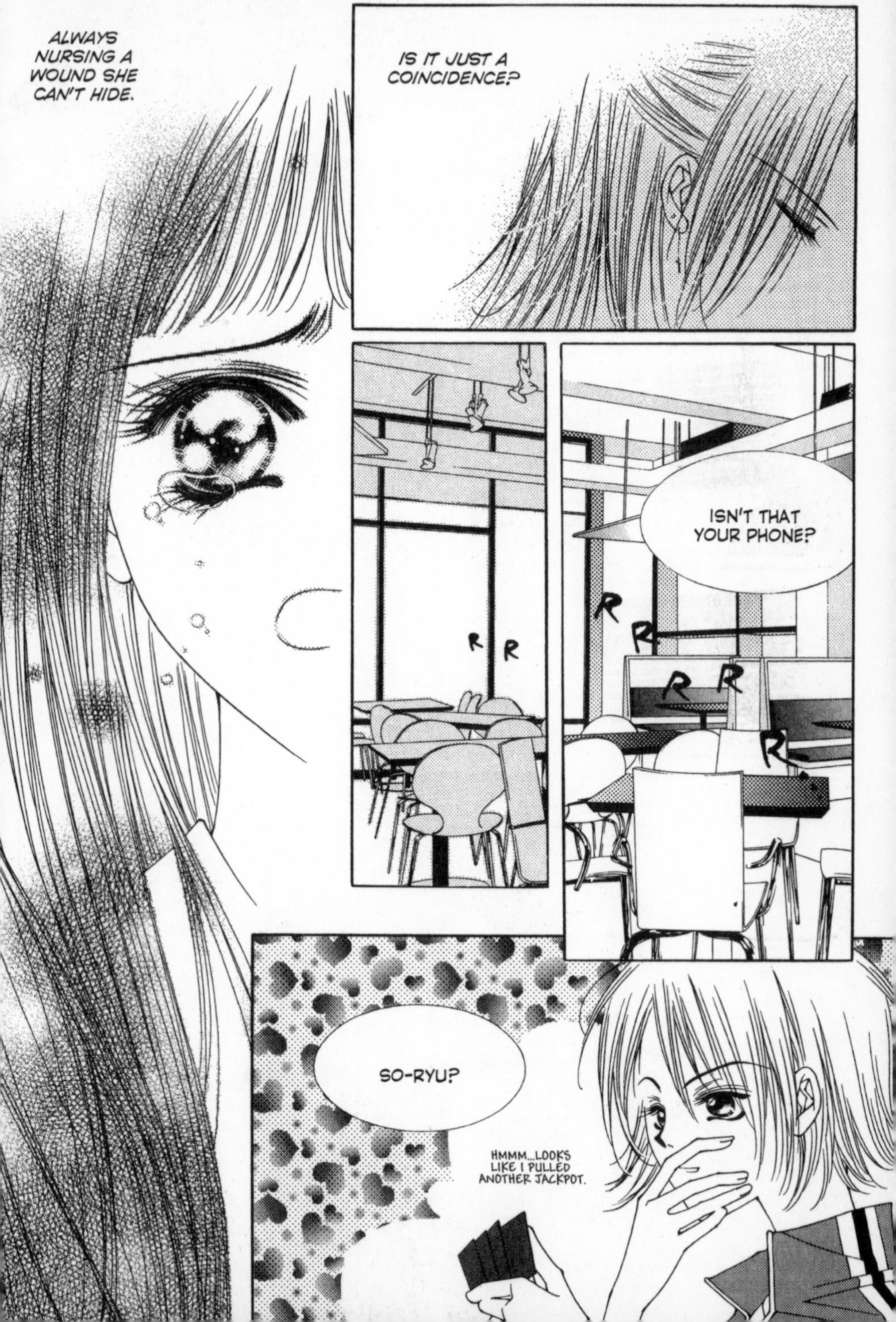
ALWAYS NURSING A WOUND SHE CAN'T HIDE.
IS IT JUST A COINCIDENCE?
R R
ISN'T THAT YOUR PHONE?
R R R R R
SO-RYU?
HMMM...LOOKS LIKE I PULLED ANOTHER JACKPOT.

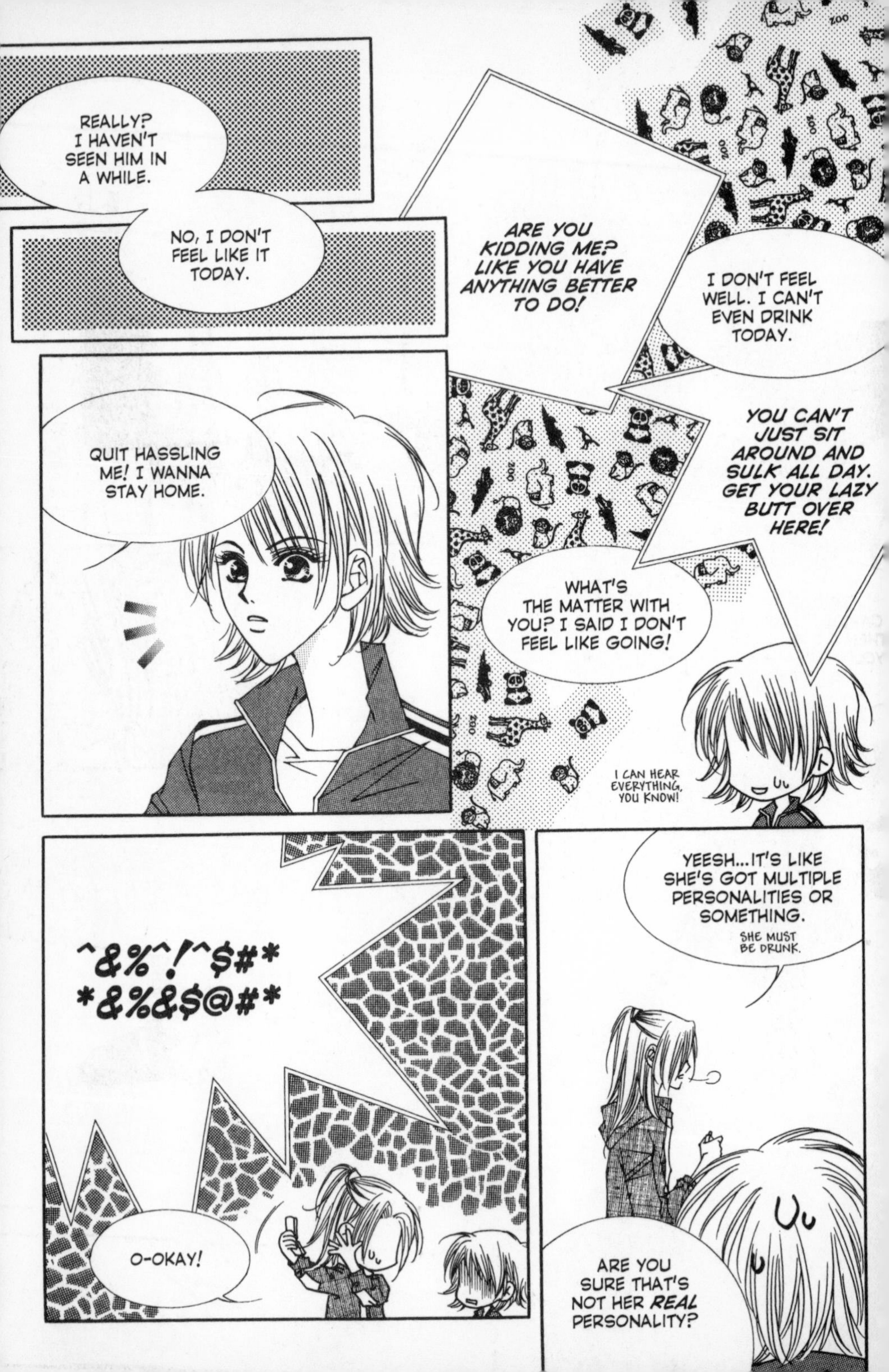
REALLY? I HAVEN'T SEEN HIM IN A WHILE.
NO, I DON'T FEEL LIKE IT TODAY.
ARE YOU KIDDING ME? LIKE YOU HAVE ANYTHING BETTER TO DO!
I DON'T FEEL WELL. I CAN'T EVEN DRINK TODAY.
QUIT HASSLING ME! I WANNA STAY HOME.
YOU CAN'T JUST SIT AROUND AND SULK ALL DAY. GET YOUR LAZY BUTT OVER HERE!
WHAT'S THE MATTER WITH YOU? I SAID I DON'T FEEL LIKE GOING!
I CAN HEAR EVERYTHING, YOU KNOW!
^&%^!^$#*
&%&$@#
O-OKAY!
YEESH...IT'S LIKE SHE'S GOT MULTIPLE PERSONALITIES OR SOMETHING.
SHE MUST BE DRUNK.
ARE YOU SURE THAT'S NOT HER REAL PERSONALITY?

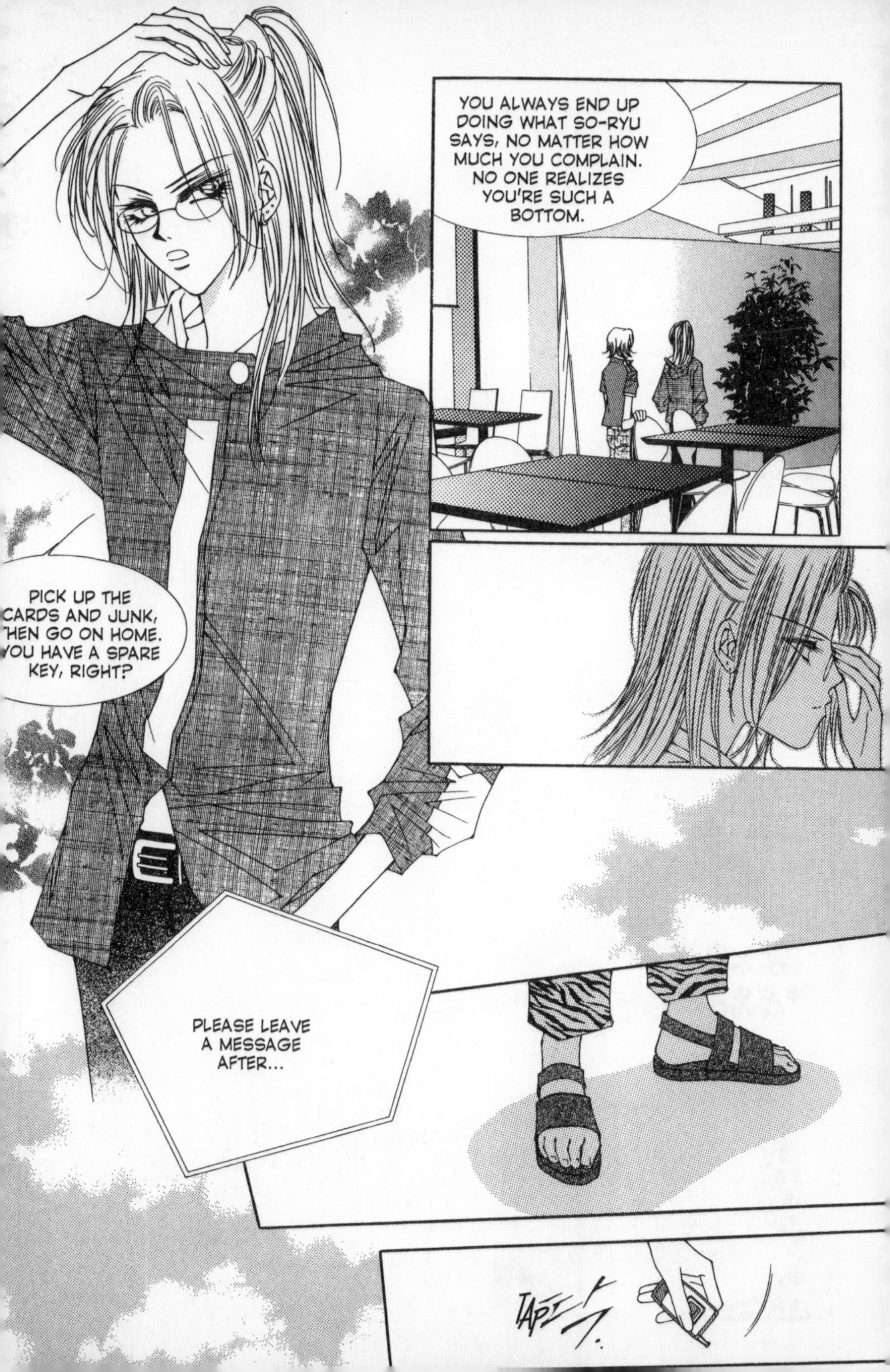
PICK UP THE CARDS AND JUNK, THEN GO ON HOME. YOU HAVE A SPARE KEY, RIGHT?
PLEASE LEAVE A MESSAGE AFTER...
YOU ALWAYS END UP DOING WHAT SO-RYU SAYS, NO MATTER HOW MUCH YOU COMPLAIN. NO ONE REALIZES YOU'RE SUCH A BOTTOM.
TAP

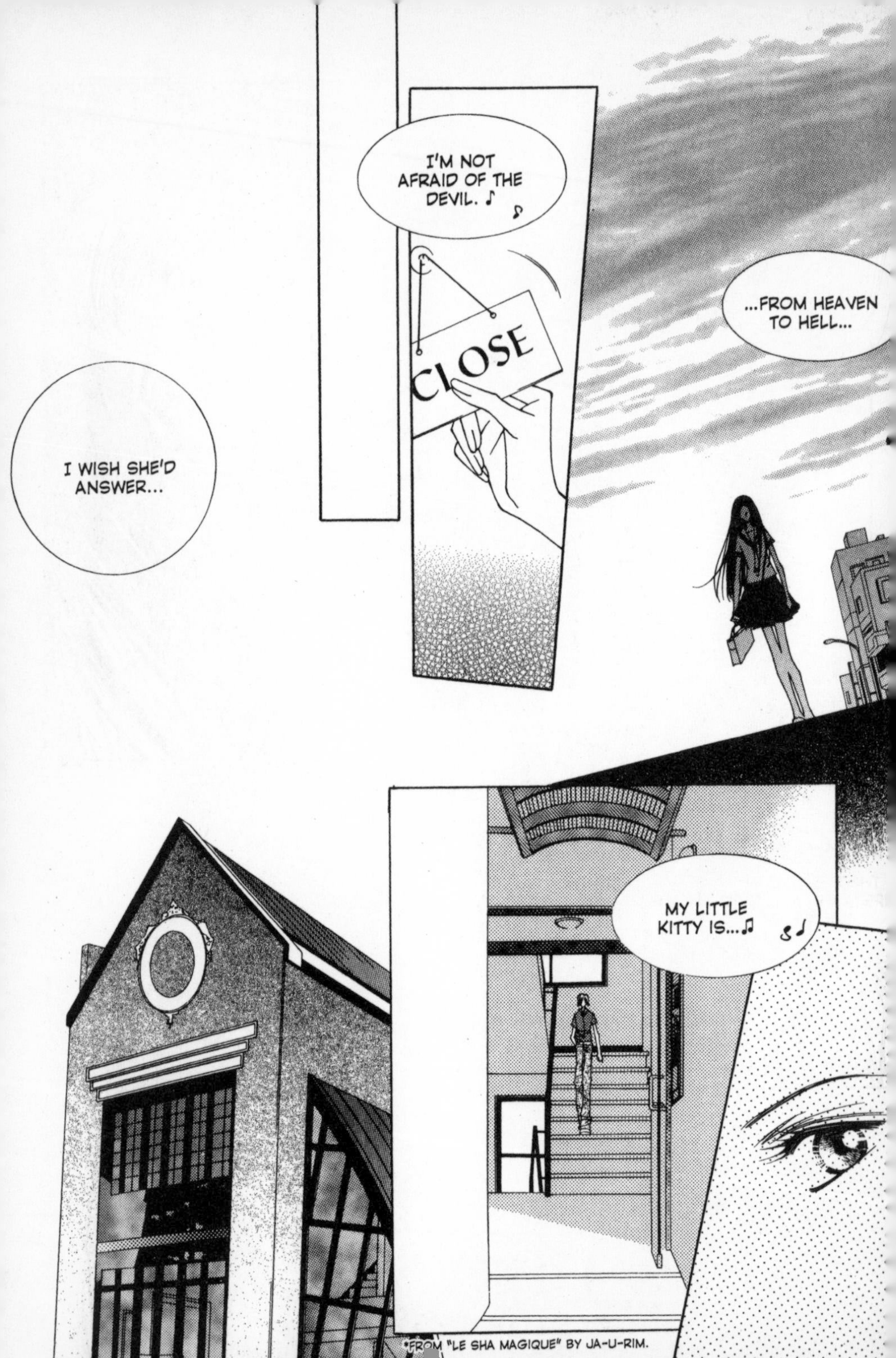
I WISH SHE'D ANSWER...
I'M NOT AFRAID OF THE DEVIL. ♪
CLOSE
...FROM HEAVEN TO HELL...
MY LITTLE KITTY IS...♫

*FROM "LE SHA MAGIQUE" BY JA-U-RIM.

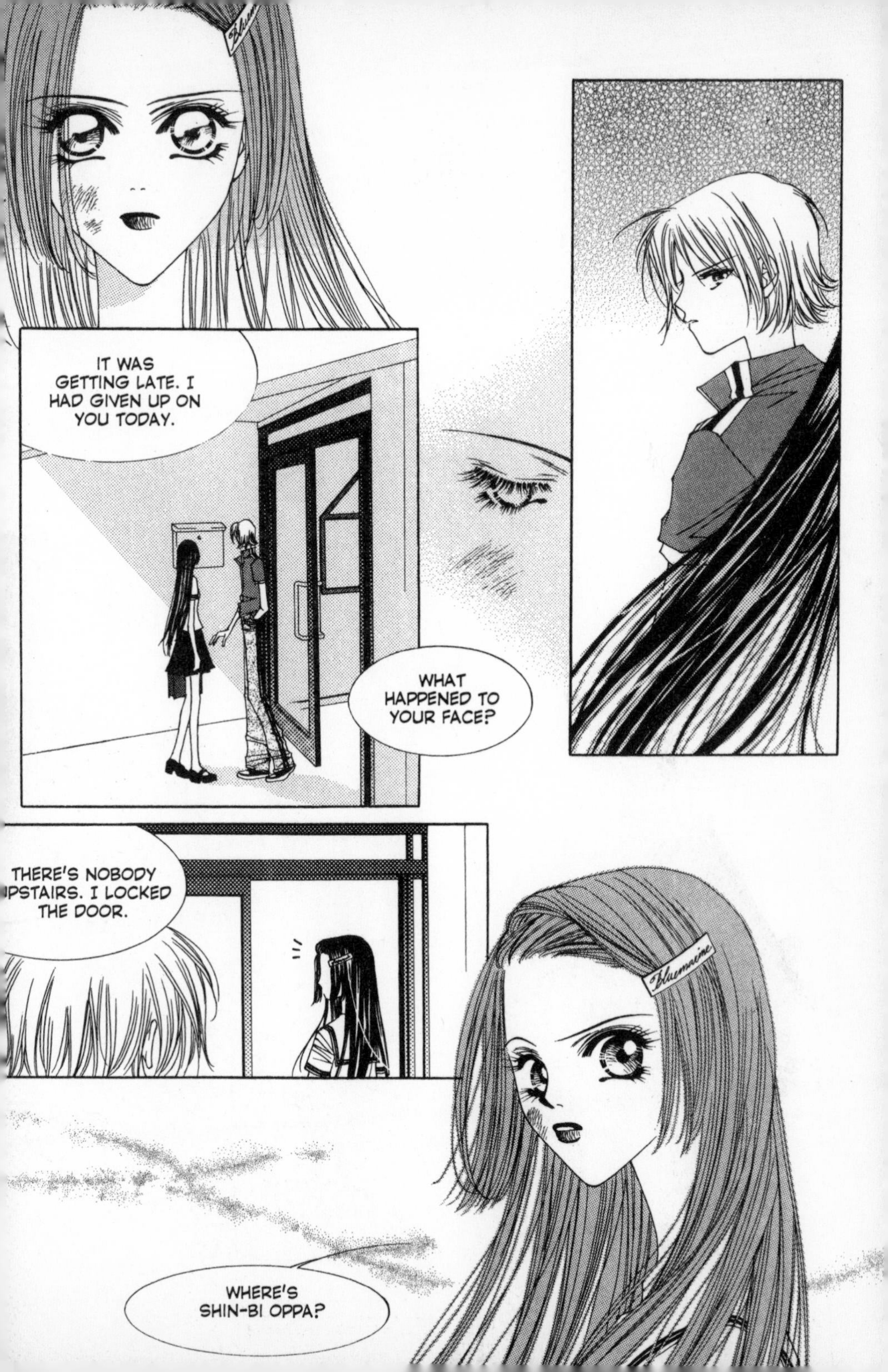
IT WAS GETTING LATE. I HAD GIVEN UP ON YOU TODAY.
WHAT HAPPENED TO YOUR FACE?
THERE'S NOBODY UPSTAIRS. I LOCKED THE DOOR.
WHERE'S SHIN-BI OPPA?

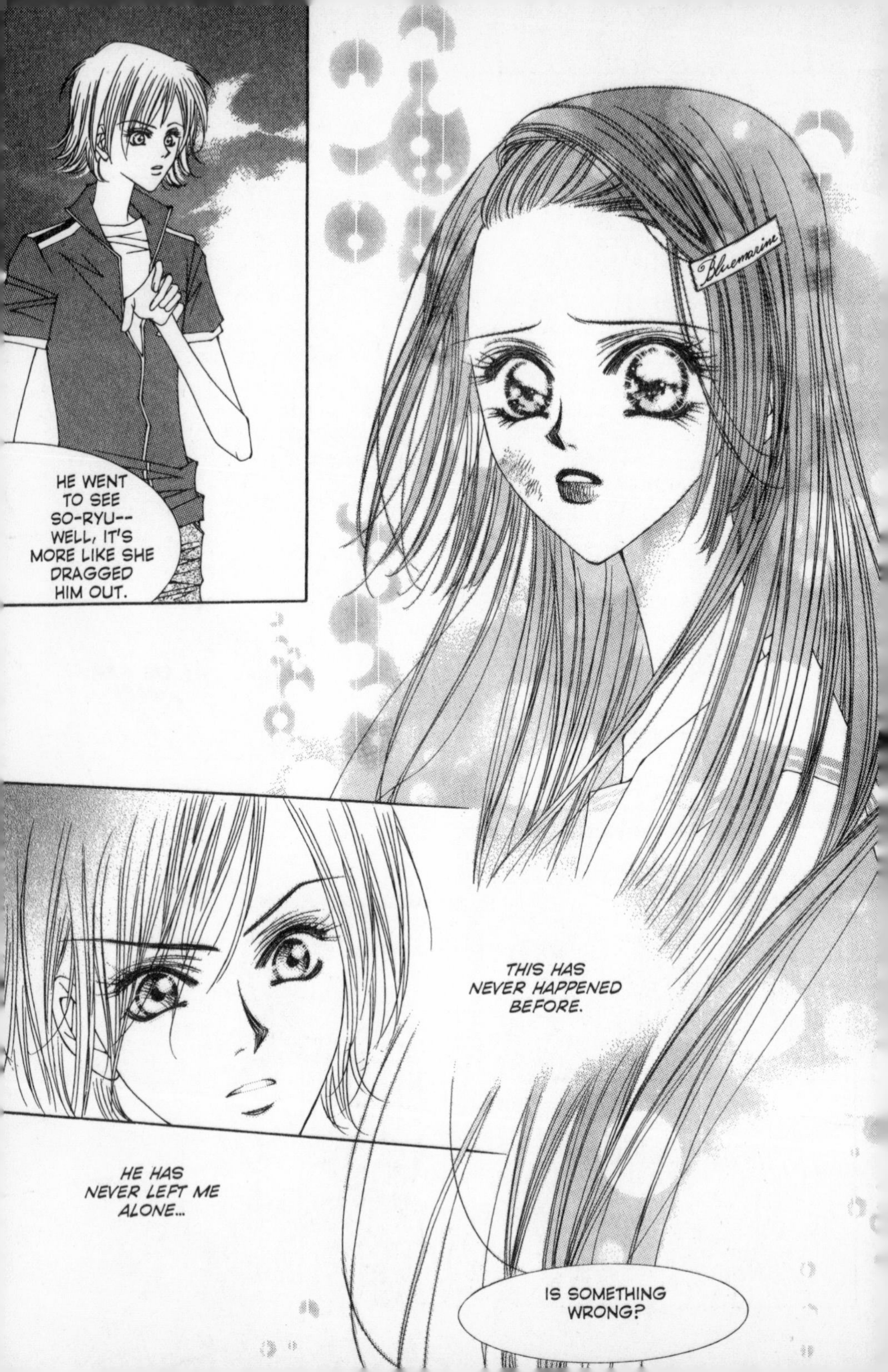
HE WENT TO SEE SO-RYU-- WELL, IT'S MORE LIKE SHE DRAGGED HIM OUT.
Bluemarine
THIS HAS NEVER HAPPENED BEFORE.
HE HAS NEVER LEFT ME ALONE...
IS SOMETHING WRONG?

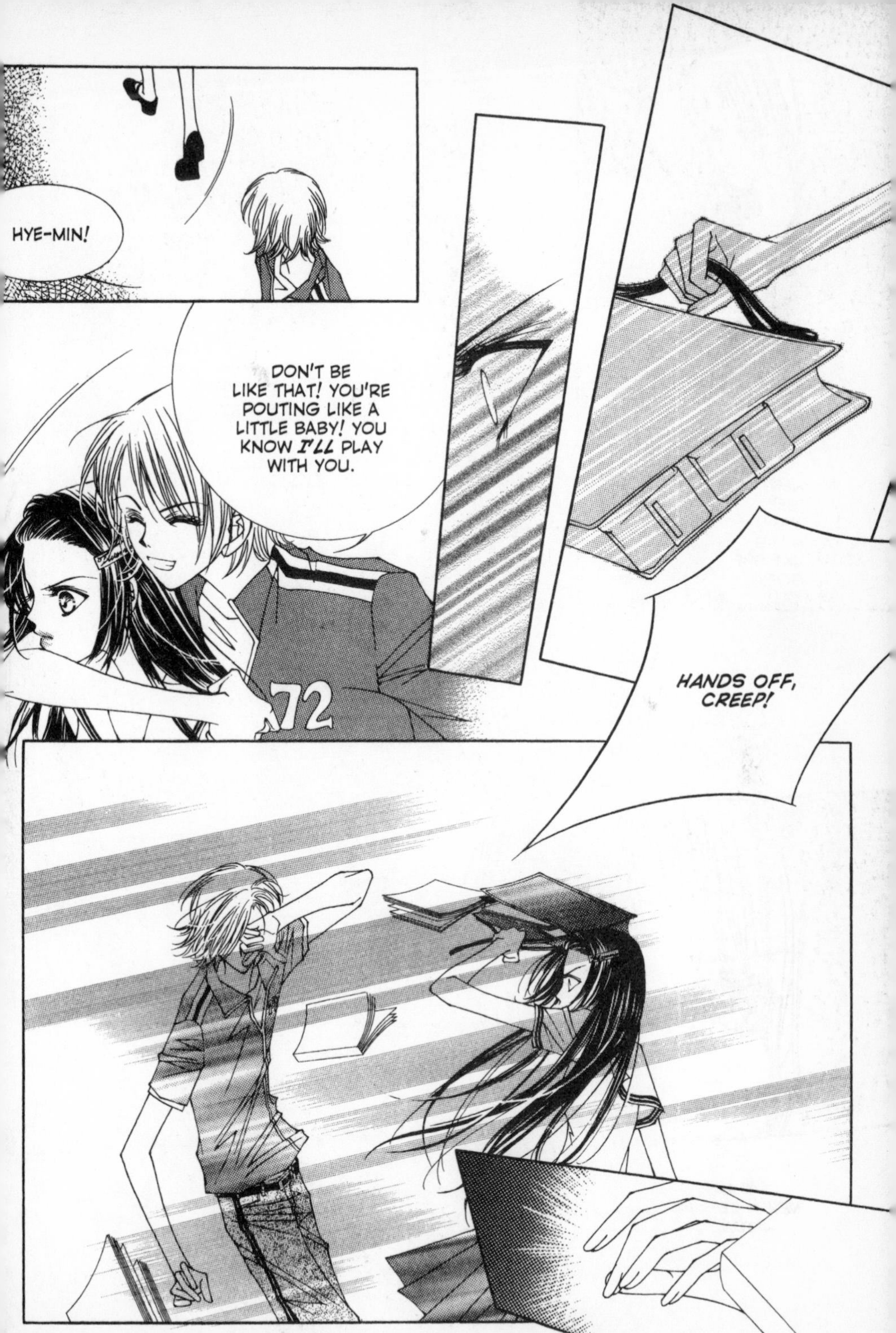
HYE-MIN!
DON'T BE LIKE THAT! YOU'RE POUTING LIKE A LITTLE BABY! YOU KNOW *I'LL* PLAY WITH YOU.
HANDS OFF, CREEP!

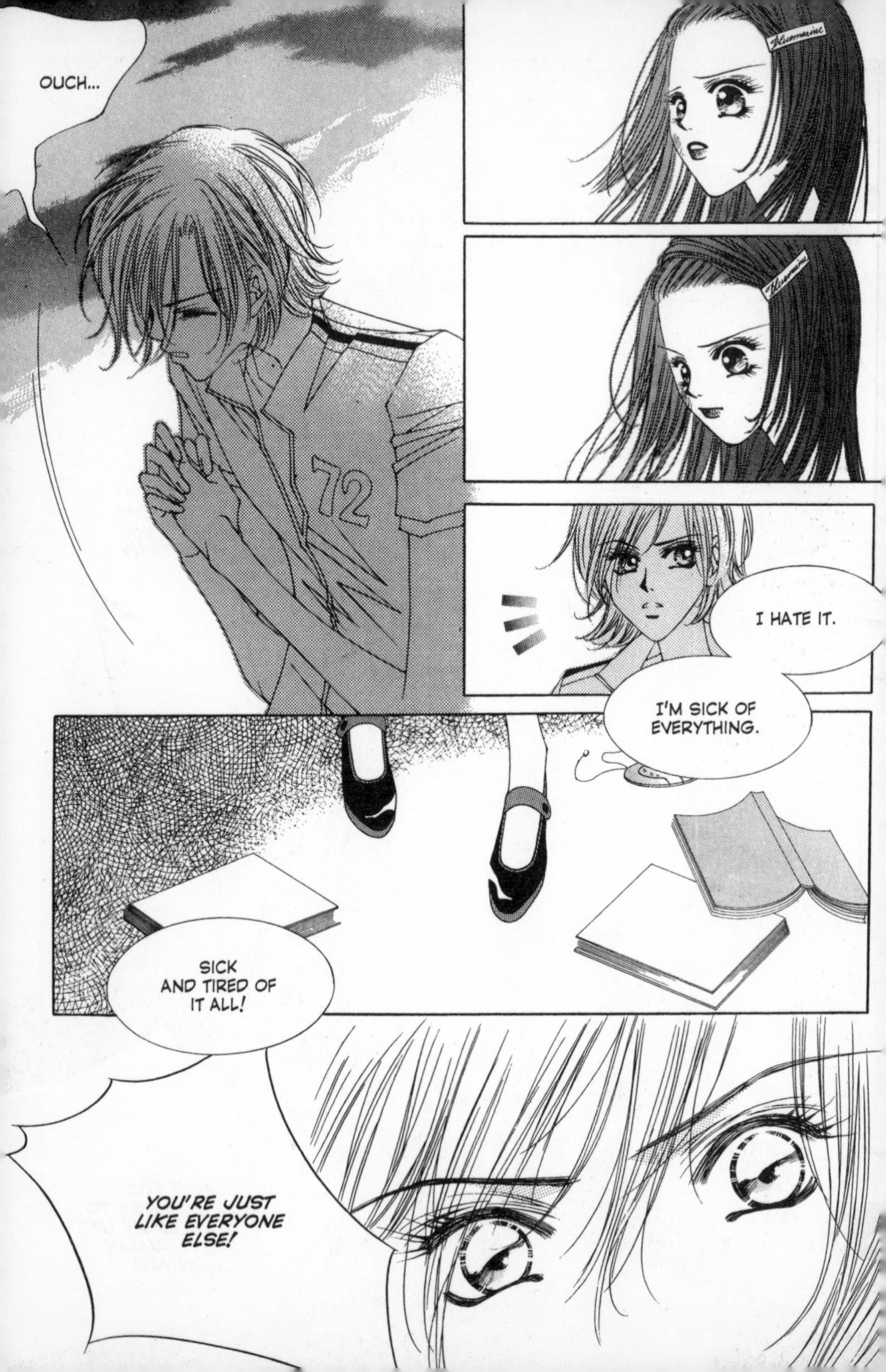
OUCH...
I HATE IT.
I'M SICK OF EVERYTHING.
SICK AND TIRED OF IT ALL!
YOU'RE JUST LIKE EVERYONE ELSE!

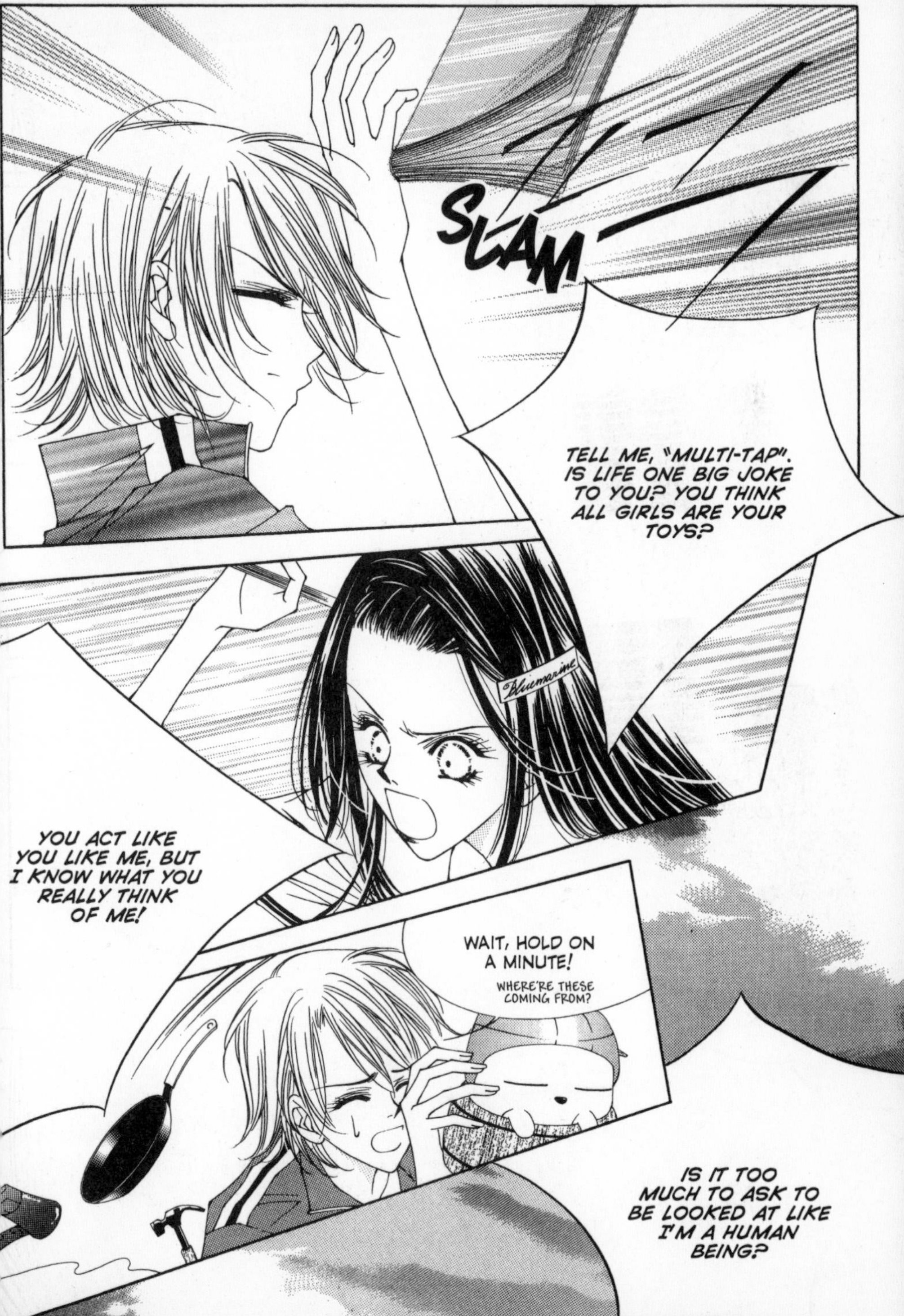
SLAM
TELL ME, "MULTI-TAP". IS LIFE ONE BIG JOKE TO YOU? YOU THINK ALL GIRLS ARE YOUR TOYS?
Bluemarine
YOU ACT LIKE YOU LIKE ME, BUT I KNOW WHAT YOU REALLY THINK OF ME!
WAIT, HOLD ON A MINUTE!
WHERE'RE THESE COMING FROM?
IS IT TOO MUCH TO ASK TO BE LOOKED AT LIKE I'M A HUMAN BEING?

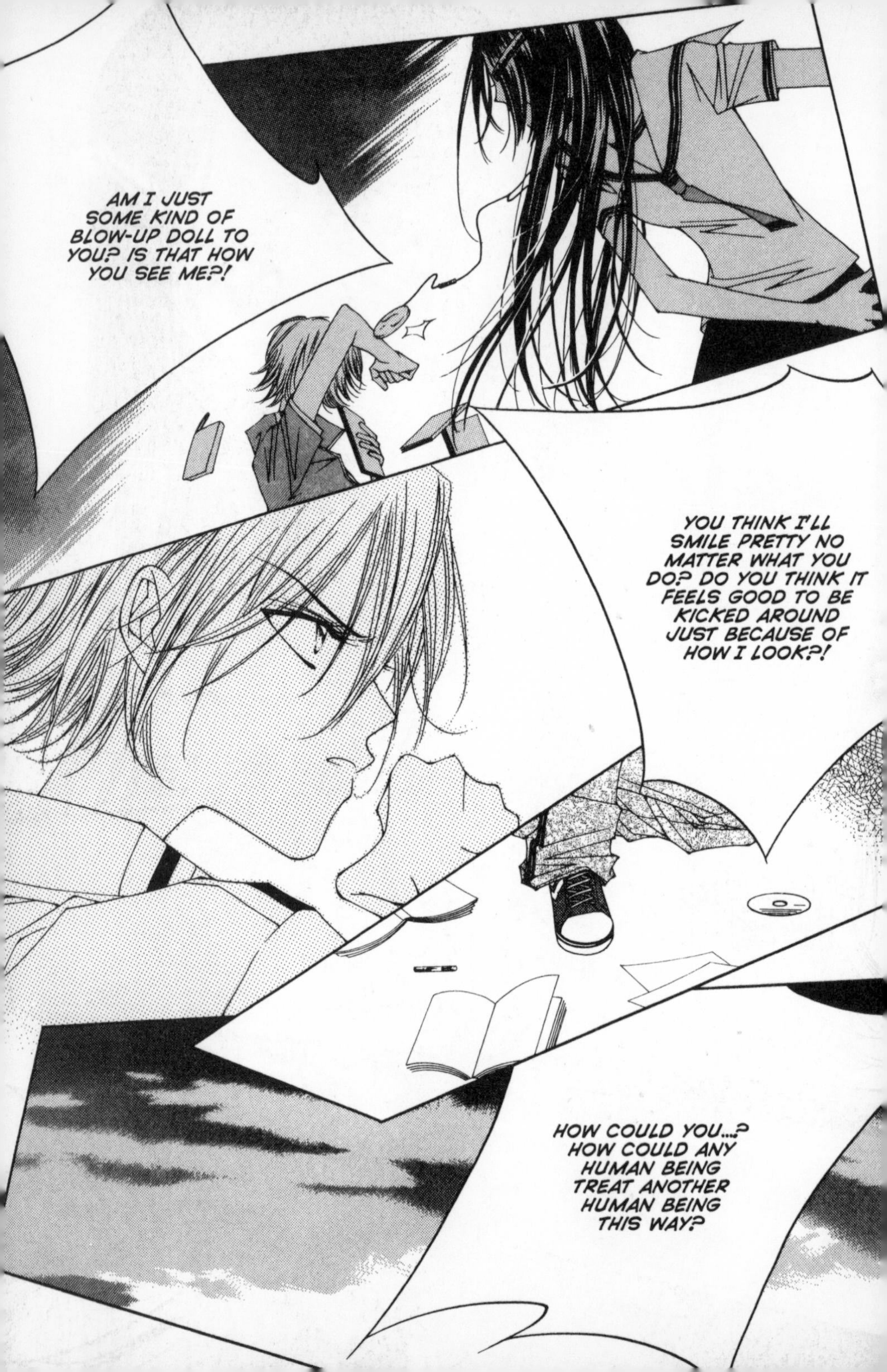
AM I JUST SOME KIND OF BLOW-UP DOLL TO YOU? IS THAT HOW YOU SEE ME?!
YOU THINK I'LL SMILE PRETTY NO MATTER WHAT YOU DO? DO YOU THINK IT FEELS GOOD TO BE KICKED AROUND JUST BECAUSE OF HOW I LOOK?!
HOW COULD YOU...? HOW COULD ANY HUMAN BEING TREAT ANOTHER HUMAN BEING THIS WAY?

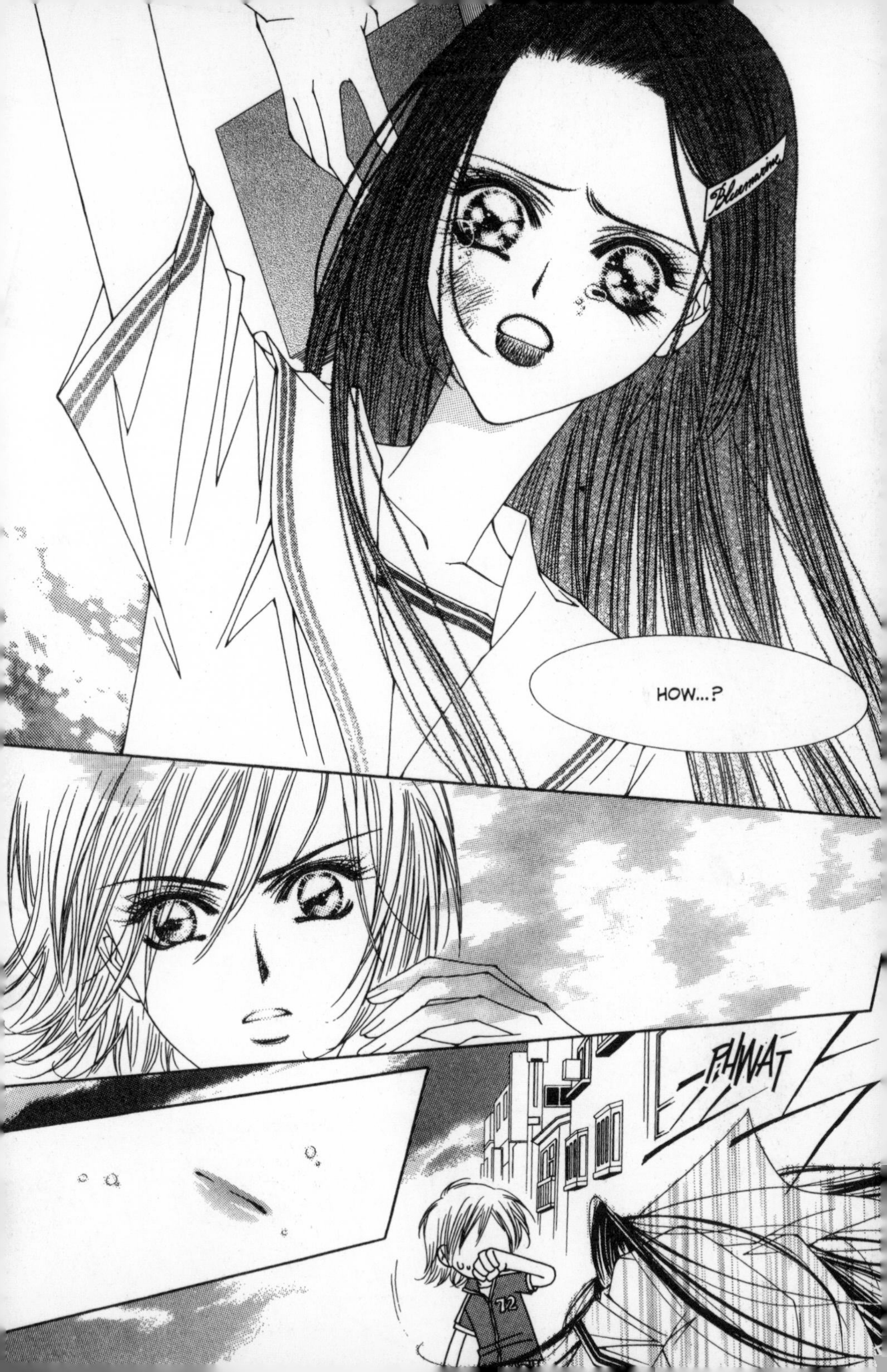
HOW...?
-PHWAT

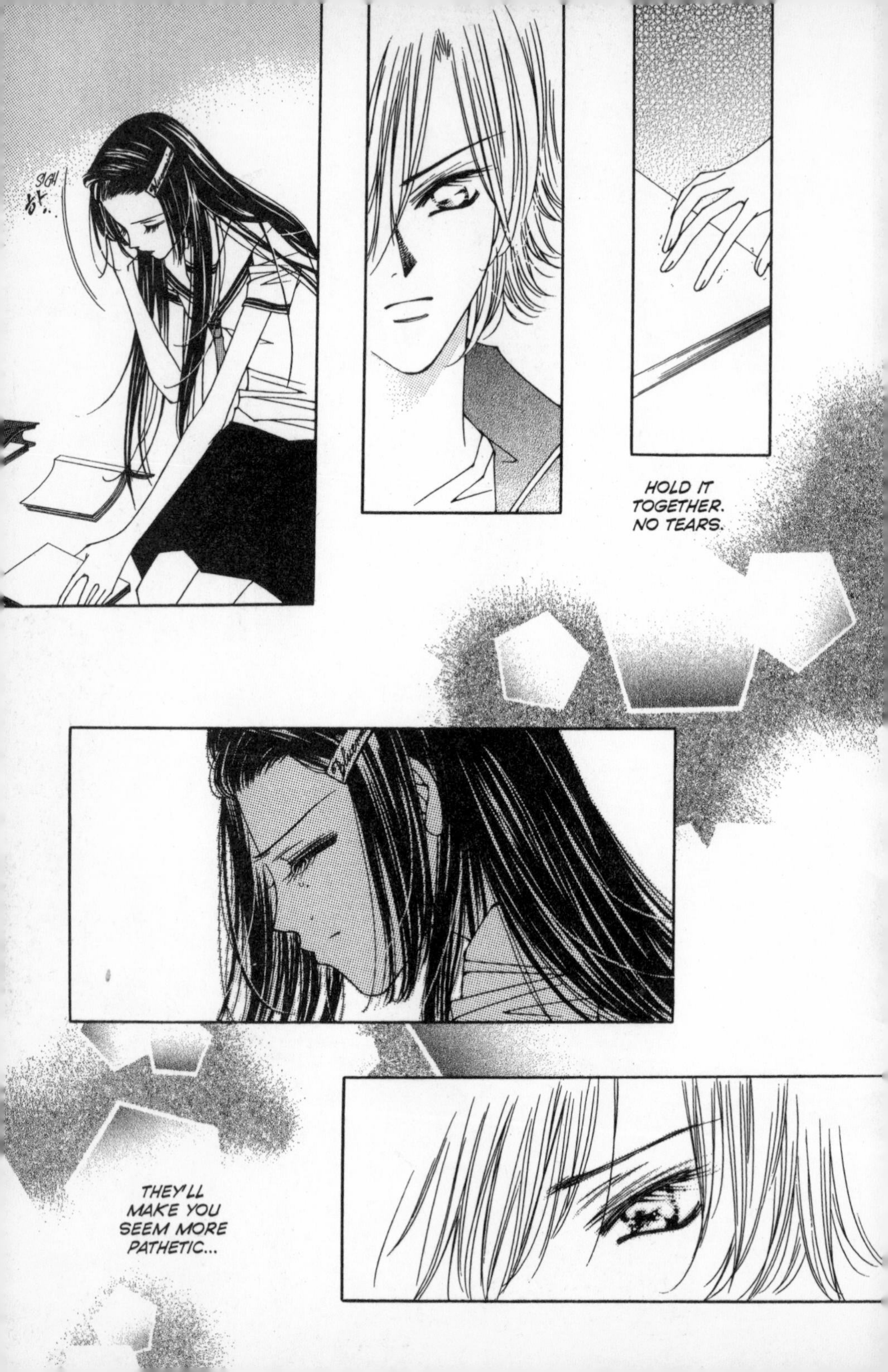
SIGH
하..
HOLD IT TOGETHER. NO TEARS.
THEY'LL MAKE YOU SEEM MORE PATHETIC...

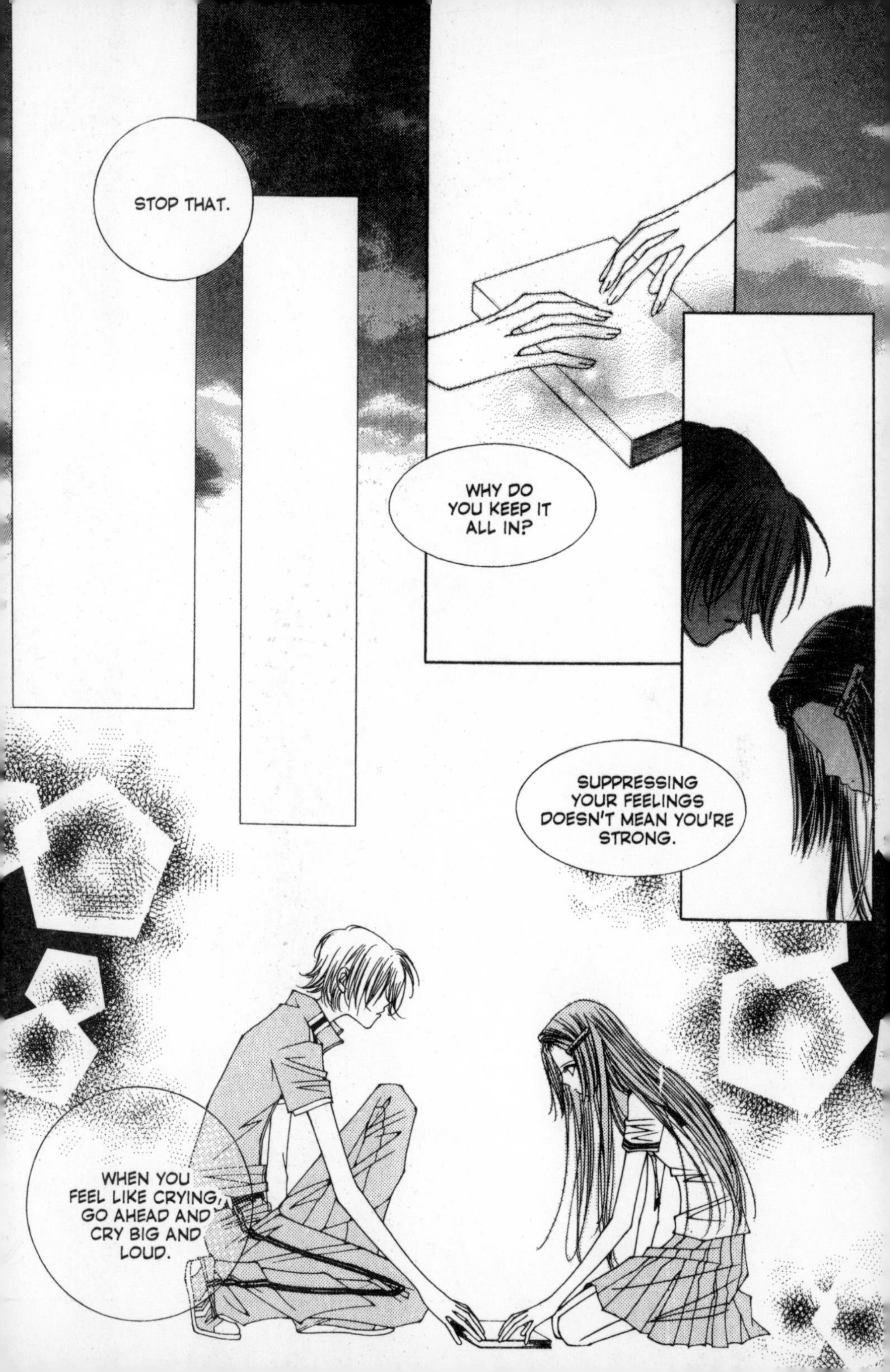
STOP THAT.
WHY DO YOU KEEP IT ALL IN?
SUPPRESSING YOUR FEELINGS DOESN'T MEAN YOU'RE STRONG.
WHEN YOU FEEL LIKE CRYING, GO AHEAD AND CRY BIG AND LOUD.

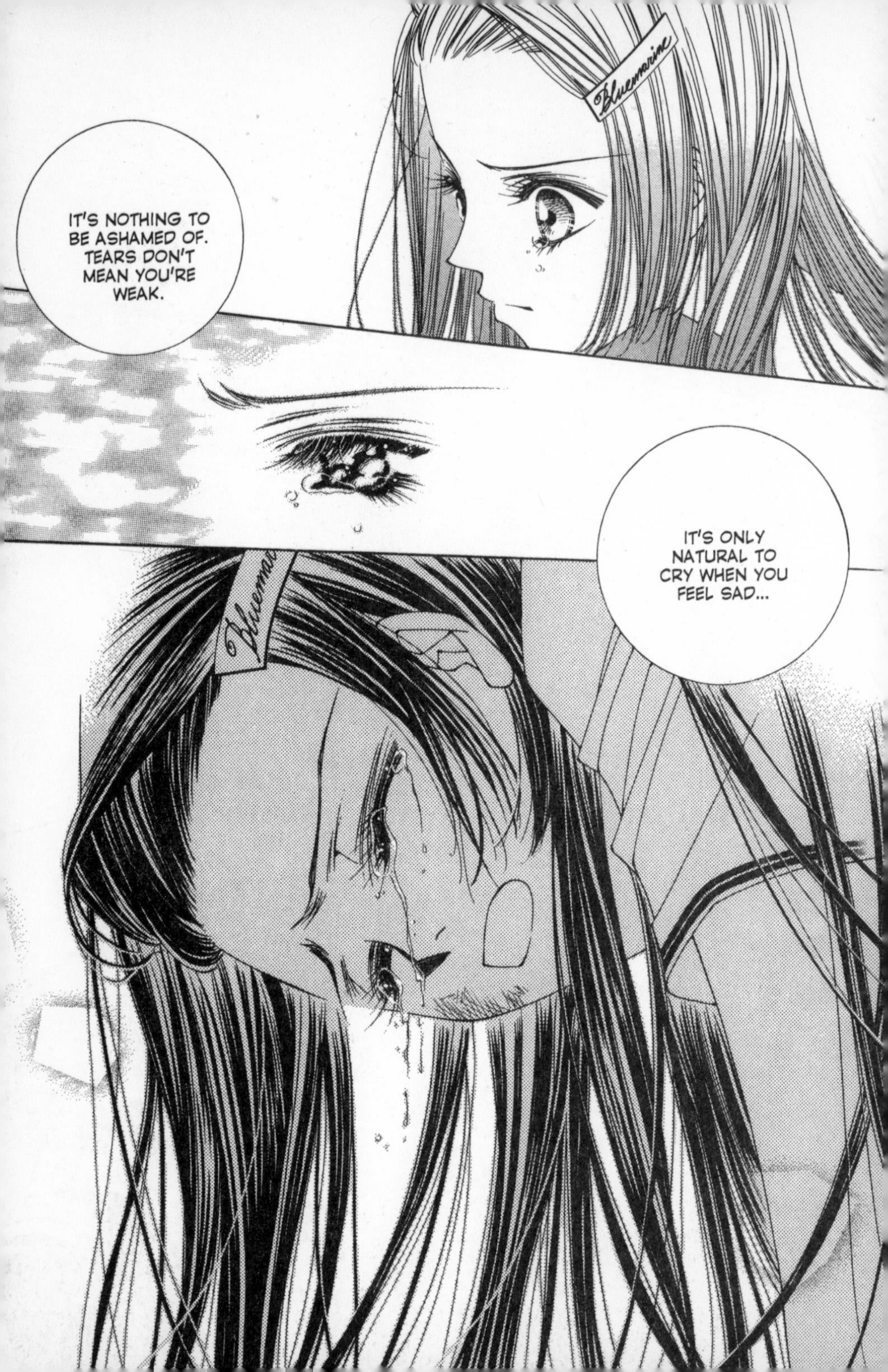
Bluemarine
IT'S NOTHING TO BE ASHAMED OF. TEARS DON'T MEAN YOU'RE WEAK.
IT'S ONLY NATURAL TO CRY WHEN YOU FEEL SAD...

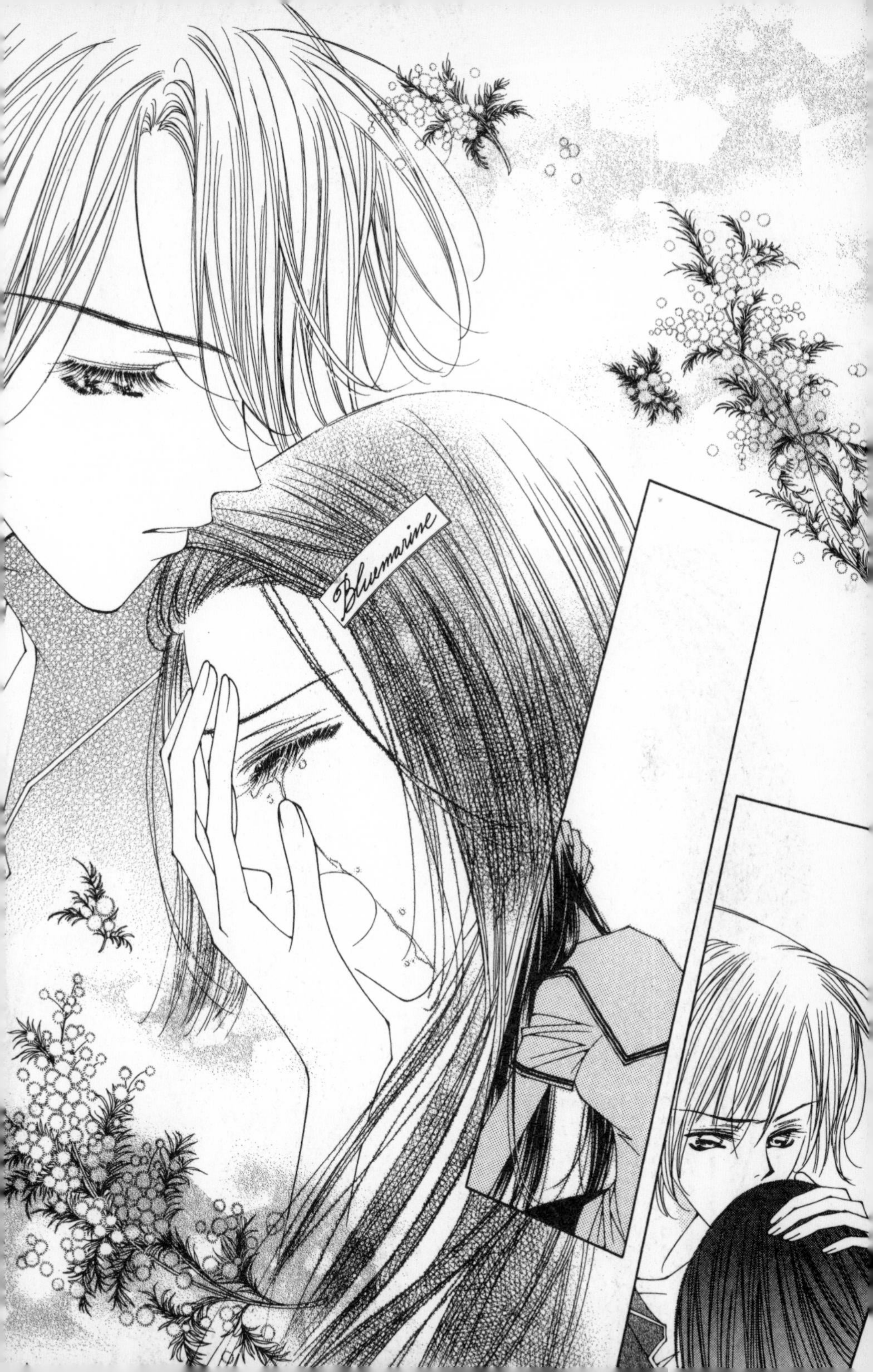
Blumarine

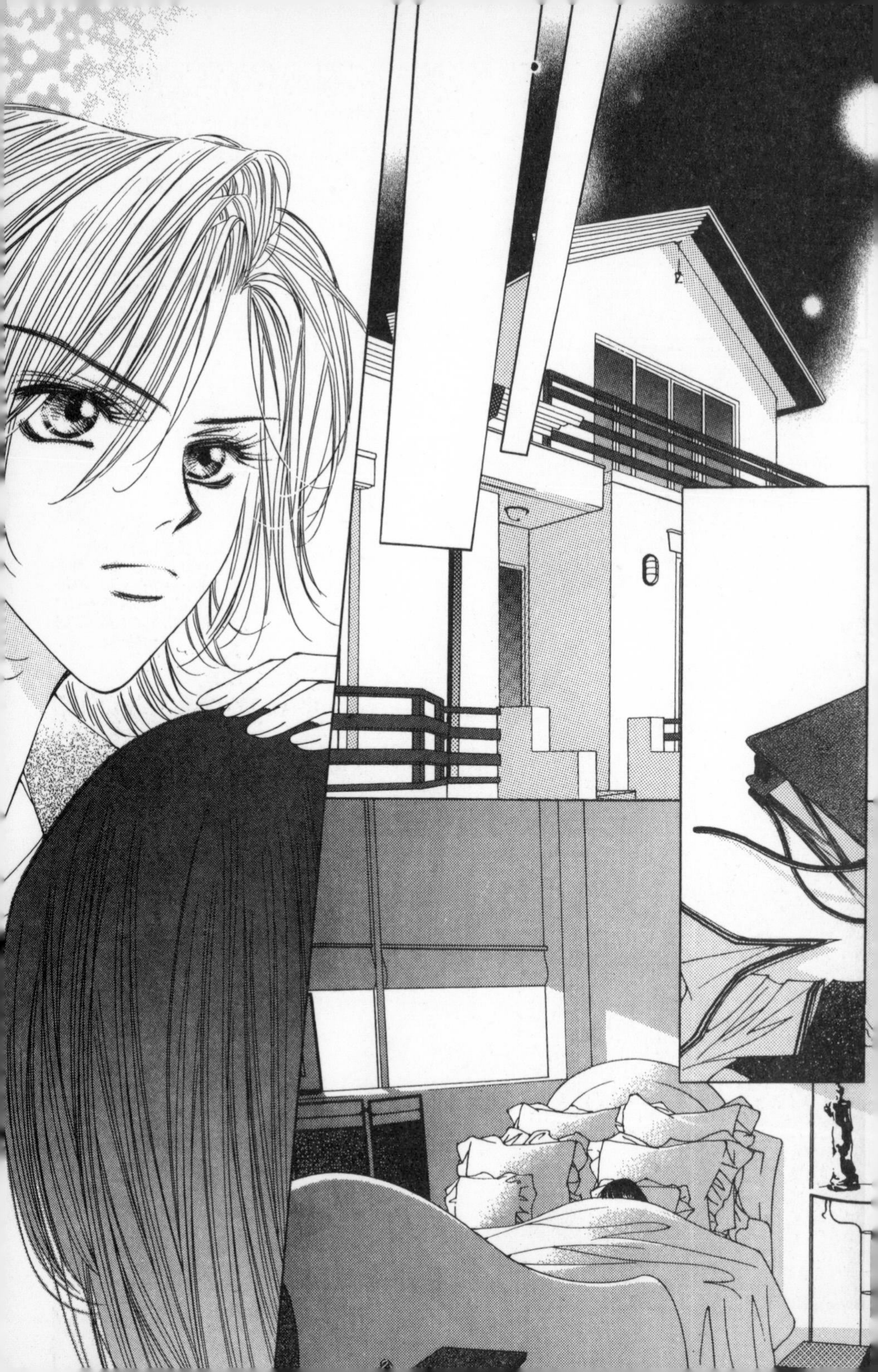

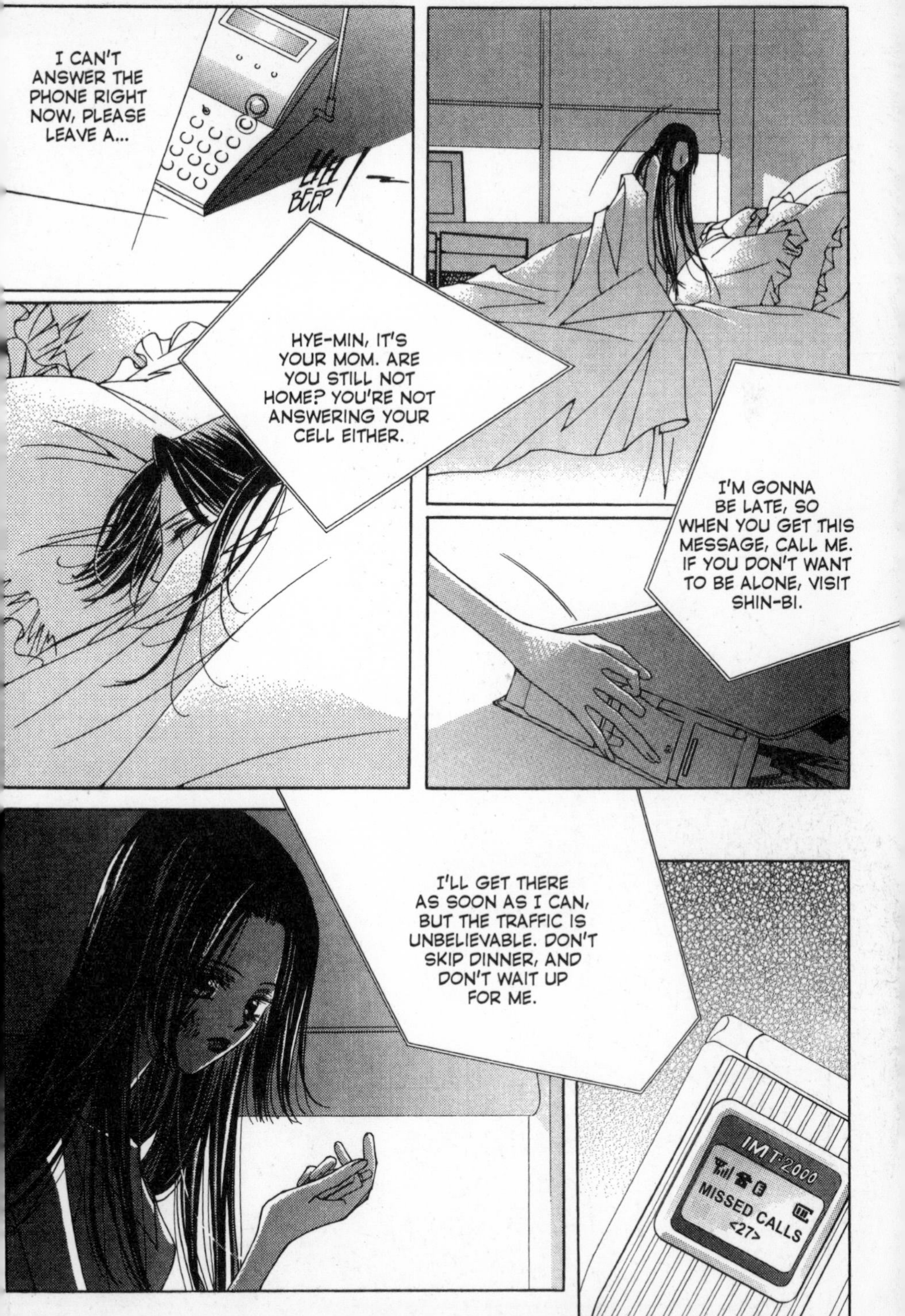
I CAN'T ANSWER THE PHONE RIGHT NOW, PLEASE LEAVE A...
BEEP
HYE-MIN, IT'S YOUR MOM. ARE YOU STILL NOT HOME? YOU'RE NOT ANSWERING YOUR CELL EITHER.
I'M GONNA BE LATE, SO WHEN YOU GET THIS MESSAGE, CALL ME. IF YOU DON'T WANT TO BE ALONE, VISIT SHIN-BI.
I'LL GET THERE AS SOON AS I CAN, BUT THE TRAFFIC IS UNBELIEVABLE. DON'T SKIP DINNER, AND DON'T WAIT UP FOR ME.
IMT2000
MISSED CALLS
<27>

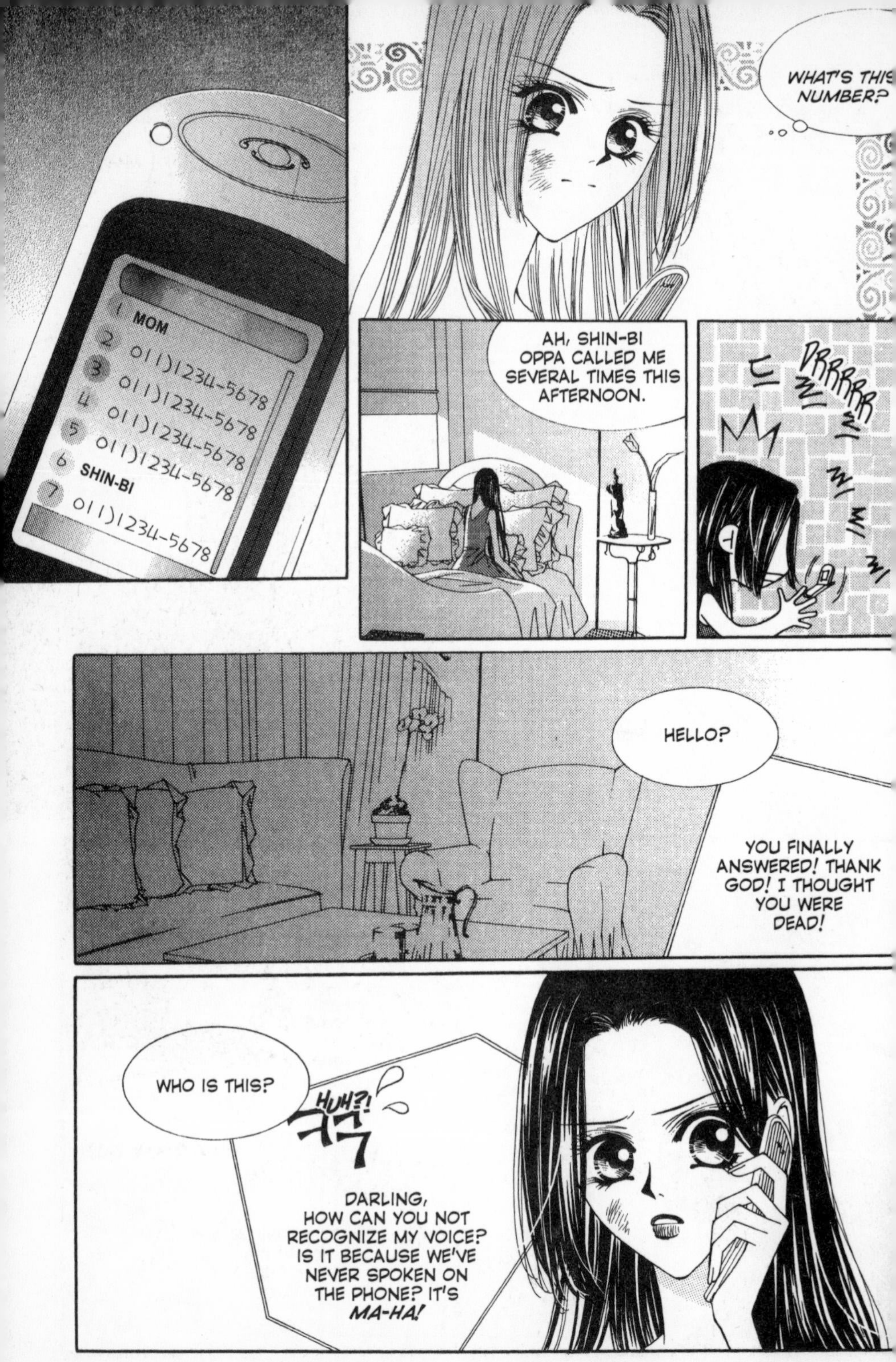
1 MOM
2 011)1234-5678
3 011)1234-5678
4 011)1234-5678
5 011)1234-5678
6 SHIN-BI
7 011)1234-5678
WHAT'S THIS NUMBER?
AH, SHIN-BI OPPA CALLED ME SEVERAL TIMES THIS AFTERNOON.
DRRRRR
HELLO?
YOU FINALLY ANSWERED! THANK GOD! I THOUGHT YOU WERE DEAD!
WHO IS THIS?
HUH?!
DARLING, HOW CAN YOU NOT RECOGNIZE MY VOICE? IS IT BECAUSE WE'VE NEVER SPOKEN ON THE PHONE? IT'S *MA-HA!*

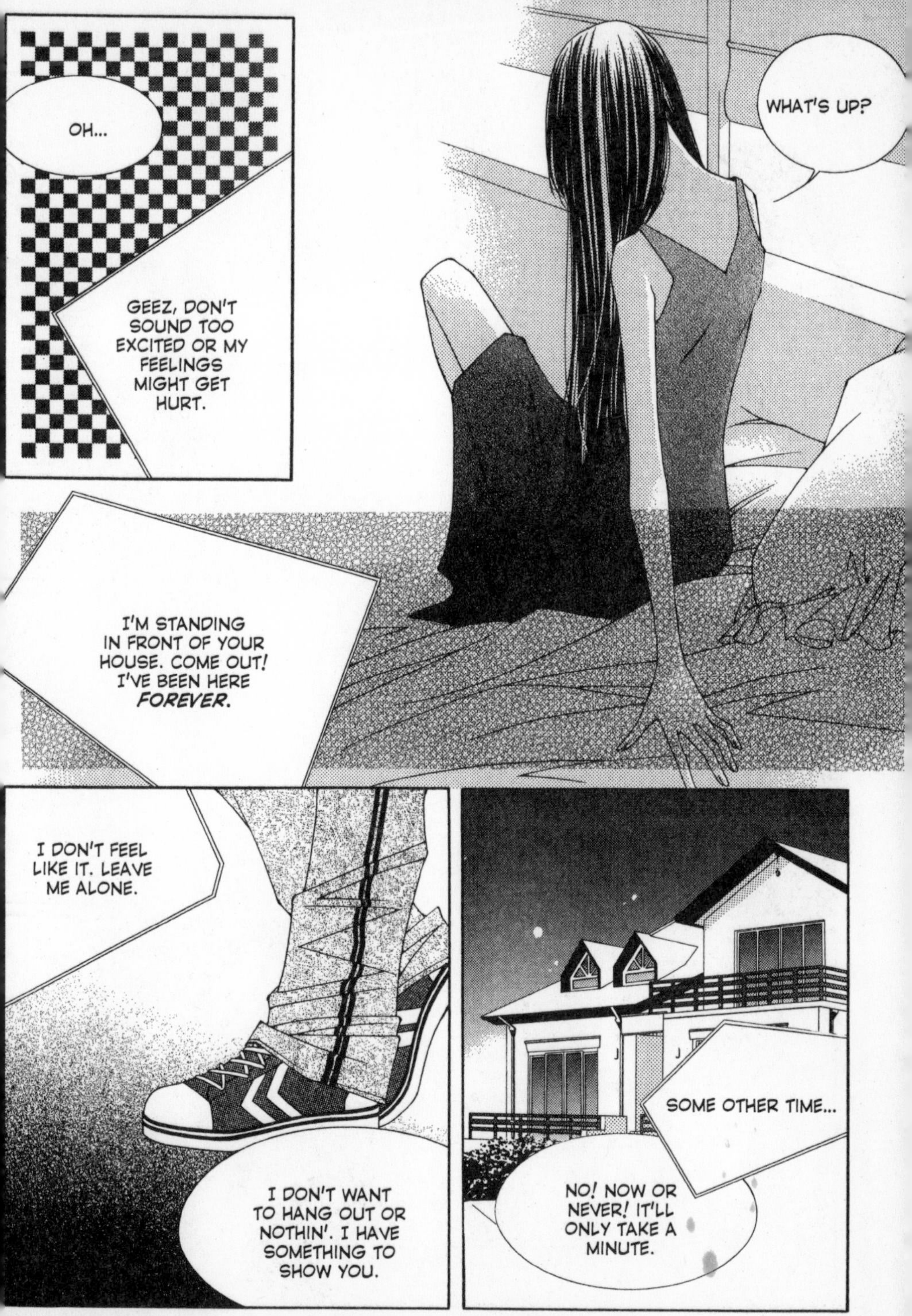
OH...
GEEZ, DON'T SOUND TOO EXCITED OR MY FEELINGS MIGHT GET HURT.
WHAT'S UP?
I'M STANDING IN FRONT OF YOUR HOUSE. COME OUT! I'VE BEEN HERE *FOREVER*.
I DON'T FEEL LIKE IT. LEAVE ME ALONE.
I DON'T WANT TO HANG OUT OR NOTHIN'. I HAVE SOMETHING TO SHOW YOU.
SOME OTHER TIME...
NO! NOW OR NEVER! IT'LL ONLY TAKE A MINUTE.

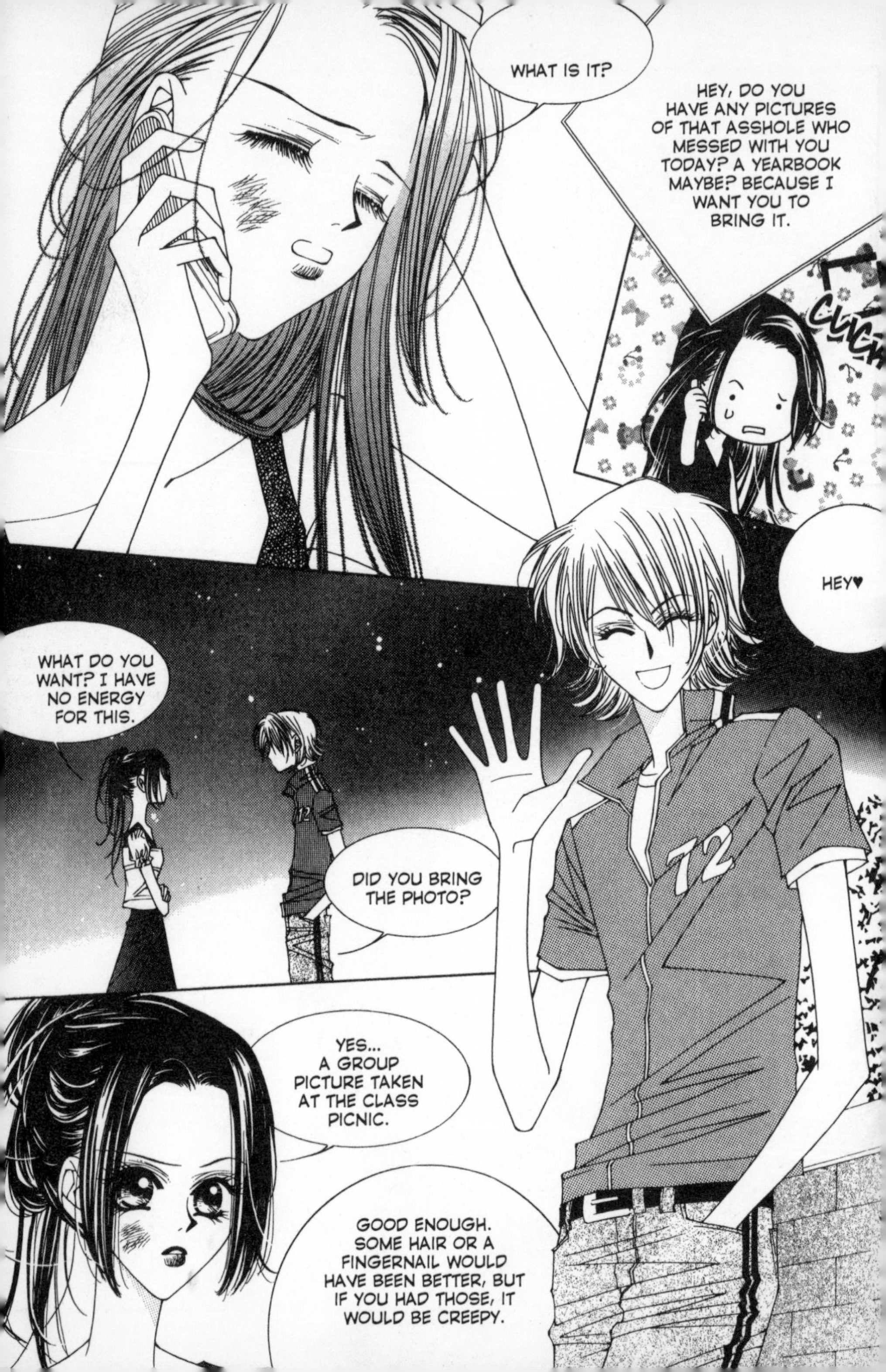
WHAT IS IT?
HEY, DO YOU HAVE ANY PICTURES OF THAT ASSHOLE WHO MESSED WITH YOU TODAY? A YEARBOOK MAYBE? BECAUSE I WANT YOU TO BRING IT.
CLICK
WHAT DO YOU WANT? I HAVE NO ENERGY FOR THIS.
DID YOU BRING THE PHOTO?
YES... A GROUP PICTURE TAKEN AT THE CLASS PICNIC.
GOOD ENOUGH. SOME HAIR OR A FINGERNAIL WOULD HAVE BEEN BETTER, BUT IF YOU HAD THOSE, IT WOULD BE CREEPY.
HEY♥

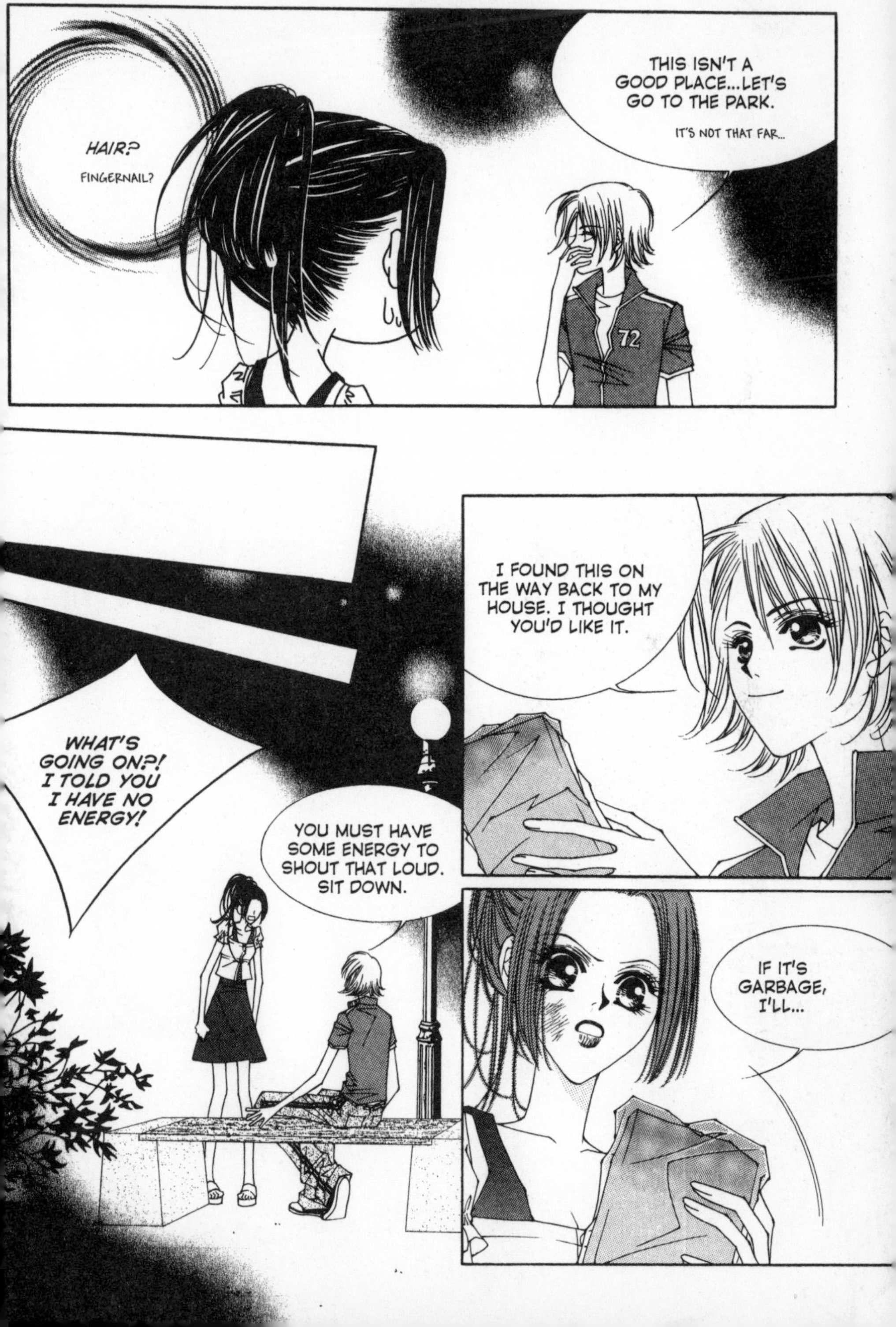
HAIR?
FINGERNAIL?
THIS ISN'T A GOOD PLACE...LET'S GO TO THE PARK.
IT'S NOT THAT FAR...
WHAT'S GOING ON?! I TOLD YOU I HAVE NO ENERGY!
YOU MUST HAVE SOME ENERGY TO SHOUT THAT LOUD. SIT DOWN.
I FOUND THIS ON THE WAY BACK TO MY HOUSE. I THOUGHT YOU'D LIKE IT.
IF IT'S GARBAGE, I'LL...

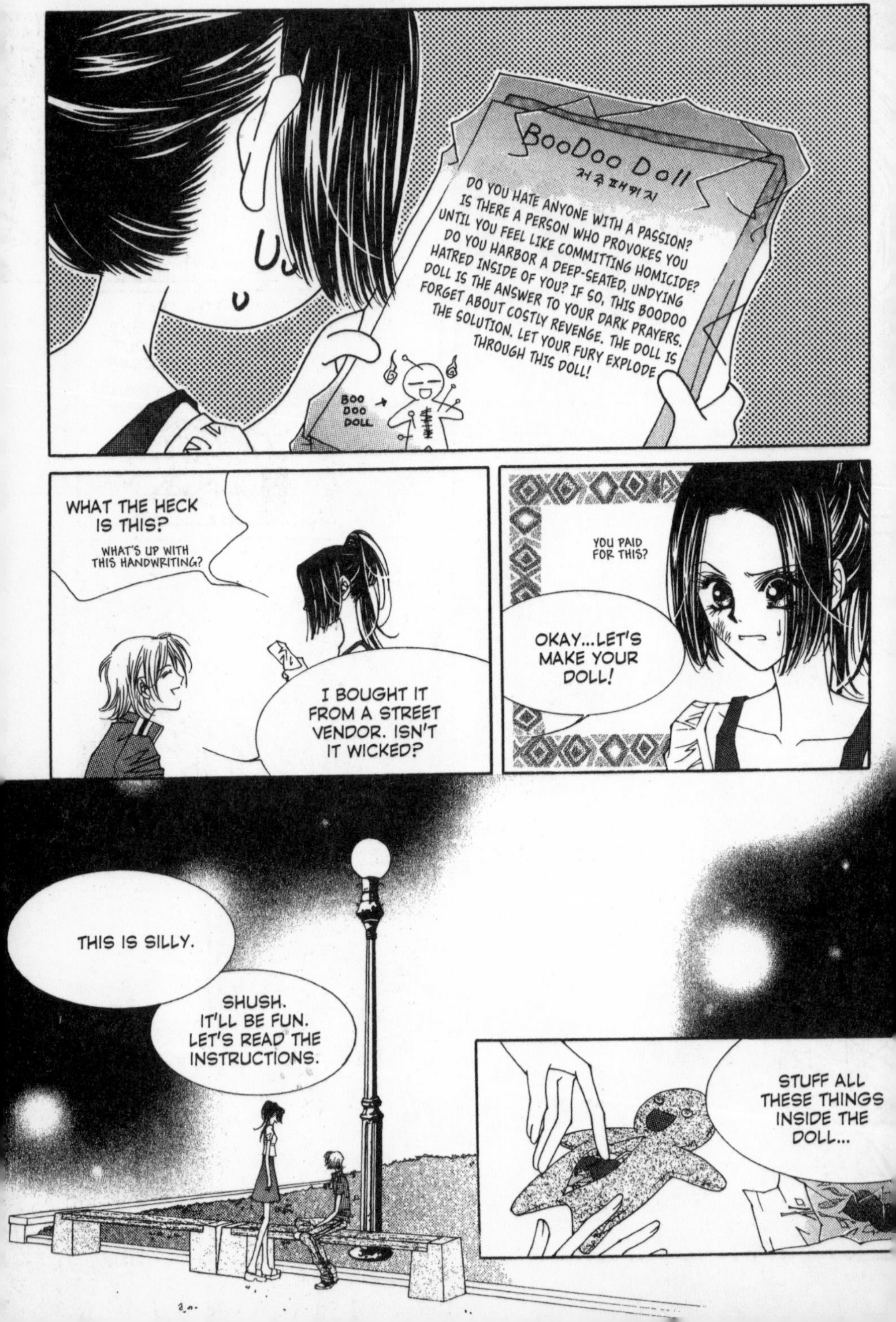
BooDoo Doll
DO YOU HATE ANYONE WITH A PASSION? IS THERE A PERSON WHO PROVOKES YOU UNTIL YOU FEEL LIKE COMMITTING HOMICIDE? DO YOU HARBOR A DEEP-SEATED, UNDYING HATRED INSIDE OF YOU? IF SO, THIS BOODOO DOLL IS THE ANSWER TO YOUR DARK PRAYERS. FORGET ABOUT COSTLY REVENGE. THE DOLL IS THE SOLUTION. LET YOUR FURY EXPLODE THROUGH THIS DOLL!
BOO DOO DOLL
WHAT THE HECK IS THIS?
WHAT'S UP WITH THIS HANDWRITING?
I BOUGHT IT FROM A STREET VENDOR. ISN'T IT WICKED?
YOU PAID FOR THIS?
OKAY...LET'S MAKE YOUR DOLL!
THIS IS SILLY.
SHUSH. IT'LL BE FUN. LET'S READ THE INSTRUCTIONS.
STUFF ALL THESE THINGS INSIDE THE DOLL...

WHICH ONE IS HE IN THE PICTURE?

UH...THERE.

NOW, WAIT JUST A SECOND!

CUT HIS FACE OUT OF THE PICTURE AND PUT IT IN THE DOLL. THEN WE'LL SEW IT UP.

AFTER THAT, LIFT YOUR RIGHT ARM AND SHOUT, "PPOROPPOROMI!"

THAT'S WHAT IT SAYS HERE.

THIS IS STUPID...

NOW, YOU CAN ABUSE THIS DOLL IN EVERY WAY YOU WANTED TO ABUSE THAT BULLY!

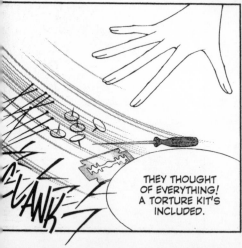

THEY THOUGHT OF EVERYTHING! A TORTURE KIT'S INCLUDED.

72

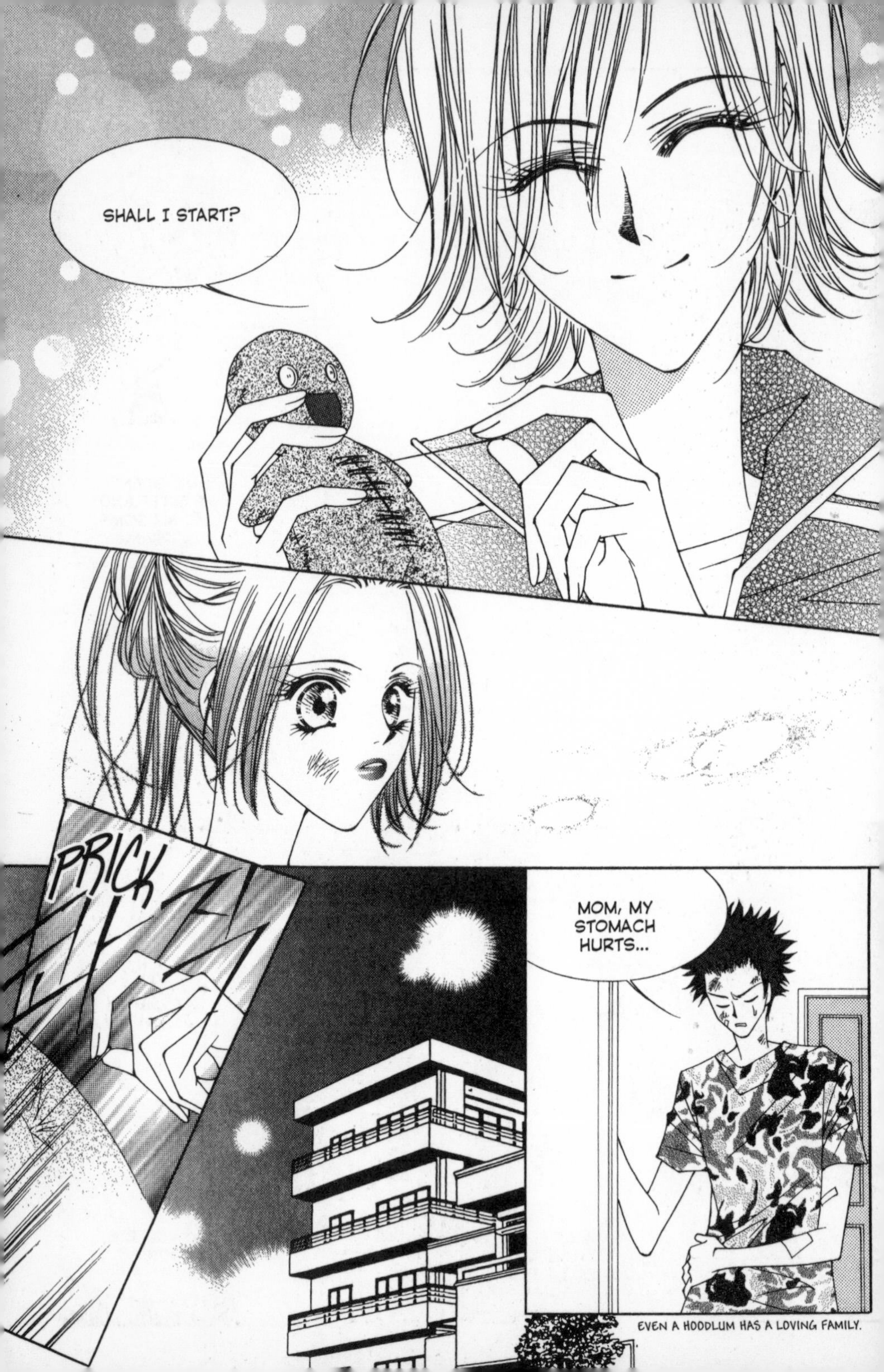
SHALL I START?
PRICK
MOM, MY STOMACH HURTS...
EVEN A HOODLUM HAS A LOVING FAMILY.

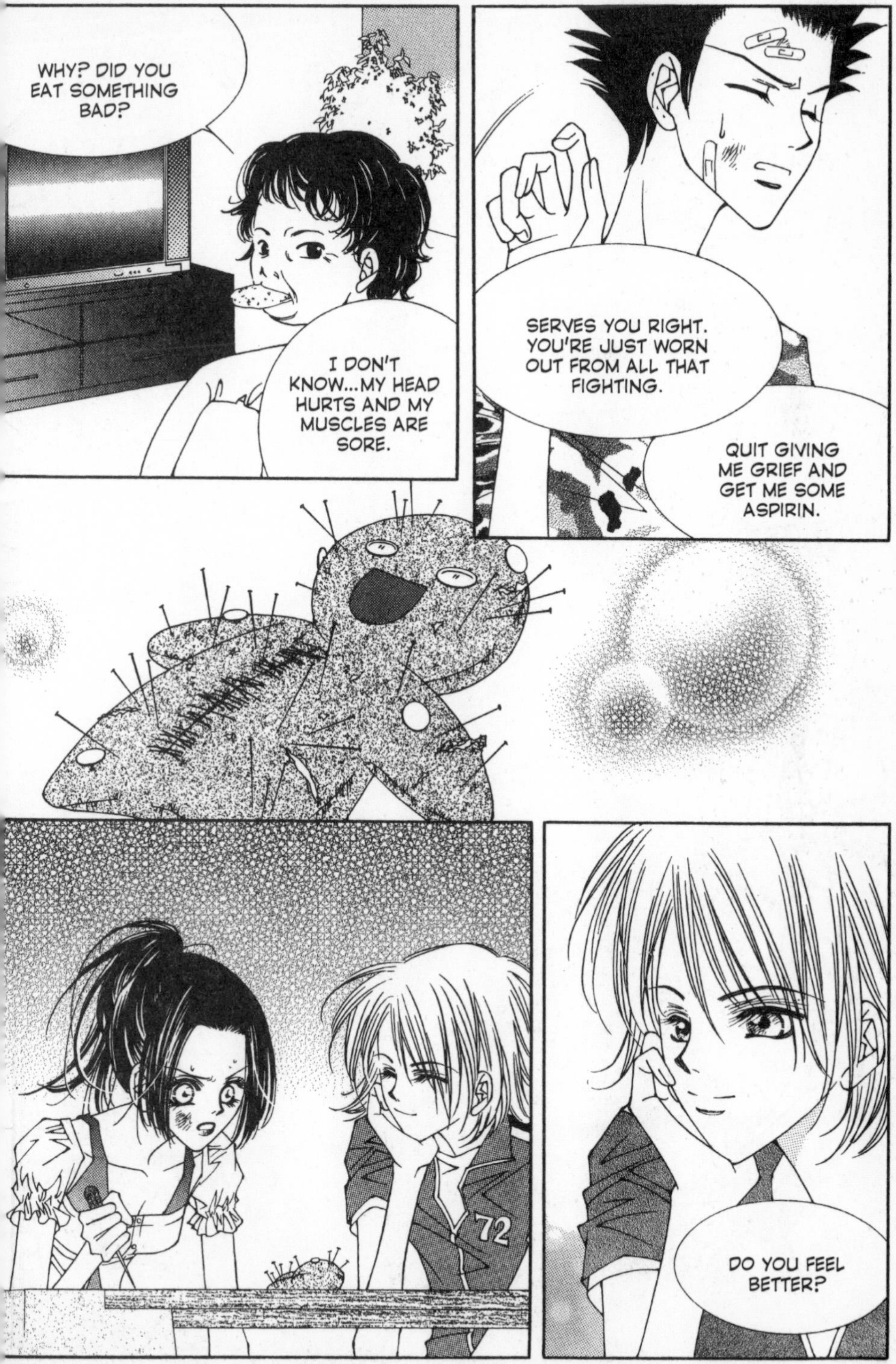
WHY? DID YOU EAT SOMETHING BAD?
I DON'T KNOW...MY HEAD HURTS AND MY MUSCLES ARE SORE.
SERVES YOU RIGHT. YOU'RE JUST WORN OUT FROM ALL THAT FIGHTING.
QUIT GIVING ME GRIEF AND GET ME SOME ASPIRIN.
72
DO YOU FEEL BETTER?

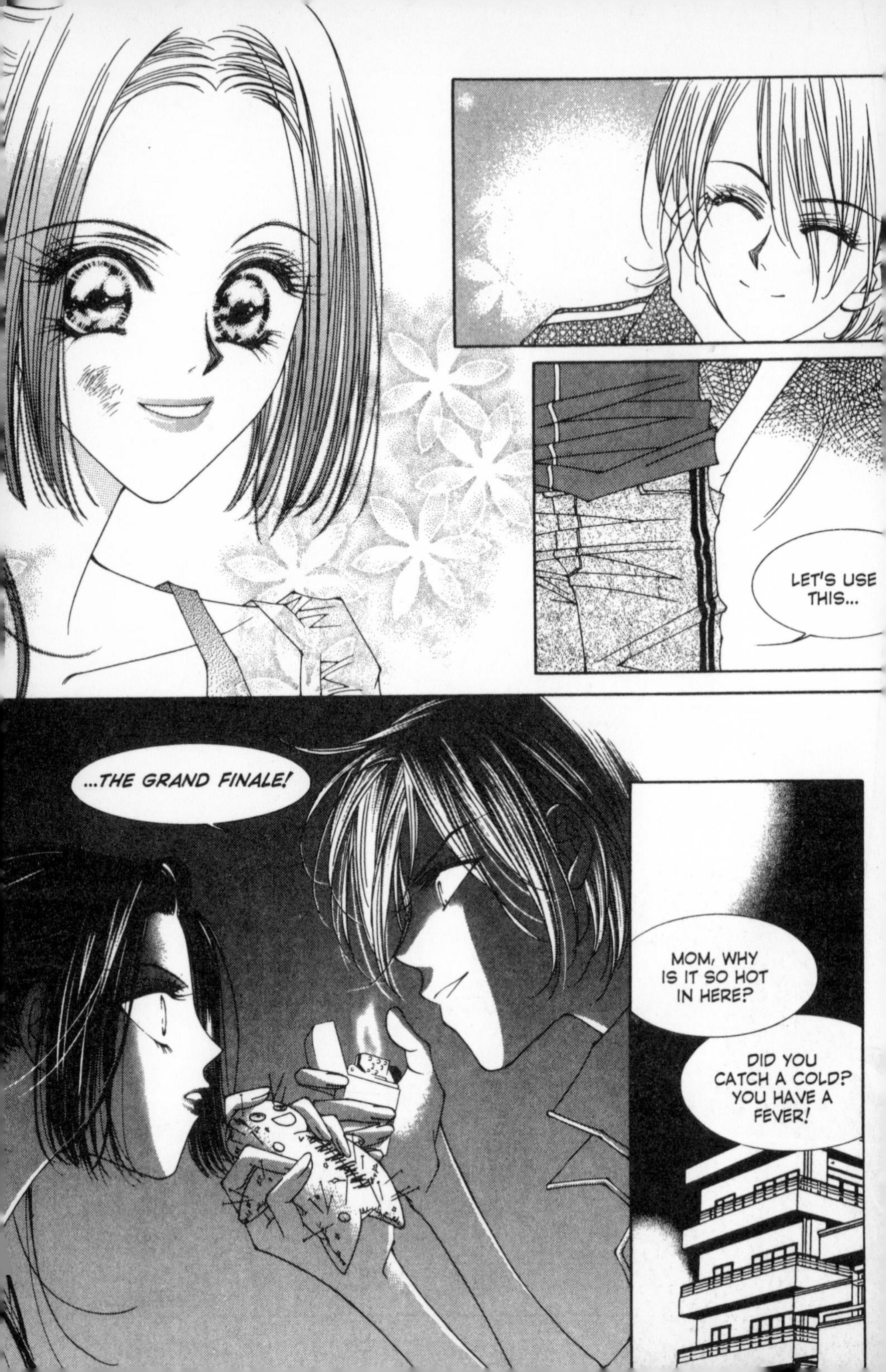
LET'S USE THIS...
...THE GRAND FINALE!
MOM, WHY IS IT SO HOT IN HERE?
DID YOU CATCH A COLD? YOU HAVE A FEVER!

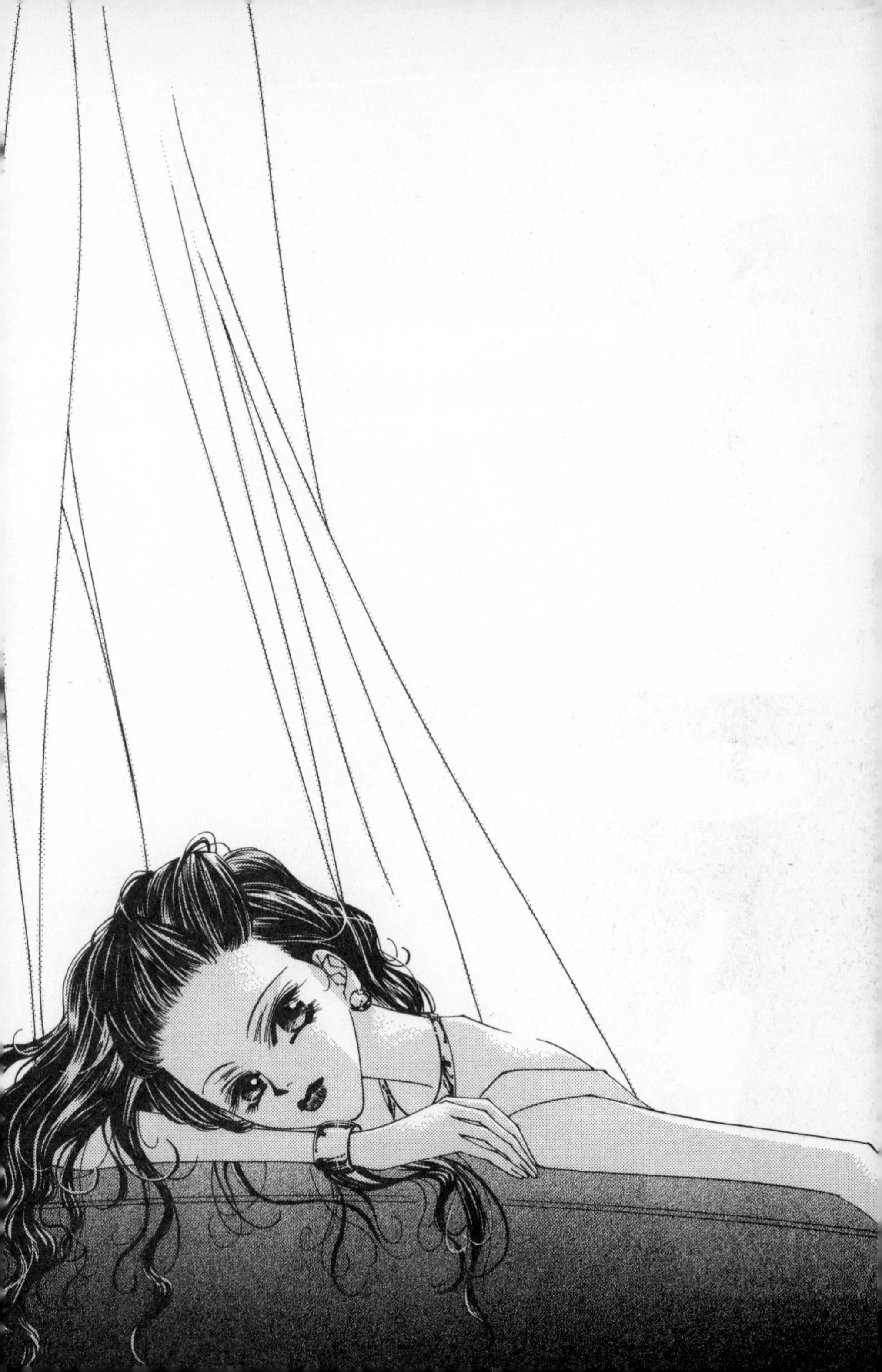

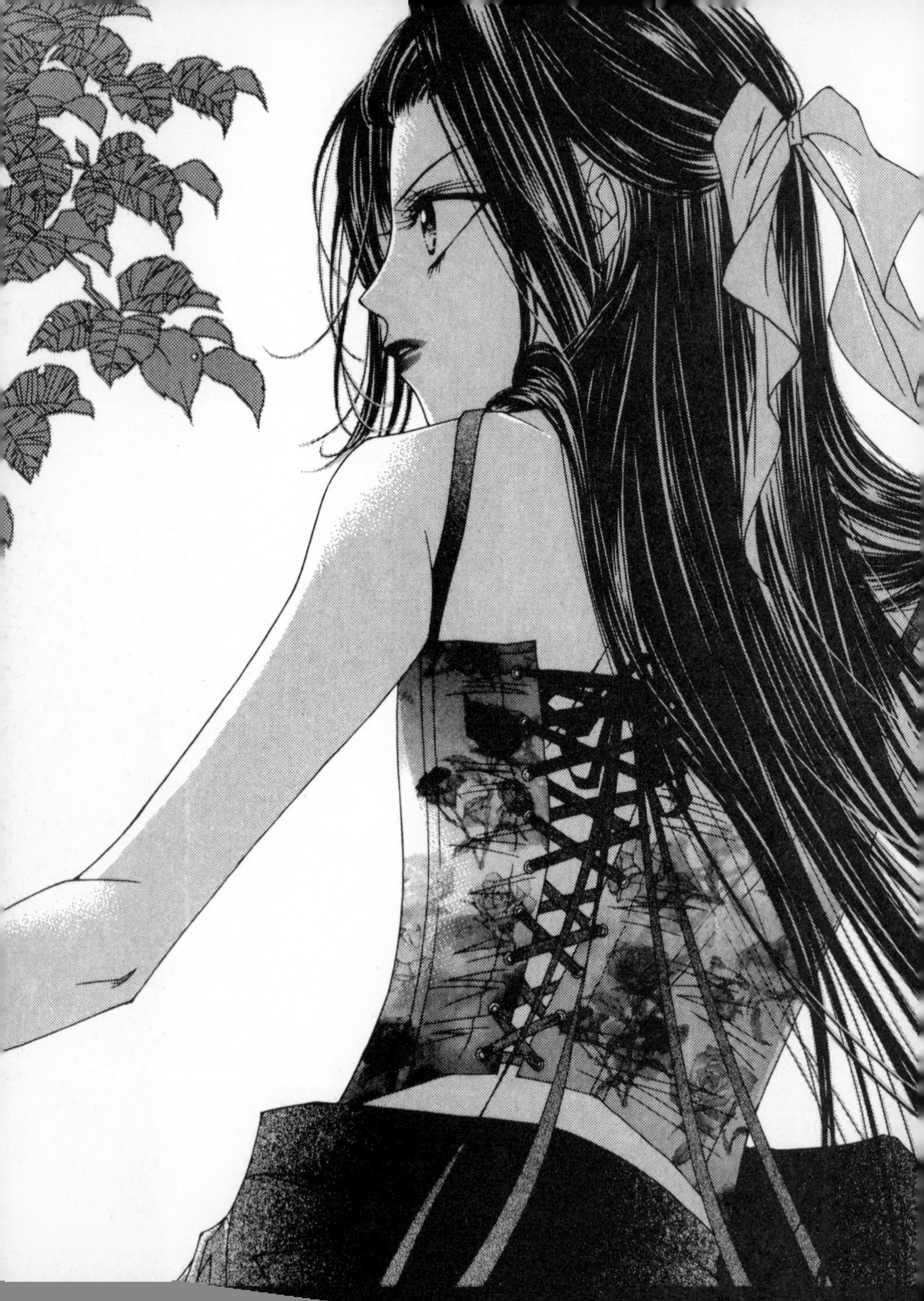

Scene.8
Intrusion

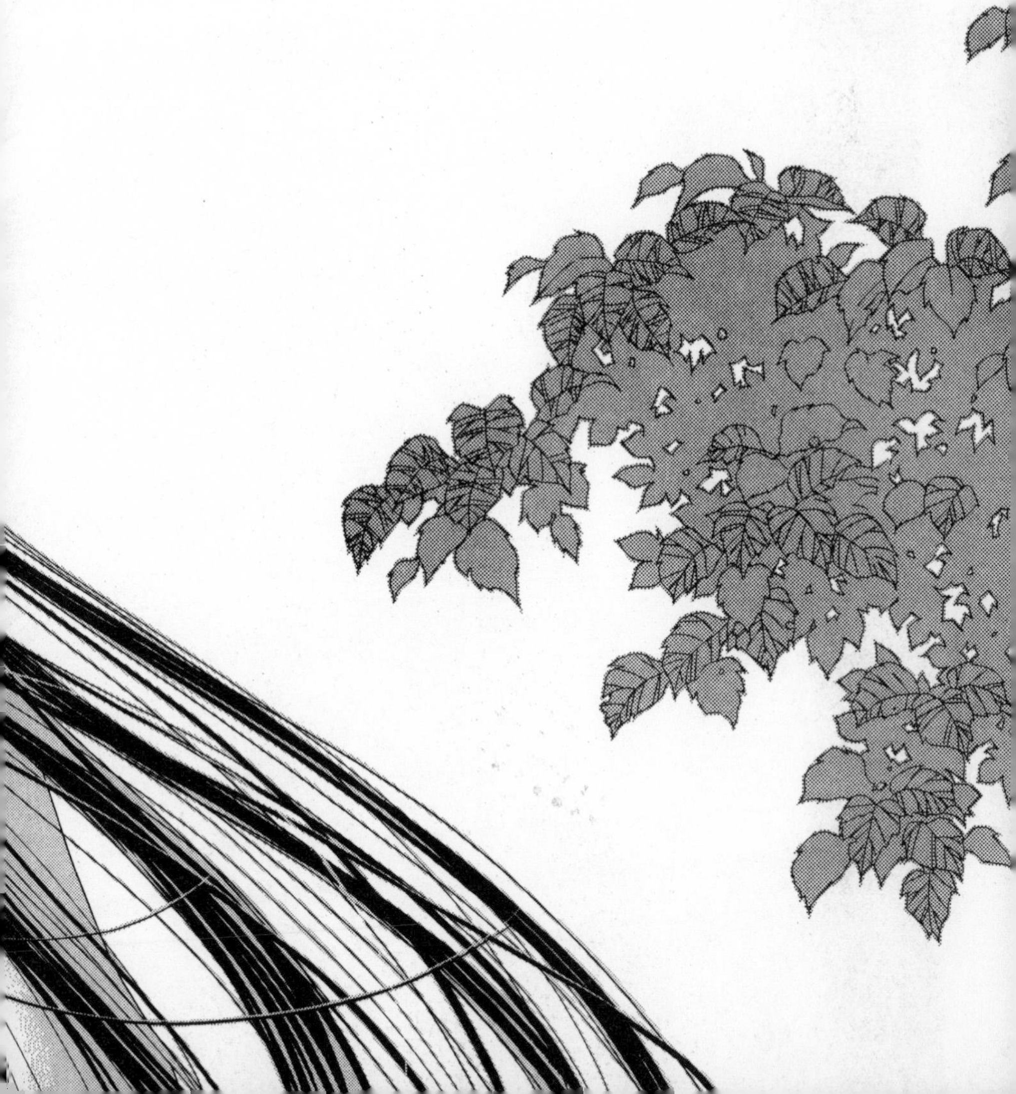

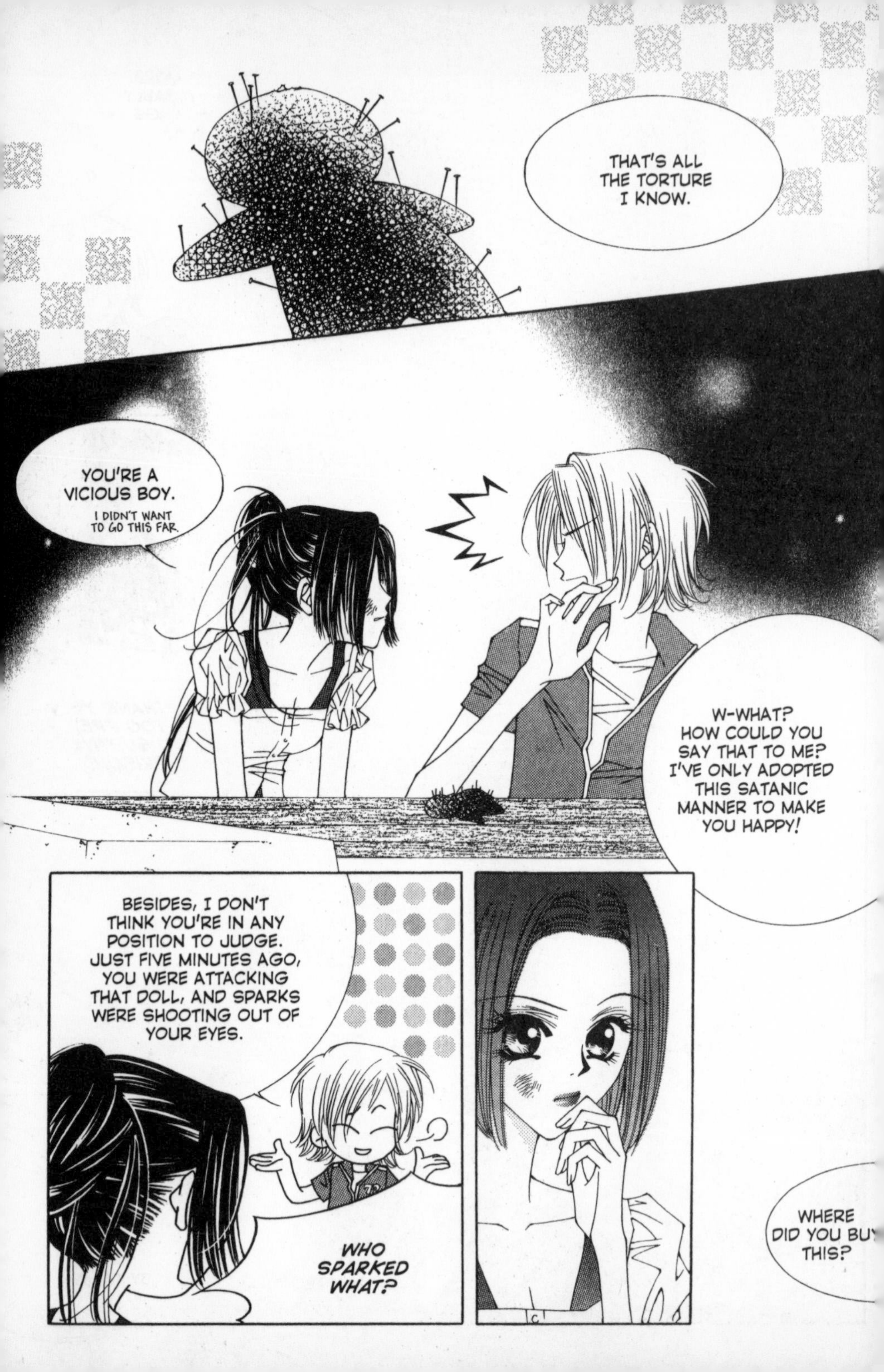
THAT'S ALL THE TORTURE I KNOW.
YOU'RE A VICIOUS BOY.
I DIDN'T WANT TO GO THIS FAR.
W-WHAT? HOW COULD YOU SAY THAT TO ME? I'VE ONLY ADOPTED THIS SATANIC MANNER TO MAKE YOU HAPPY!
BESIDES, I DON'T THINK YOU'RE IN ANY POSITION TO JUDGE. JUST FIVE MINUTES AGO, YOU WERE ATTACKING THAT DOLL, AND SPARKS WERE SHOOTING OUT OF YOUR EYES.
WHO SPARKED WHAT?
WHERE DID YOU BUY THIS?

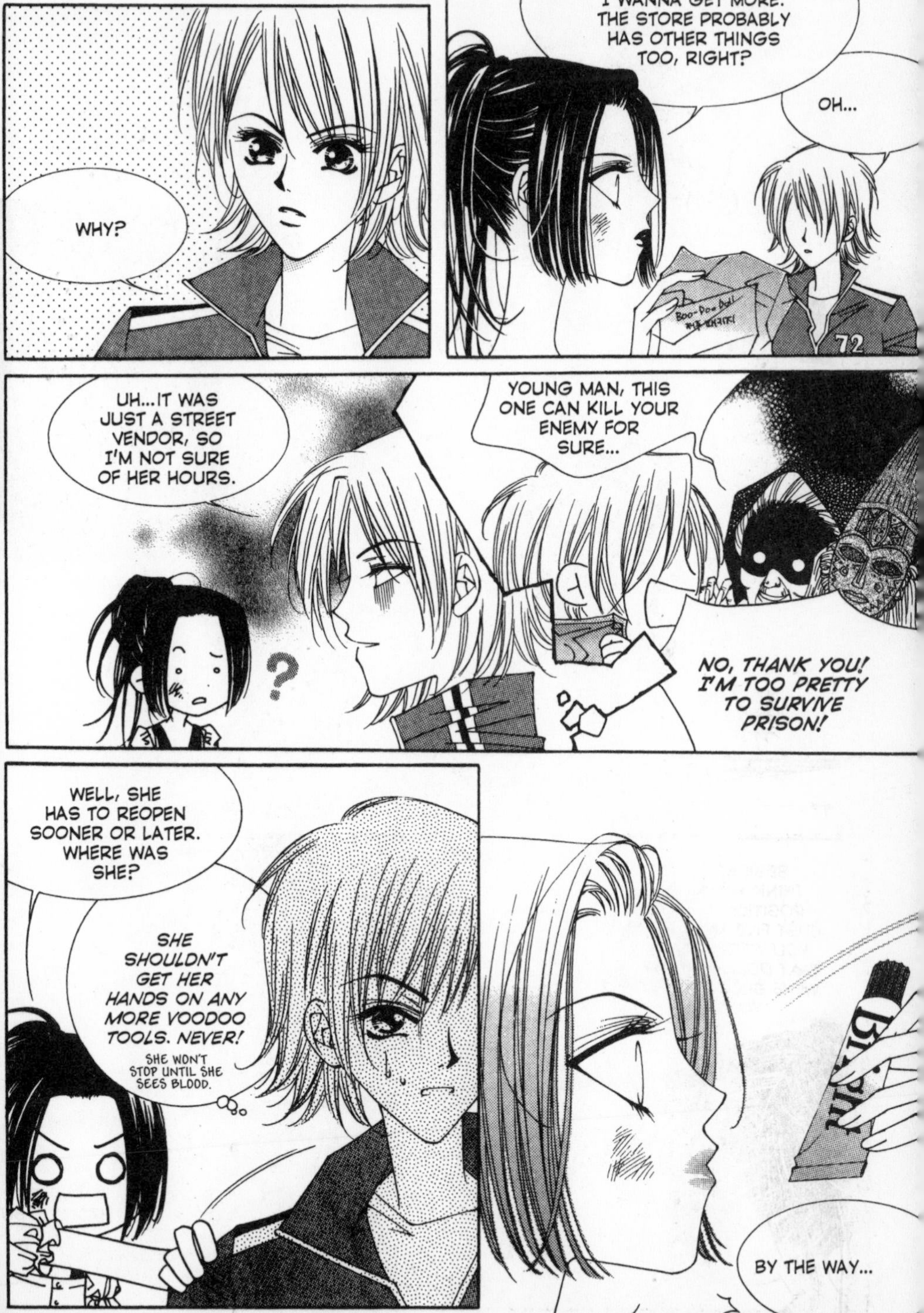
WHY?
I WANNA GET MORE. THE STORE PROBABLY HAS OTHER THINGS TOO, RIGHT?
OH...
Boo-Doo Doll
UH...IT WAS JUST A STREET VENDOR, SO I'M NOT SURE OF HER HOURS.
YOUNG MAN, THIS ONE CAN KILL YOUR ENEMY FOR SURE...
NO, THANK YOU! I'M TOO PRETTY TO SURVIVE PRISON!
WELL, SHE HAS TO REOPEN SOONER OR LATER. WHERE WAS SHE?
SHE SHOULDN'T GET HER HANDS ON ANY MORE VOODOO TOOLS. NEVER!
SHE WON'T STOP UNTIL SHE SEES BLOOD.
BY THE WAY...

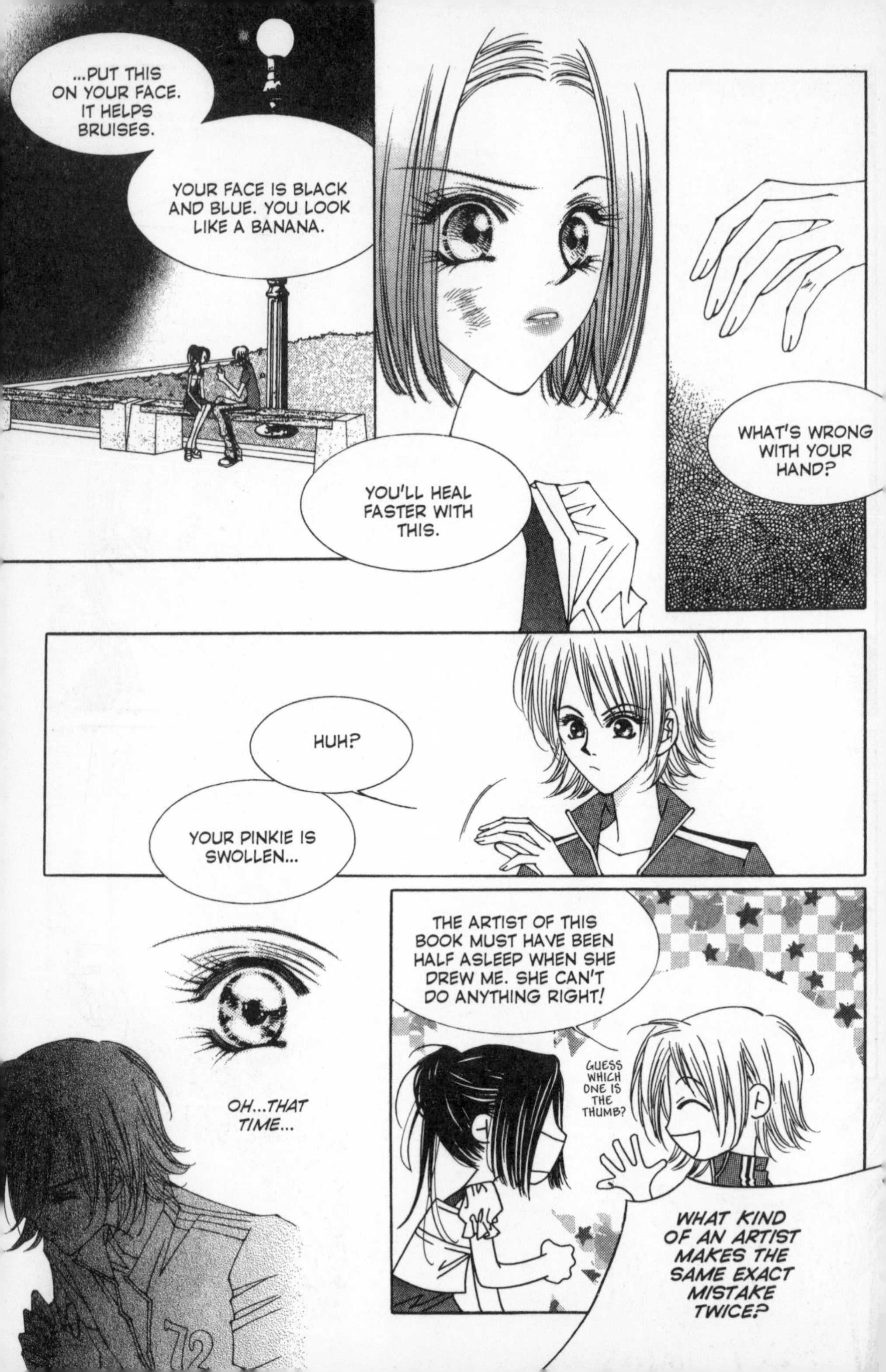
...PUT THIS ON YOUR FACE. IT HELPS BRUISES.
YOUR FACE IS BLACK AND BLUE. YOU LOOK LIKE A BANANA.
YOU'LL HEAL FASTER WITH THIS.
WHAT'S WRONG WITH YOUR HAND?
HUH?
YOUR PINKIE IS SWOLLEN...
OH...THAT TIME...
THE ARTIST OF THIS BOOK MUST HAVE BEEN HALF ASLEEP WHEN SHE DREW ME. SHE CAN'T DO ANYTHING RIGHT!
GUESS WHICH ONE IS THE THUMB?
WHAT KIND OF AN ARTIST MAKES THE SAME EXACT MISTAKE TWICE?

GET UP. IT MIGHT BE BROKEN. YOU NEED TO SEE A DOCTOR.

IT'S A BIG DEAL IF IT IS BROKEN.

CRAP! THE CLINICS ARE PROBABLY CLOSED. WHAT SHOULD WE DO?

A PHARMACY! THEY'LL HAVE SOMETHING FOR IT. LET'S GO!

W-WHAT'S GOTTEN INTO YOU? USUALLY YOU BEAT THE CRAP OUT OF ME AND YOU DON'T EVEN BLINK.

THIS IS WAY SCARIER...

THOSE TIMES YOU DESERVED WHAT YOU GOT!

BESIDES, IT WAS ALL FOR COMEDIC EFFECT.

ON TOP OF THAT...

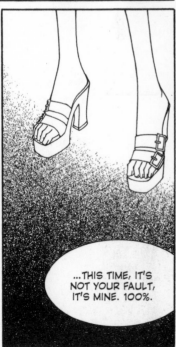

...THIS TIME, IT'S NOT YOUR FAULT, IT'S MINE. 100%.

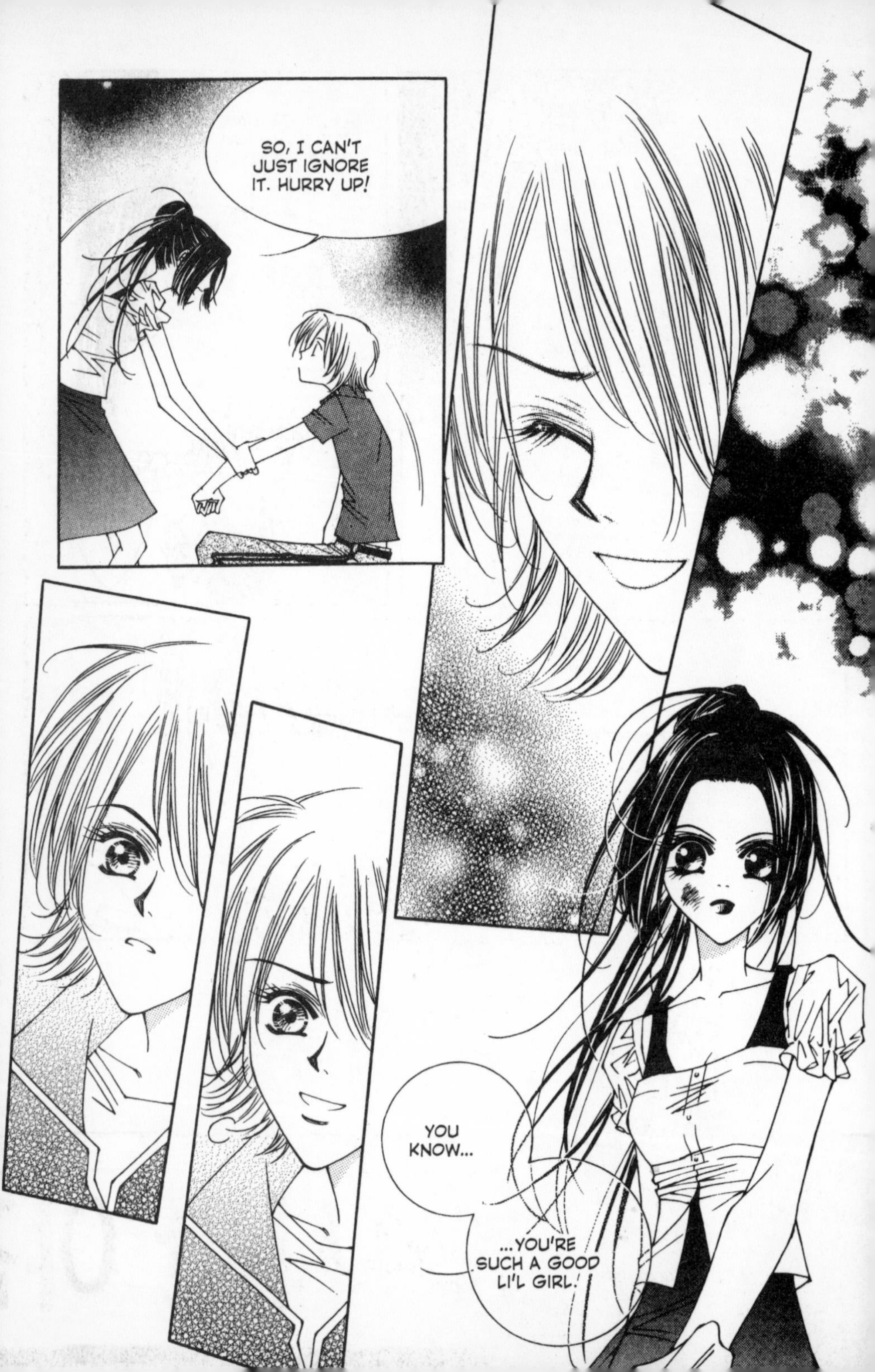
SO, I CAN'T JUST IGNORE IT. HURRY UP!
YOU KNOW...
...YOU'RE SUCH A GOOD LI'L GIRL!

WHAT?

DON'T TALK TO ME LIKE I'M A LITTLE KI--.

DON'T CHANGE THE SUBJECT BY AGREEING WITH ME!

WAIT A MINUTE...TODAY IS WEDNESDAY, RIGHT?

SINCE WE'VE STARTED TALKING ABOUT IT, IT'S STARTED HURTING. LET'S GET TO A DOCTOR.

I KNOW A DOCTOR'S OFFICE THAT'S OPEN THIS LATE. LET'S GO THERE.

THAT CAREFREE LOOK ON HIS FACE...

...NEVER FAILS TO DRAW ME IN.

24 HOURS - DAY & NIGHT

24시간 야ᄀ

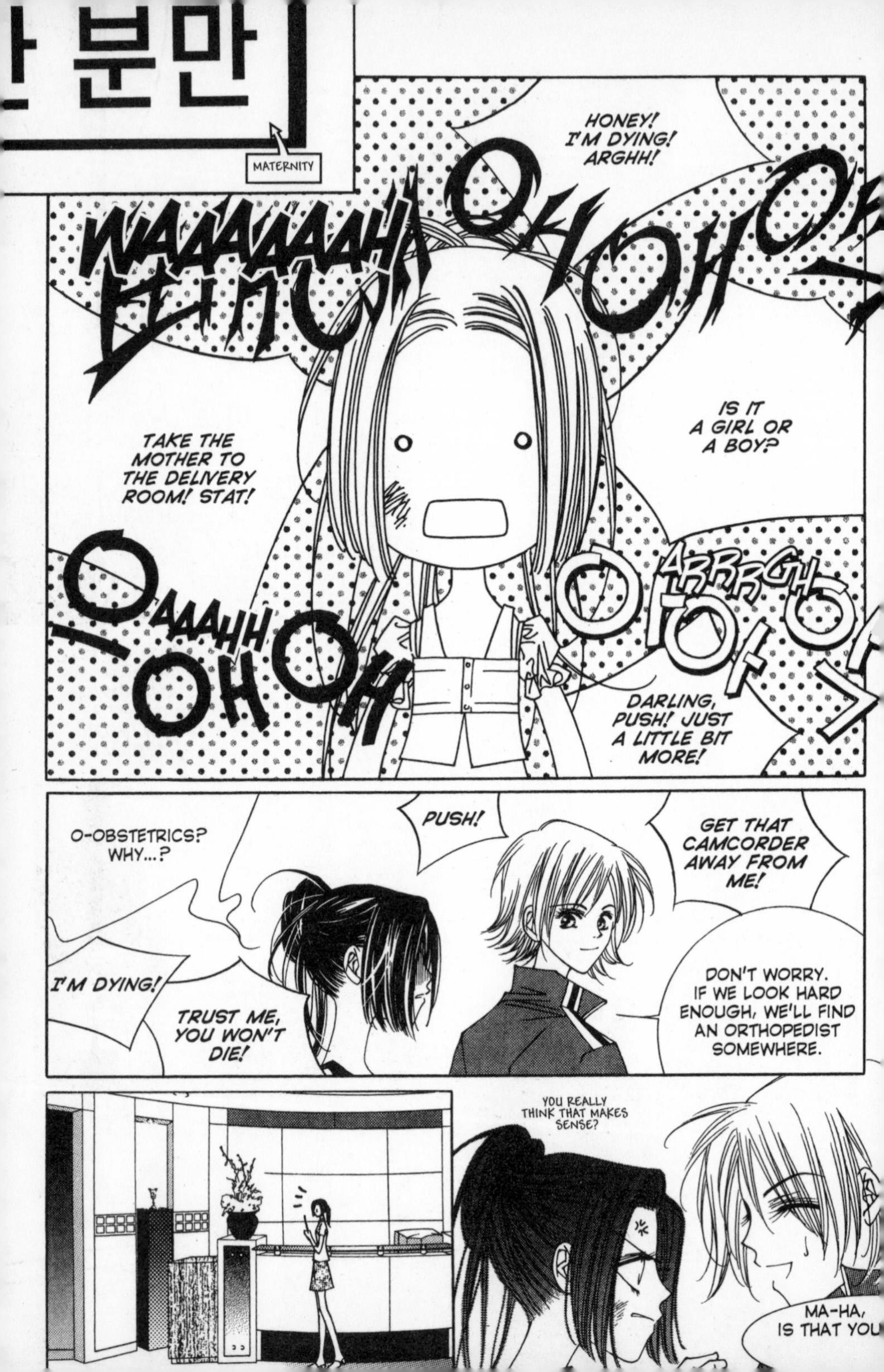
분만
MATERNITY
HONEY! I'M DYING! ARGHH!
TAKE THE MOTHER TO THE DELIVERY ROOM! STAT!
IS IT A GIRL OR A BOY?
ARRRGH
DARLING, PUSH! JUST A LITTLE BIT MORE!
O-OBSTETRICS? WHY...?
PUSH!
GET THAT CAMCORDER AWAY FROM ME!
I'M DYING!
TRUST ME, YOU WON'T DIE!
DON'T WORRY. IF WE LOOK HARD ENOUGH, WE'LL FIND AN ORTHOPEDIST SOMEWHERE.
YOU REALLY THINK THAT MAKES SENSE?
MA-HA, IS THAT YOU

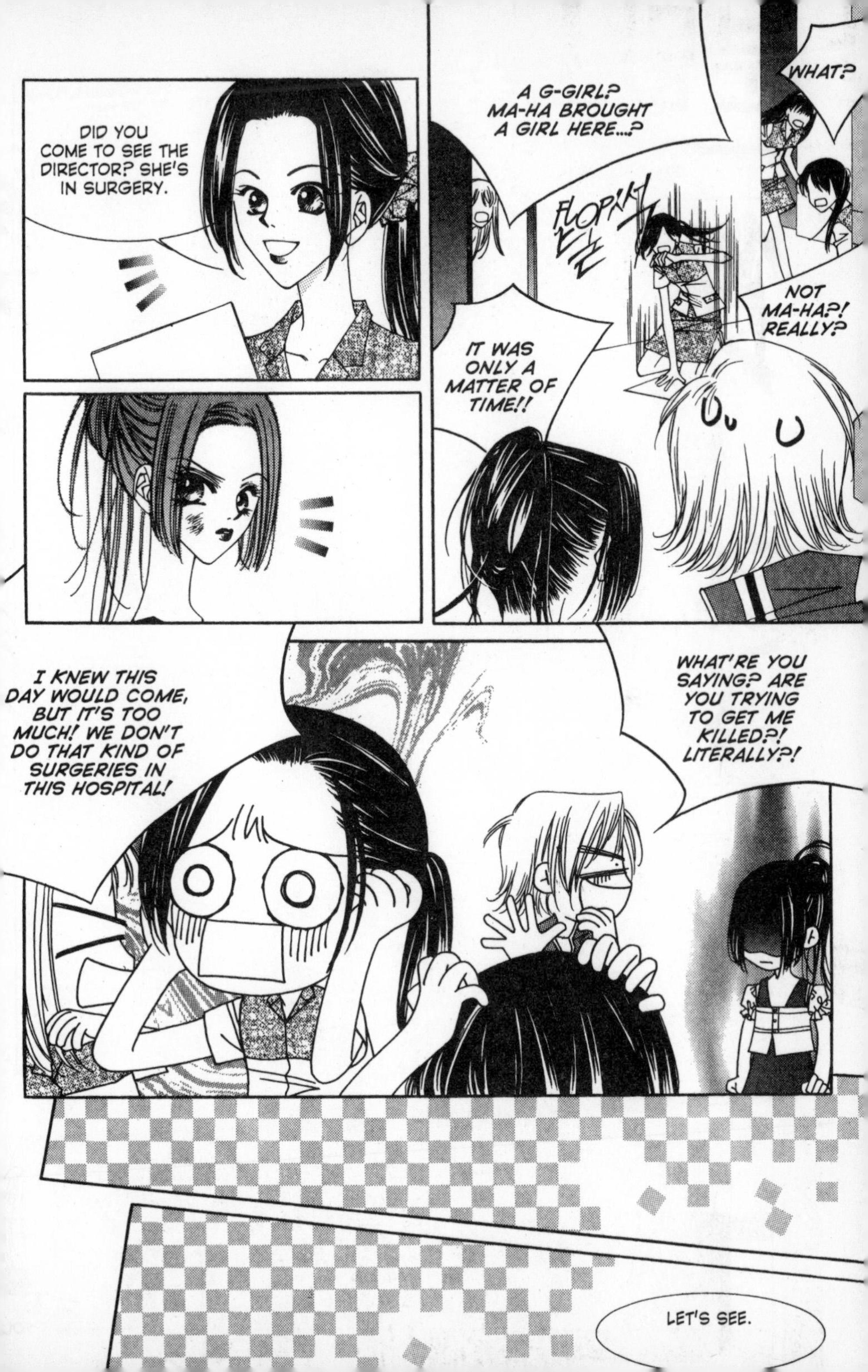
DID YOU COME TO SEE THE DIRECTOR? SHE'S IN SURGERY.
A G-GIRL? MA-HA BROUGHT A GIRL HERE...?
WHAT?
FLOP
NOT MA-HA?! REALLY?
IT WAS ONLY A MATTER OF TIME!!
I KNEW THIS DAY WOULD COME, BUT IT'S TOO MUCH! WE DON'T DO THAT KIND OF SURGERIES IN THIS HOSPITAL!
WHAT'RE YOU SAYING? ARE YOU TRYING TO GET ME KILLED?! LITERALLY?!
LET'S SEE.

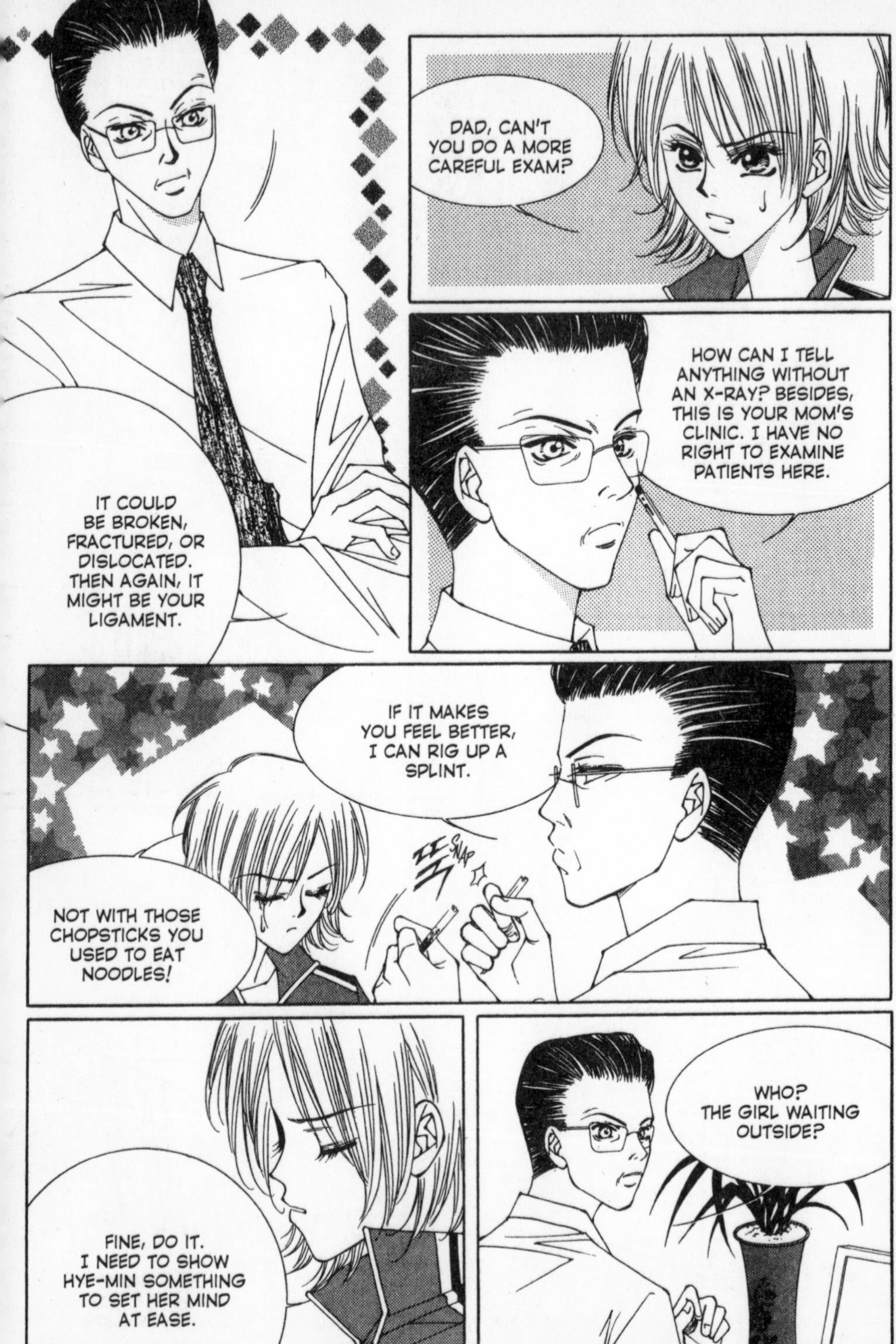
IT COULD BE BROKEN, FRACTURED, OR DISLOCATED. THEN AGAIN, IT MIGHT BE YOUR LIGAMENT.
DAD, CAN'T YOU DO A MORE CAREFUL EXAM?
HOW CAN I TELL ANYTHING WITHOUT AN X-RAY? BESIDES, THIS IS YOUR MOM'S CLINIC. I HAVE NO RIGHT TO EXAMINE PATIENTS HERE.
IF IT MAKES YOU FEEL BETTER, I CAN RIG UP A SPLINT.
SNAP
NOT WITH THOSE CHOPSTICKS YOU USED TO EAT NOODLES!
FINE, DO IT. I NEED TO SHOW HYE-MIN SOMETHING TO SET HER MIND AT EASE.
WHO? THE GIRL WAITING OUTSIDE?

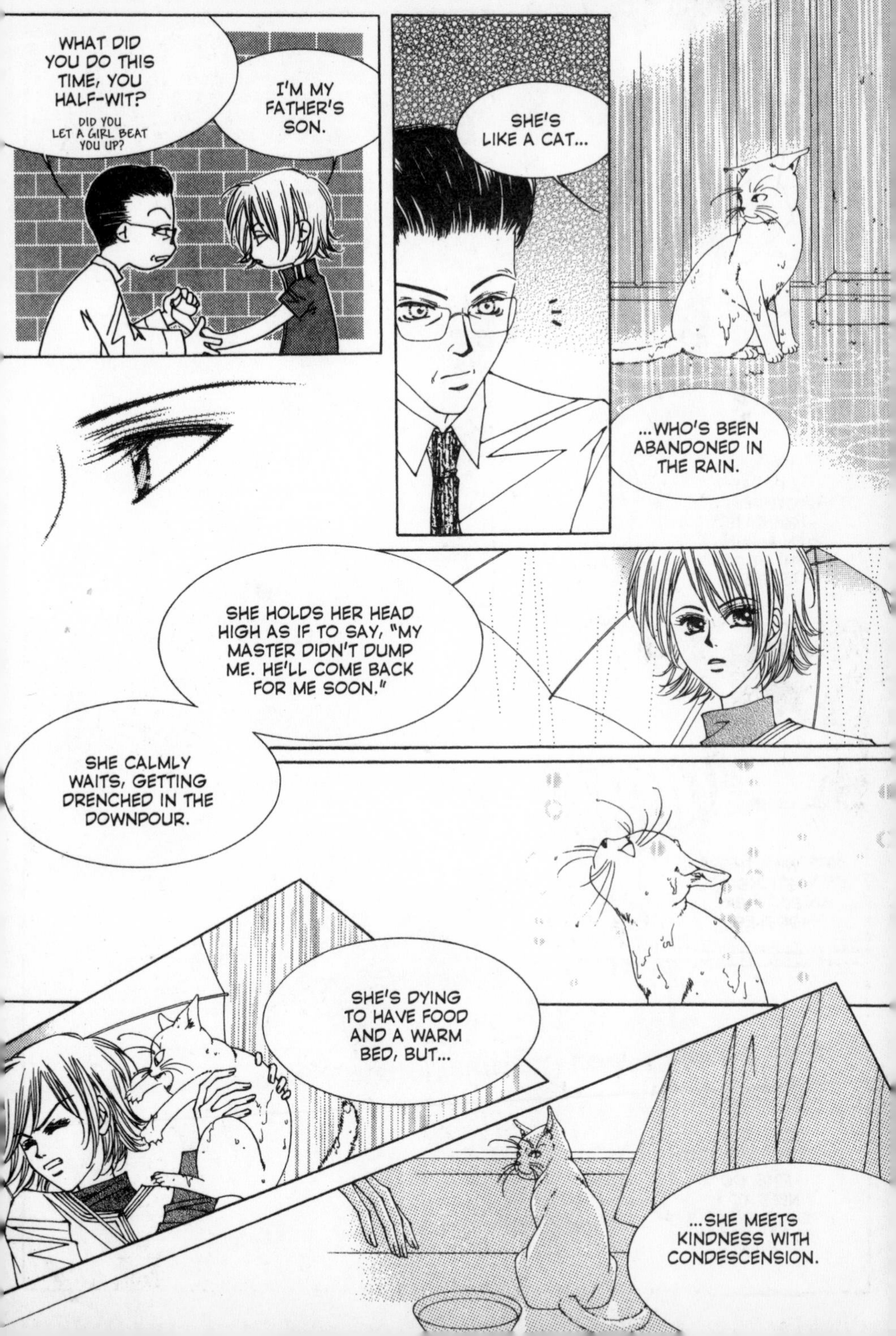
WHAT DID YOU DO THIS TIME, YOU HALF-WIT?
DID YOU LET A GIRL BEAT YOU UP?
I'M MY FATHER'S SON.
SHE'S LIKE A CAT...
...WHO'S BEEN ABANDONED IN THE RAIN.
SHE HOLDS HER HEAD HIGH AS IF TO SAY, "MY MASTER DIDN'T DUMP ME. HE'LL COME BACK FOR ME SOON."
SHE CALMLY WAITS, GETTING DRENCHED IN THE DOWNPOUR.
SHE'S DYING TO HAVE FOOD AND A WARM BED, BUT...
...SHE MEETS KINDNESS WITH CONDESCENSION.

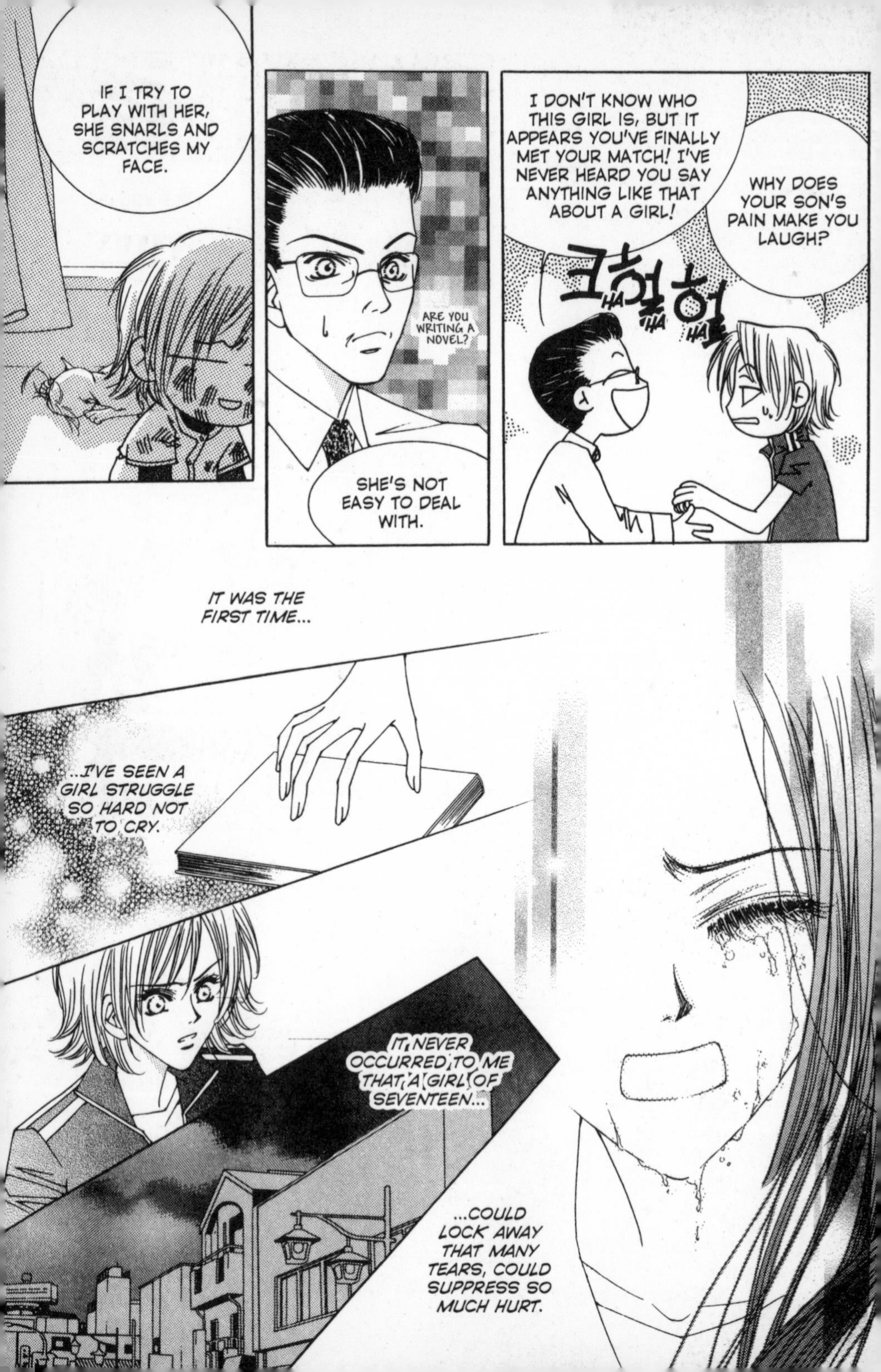
IF I TRY TO PLAY WITH HER, SHE SNARLS AND SCRATCHES MY FACE.
ARE YOU WRITING A NOVEL?
SHE'S NOT EASY TO DEAL WITH.
I DON'T KNOW WHO THIS GIRL IS, BUT IT APPEARS YOU'VE FINALLY MET YOUR MATCH! I'VE NEVER HEARD YOU SAY ANYTHING LIKE THAT ABOUT A GIRL!
HA HA HA
WHY DOES YOUR SON'S PAIN MAKE YOU LAUGH?
IT WAS THE FIRST TIME...
...I'VE SEEN A GIRL STRUGGLE SO HARD NOT TO CRY.
IT NEVER OCCURRED TO ME THAT A GIRL OF SEVENTEEN...
...COULD LOCK AWAY THAT MANY TEARS, COULD SUPPRESS SO MUCH HURT.

I THOUGHT THAT GIRLS CRIED JUST TO MAKE OTHER PEOPLE FEEL SORRY FOR THEM.

JUST THE HINT OF WATER IN THEIR EYES ANNOYED ME.

HERE YOU GO.

ALL OF THIS HAPPENED BECAUSE YOU LACK EMPATHY. TRY TO TAKE PITY ON SOME OF THE GIRLS YOU ENSNARE IN YOUR WEB. YOU'LL FIND LIFE GOES BETTER THAT WAY.

IS THAT HOW YOU GET BY, OLD MAN?

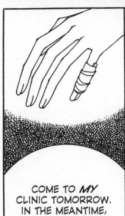

COME TO *MY* CLINIC TOMORROW. IN THE MEANTIME, DON'T USE THAT FINGER.

HAVE I EVER FELT SYMPATHY FOR ANYONE TILL NOW?

MAYBE HE'S RIGHT.

TAP!

THERE'S A GIRL WAITING OUTSIDE.

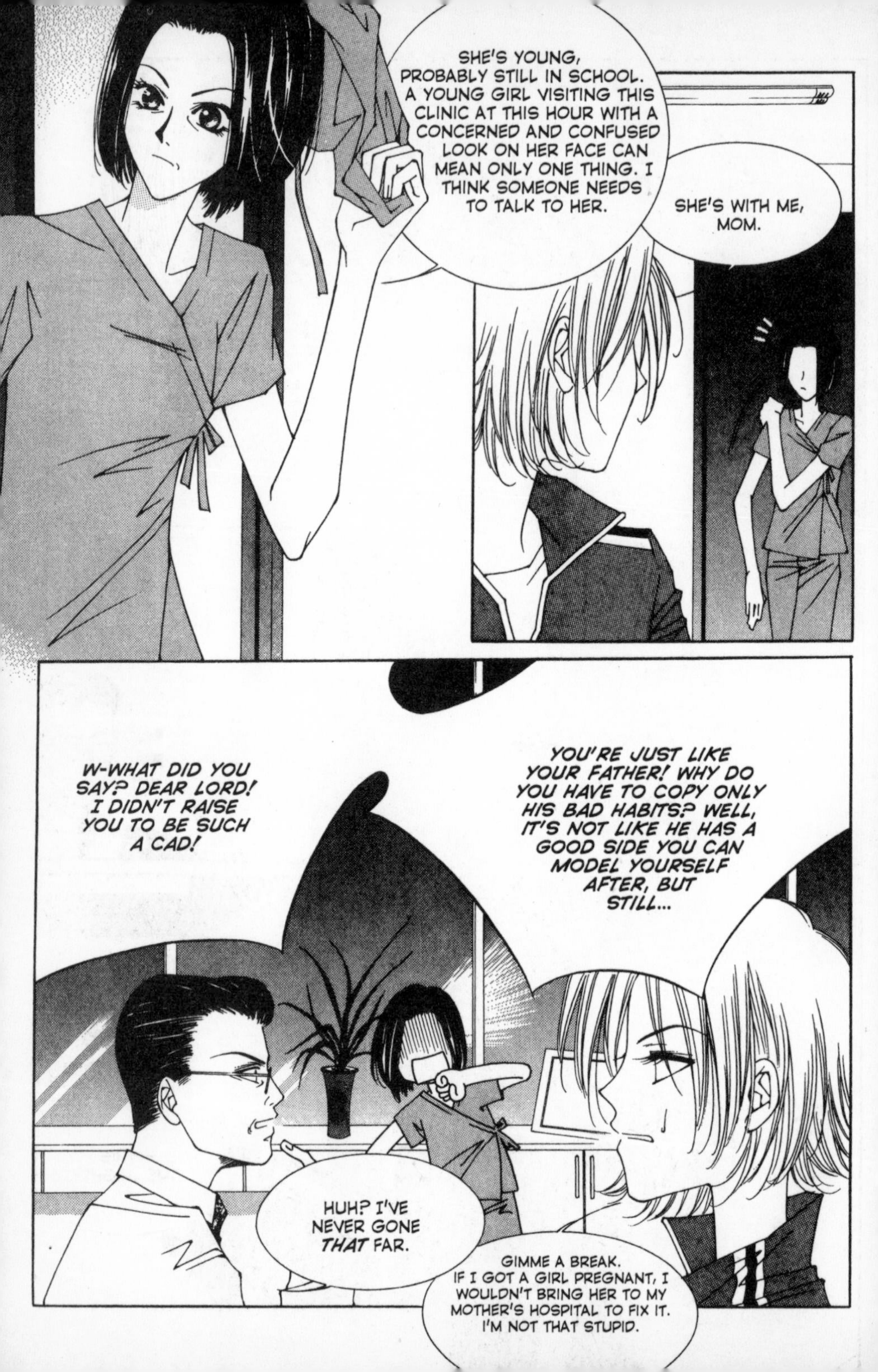
SHE'S YOUNG, PROBABLY STILL IN SCHOOL. A YOUNG GIRL VISITING THIS CLINIC AT THIS HOUR WITH A CONCERNED AND CONFUSED LOOK ON HER FACE CAN MEAN ONLY ONE THING. I THINK SOMEONE NEEDS TO TALK TO HER.
SHE'S WITH ME, MOM.
W-WHAT DID YOU SAY? DEAR LORD! I DIDN'T RAISE YOU TO BE SUCH A CAD!
YOU'RE JUST LIKE YOUR FATHER! WHY DO YOU HAVE TO COPY ONLY HIS BAD HABITS? WELL, IT'S NOT LIKE HE HAS A GOOD SIDE YOU CAN MODEL YOURSELF AFTER, BUT STILL...
HUH? I'VE NEVER GONE *THAT* FAR.
GIMME A BREAK. IF I GOT A GIRL PREGNANT, I WOULDN'T BRING HER TO MY MOTHER'S HOSPITAL TO FIX IT. I'M NOT THAT STUPID.

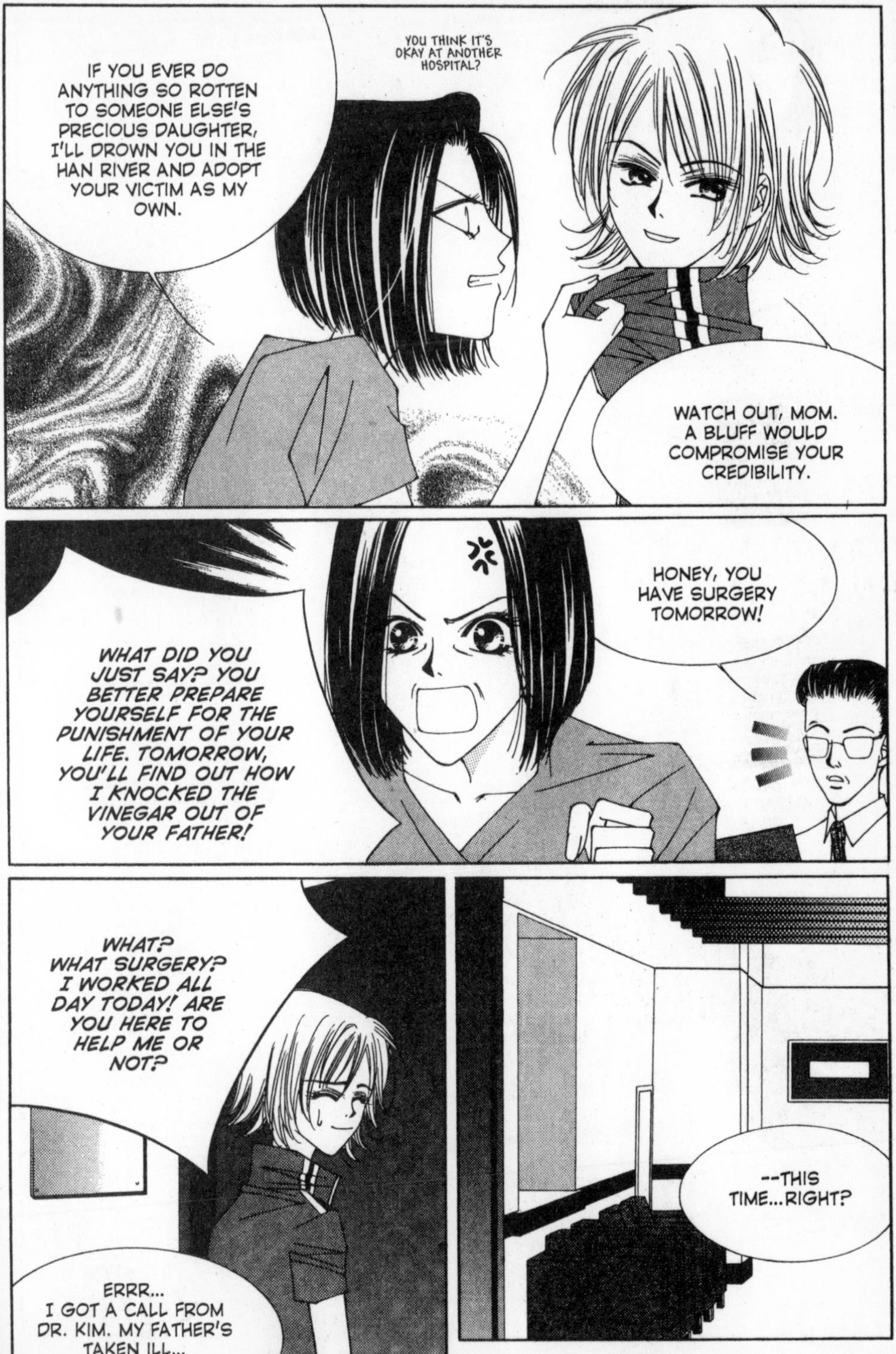
IF YOU EVER DO ANYTHING SO ROTTEN TO SOMEONE ELSE'S PRECIOUS DAUGHTER, I'LL DROWN YOU IN THE HAN RIVER AND ADOPT YOUR VICTIM AS MY OWN.
YOU THINK IT'S OKAY AT ANOTHER HOSPITAL?
WATCH OUT, MOM. A BLUFF WOULD COMPROMISE YOUR CREDIBILITY.
WHAT DID YOU JUST SAY? YOU BETTER PREPARE YOURSELF FOR THE PUNISHMENT OF YOUR LIFE. TOMORROW, YOU'LL FIND OUT HOW I KNOCKED THE VINEGAR OUT OF YOUR FATHER!
HONEY, YOU HAVE SURGERY TOMORROW!
WHAT? WHAT SURGERY? I WORKED ALL DAY TODAY! ARE YOU HERE TO HELP ME OR NOT?
ERRR... I GOT A CALL FROM DR. KIM. MY FATHER'S TAKEN ILL...
--THIS TIME...RIGHT?

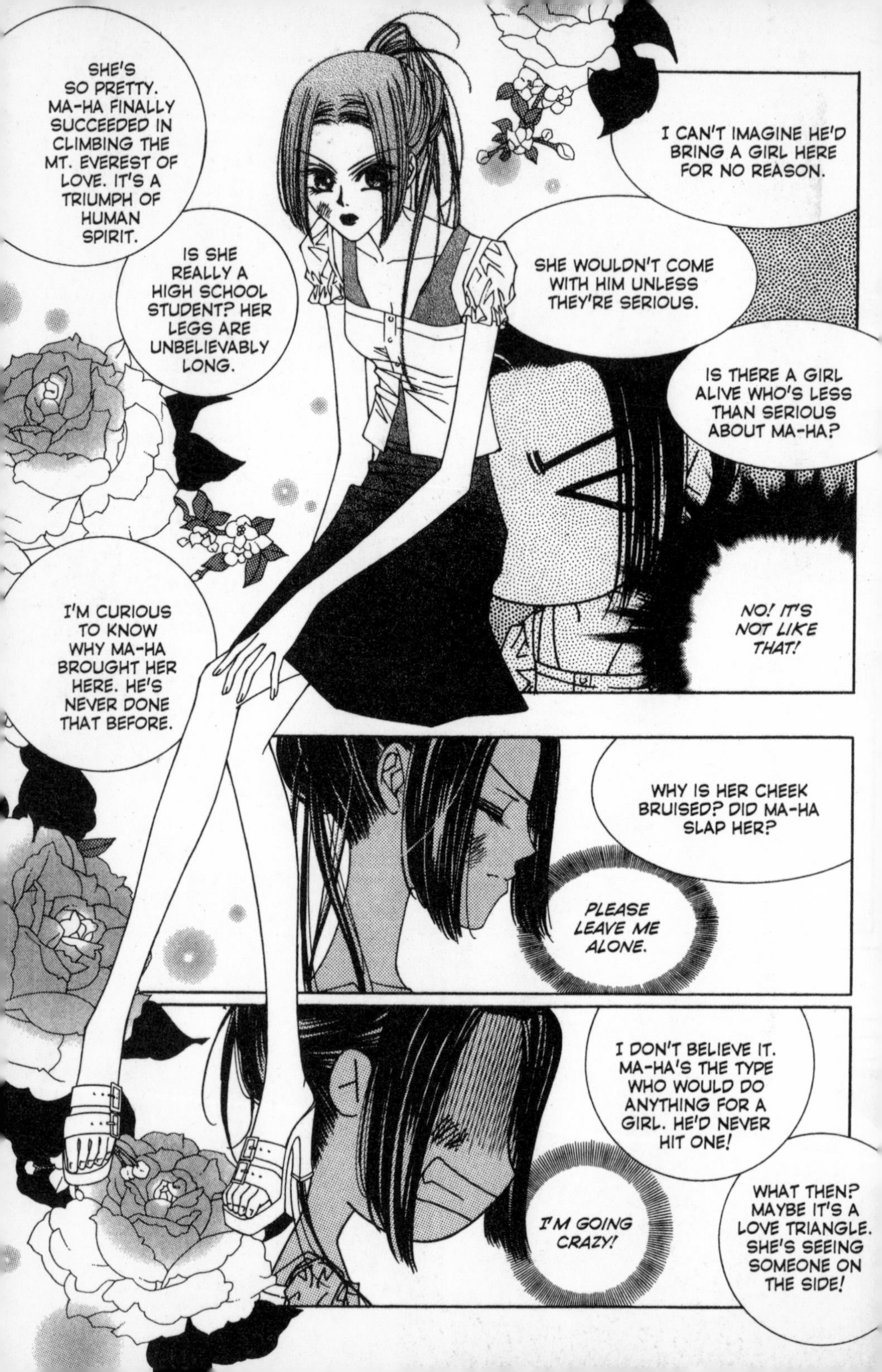
SHE'S SO PRETTY. MA-HA FINALLY SUCCEEDED IN CLIMBING THE MT. EVEREST OF LOVE. IT'S A TRIUMPH OF HUMAN SPIRIT.
IS SHE REALLY A HIGH SCHOOL STUDENT? HER LEGS ARE UNBELIEVABLY LONG.
I'M CURIOUS TO KNOW WHY MA-HA BROUGHT HER HERE. HE'S NEVER DONE THAT BEFORE.
I CAN'T IMAGINE HE'D BRING A GIRL HERE FOR NO REASON.
SHE WOULDN'T COME WITH HIM UNLESS THEY'RE SERIOUS.
IS THERE A GIRL ALIVE WHO'S LESS THAN SERIOUS ABOUT MA-HA?
NO! IT'S NOT LIKE THAT!
WHY IS HER CHEEK BRUISED? DID MA-HA SLAP HER?
PLEASE LEAVE ME ALONE.
I DON'T BELIEVE IT. MA-HA'S THE TYPE WHO WOULD DO ANYTHING FOR A GIRL. HE'D NEVER HIT ONE!
I'M GOING CRAZY!
WHAT THEN? MAYBE IT'S A LOVE TRIANGLE. SHE'S SEEING SOMEONE ON THE SIDE!

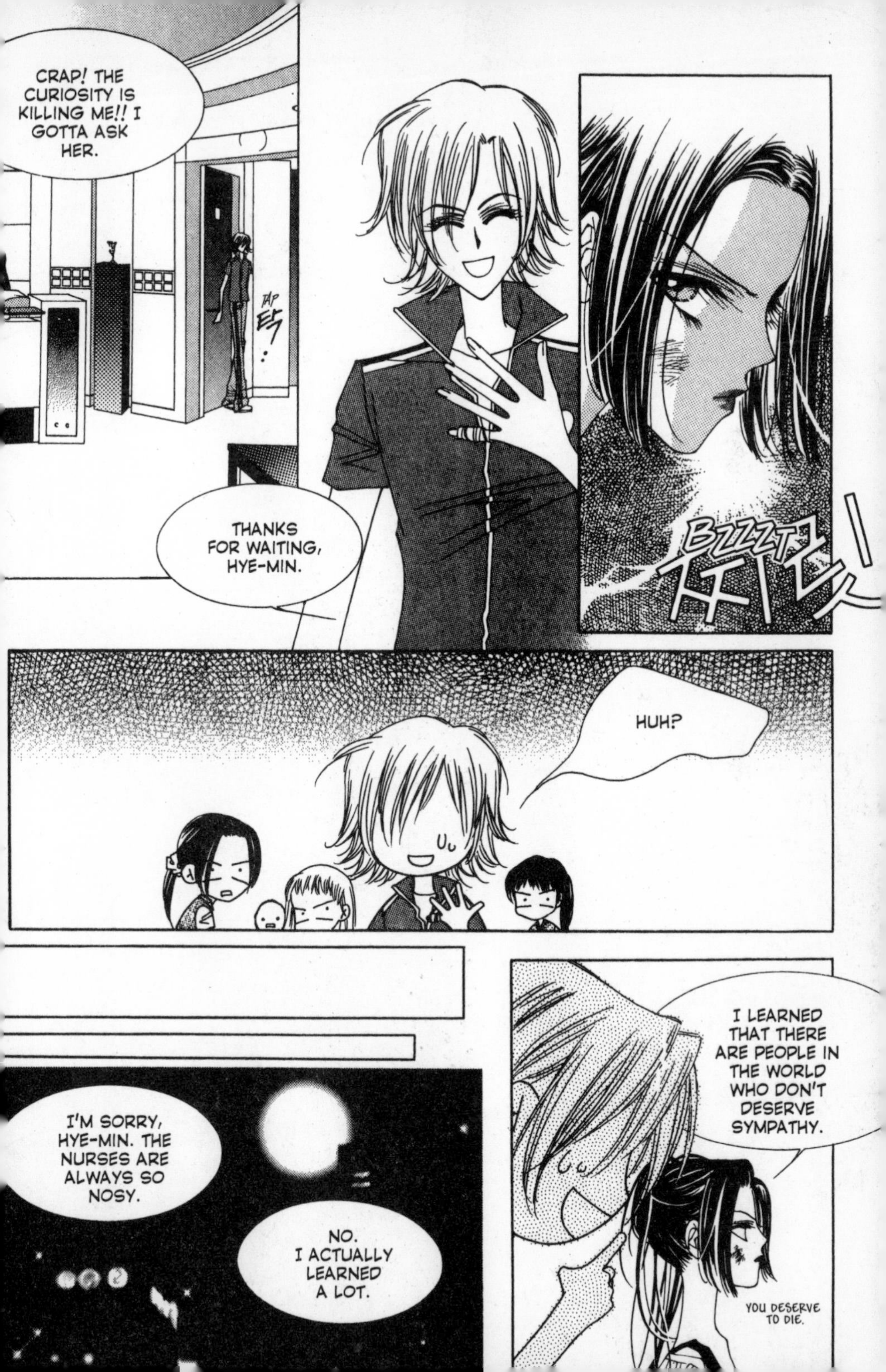
CRAP! THE CURIOSITY IS KILLING ME!! I GOTTA ASK HER.
TAP
THANKS FOR WAITING, HYE-MIN.
BZZZT
HUH?
I'M SORRY, HYE-MIN. THE NURSES ARE ALWAYS SO NOSY.
NO. I ACTUALLY LEARNED A LOT.
I LEARNED THAT THERE ARE PEOPLE IN THE WORLD WHO DON'T DESERVE SYMPATHY.
YOU DESERVE TO DIE.

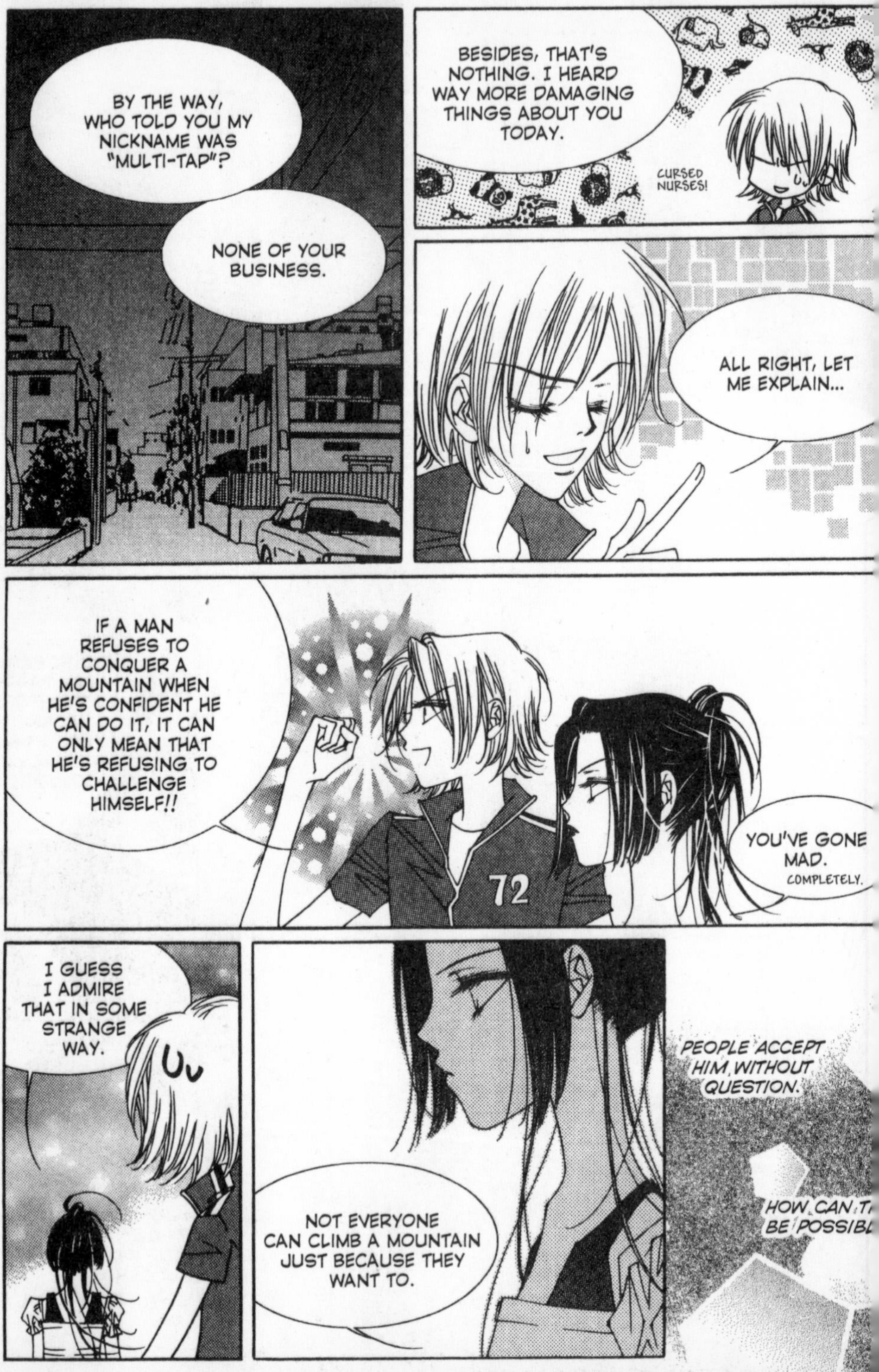
BY THE WAY, WHO TOLD YOU MY NICKNAME WAS "MULTI-TAP"?
NONE OF YOUR BUSINESS.
BESIDES, THAT'S NOTHING. I HEARD WAY MORE DAMAGING THINGS ABOUT YOU TODAY.
CURSED NURSES!
ALL RIGHT, LET ME EXPLAIN...
IF A MAN REFUSES TO CONQUER A MOUNTAIN WHEN HE'S CONFIDENT HE CAN DO IT, IT CAN ONLY MEAN THAT HE'S REFUSING TO CHALLENGE HIMSELF!!
YOU'VE GONE MAD.
COMPLETELY.
I GUESS I ADMIRE THAT IN SOME STRANGE WAY.
NOT EVERYONE CAN CLIMB A MOUNTAIN JUST BECAUSE THEY WANT TO.
PEOPLE ACCEPT HIM, WITHOUT QUESTION.
HOW CAN T
BE POSSIBL

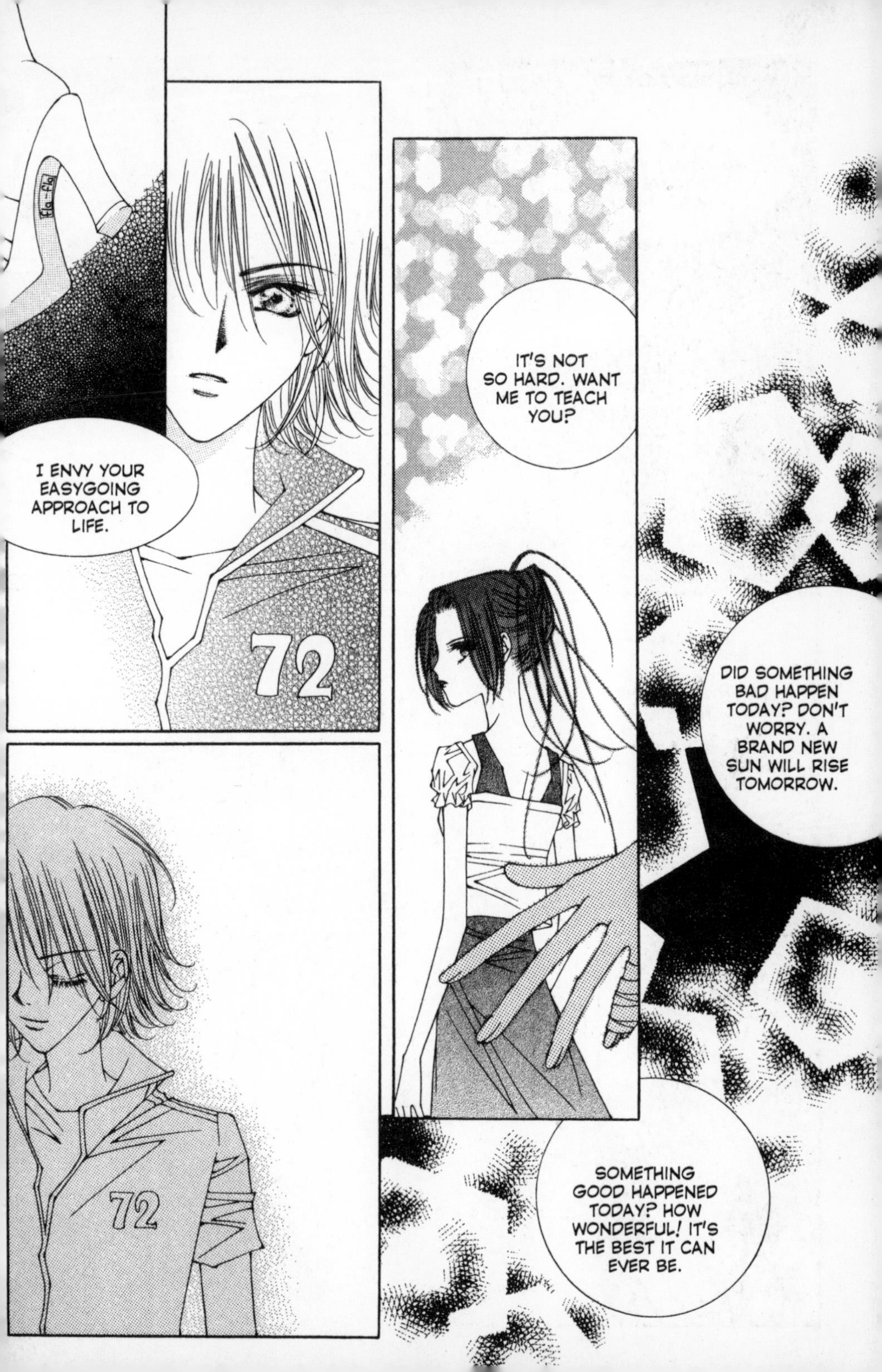
I ENVY YOUR EASYGOING APPROACH TO LIFE.
IT'S NOT SO HARD. WANT ME TO TEACH YOU?
DID SOMETHING BAD HAPPEN TODAY? DON'T WORRY. A BRAND NEW SUN WILL RISE TOMORROW.
SOMETHING GOOD HAPPENED TODAY? HOW WONDERFUL! IT'S THE BEST IT CAN EVER BE.

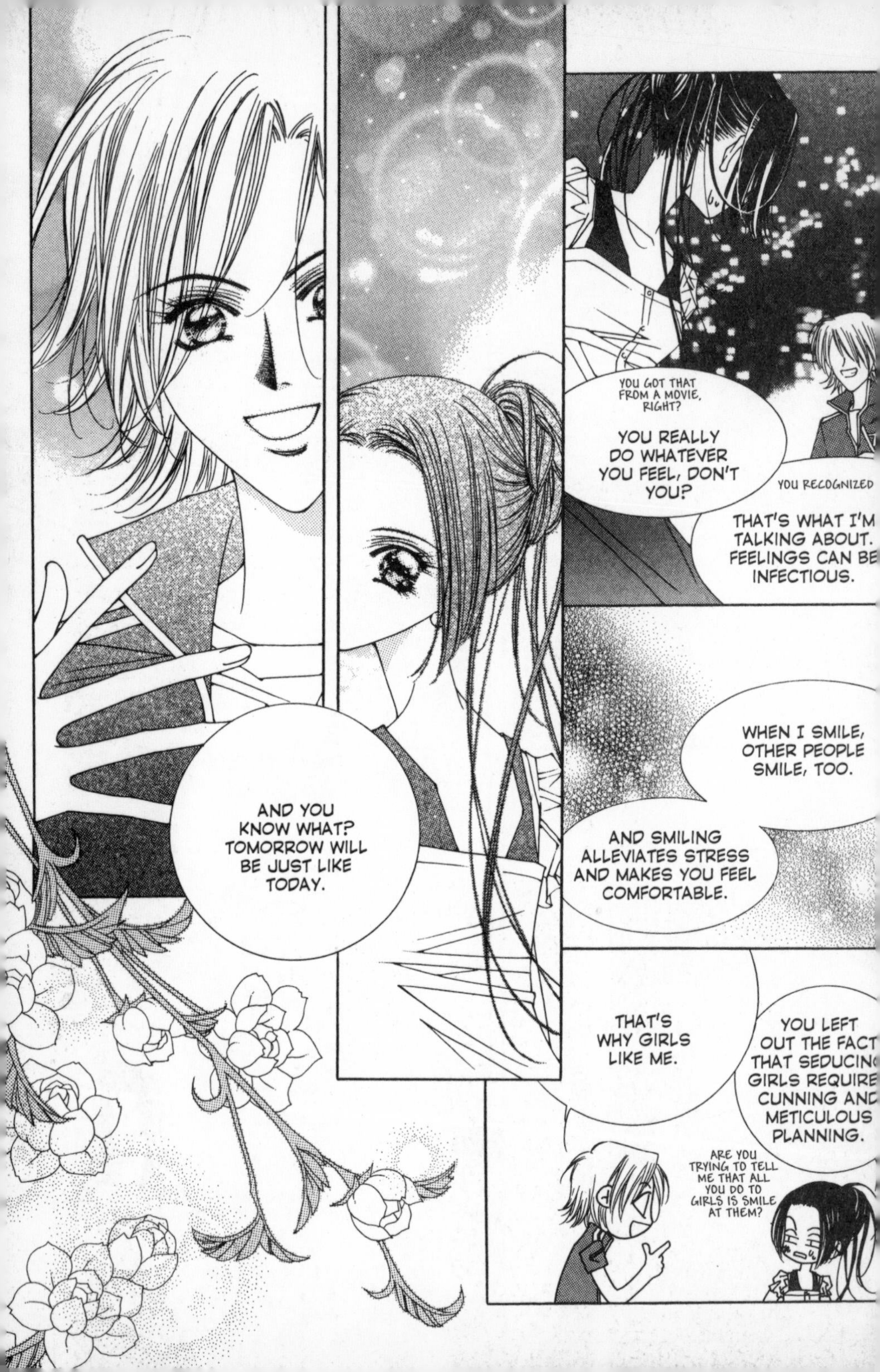
AND YOU KNOW WHAT? TOMORROW WILL BE JUST LIKE TODAY.
YOU GOT THAT FROM A MOVIE, RIGHT?
YOU REALLY DO WHATEVER YOU FEEL, DON'T YOU?
YOU RECOGNIZED
THAT'S WHAT I'M TALKING ABOUT. FEELINGS CAN BE INFECTIOUS.
WHEN I SMILE, OTHER PEOPLE SMILE, TOO.
AND SMILING ALLEVIATES STRESS AND MAKES YOU FEEL COMFORTABLE.
THAT'S WHY GIRLS LIKE ME.
YOU LEFT OUT THE FACT THAT SEDUCIN GIRLS REQUIRE CUNNING AND METICULOUS PLANNING.
ARE YOU TRYING TO TELL ME THAT ALL YOU DO TO GIRLS IS SMILE AT THEM?

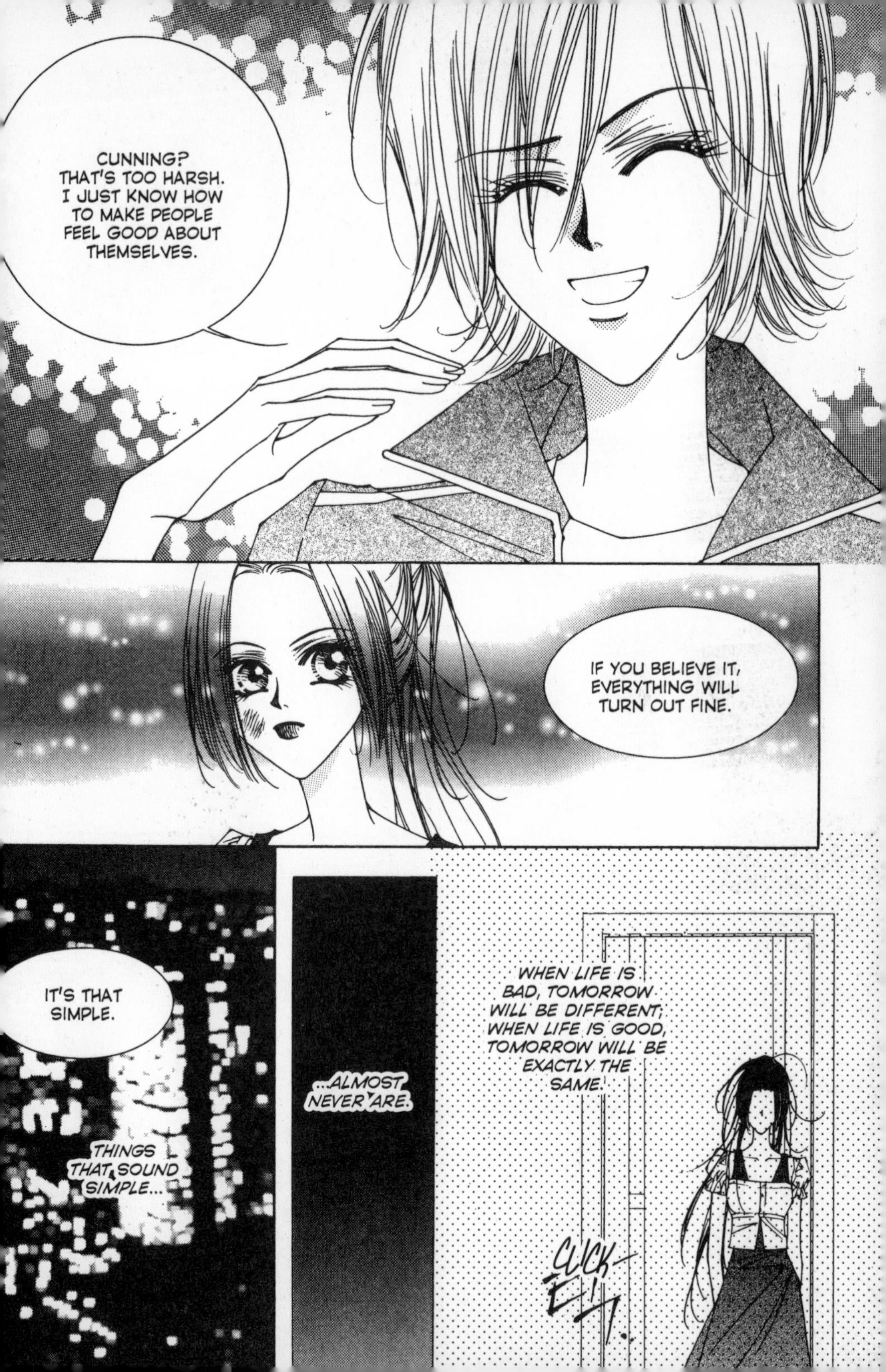
CUNNING? THAT'S TOO HARSH. I JUST KNOW HOW TO MAKE PEOPLE FEEL GOOD ABOUT THEMSELVES.
IF YOU BELIEVE IT, EVERYTHING WILL TURN OUT FINE.
IT'S THAT SIMPLE.
THINGS THAT SOUND SIMPLE...
...ALMOST NEVER ARE.
WHEN LIFE IS BAD, TOMORROW WILL BE DIFFERENT; WHEN LIFE IS GOOD, TOMORROW WILL BE EXACTLY THE SAME.
CLICK-E!

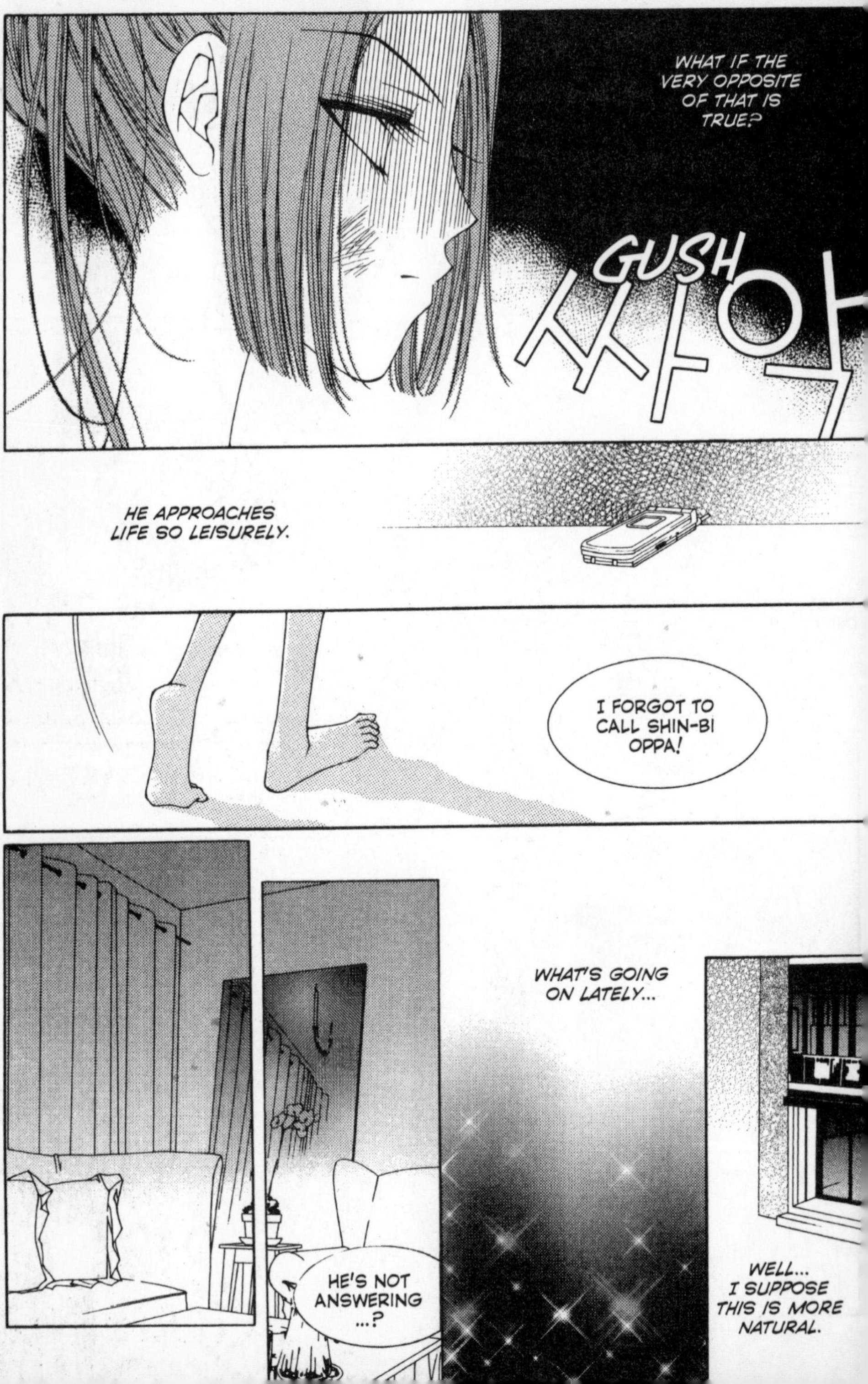
WHAT IF THE VERY OPPOSITE OF THAT IS TRUE?
GUSH
HE APPROACHES LIFE SO LEISURELY.
I FORGOT TO CALL SHIN-BI OPPA!
HE'S NOT ANSWERING ...?
WHAT'S GOING ON LATELY...
WELL... I SUPPOSE THIS IS MORE NATURAL.

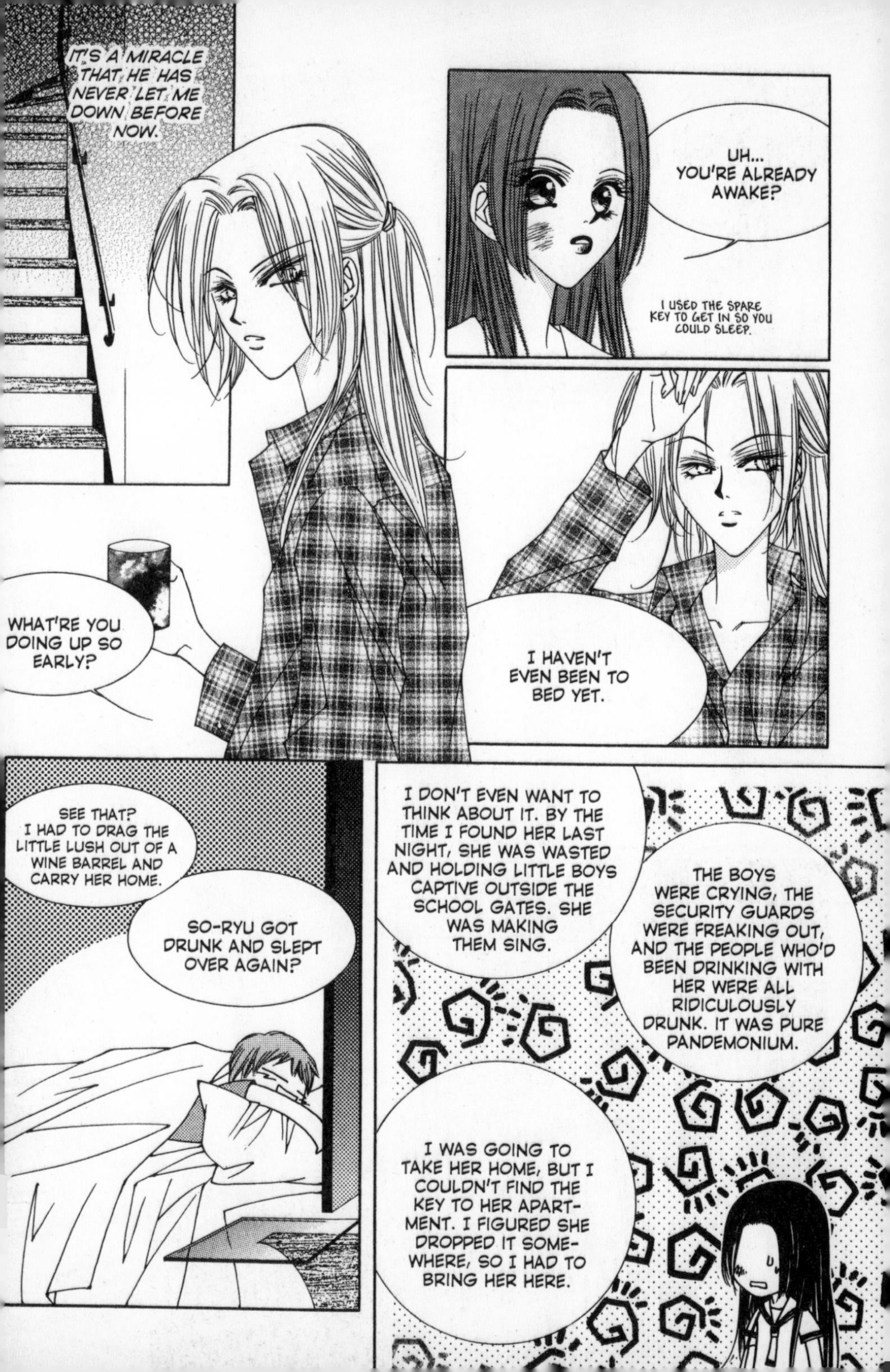
IT'S A MIRACLE THAT HE HAS NEVER LET ME DOWN BEFORE NOW.
WHAT'RE YOU DOING UP SO EARLY?
UH... YOU'RE ALREADY AWAKE?
I USED THE SPARE KEY TO GET IN SO YOU COULD SLEEP.
I HAVEN'T EVEN BEEN TO BED YET.
SEE THAT? I HAD TO DRAG THE LITTLE LUSH OUT OF A WINE BARREL AND CARRY HER HOME.
SO-RYU GOT DRUNK AND SLEPT OVER AGAIN?
I DON'T EVEN WANT TO THINK ABOUT IT. BY THE TIME I FOUND HER LAST NIGHT, SHE WAS WASTED AND HOLDING LITTLE BOYS CAPTIVE OUTSIDE THE SCHOOL GATES. SHE WAS MAKING THEM SING.
THE BOYS WERE CRYING, THE SECURITY GUARDS WERE FREAKING OUT, AND THE PEOPLE WHO'D BEEN DRINKING WITH HER WERE ALL RIDICULOUSLY DRUNK. IT WAS PURE PANDEMONIUM.
I WAS GOING TO TAKE HER HOME, BUT I COULDN'T FIND THE KEY TO HER APARTMENT. I FIGURED SHE DROPPED IT SOMEWHERE, SO I HAD TO BRING HER HERE.

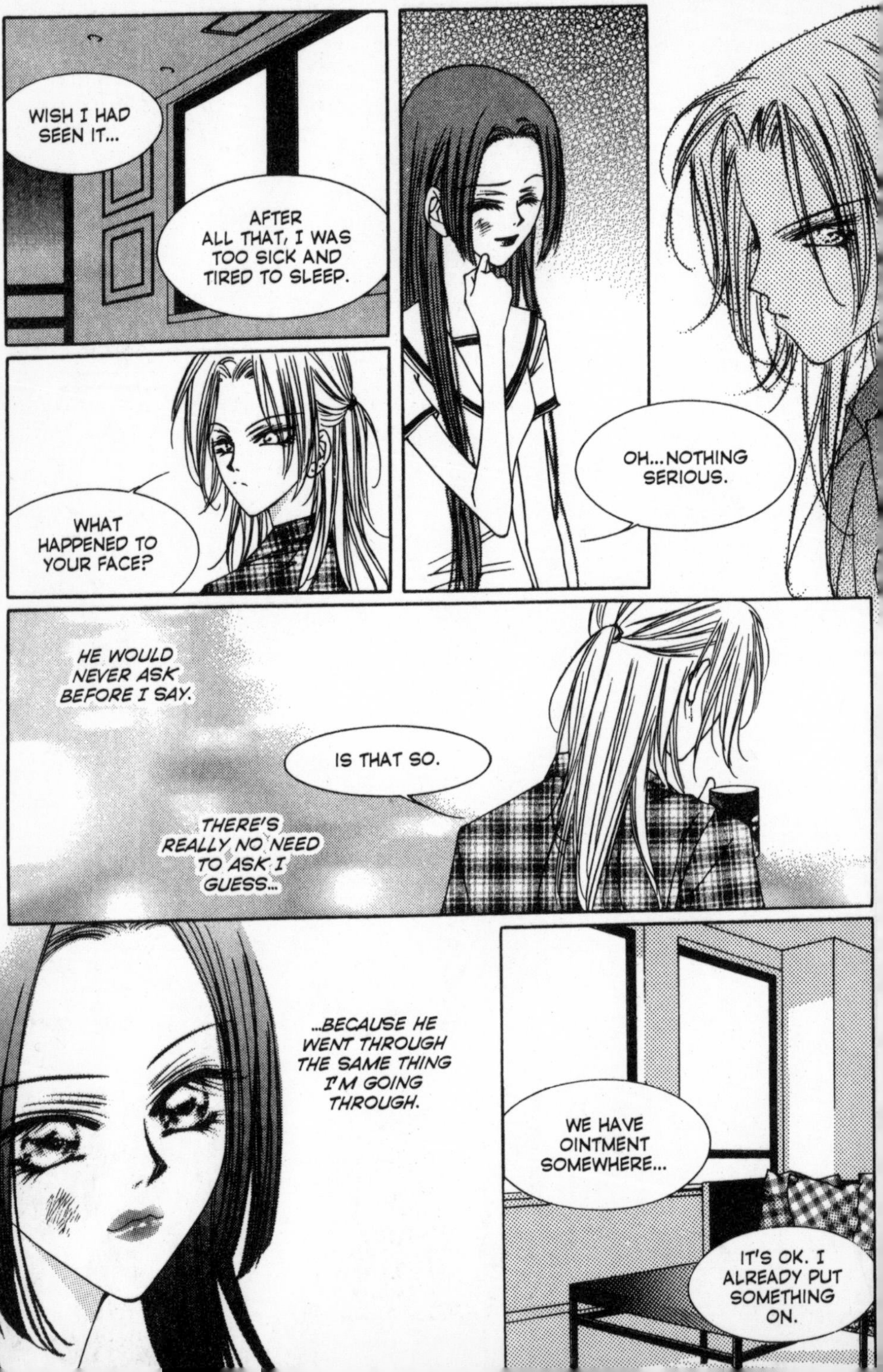
WISH I HAD SEEN IT...
AFTER ALL THAT, I WAS TOO SICK AND TIRED TO SLEEP.
WHAT HAPPENED TO YOUR FACE?
OH...NOTHING SERIOUS.
HE WOULD NEVER ASK BEFORE I SAY.
IS THAT SO.
THERE'S REALLY NO NEED TO ASK I GUESS...
...BECAUSE HE WENT THROUGH THE SAME THING I'M GOING THROUGH.
WE HAVE OINTMENT SOMEWHERE...
IT'S OK. I ALREADY PUT SOMETHING ON.

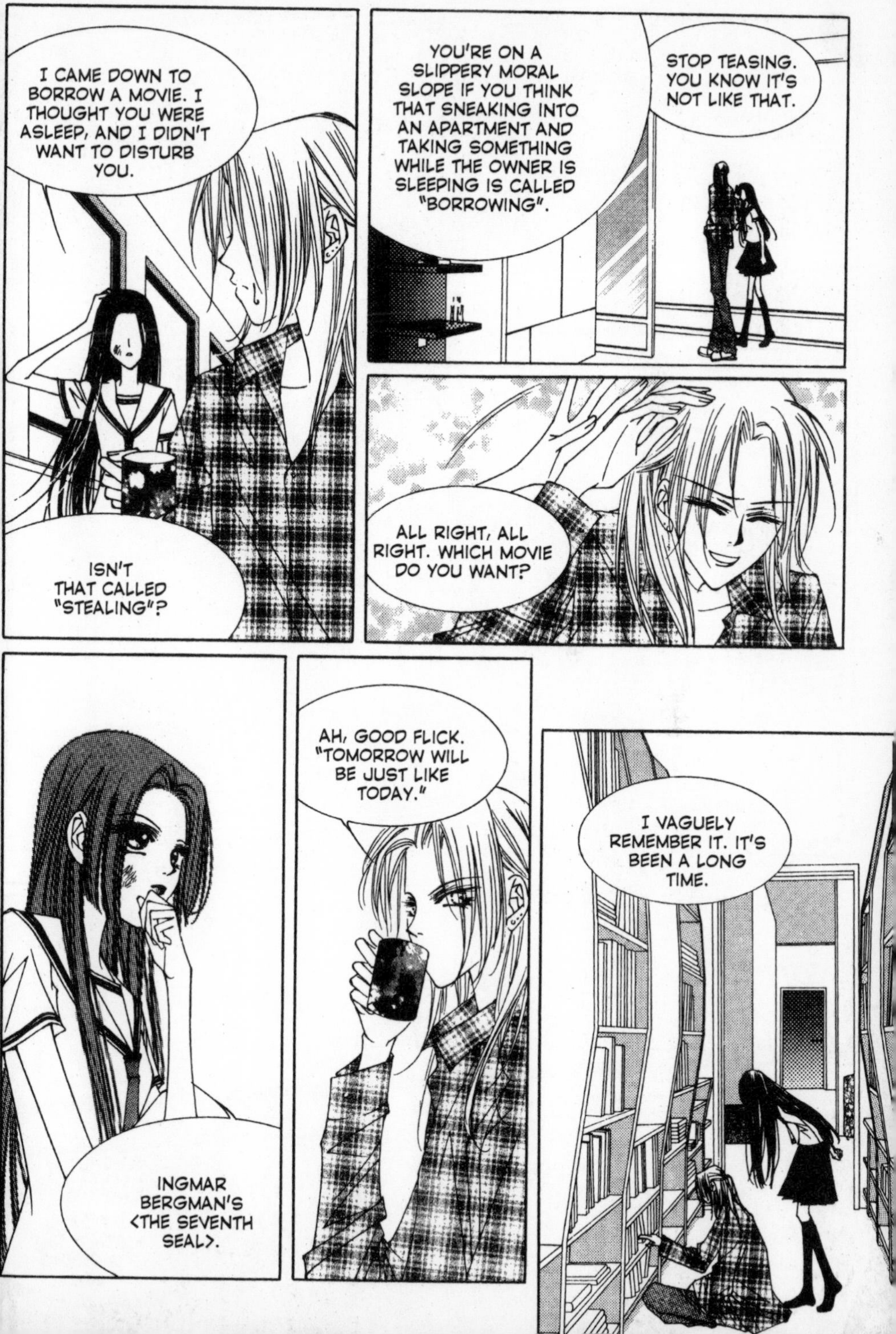
I CAME DOWN TO BORROW A MOVIE. I THOUGHT YOU WERE ASLEEP, AND I DIDN'T WANT TO DISTURB YOU.
ISN'T THAT CALLED "STEALING"?
YOU'RE ON A SLIPPERY MORAL SLOPE IF YOU THINK THAT SNEAKING INTO AN APARTMENT AND TAKING SOMETHING WHILE THE OWNER IS SLEEPING IS CALLED "BORROWING".
STOP TEASING. YOU KNOW IT'S NOT LIKE THAT.
ALL RIGHT, ALL RIGHT. WHICH MOVIE DO YOU WANT?
INGMAR BERGMAN'S <THE SEVENTH SEAL>.
AH, GOOD FLICK. "TOMORROW WILL BE JUST LIKE TODAY."
I VAGUELY REMEMBER IT. IT'S BEEN A LONG TIME.

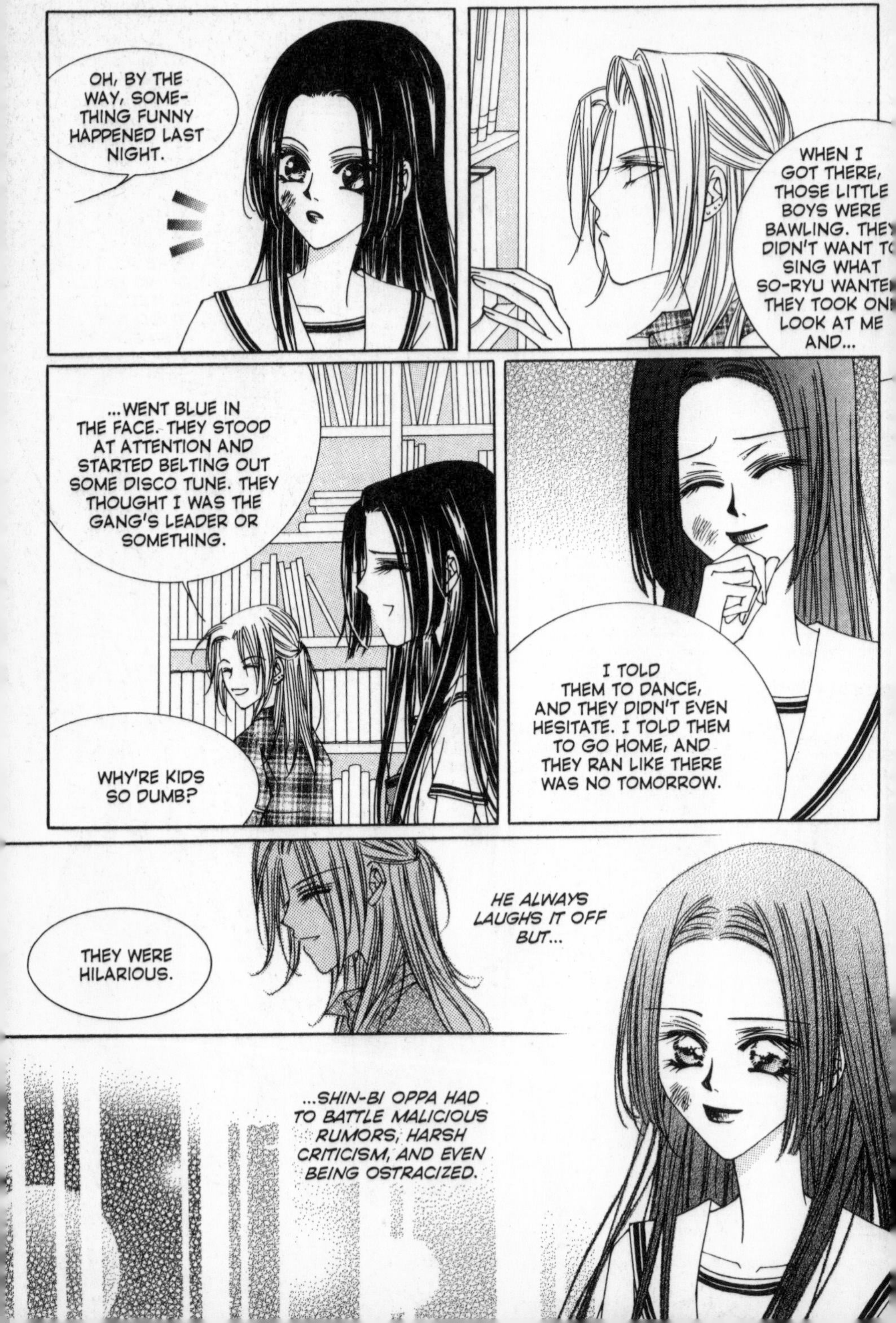
OH, BY THE WAY, SOME-THING FUNNY HAPPENED LAST NIGHT.
WHEN I GOT THERE, THOSE LITTLE BOYS WERE BAWLING. THE DIDN'T WANT T SING WHAT SO-RYU WANTE THEY TOOK ON LOOK AT ME AND...
...WENT BLUE IN THE FACE. THEY STOOD AT ATTENTION AND STARTED BELTING OUT SOME DISCO TUNE. THEY THOUGHT I WAS THE GANG'S LEADER OR SOMETHING.
WHY'RE KIDS SO DUMB?
I TOLD THEM TO DANCE, AND THEY DIDN'T EVEN HESITATE. I TOLD THEM TO GO HOME, AND THEY RAN LIKE THERE WAS NO TOMORROW.
THEY WERE HILARIOUS.
HE ALWAYS LAUGHS IT OFF BUT...
...SHIN-BI OPPA HAD TO BATTLE MALICIOUS RUMORS, HARSH CRITICISM, AND EVEN BEING OSTRACIZED.

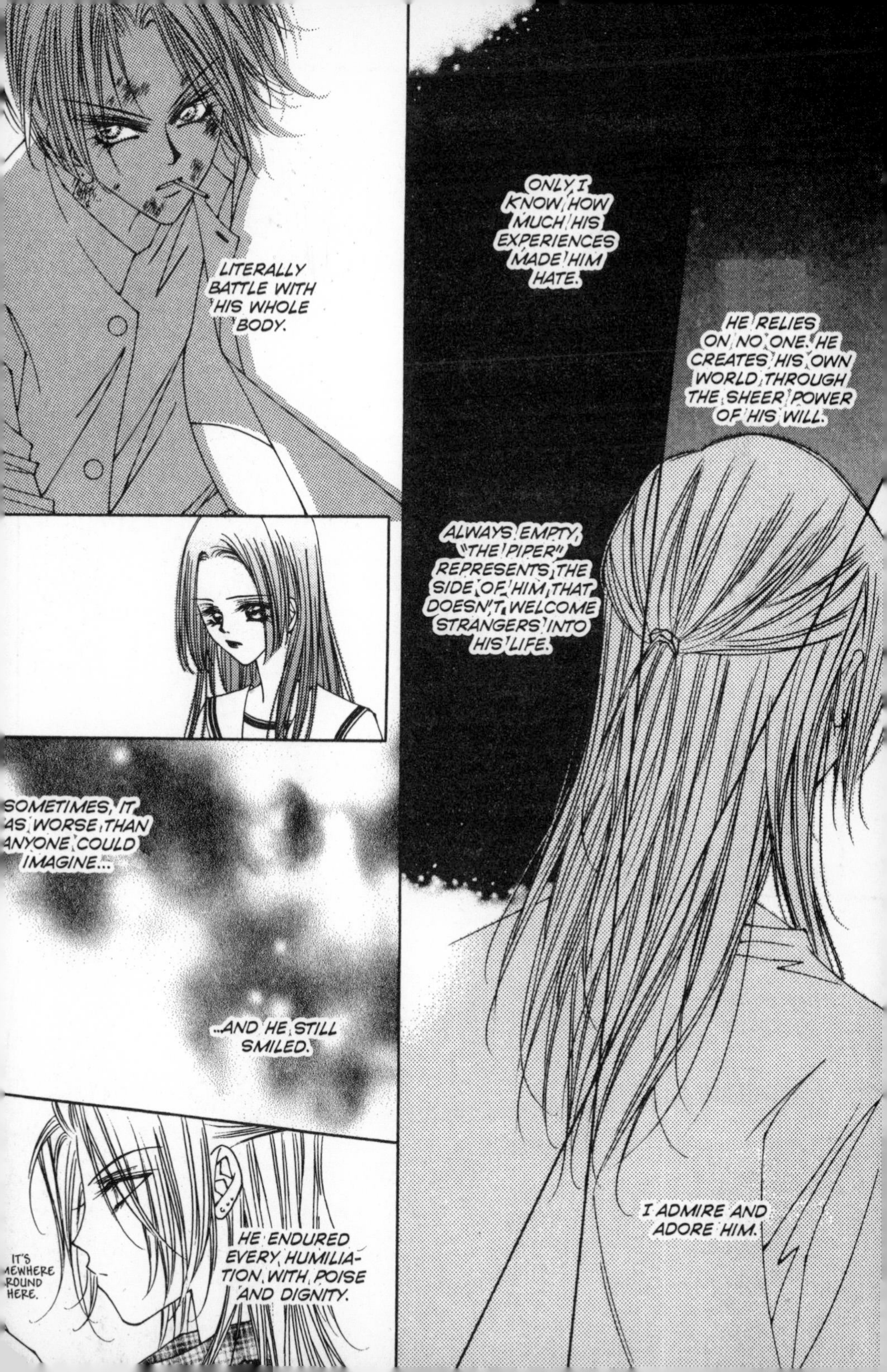
LITERALLY BATTLE WITH HIS WHOLE BODY.
SOMETIMES, IT AS WORSE THAN ANYONE COULD IMAGINE...
...AND HE STILL SMILED.
IT'S MEWHERE ROUND HERE.
HE ENDURED EVERY HUMILIATION WITH POISE AND DIGNITY.
ONLY I KNOW HOW MUCH HIS EXPERIENCES MADE HIM HATE.
HE RELIES ON NO ONE. HE CREATES HIS OWN WORLD THROUGH THE SHEER POWER OF HIS WILL.
ALWAYS EMPTY, "THE PIPER" REPRESENTS THE SIDE OF HIM THAT DOESN'T WELCOME STRANGERS INTO HIS LIFE.
I ADMIRE AND ADORE HIM.

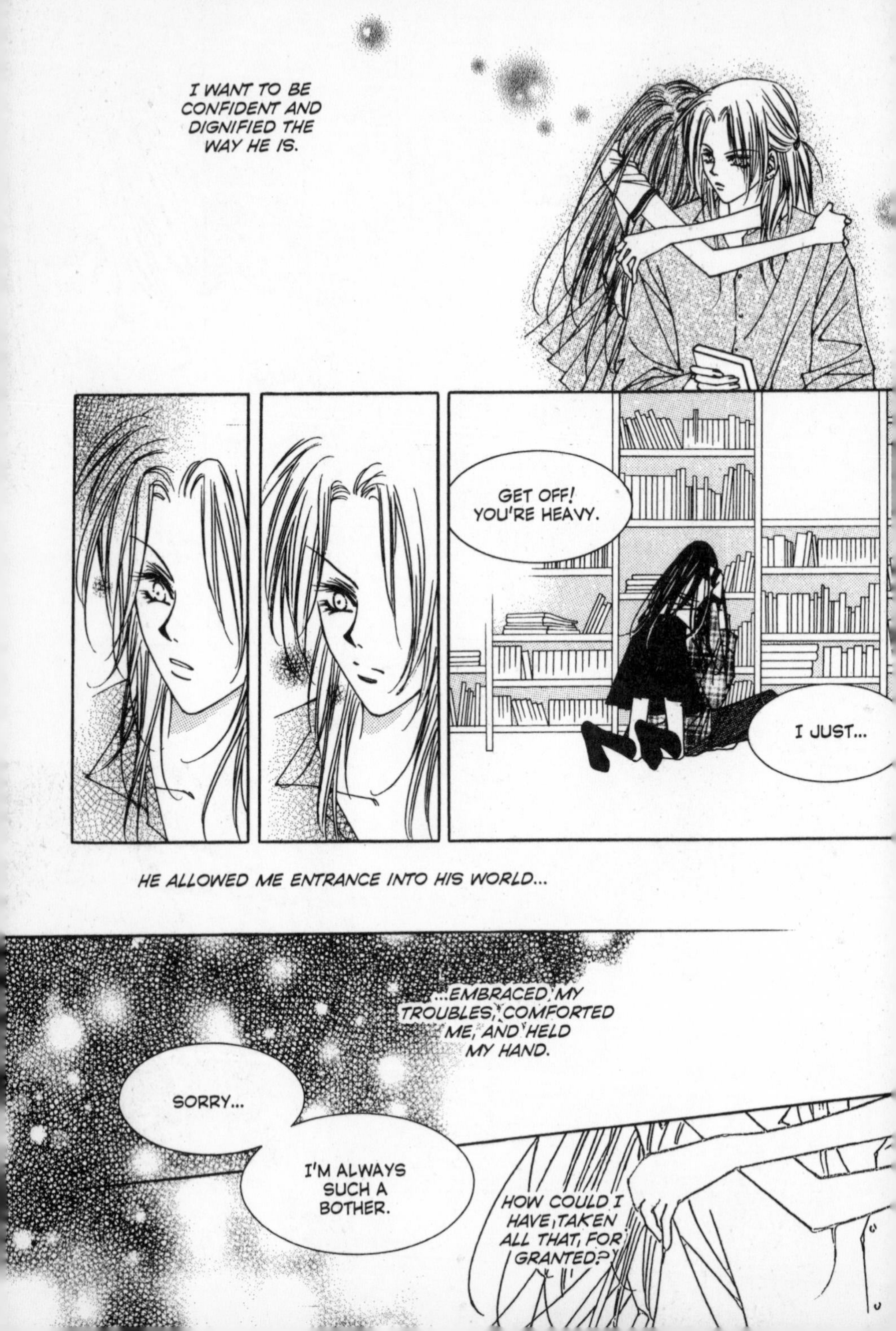
I WANT TO BE CONFIDENT AND DIGNIFIED THE WAY HE IS.
GET OFF! YOU'RE HEAVY.
I JUST...
HE ALLOWED ME ENTRANCE INTO HIS WORLD...
...EMBRACED MY TROUBLES, COMFORTED ME, AND HELD MY HAND.
SORRY...
I'M ALWAYS SUCH A BOTHER.
HOW COULD I HAVE TAKEN ALL THAT FOR GRANTED?

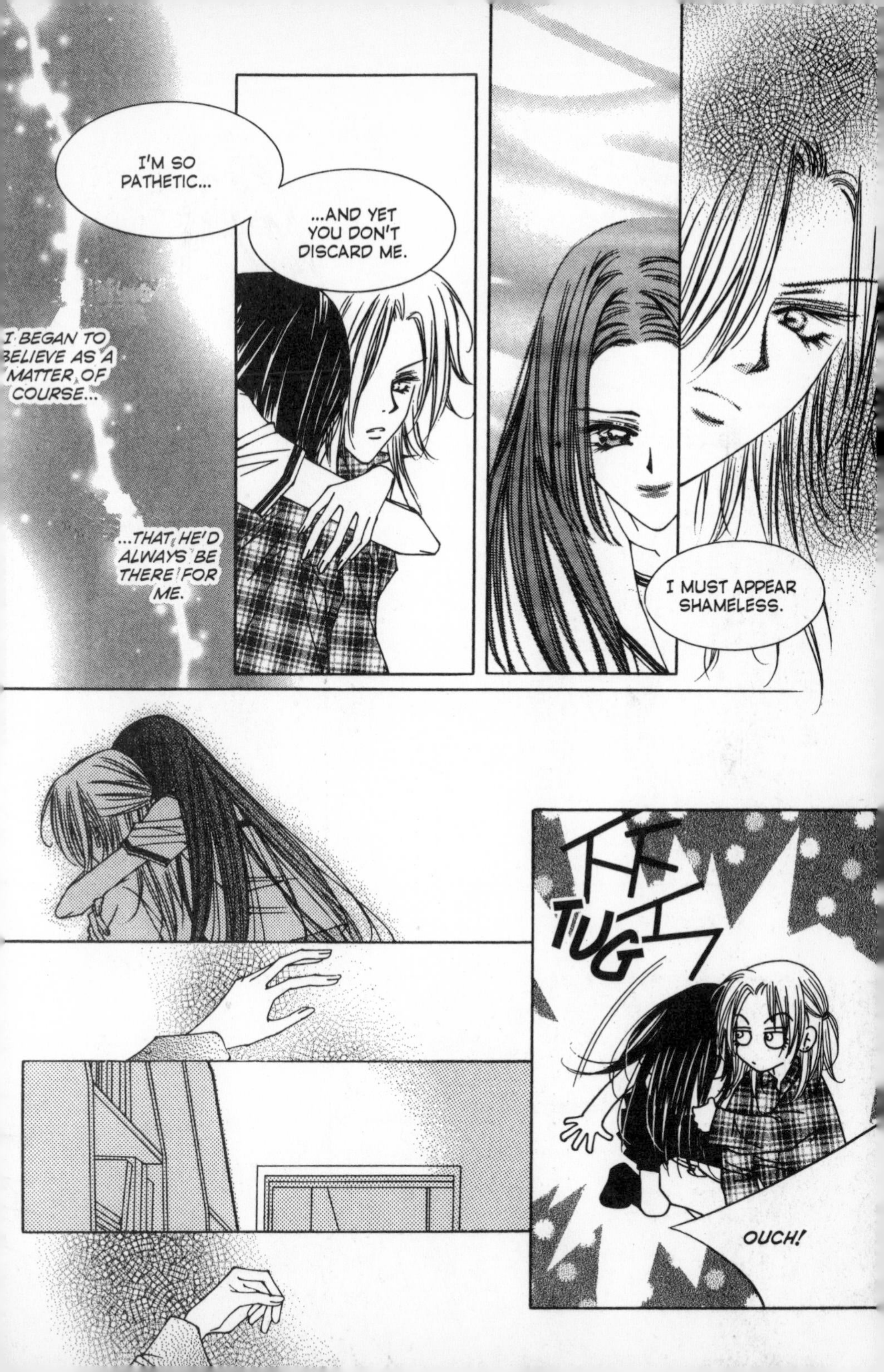
I BEGAN TO BELIEVE AS A MATTER OF COURSE...
...THAT HE'D ALWAYS BE THERE FOR ME.
I'M SO PATHETIC...
...AND YET YOU DON'T DISCARD ME.
I MUST APPEAR SHAMELESS.
TUG
OUCH!

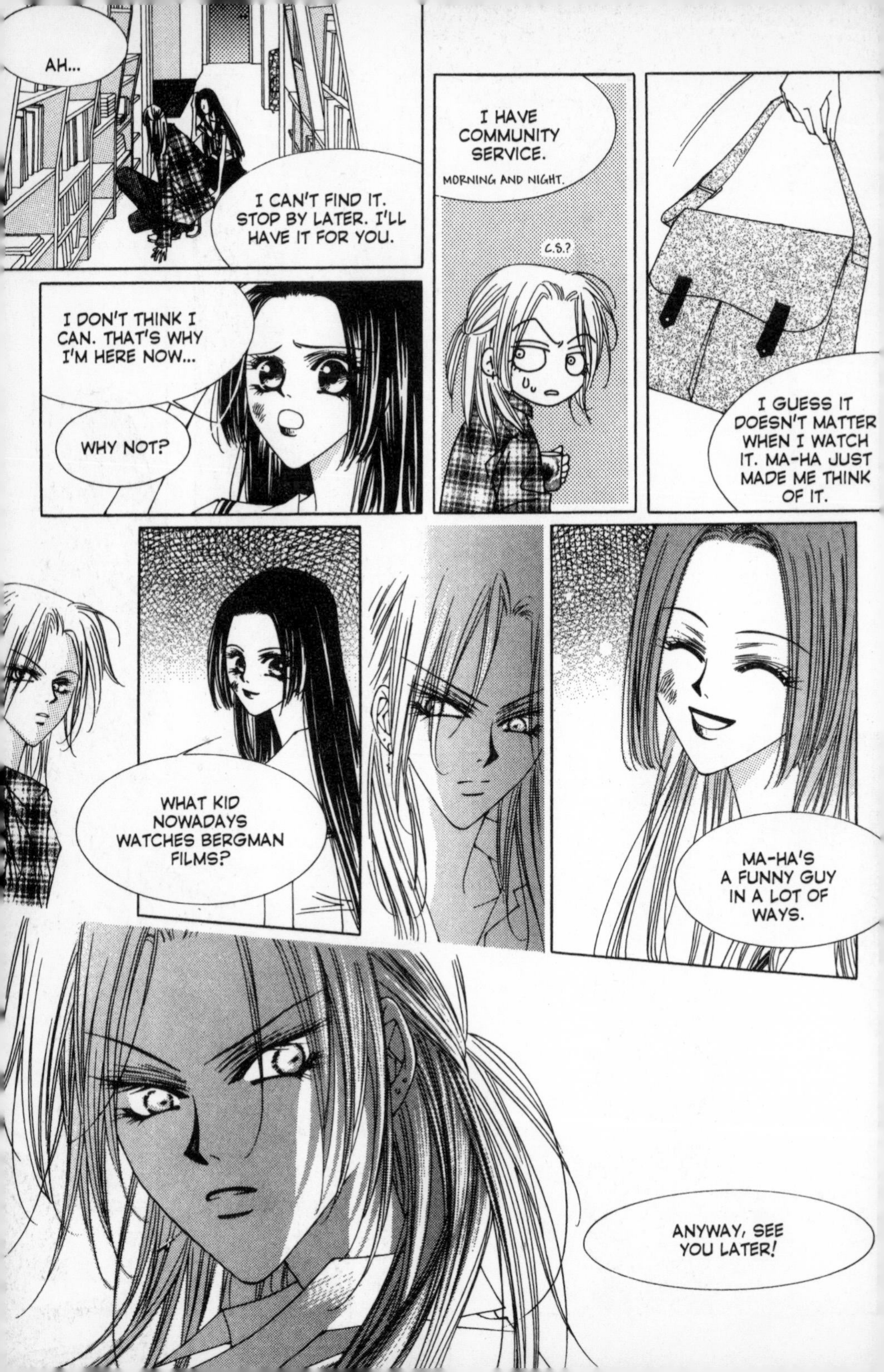
AH...
I CAN'T FIND IT. STOP BY LATER. I'LL HAVE IT FOR YOU.
I DON'T THINK I CAN. THAT'S WHY I'M HERE NOW...
WHY NOT?
I HAVE COMMUNITY SERVICE.
MORNING AND NIGHT.
C.S.?
I GUESS IT DOESN'T MATTER WHEN I WATCH IT. MA-HA JUST MADE ME THINK OF IT.
WHAT KID NOWADAYS WATCHES BERGMAN FILMS?
MA-HA'S A FUNNY GUY IN A LOT OF WAYS.
ANYWAY, SEE YOU LATER!

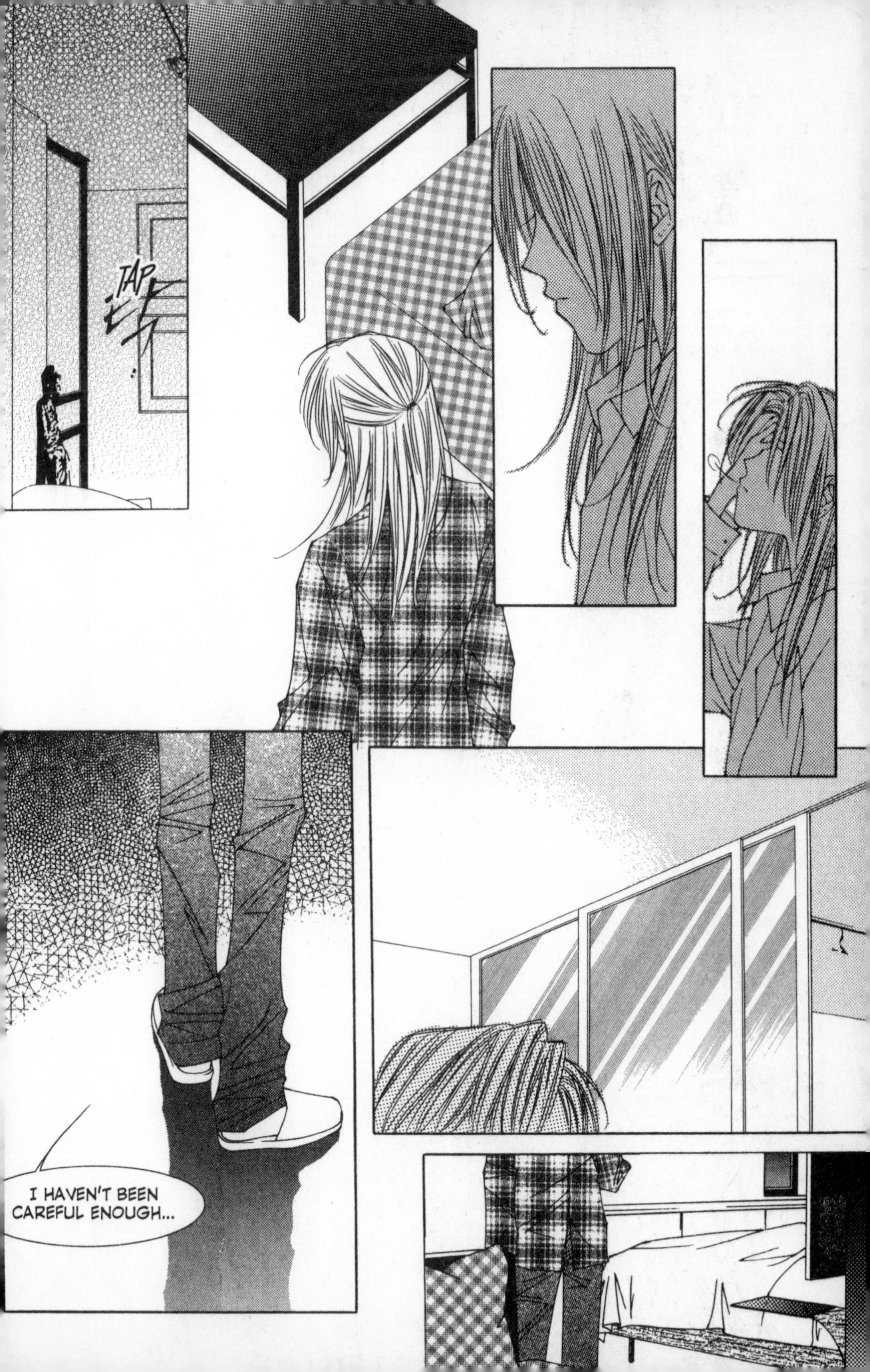
TAP
I HAVEN'T BEEN CAREFUL ENOUGH...

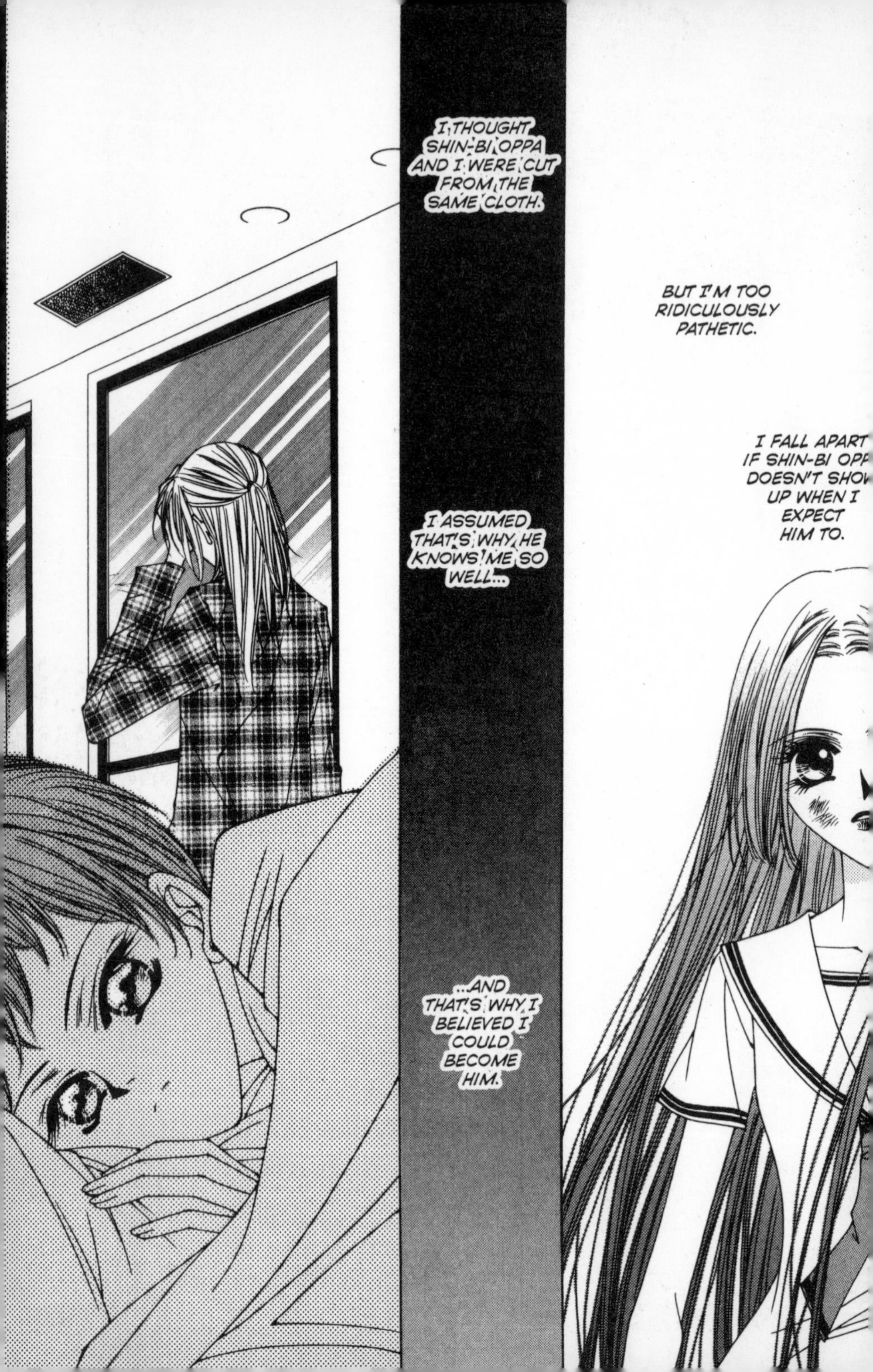
I THOUGHT SHIN-BI OPPA AND I WERE CUT FROM THE SAME CLOTH.
I ASSUMED THAT'S WHY HE KNOWS ME SO WELL...
...AND THAT'S WHY I BELIEVED I COULD BECOME HIM.
BUT I'M TOO RIDICULOUSLY PATHETIC.
I FALL APART IF SHIN-BI OPP DOESN'T SHOW UP WHEN I EXPECT HIM TO.

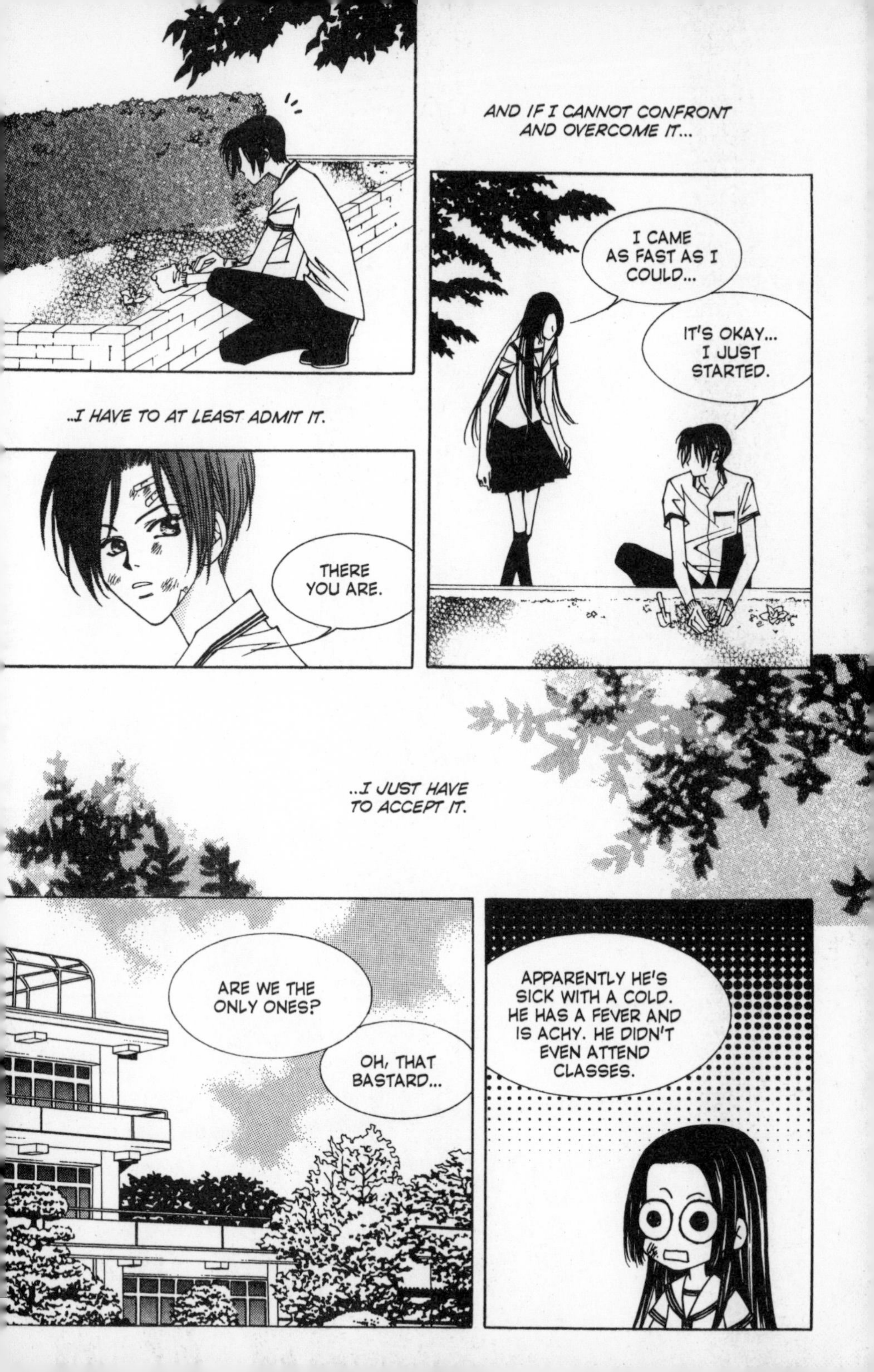
AND IF I CANNOT CONFRONT AND OVERCOME IT...
..I HAVE TO AT LEAST ADMIT IT.
THERE YOU ARE.
I CAME AS FAST AS I COULD...
IT'S OKAY... I JUST STARTED.
..I JUST HAVE TO ACCEPT IT.
ARE WE THE ONLY ONES?
OH, THAT BASTARD...
APPARENTLY HE'S SICK WITH A COLD. HE HAS A FEVER AND IS ACHY. HE DIDN'T EVEN ATTEND CLASSES.

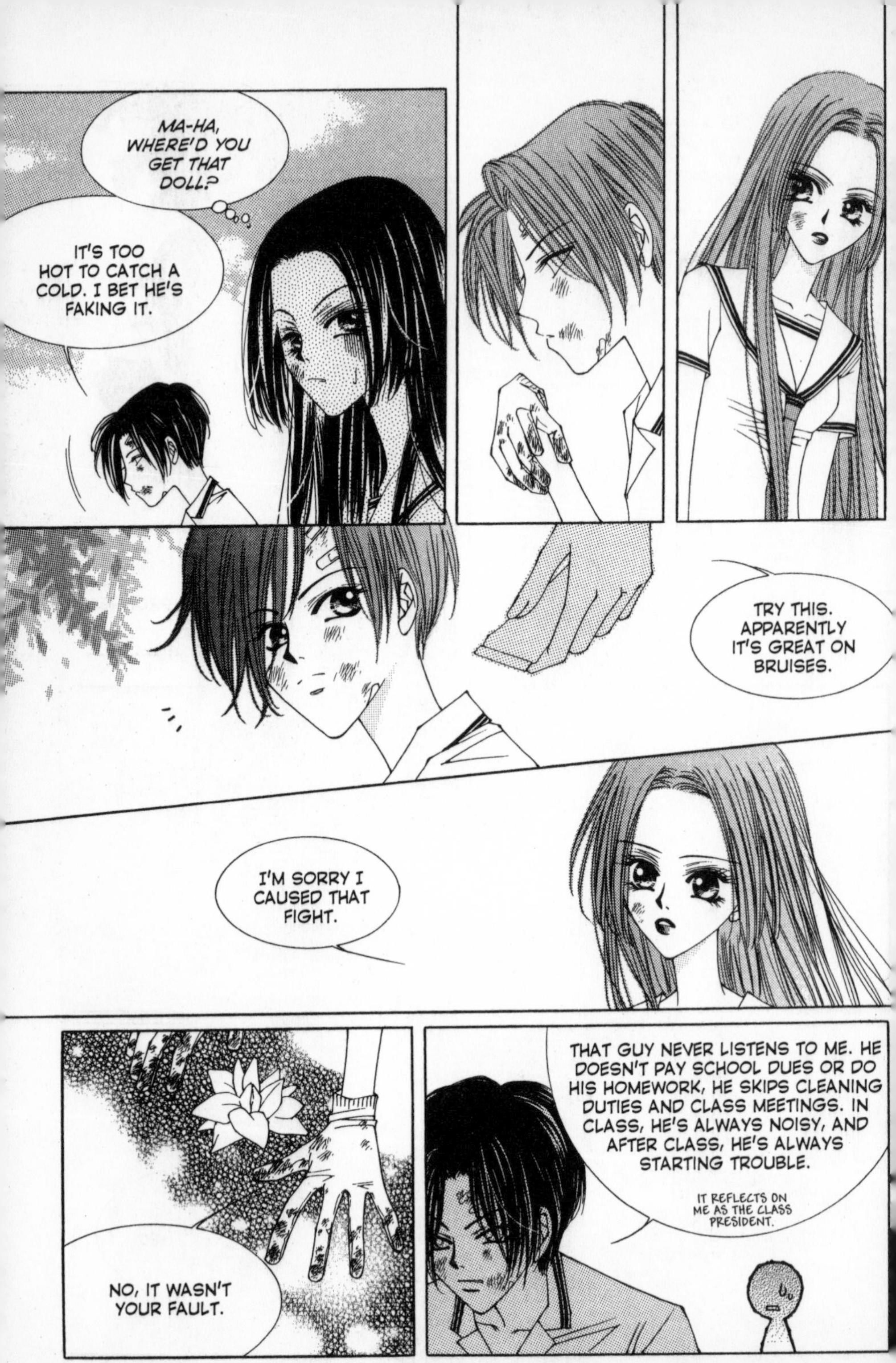
MA-HA, WHERE'D YOU GET THAT DOLL?
IT'S TOO HOT TO CATCH A COLD. I BET HE'S FAKING IT.
TRY THIS. APPARENTLY IT'S GREAT ON BRUISES.
I'M SORRY I CAUSED THAT FIGHT.
NO, IT WASN'T YOUR FAULT.
THAT GUY NEVER LISTENS TO ME. HE DOESN'T PAY SCHOOL DUES OR DO HIS HOMEWORK, HE SKIPS CLEANING DUTIES AND CLASS MEETINGS. IN CLASS, HE'S ALWAYS NOISY, AND AFTER CLASS, HE'S ALWAYS STARTING TROUBLE.
IT REFLECTS ON ME AS THE CLASS PRESIDENT.

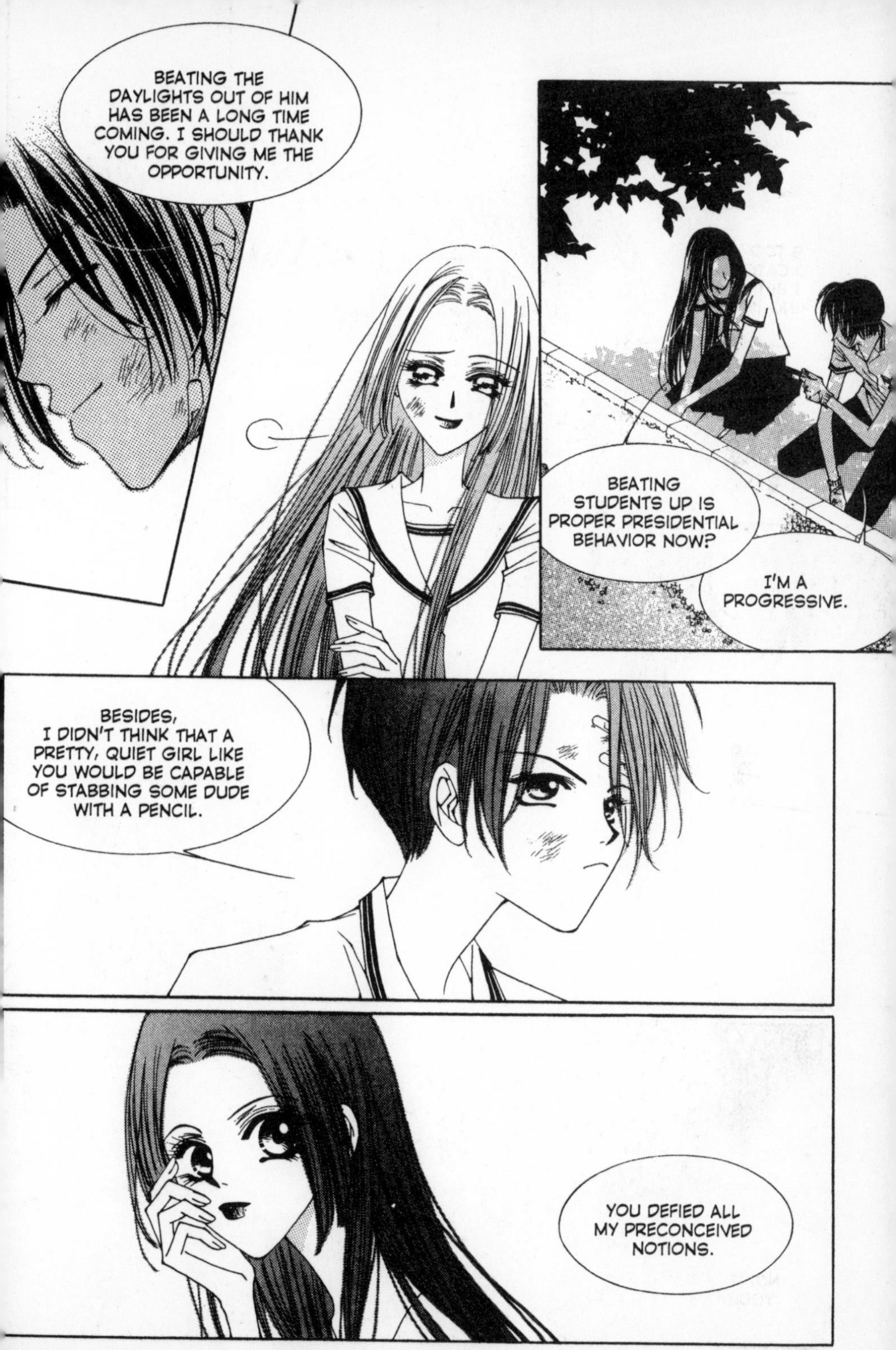
BEATING THE DAYLIGHTS OUT OF HIM HAS BEEN A LONG TIME COMING. I SHOULD THANK YOU FOR GIVING ME THE OPPORTUNITY.
BEATING STUDENTS UP IS PROPER PRESIDENTIAL BEHAVIOR NOW?
I'M A PROGRESSIVE.
BESIDES, I DIDN'T THINK THAT A PRETTY, QUIET GIRL LIKE YOU WOULD BE CAPABLE OF STABBING SOME DUDE WITH A PENCIL.
YOU DEFIED ALL MY PRECONCEIVED NOTIONS.

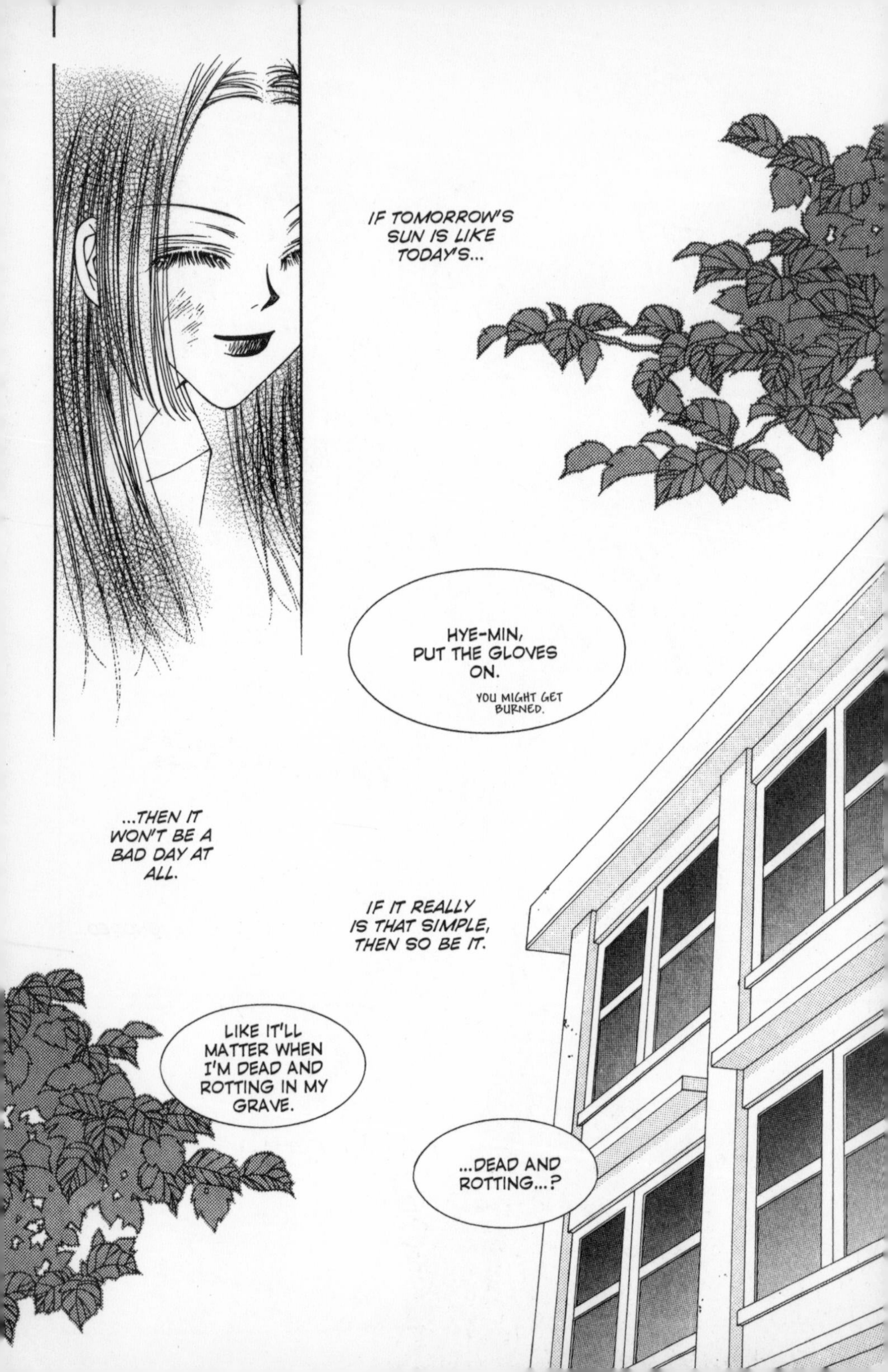

IF TOMORROW'S SUN IS LIKE TODAY'S...
HYE-MIN, PUT THE GLOVES ON.
YOU MIGHT GET BURNED.
...THEN IT WON'T BE A BAD DAY AT ALL.
IF IT REALLY IS THAT SIMPLE, THEN SO BE IT.
LIKE IT'LL MATTER WHEN I'M DEAD AND ROTTING IN MY GRAVE.
...DEAD AND ROTTING...?

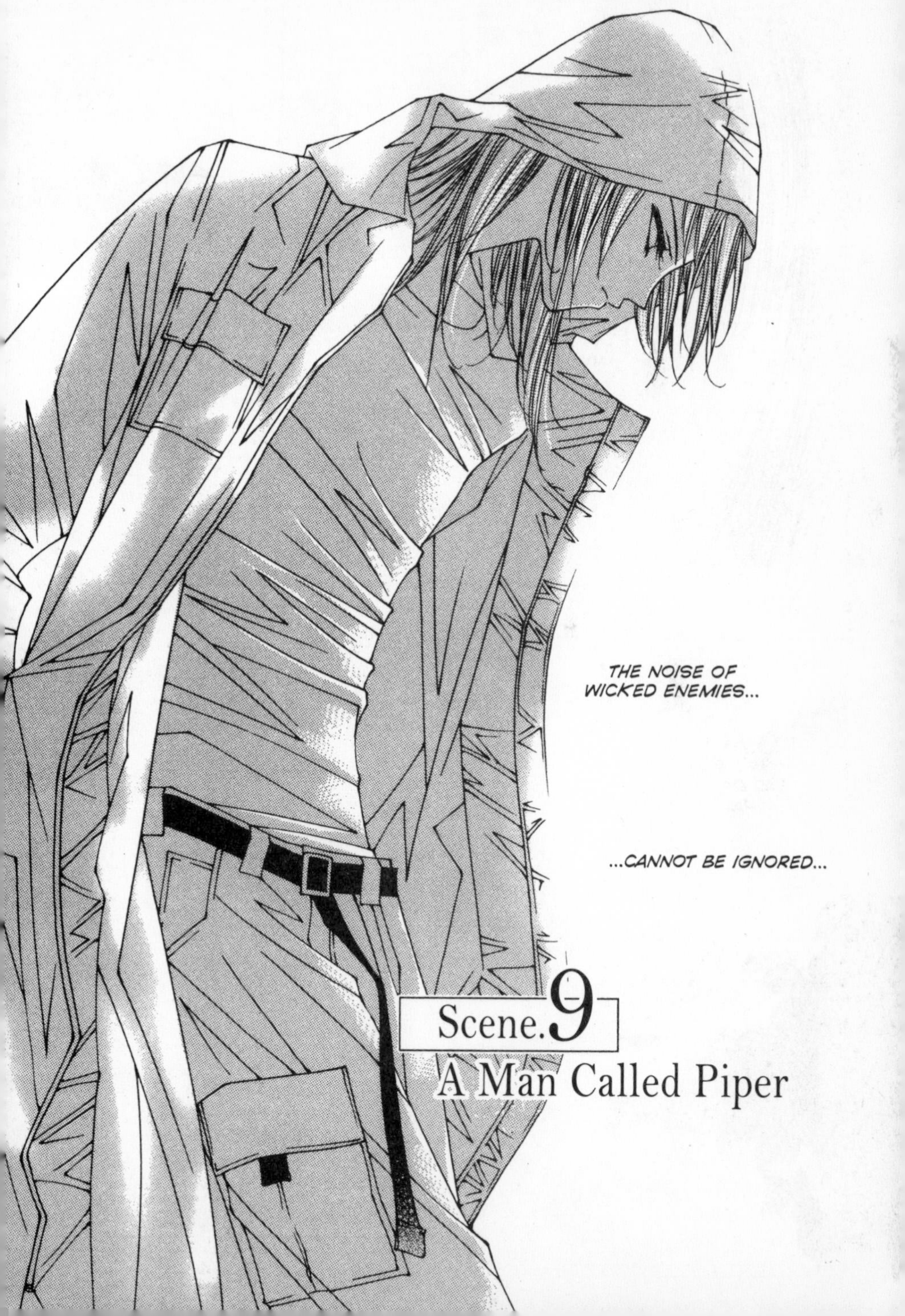
THE NOISE OF WICKED ENEMIES...
...CANNOT BE IGNORED...
Scene.9
A Man Called Piper

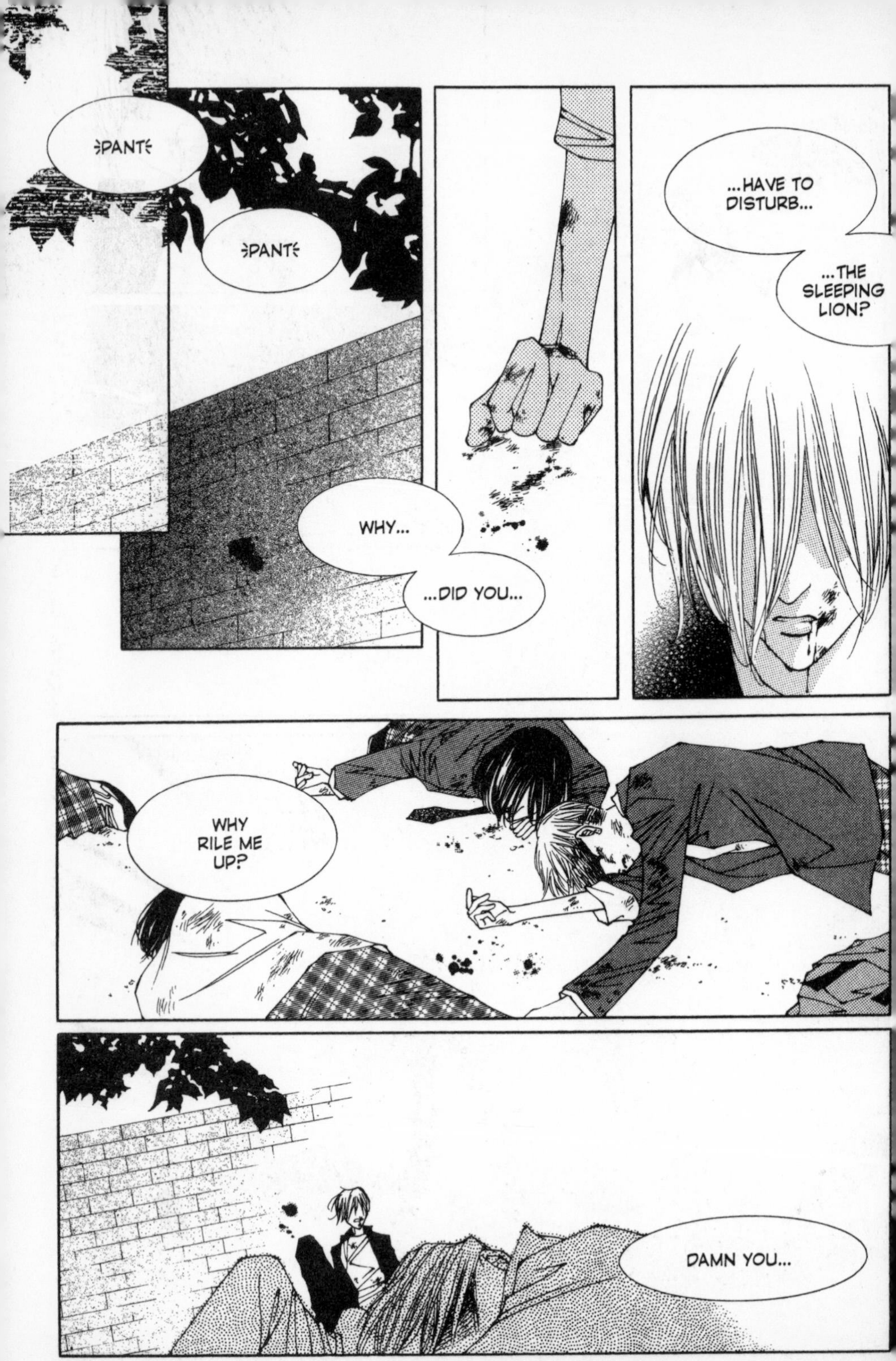

PANT
PANT
WHY...
...DID YOU...
...HAVE TO DISTURB...
...THE SLEEPING LION?
WHY RILE ME UP?
DAMN YOU...

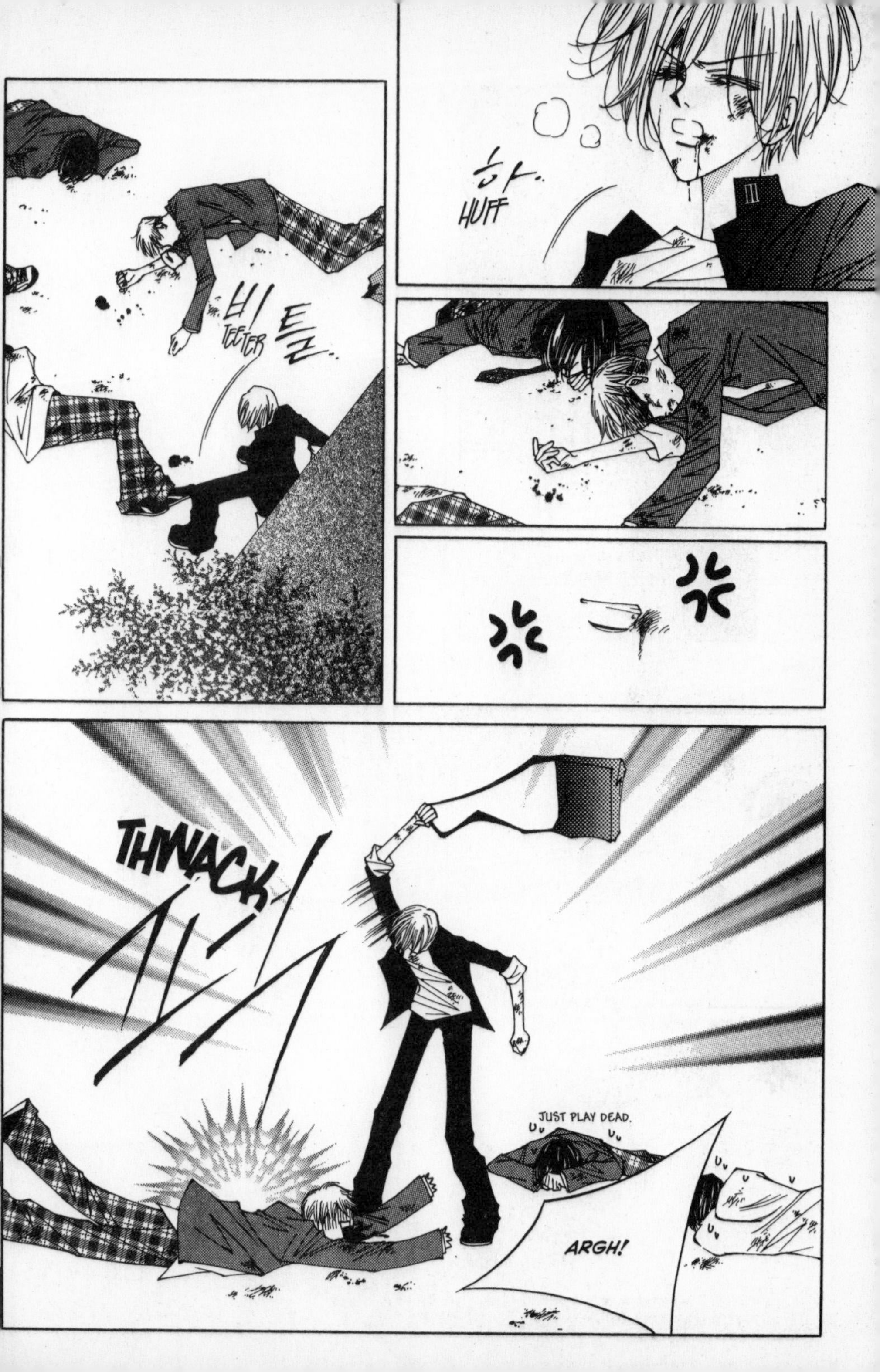
비틀
TEETER
하
HUFF
THWACK
JUST PLAY DEAD.
ARGH!

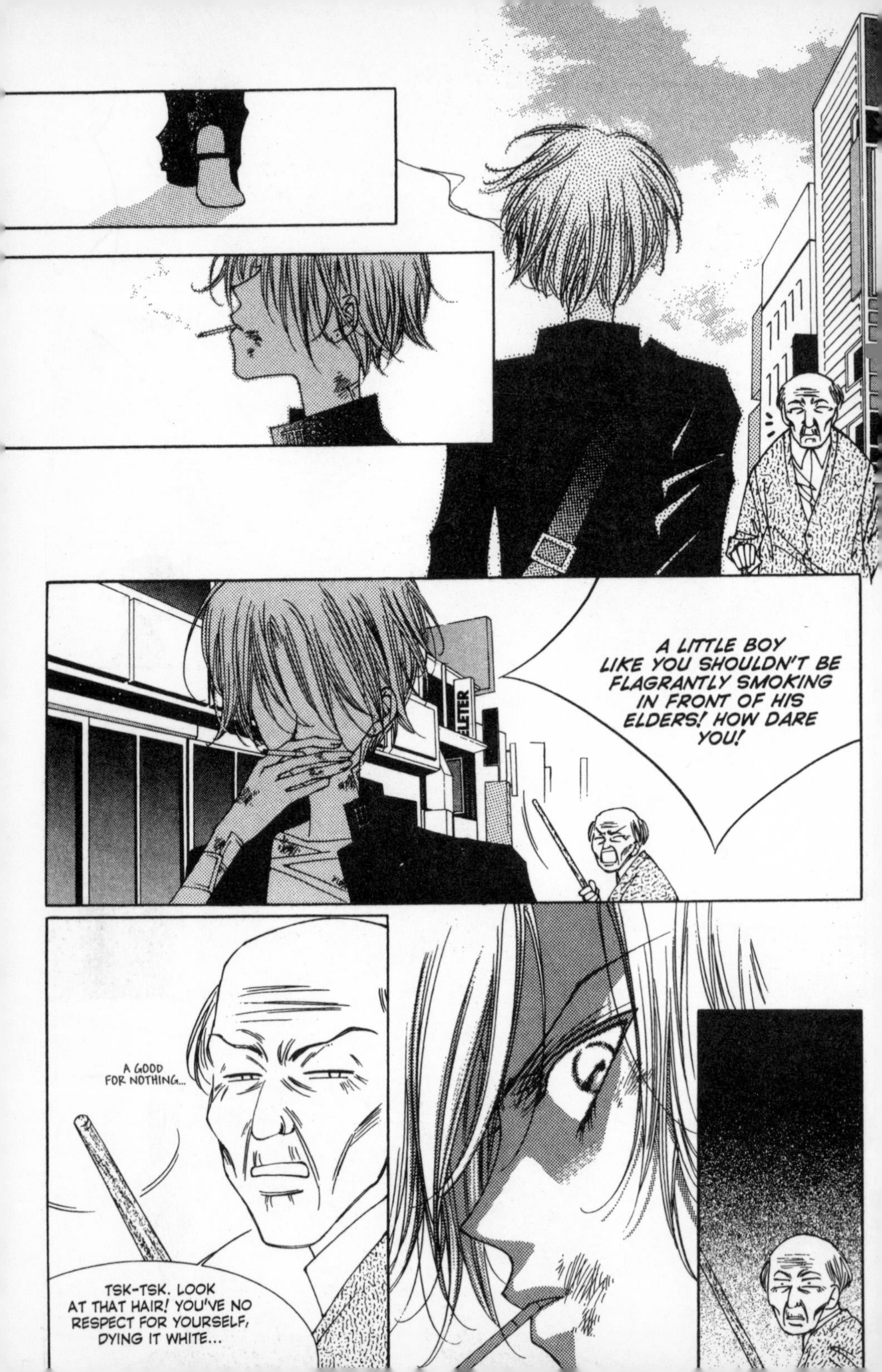
A LITTLE BOY LIKE YOU SHOULDN'T BE FLAGRANTLY SMOKING IN FRONT OF HIS ELDERS! HOW DARE YOU!
A GOOD FOR NOTHING...
TSK-TSK. LOOK AT THAT HAIR! YOU'VE NO RESPECT FOR YOURSELF, DYING IT WHITE...

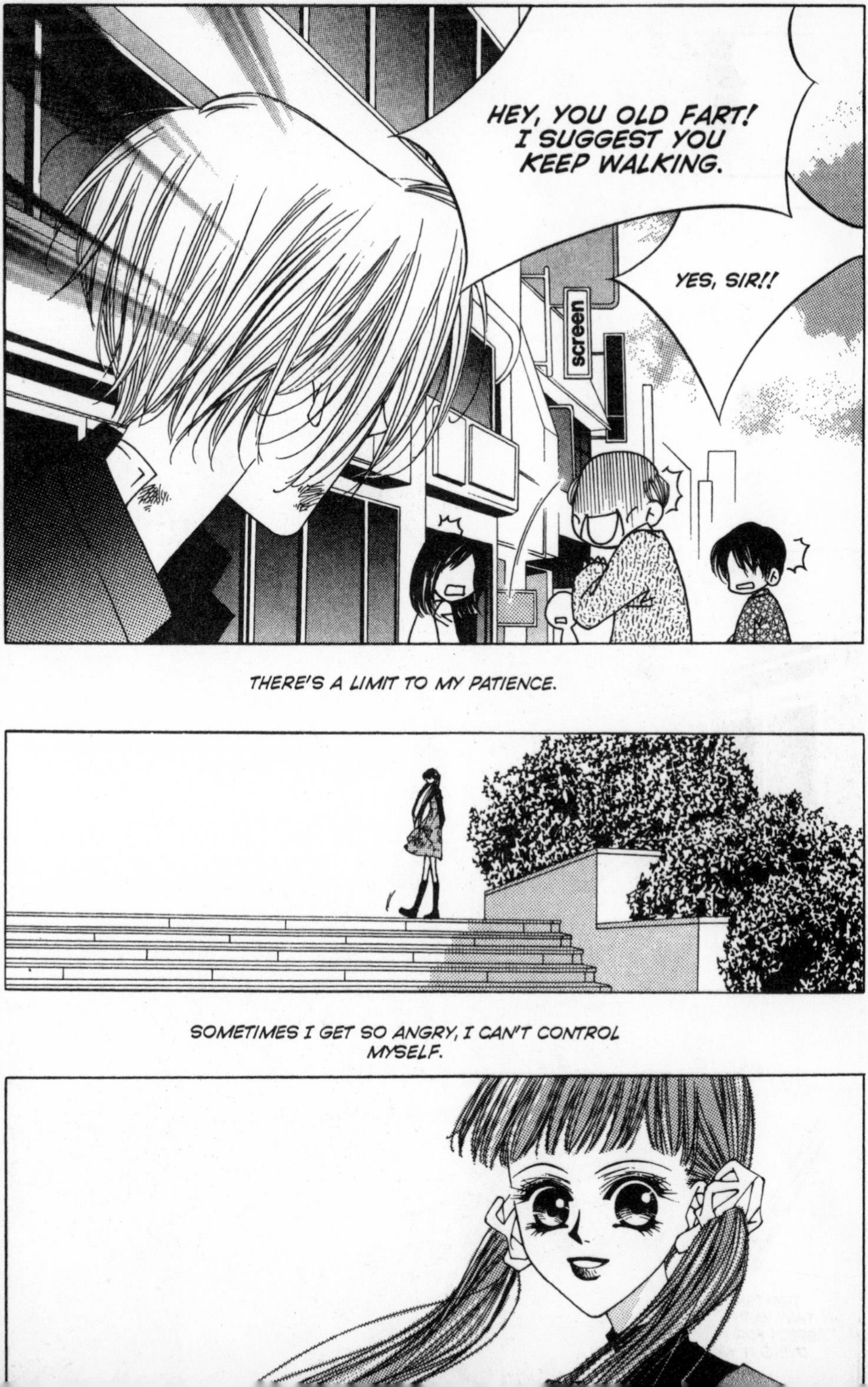
HEY, YOU OLD FART! I SUGGEST YOU KEEP WALKING.
screen
YES, SIR!!
THERE'S A LIMIT TO MY PATIENCE.
SOMETIMES I GET SO ANGRY, I CAN'T CONTROL MYSELF.

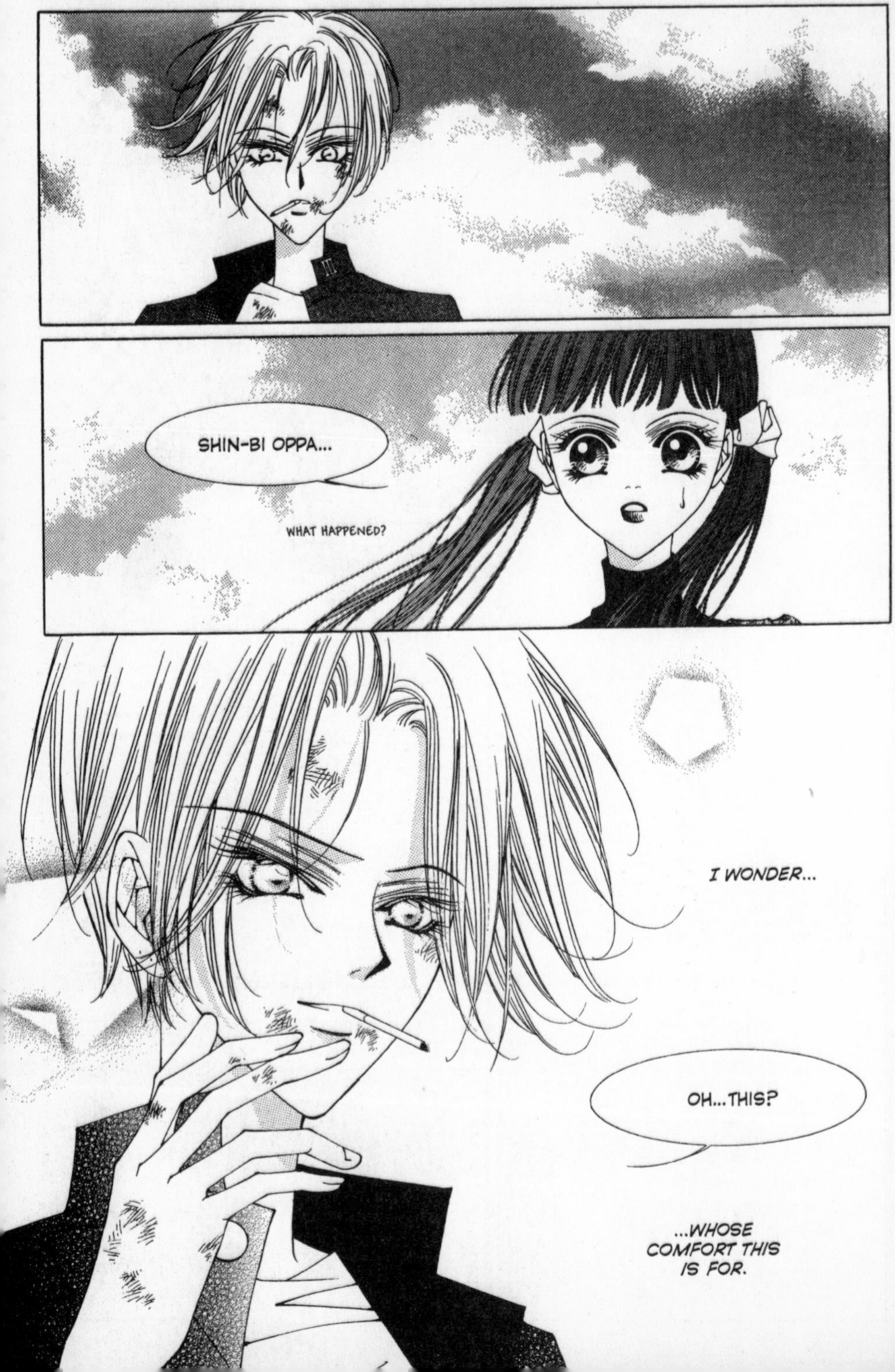
SHIN-BI OPPA...
WHAT HAPPENED?
I WONDER...
OH...THIS?
...WHOSE COMFORT THIS IS FOR.

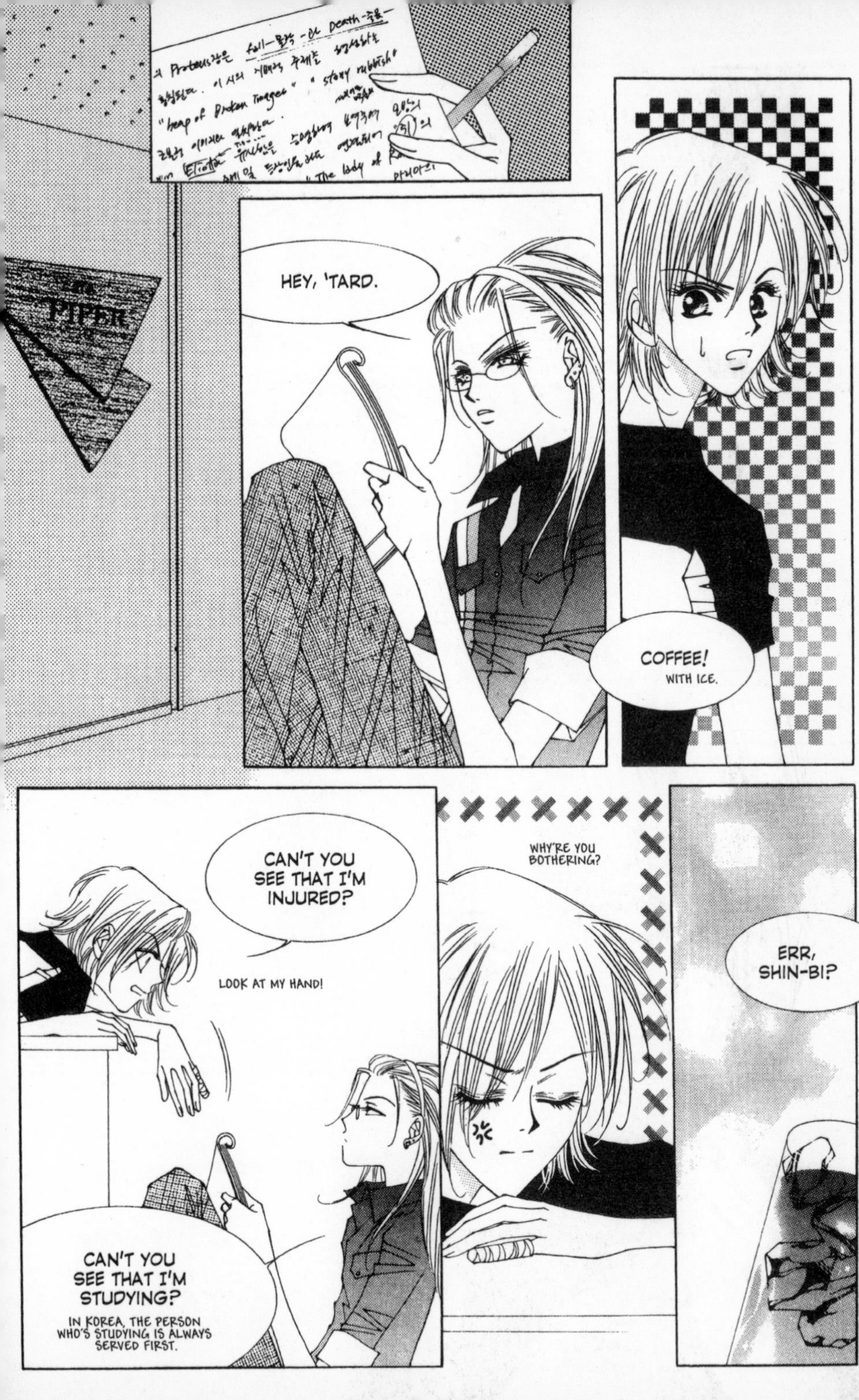
PIPER
HEY, 'TARD.
COFFEE!
WITH ICE.
CAN'T YOU SEE THAT I'M INJURED?
LOOK AT MY HAND!
CAN'T YOU SEE THAT I'M STUDYING?
IN KOREA, THE PERSON WHO'S STUDYING IS ALWAYS SERVED FIRST.
WHY'RE YOU BOTHERING?
ERR, SHIN-BI?

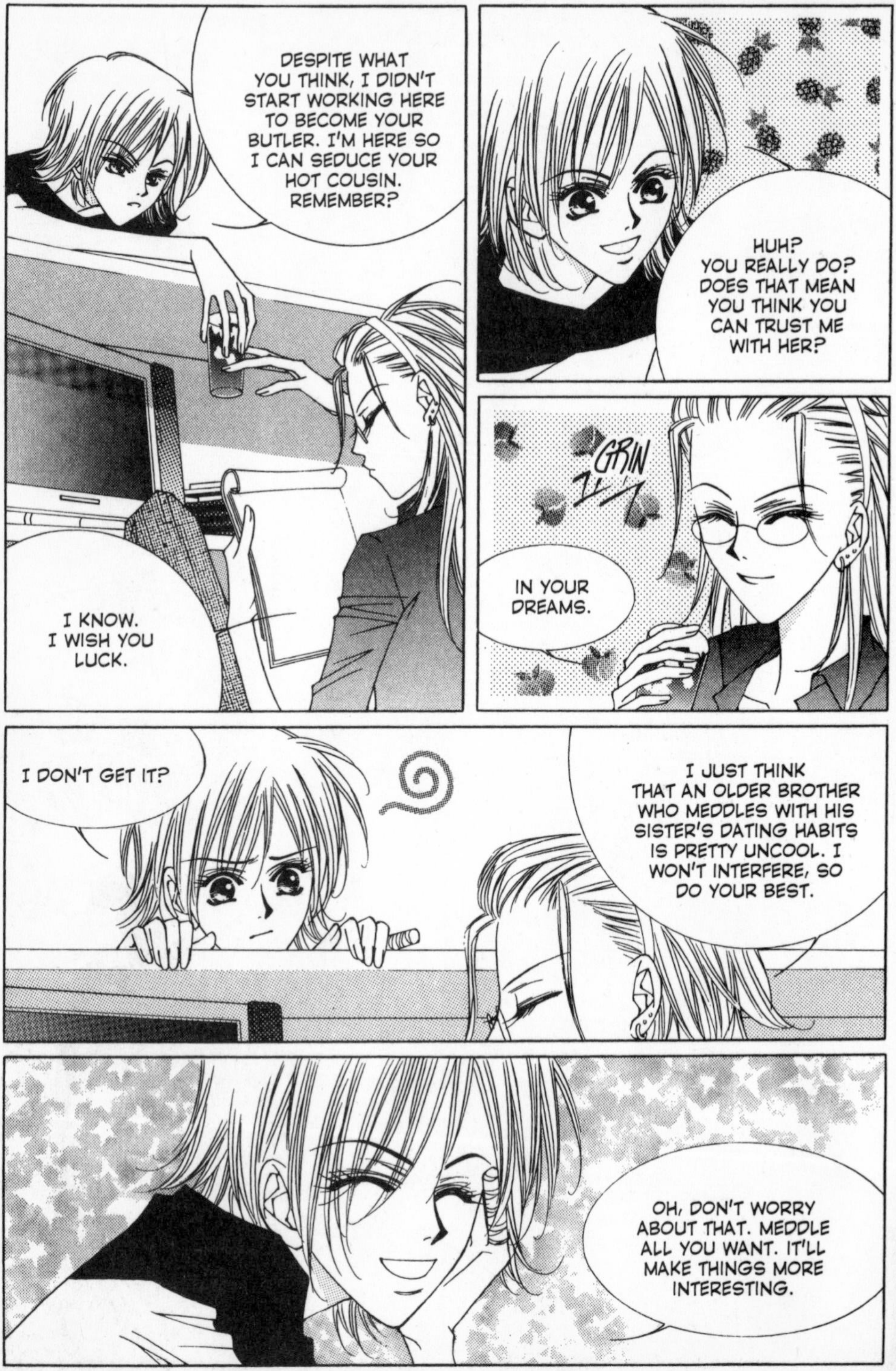
DESPITE WHAT YOU THINK, I DIDN'T START WORKING HERE TO BECOME YOUR BUTLER. I'M HERE SO I CAN SEDUCE YOUR HOT COUSIN. REMEMBER?
I KNOW. I WISH YOU LUCK.
HUH? YOU REALLY DO? DOES THAT MEAN YOU THINK YOU CAN TRUST ME WITH HER?
GRIN
IN YOUR DREAMS.
I DON'T GET IT?
I JUST THINK THAT AN OLDER BROTHER WHO MEDDLES WITH HIS SISTER'S DATING HABITS IS PRETTY UNCOOL. I WON'T INTERFERE, SO DO YOUR BEST.
OH, DON'T WORRY ABOUT THAT. MEDDLE ALL YOU WANT. IT'LL MAKE THINGS MORE INTERESTING.

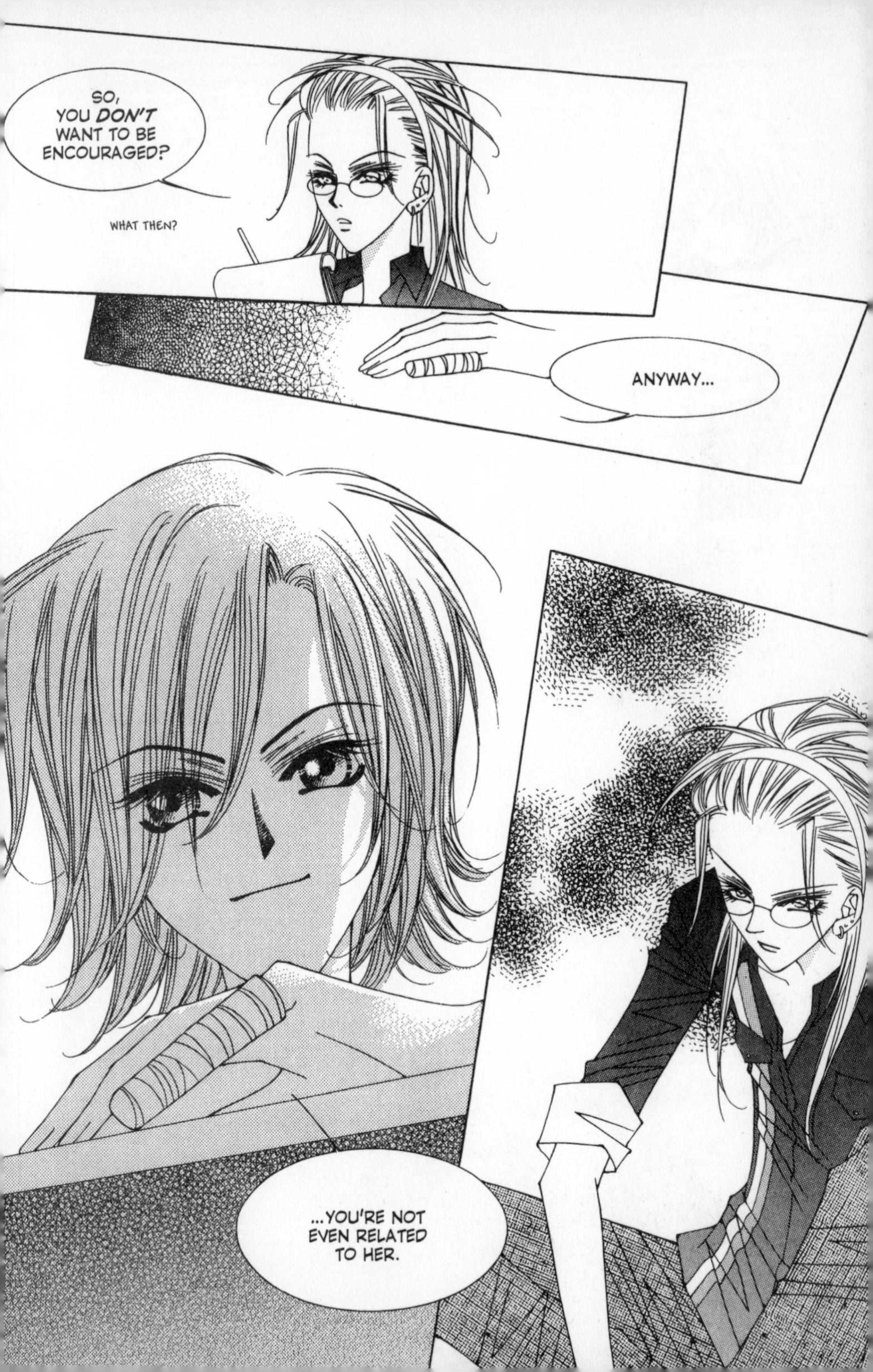
SO, YOU **DON'T** WANT TO BE ENCOURAGED?
WHAT THEN?
ANYWAY...
...YOU'RE NOT EVEN RELATED TO HER.

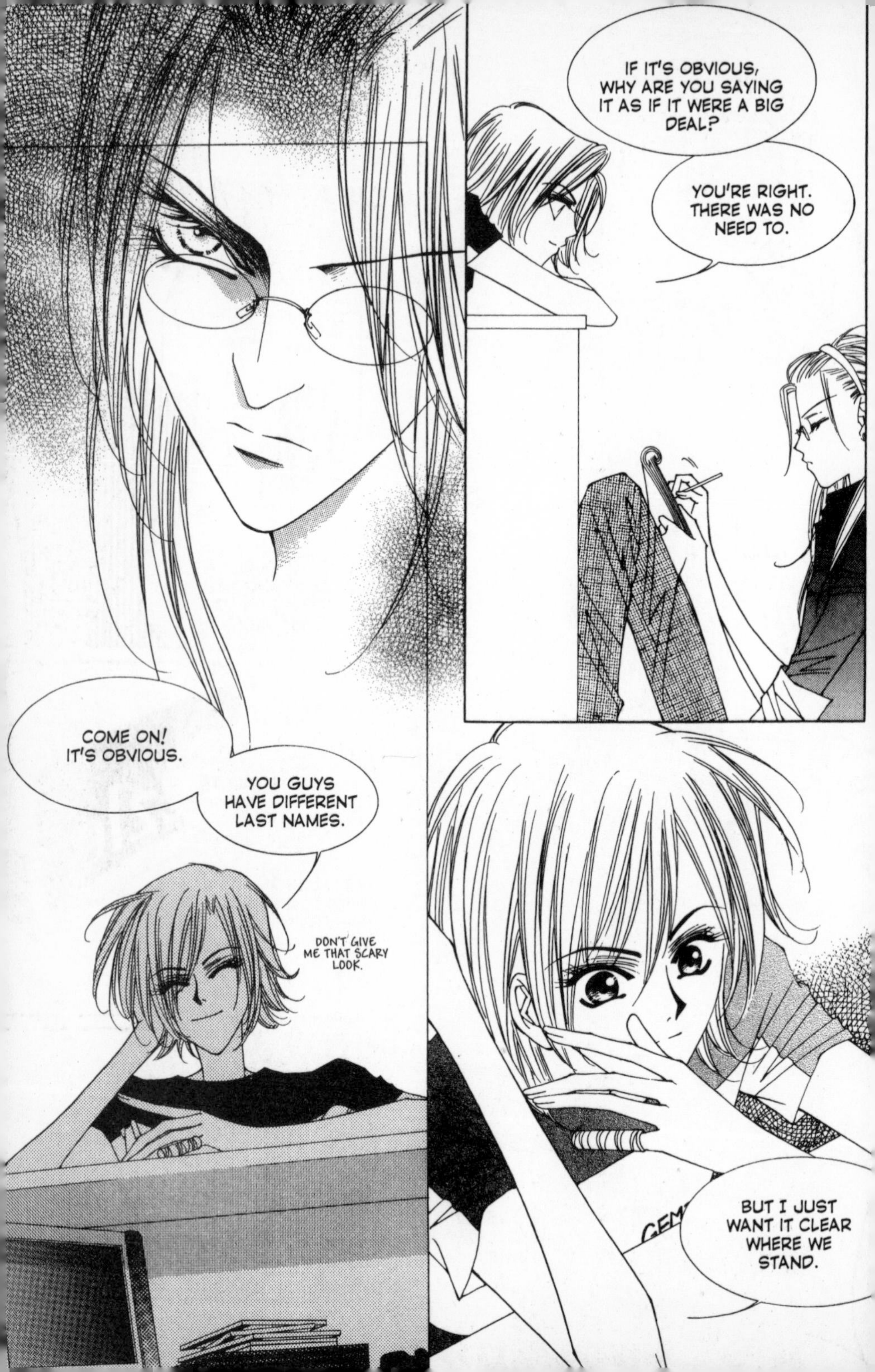
COME ON! IT'S OBVIOUS.
YOU GUYS HAVE DIFFERENT LAST NAMES.
DON'T GIVE ME THAT SCARY LOOK.
IF IT'S OBVIOUS, WHY ARE YOU SAYING IT AS IF IT WERE A BIG DEAL?
YOU'RE RIGHT. THERE WAS NO NEED TO.
BUT I JUST WANT IT CLEAR WHERE WE STAND.

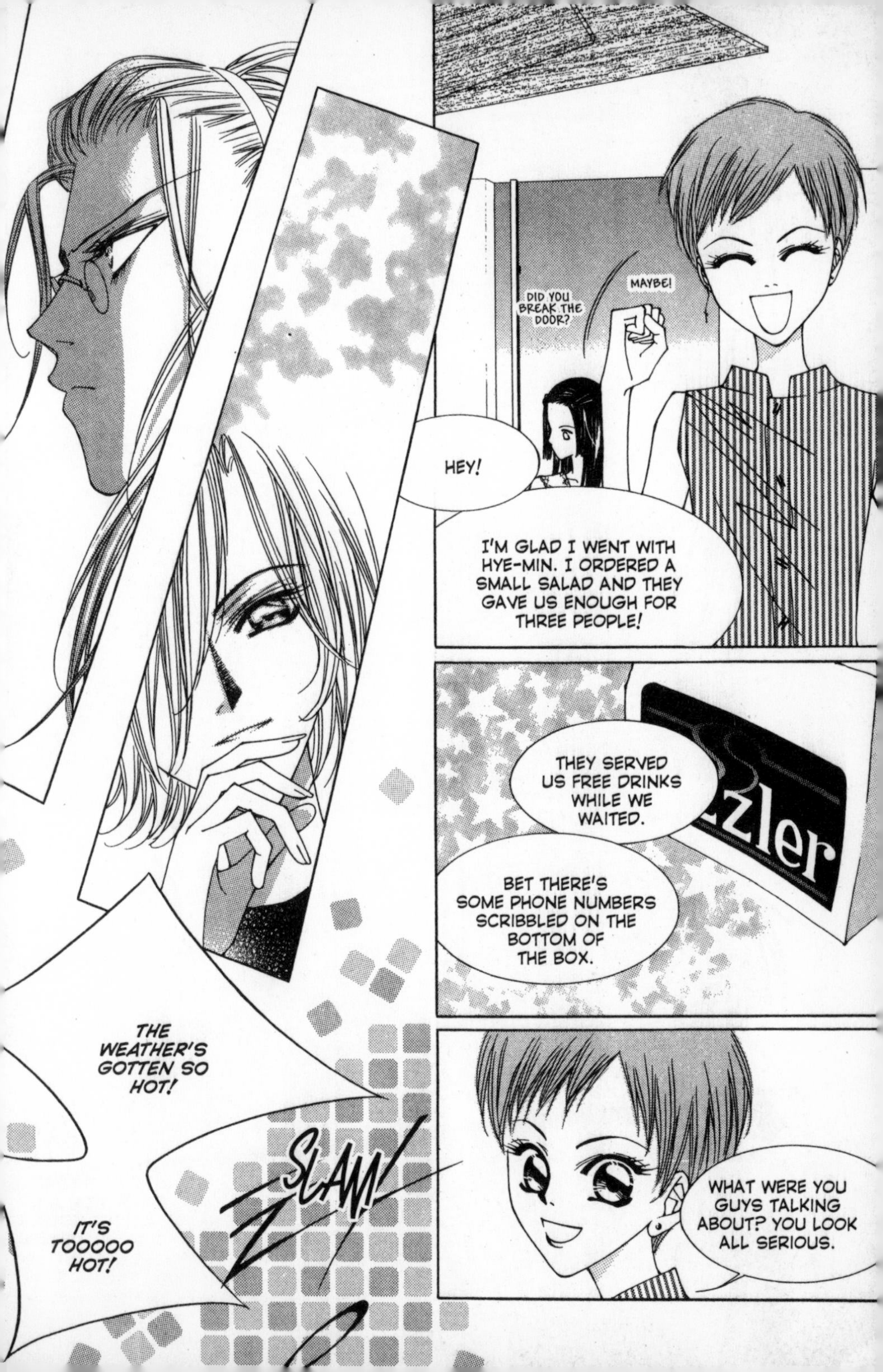
THE WEATHER'S GOTTEN SO HOT!
SLAM
IT'S TOOOOO HOT!
DID YOU BREAK THE DOOR?
MAYBE!
HEY!
I'M GLAD I WENT WITH HYE-MIN. I ORDERED A SMALL SALAD AND THEY GAVE US ENOUGH FOR THREE PEOPLE!
THEY SERVED US FREE DRINKS WHILE WE WAITED.
BET THERE'S SOME PHONE NUMBERS SCRIBBLED ON THE BOTTOM OF THE BOX.
WHAT WERE YOU GUYS TALKING ABOUT? YOU LOOK ALL SERIOUS.

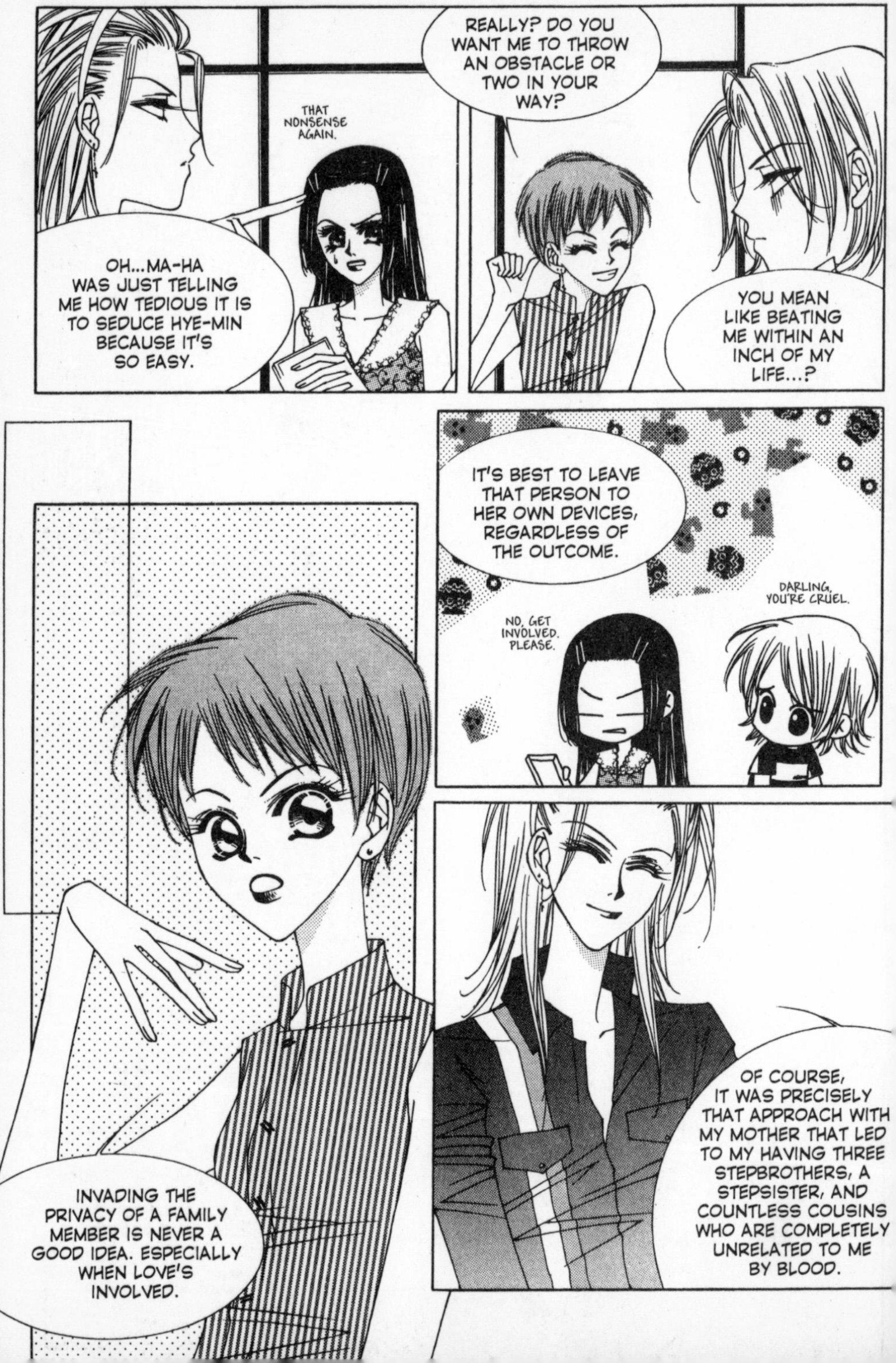

OH...MA-HA WAS JUST TELLING ME HOW TEDIOUS IT IS TO SEDUCE HYE-MIN BECAUSE IT'S SO EASY.
THAT NONSENSE AGAIN.
REALLY? DO YOU WANT ME TO THROW AN OBSTACLE OR TWO IN YOUR WAY?
YOU MEAN LIKE BEATING ME WITHIN AN INCH OF MY LIFE...?
INVADING THE PRIVACY OF A FAMILY MEMBER IS NEVER A GOOD IDEA. ESPECIALLY WHEN LOVE'S INVOLVED.
IT'S BEST TO LEAVE THAT PERSON TO HER OWN DEVICES, REGARDLESS OF THE OUTCOME.
NO, GET INVOLVED. PLEASE.
DARLING, YOU'RE CRUEL.
OF COURSE, IT WAS PRECISELY THAT APPROACH WITH MY MOTHER THAT LED TO MY HAVING THREE STEPBROTHERS, A STEPSISTER, AND COUNTLESS COUSINS WHO ARE COMPLETELY UNRELATED TO ME BY BLOOD.

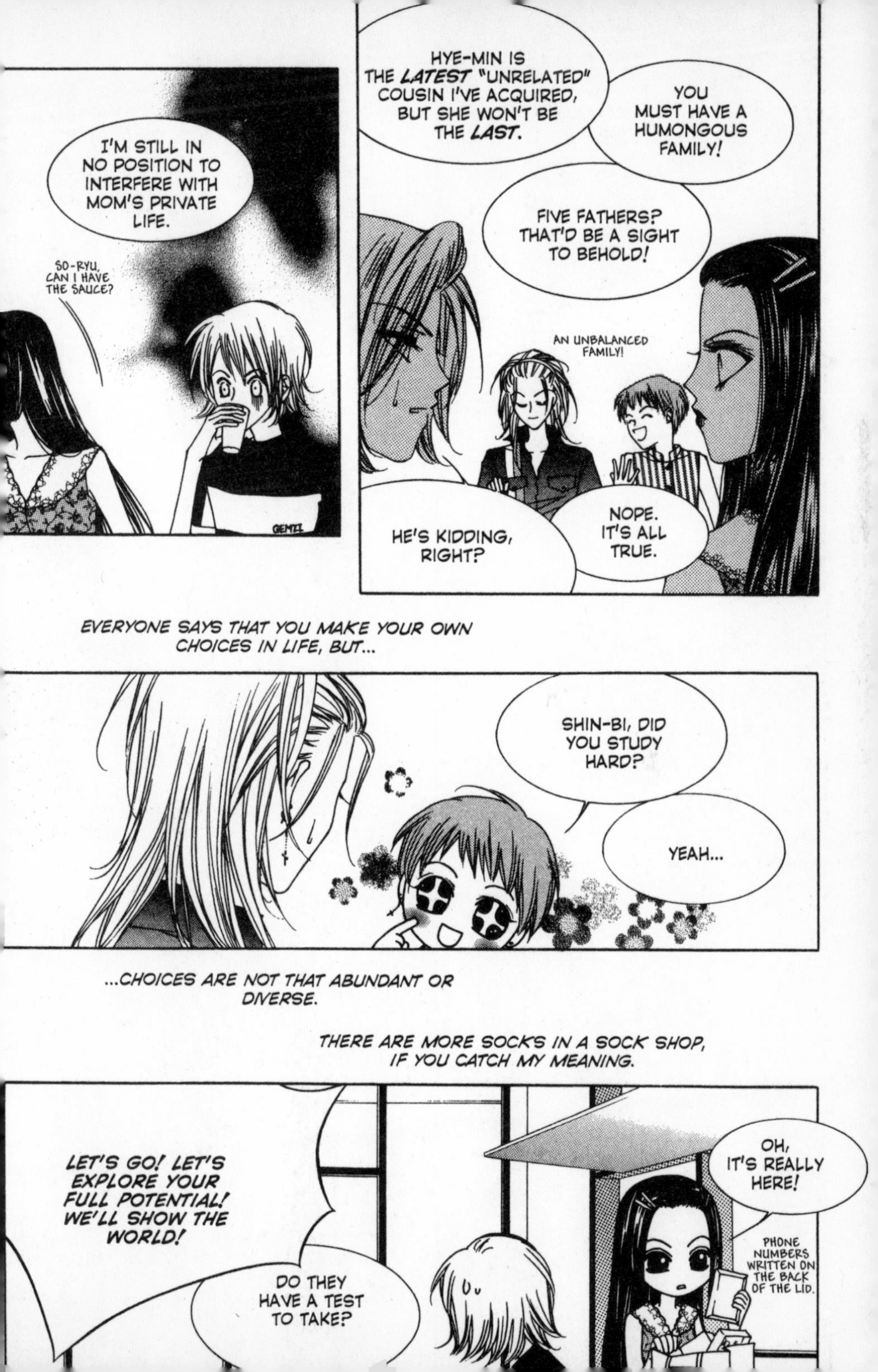
I'M STILL IN NO POSITION TO INTERFERE WITH MOM'S PRIVATE LIFE.
SO-RYU, CAN I HAVE THE SAUCE?
HYE-MIN IS THE LATEST "UNRELATED" COUSIN I'VE ACQUIRED, BUT SHE WON'T BE THE LAST.
YOU MUST HAVE A HUMONGOUS FAMILY!
FIVE FATHERS? THAT'D BE A SIGHT TO BEHOLD!
AN UNBALANCED FAMILY!
HE'S KIDDING, RIGHT?
NOPE. IT'S ALL TRUE.
EVERYONE SAYS THAT YOU MAKE YOUR OWN CHOICES IN LIFE, BUT...
SHIN-BI, DID YOU STUDY HARD?
YEAH...
...CHOICES ARE NOT THAT ABUNDANT OR DIVERSE.
THERE ARE MORE SOCKS IN A SOCK SHOP, IF YOU CATCH MY MEANING.
LET'S GO! LET'S EXPLORE YOUR FULL POTENTIAL! WE'LL SHOW THE WORLD!
DO THEY HAVE A TEST TO TAKE?
OH, IT'S REALLY HERE!
PHONE NUMBERS WRITTEN ON THE BACK OF THE LID.

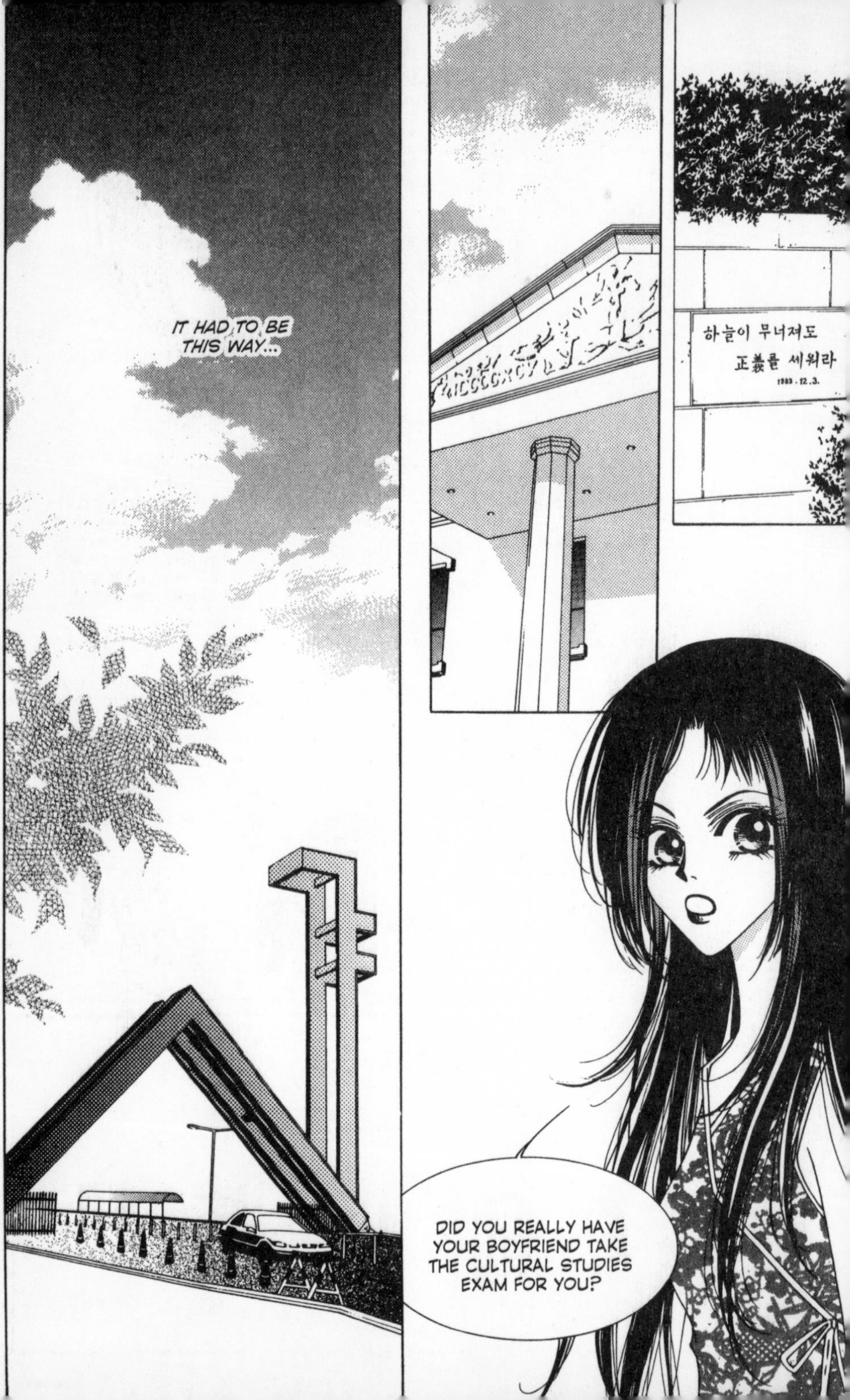
IT HAD TO BE THIS WAY...
하늘이 무너져도
正義를 세워라
1983.12.3.
DID YOU REALLY HAVE YOUR BOYFRIEND TAKE THE CULTURAL STUDIES EXAM FOR YOU?

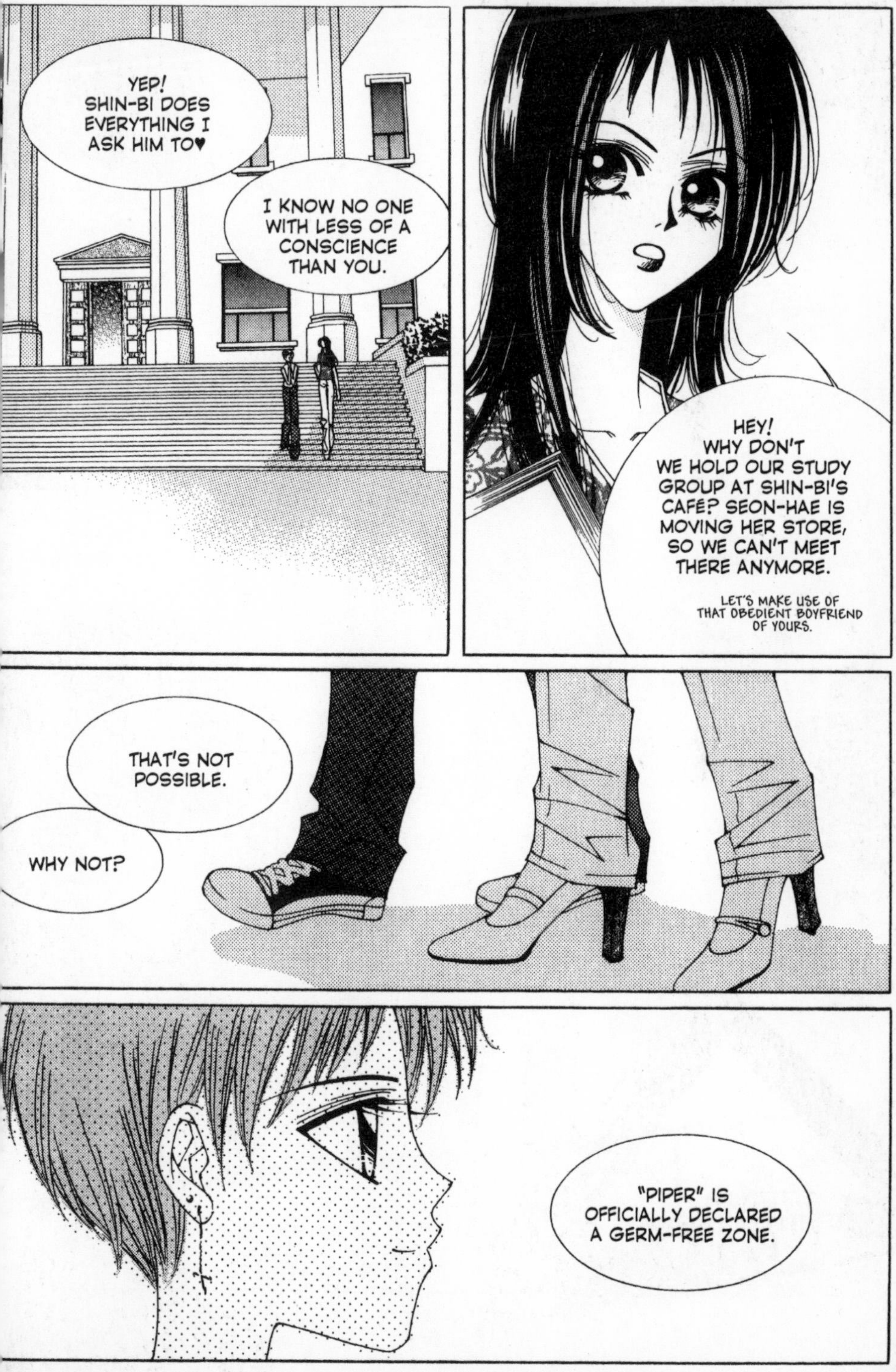
YEP! SHIN-BI DOES EVERYTHING I ASK HIM TO♥
I KNOW NO ONE WITH LESS OF A CONSCIENCE THAN YOU.
HEY! WHY DON'T WE HOLD OUR STUDY GROUP AT SHIN-BI'S CAFÉ? SEON-HAE IS MOVING HER STORE, SO WE CAN'T MEET THERE ANYMORE.
LET'S MAKE USE OF THAT OBEDIENT BOYFRIEND OF YOURS.
THAT'S NOT POSSIBLE.
WHY NOT?
"PIPER" IS OFFICIALLY DECLARED A GERM-FREE ZONE.

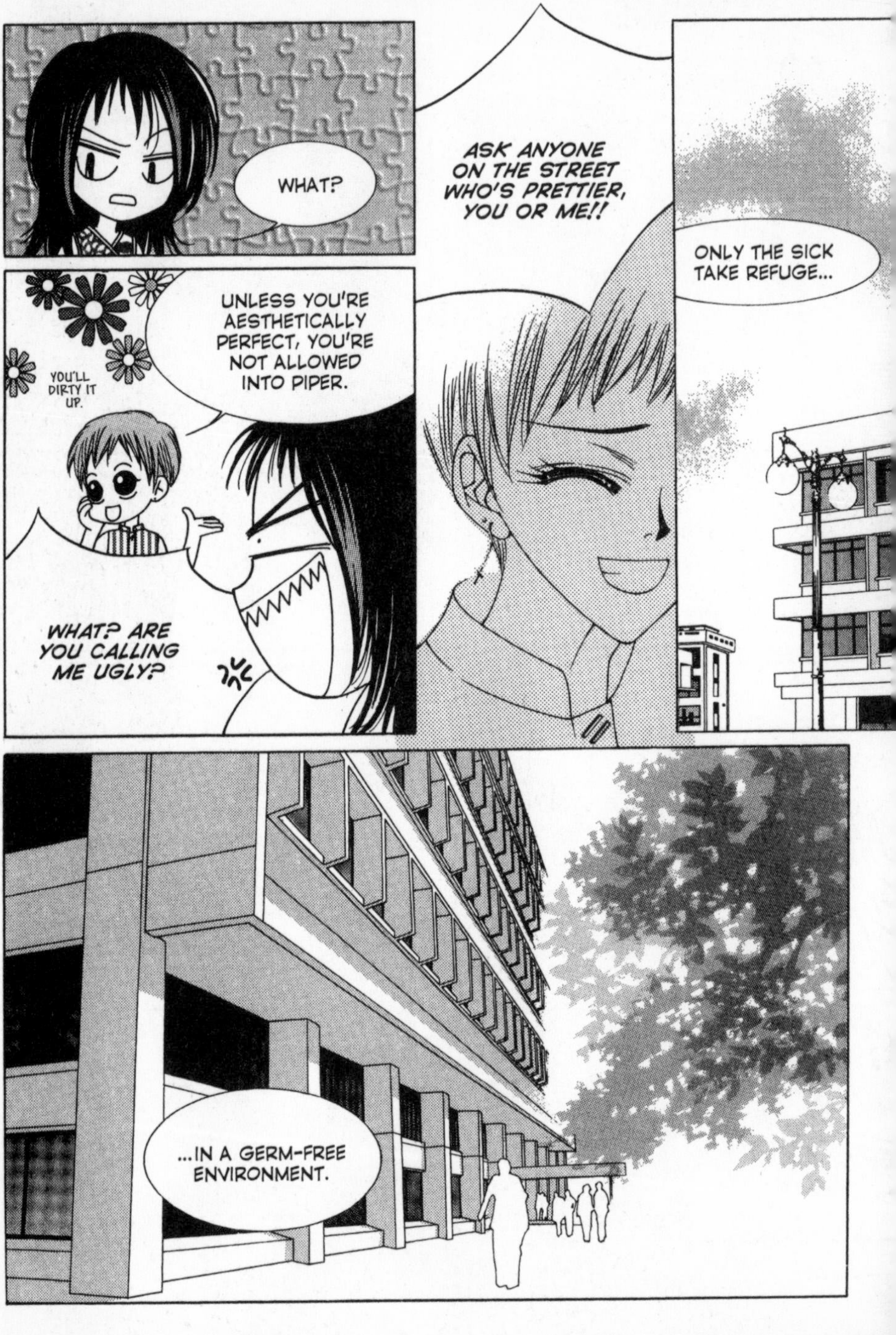
WHAT?
UNLESS YOU'RE AESTHETICALLY PERFECT, YOU'RE NOT ALLOWED INTO PIPER.
YOU'LL DIRTY IT UP.
WHAT? ARE YOU CALLING ME UGLY?
ASK ANYONE ON THE STREET WHO'S PRETTIER, YOU OR ME!!
ONLY THE SICK TAKE REFUGE...
...IN A GERM-FREE ENVIRONMENT.

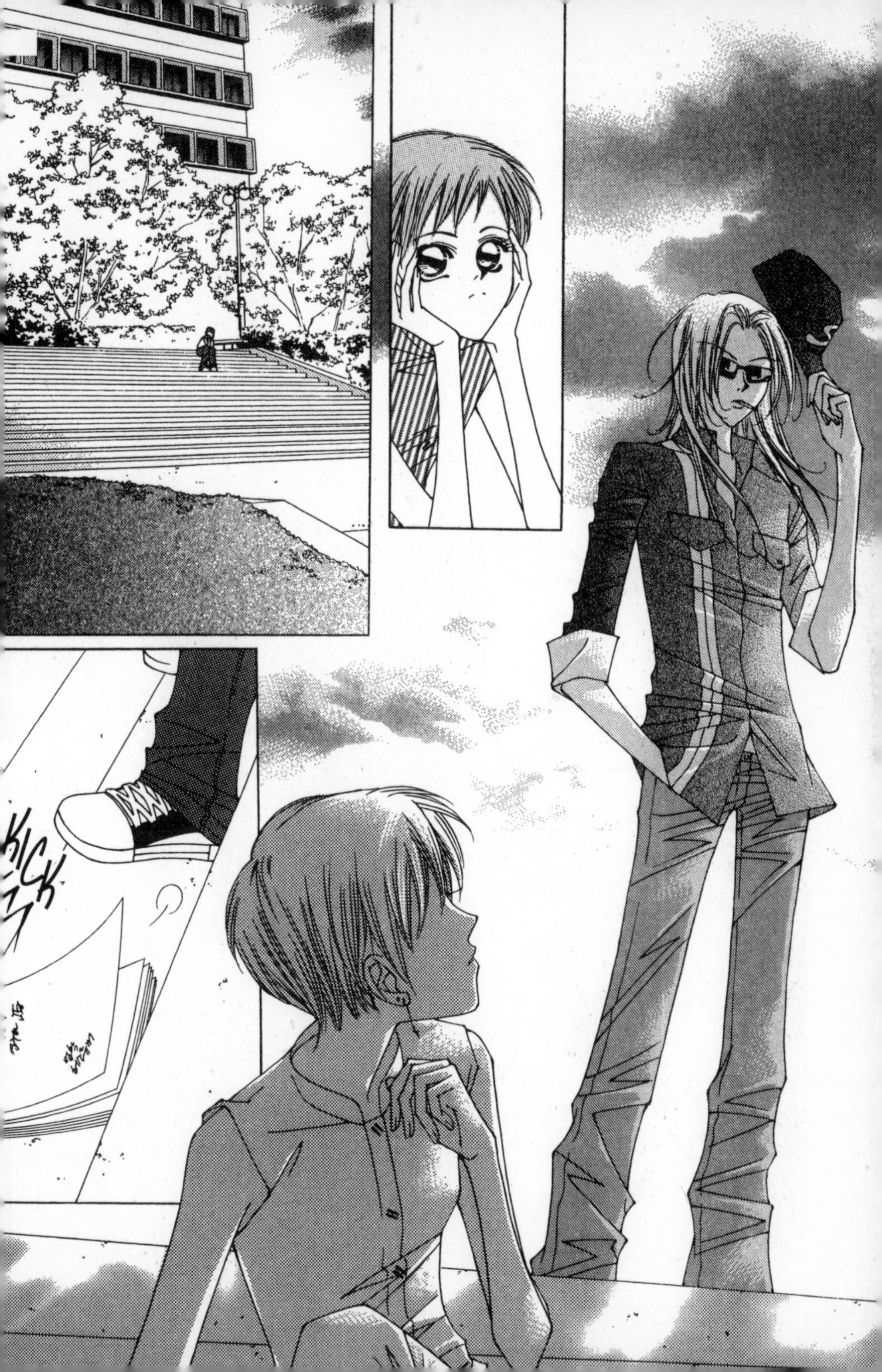
KICK

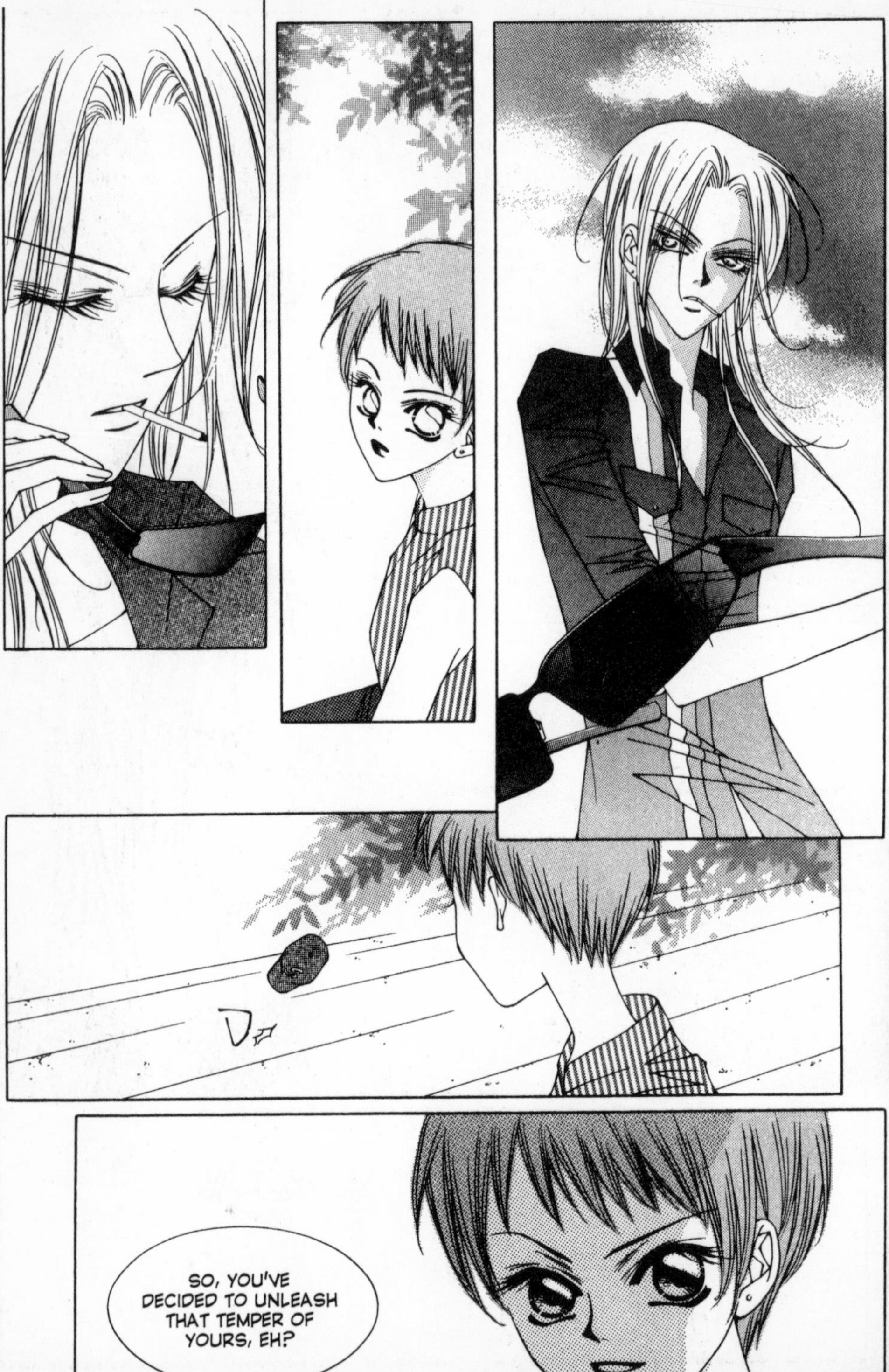
SO, YOU'VE DECIDED TO UNLEASH THAT TEMPER OF YOURS, EH?

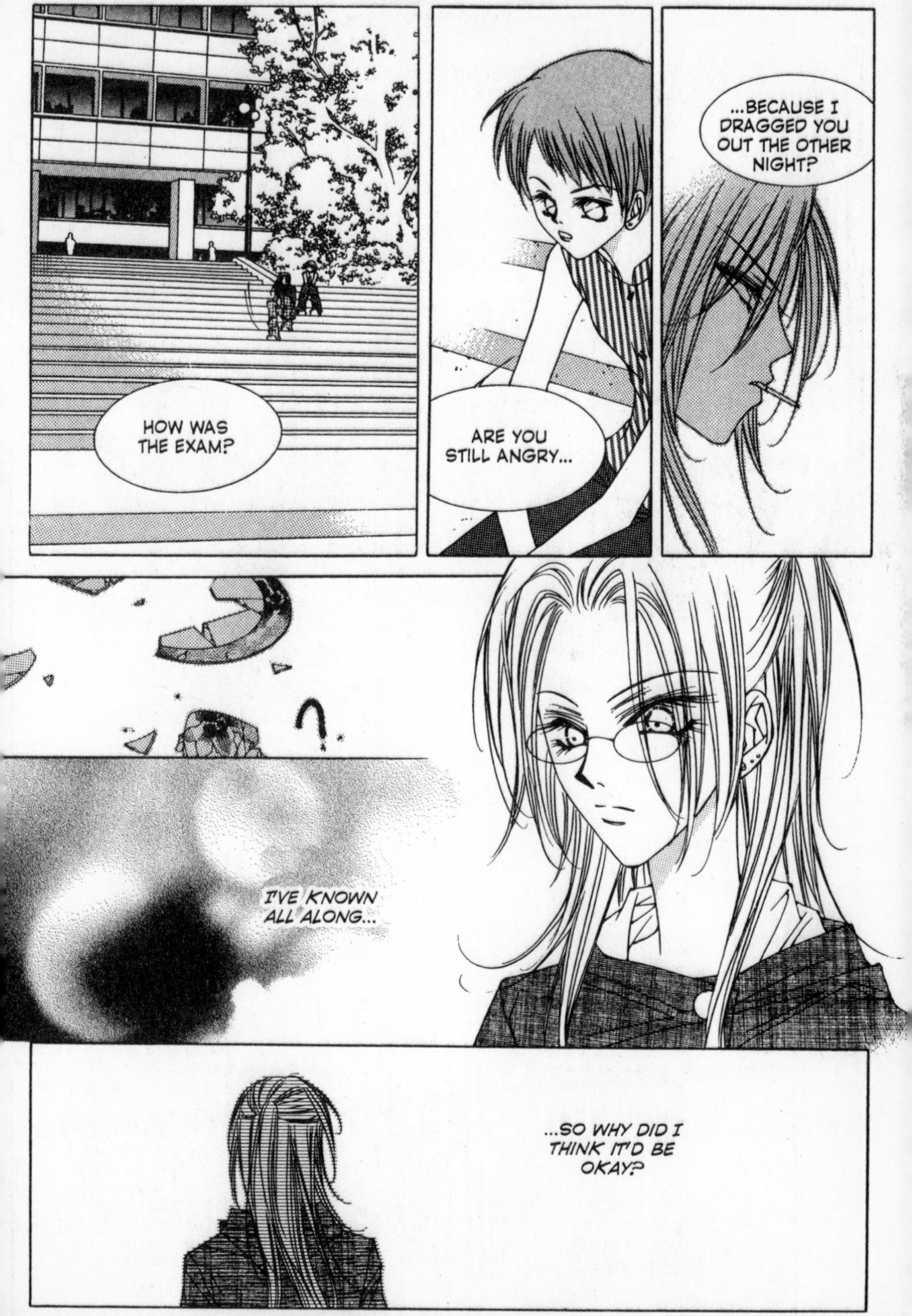
HOW WAS THE EXAM?
ARE YOU STILL ANGRY...
...BECAUSE I DRAGGED YOU OUT THE OTHER NIGHT?
?
I'VE KNOWN ALL ALONG...
...SO WHY DID I THINK IT'D BE OKAY?

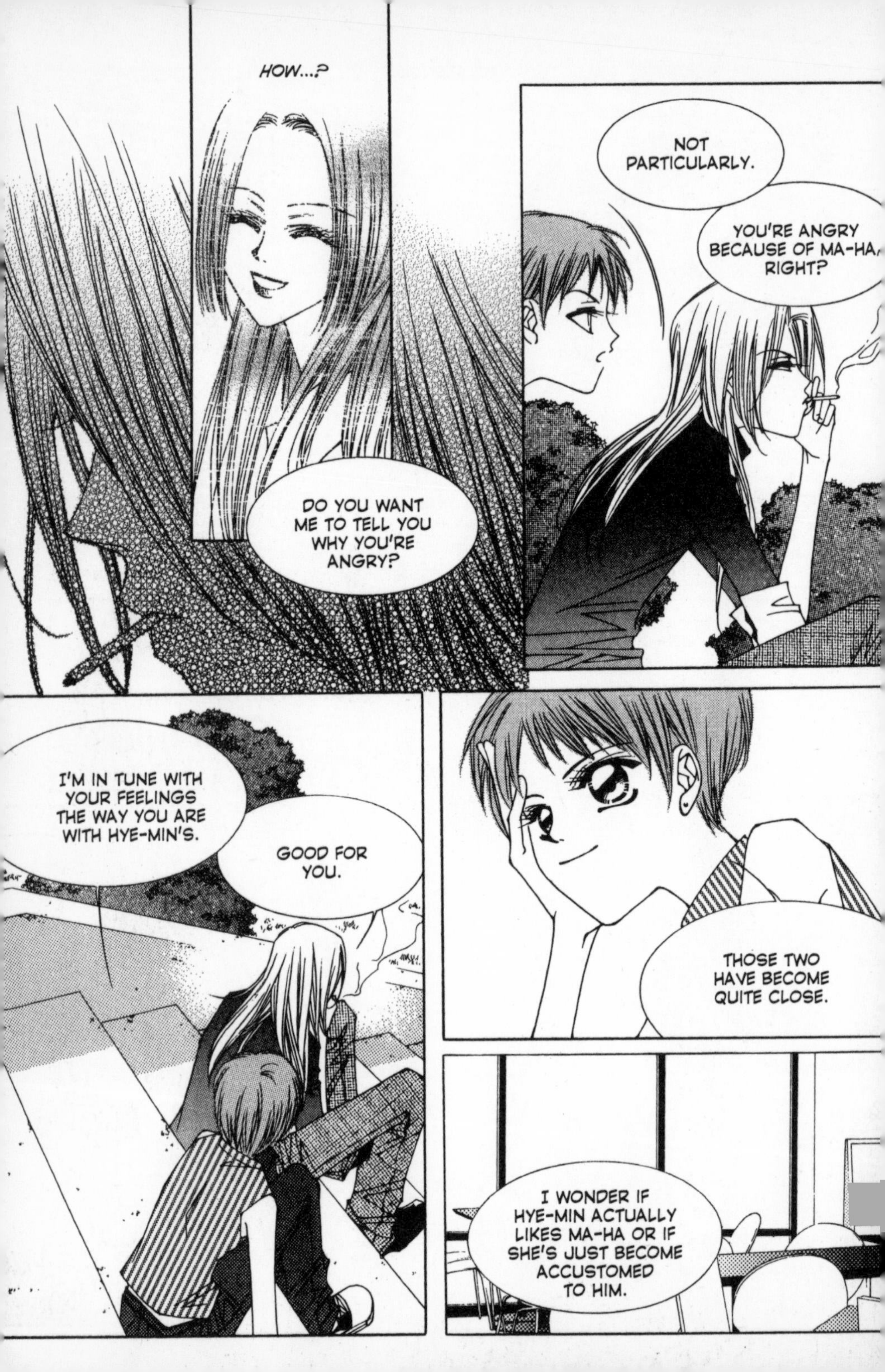
HOW...?
DO YOU WANT ME TO TELL YOU WHY YOU'RE ANGRY?
NOT PARTICULARLY.
YOU'RE ANGRY BECAUSE OF MA-HA, RIGHT?
I'M IN TUNE WITH YOUR FEELINGS THE WAY YOU ARE WITH HYE-MIN'S.
GOOD FOR YOU.
THOSE TWO HAVE BECOME QUITE CLOSE.
I WONDER IF HYE-MIN ACTUALLY LIKES MA-HA OR IF SHE'S JUST BECOME ACCUSTOMED TO HIM.

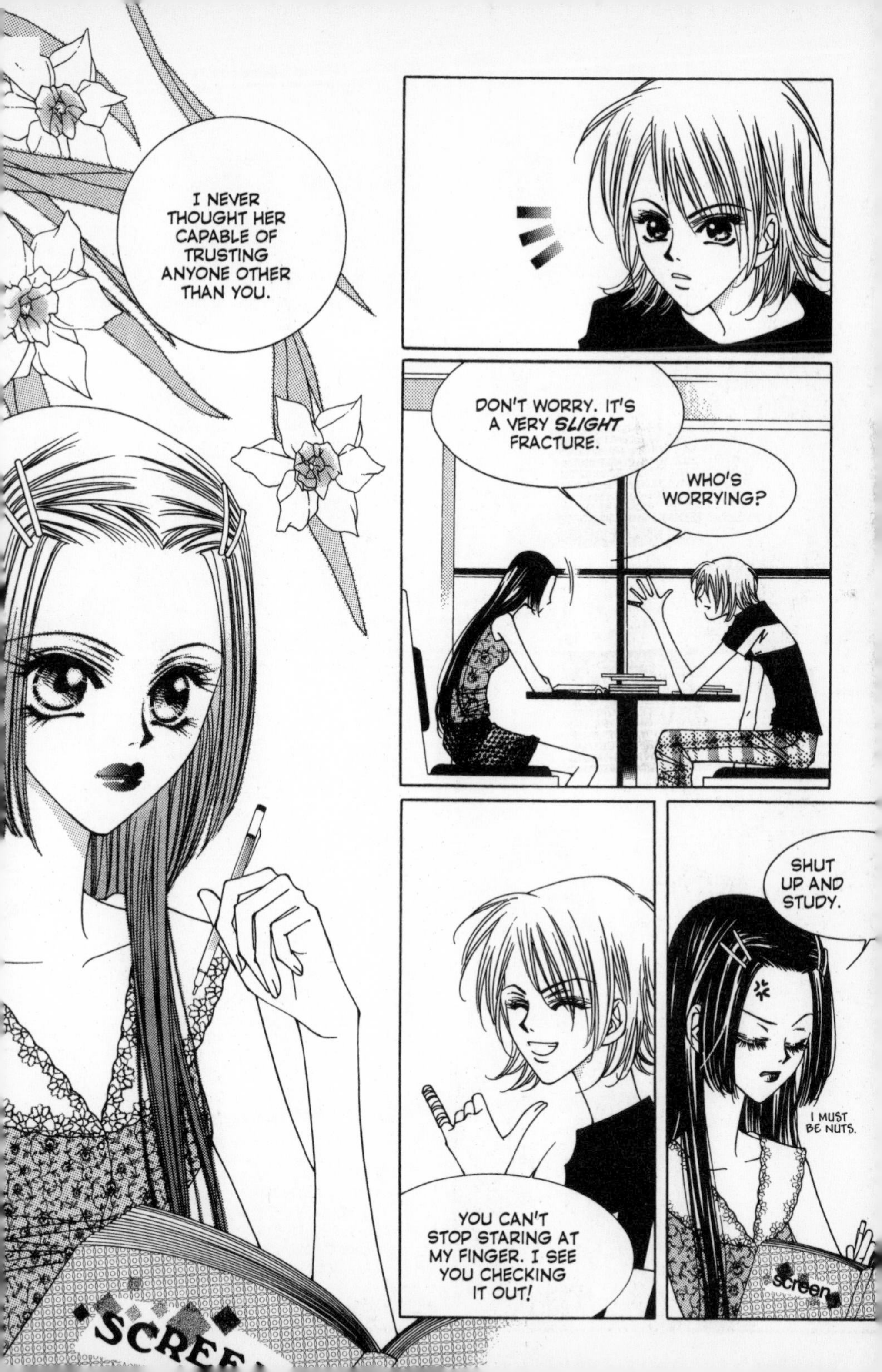
I NEVER THOUGHT HER CAPABLE OF TRUSTING ANYONE OTHER THAN YOU.
DON'T WORRY. IT'S A VERY *SLIGHT* FRACTURE.
WHO'S WORRYING?
YOU CAN'T STOP STARING AT MY FINGER. I SEE YOU CHECKING IT OUT!
SHUT UP AND STUDY.
I MUST BE NUTS.
screen

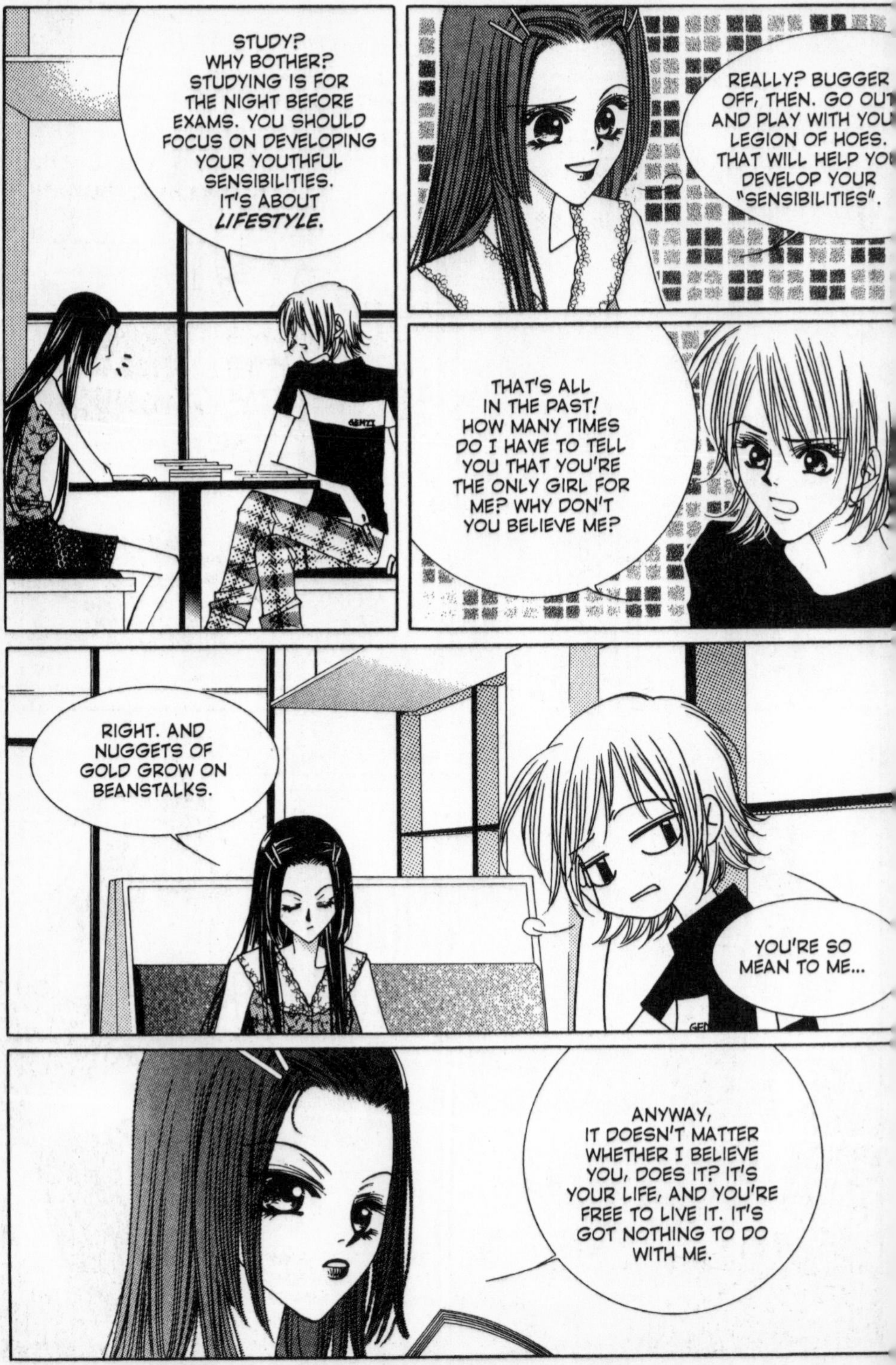
STUDY? WHY BOTHER? STUDYING IS FOR THE NIGHT BEFORE EXAMS. YOU SHOULD FOCUS ON DEVELOPING YOUR YOUTHFUL SENSIBILITIES. IT'S ABOUT *LIFESTYLE*.
REALLY? BUGGER OFF, THEN. GO OUT AND PLAY WITH YOU LEGION OF HOES. THAT WILL HELP YO DEVELOP YOUR "SENSIBILITIES".
THAT'S ALL IN THE PAST! HOW MANY TIMES DO I HAVE TO TELL YOU THAT YOU'RE THE ONLY GIRL FOR ME? WHY DON'T YOU BELIEVE ME?
RIGHT. AND NUGGETS OF GOLD GROW ON BEANSTALKS.
YOU'RE SO MEAN TO ME...
ANYWAY, IT DOESN'T MATTER WHETHER I BELIEVE YOU, DOES IT? IT'S YOUR LIFE, AND YOU'RE FREE TO LIVE IT. IT'S GOT NOTHING TO DO WITH ME.

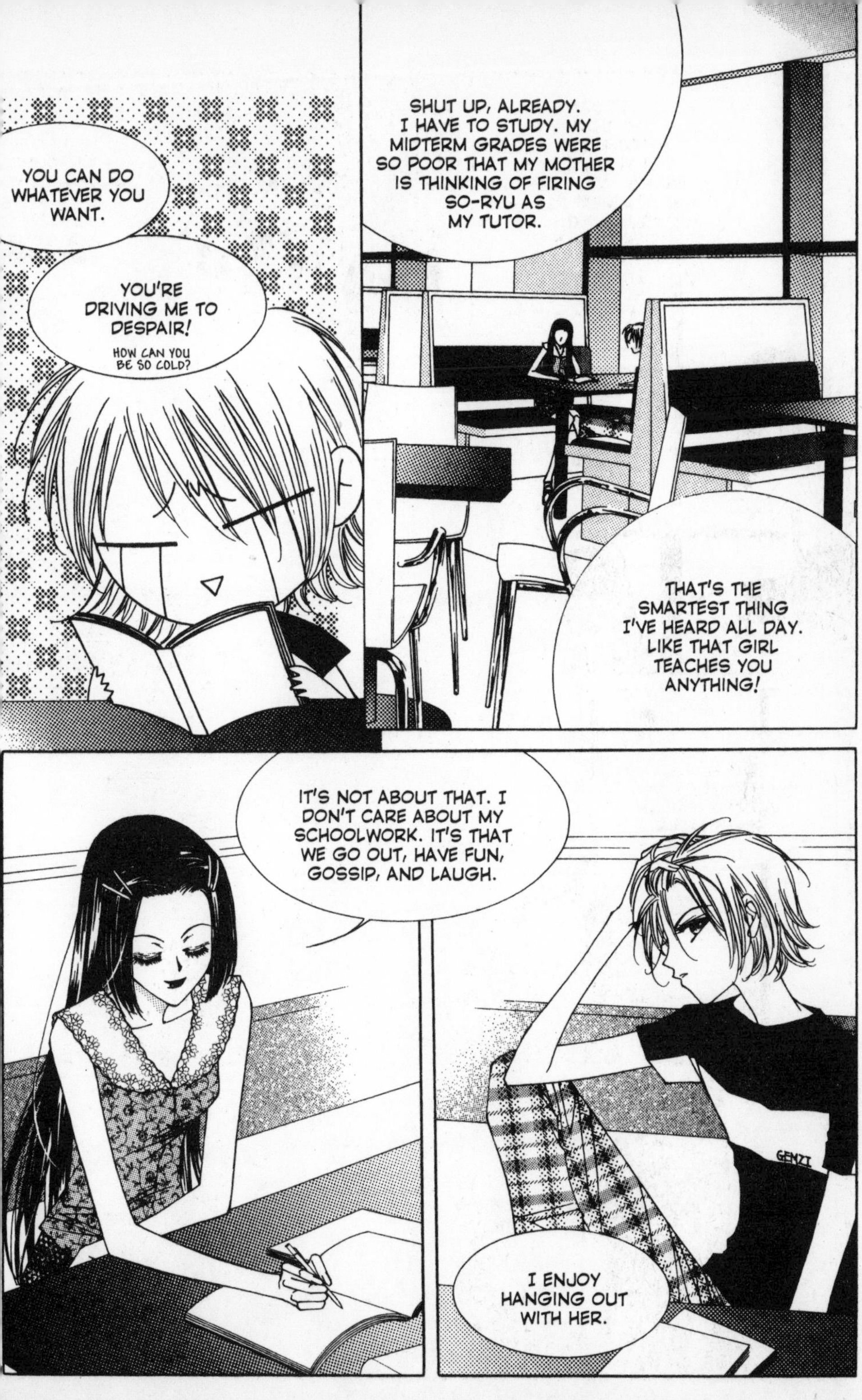

YOU CAN DO WHATEVER YOU WANT.
YOU'RE DRIVING ME TO DESPAIR!
HOW CAN YOU BE SO COLD?
SHUT UP, ALREADY. I HAVE TO STUDY. MY MIDTERM GRADES WERE SO POOR THAT MY MOTHER IS THINKING OF FIRING SO-RYU AS MY TUTOR.
THAT'S THE SMARTEST THING I'VE HEARD ALL DAY. LIKE THAT GIRL TEACHES YOU ANYTHING!
IT'S NOT ABOUT THAT. I DON'T CARE ABOUT MY SCHOOLWORK. IT'S THAT WE GO OUT, HAVE FUN, GOSSIP, AND LAUGH.
GENZI
I ENJOY HANGING OUT WITH HER.

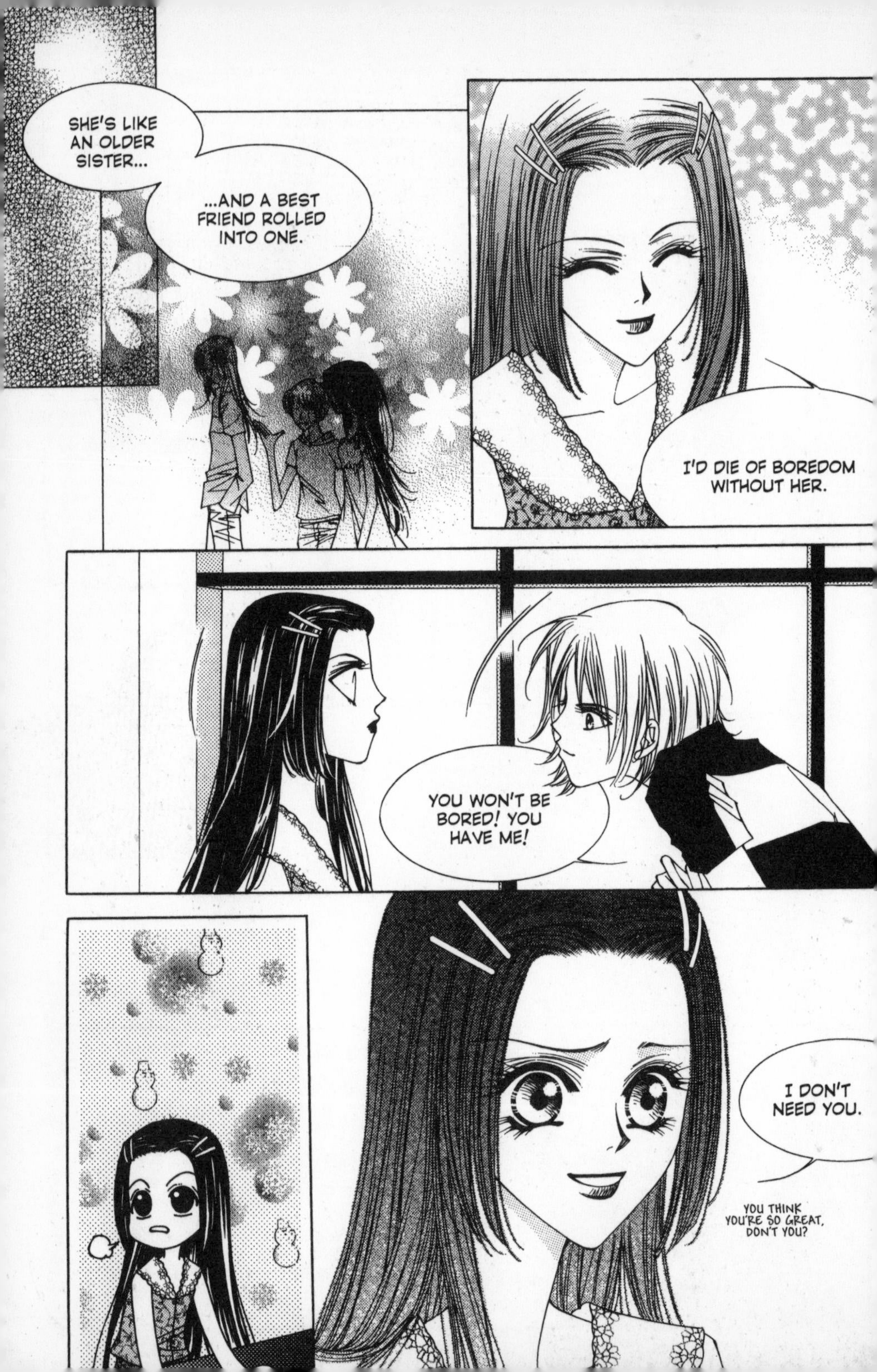
SHE'S LIKE AN OLDER SISTER...
...AND A BEST FRIEND ROLLED INTO ONE.
I'D DIE OF BOREDOM WITHOUT HER.
YOU WON'T BE BORED! YOU HAVE ME!
I DON'T NEED YOU.
YOU THINK YOU'RE SO GREAT, DON'T YOU?

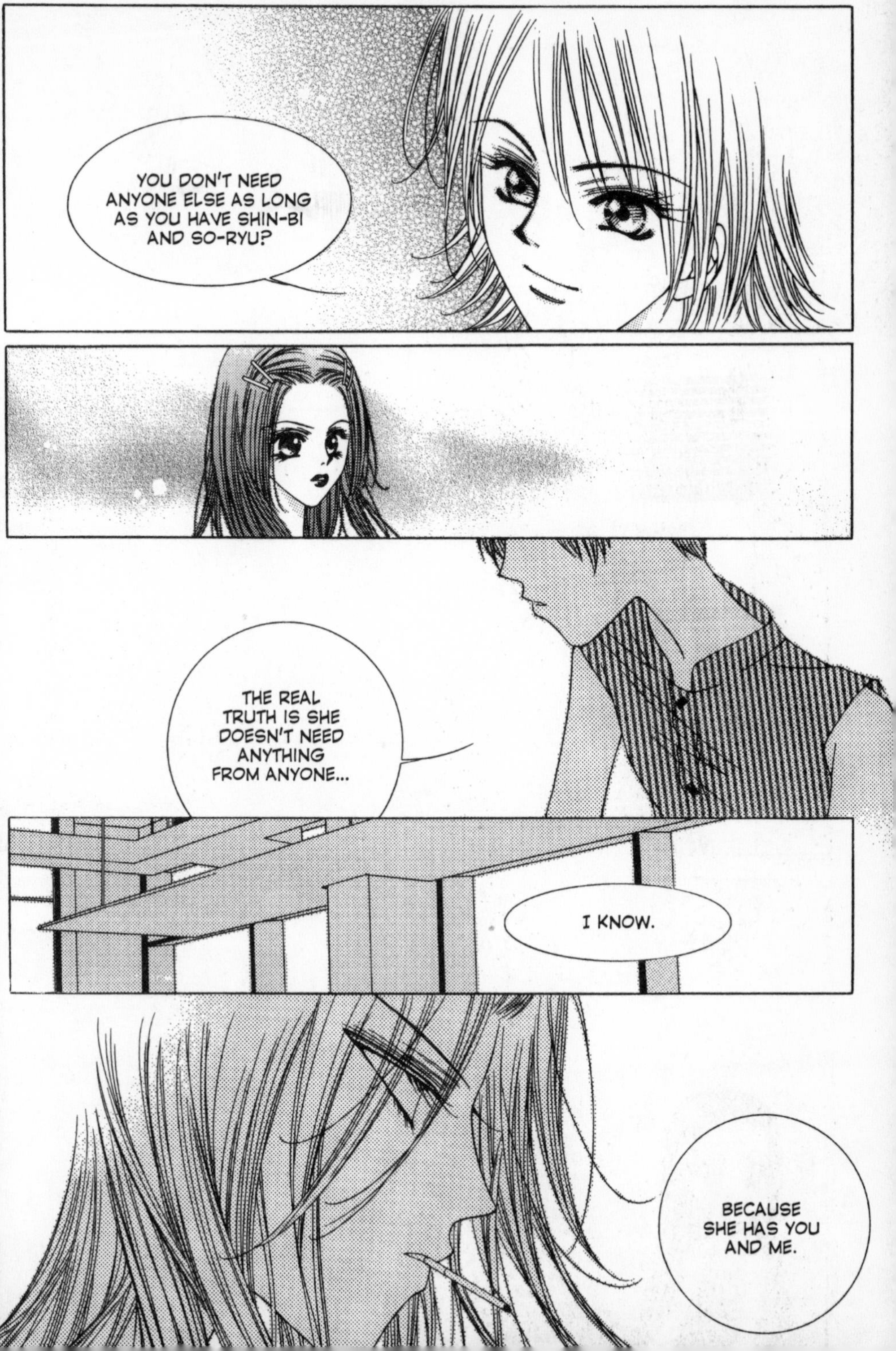
YOU DON'T NEED ANYONE ELSE AS LONG AS YOU HAVE SHIN-BI AND SO-RYU?
THE REAL TRUTH IS SHE DOESN'T NEED ANYTHING FROM ANYONE...
I KNOW.
BECAUSE SHE HAS YOU AND ME.

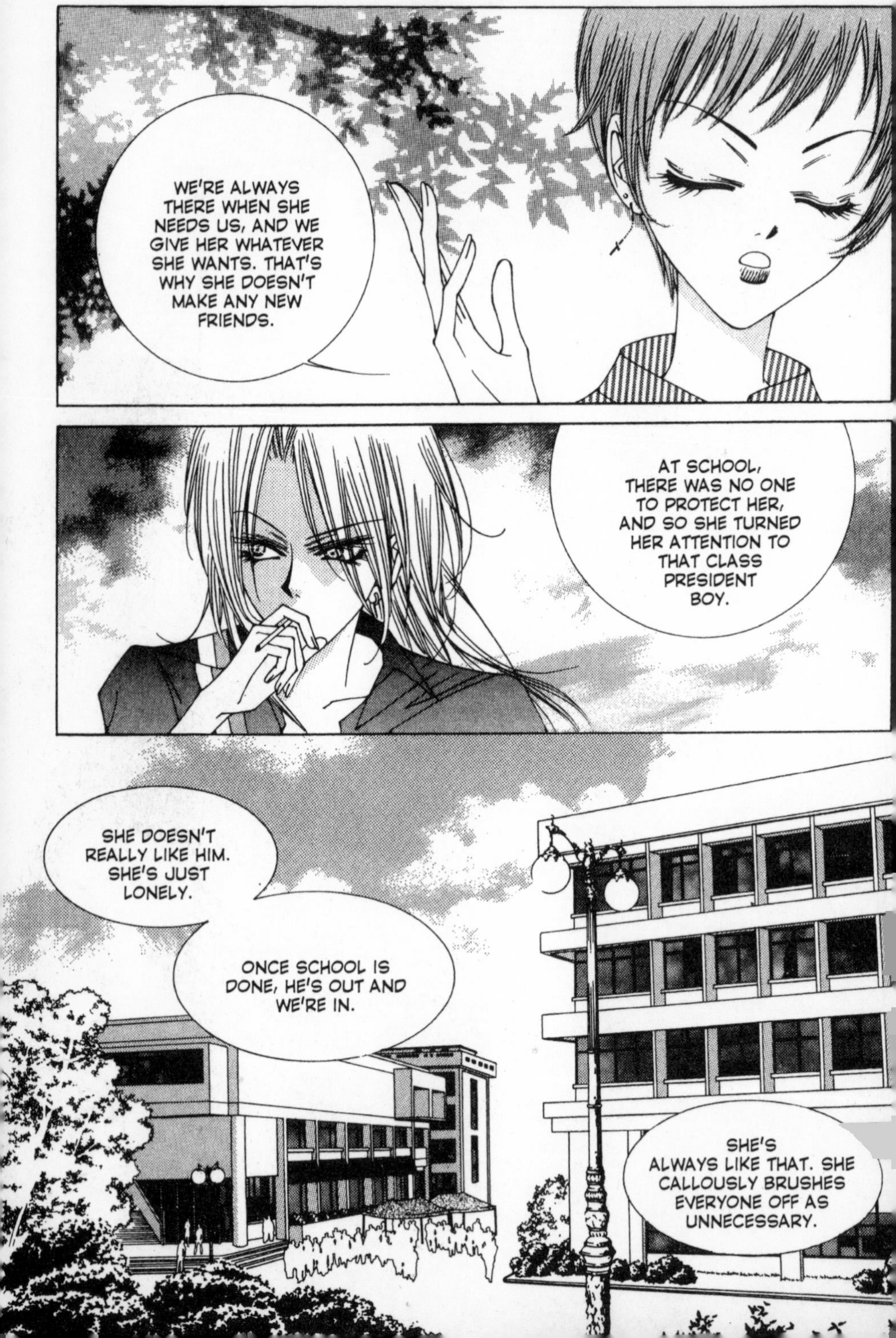
WE'RE ALWAYS THERE WHEN SHE NEEDS US, AND WE GIVE HER WHATEVER SHE WANTS. THAT'S WHY SHE DOESN'T MAKE ANY NEW FRIENDS.
AT SCHOOL, THERE WAS NO ONE TO PROTECT HER, AND SO SHE TURNED HER ATTENTION TO THAT CLASS PRESIDENT BOY.
SHE DOESN'T REALLY LIKE HIM. SHE'S JUST LONELY.
ONCE SCHOOL IS DONE, HE'S OUT AND WE'RE IN.
SHE'S ALWAYS LIKE THAT. SHE CALLOUSLY BRUSHES EVERYONE OFF AS UNNECESSARY.

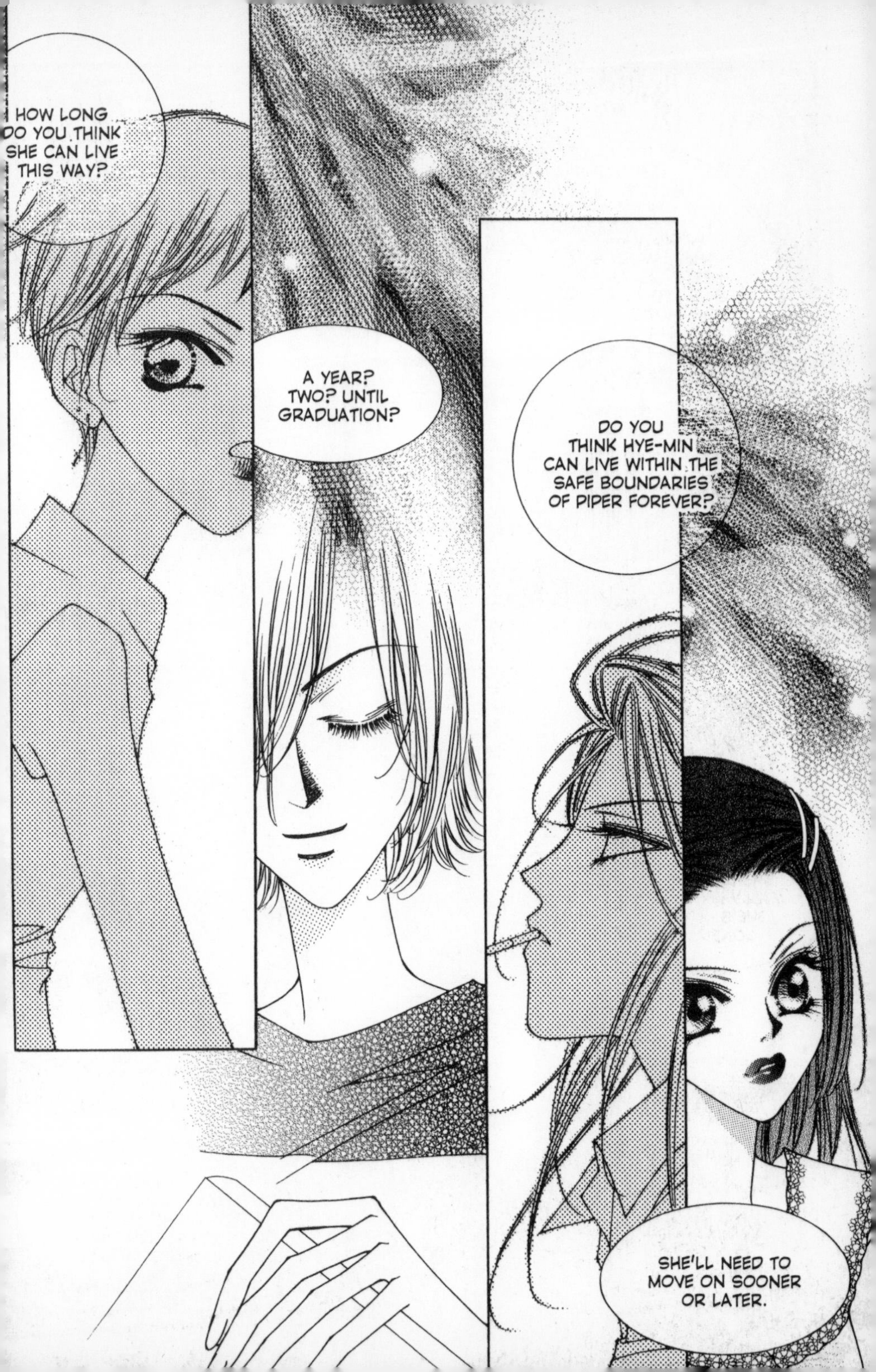
HOW LONG DO YOU THINK SHE CAN LIVE THIS WAY?
A YEAR? TWO? UNTIL GRADUATION?
DO YOU THINK HYE-MIN CAN LIVE WITHIN THE SAFE BOUNDARIES OF PIPER FOREVER?
SHE'LL NEED TO MOVE ON SOONER OR LATER.

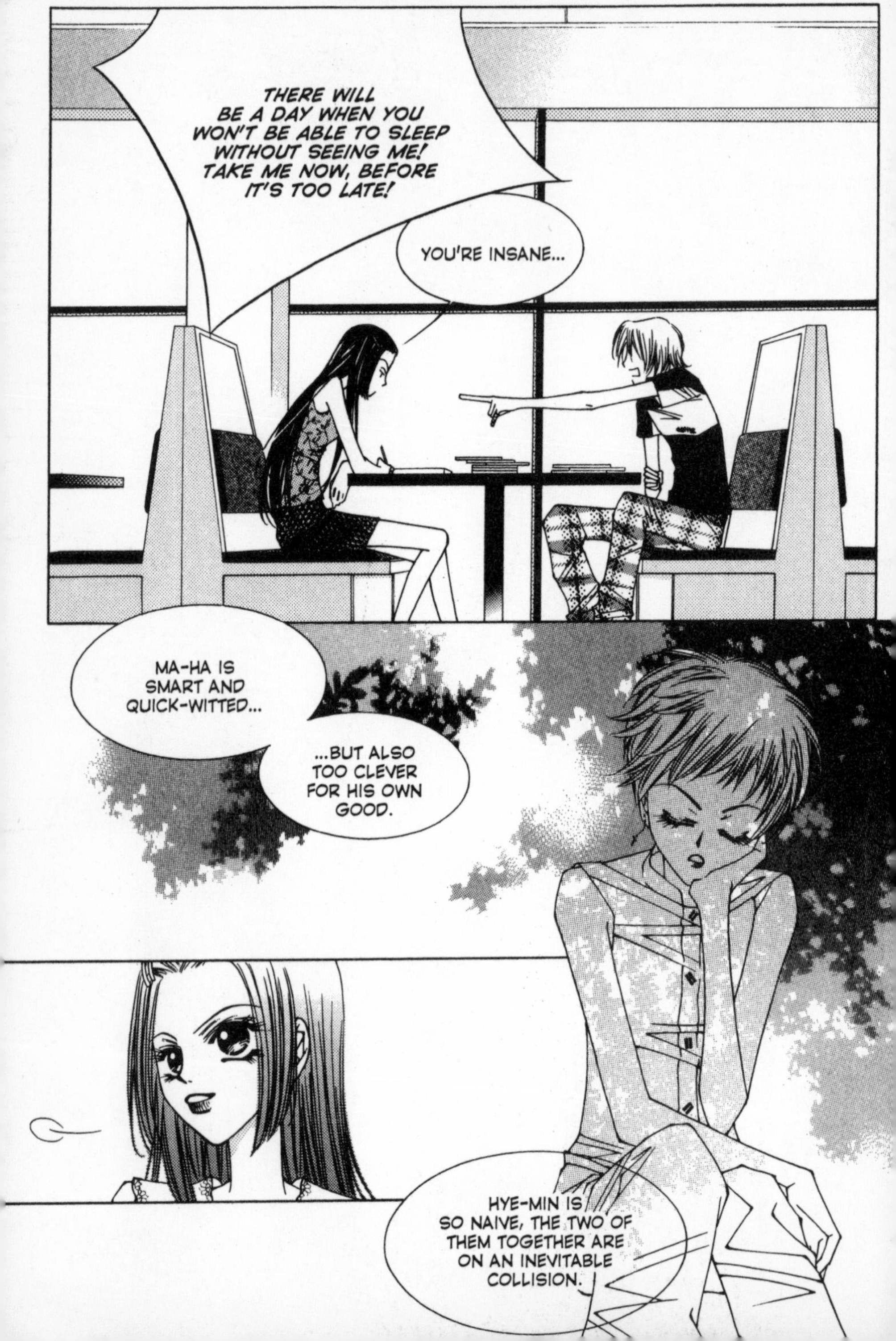
THERE WILL BE A DAY WHEN YOU WON'T BE ABLE TO SLEEP WITHOUT SEEING ME! TAKE ME NOW, BEFORE IT'S TOO LATE!
YOU'RE INSANE...
MA-HA IS SMART AND QUICK-WITTED...
...BUT ALSO TOO CLEVER FOR HIS OWN GOOD.
HYE-MIN IS SO NAIVE, THE TWO OF THEM TOGETHER ARE ON AN INEVITABLE COLLISION.

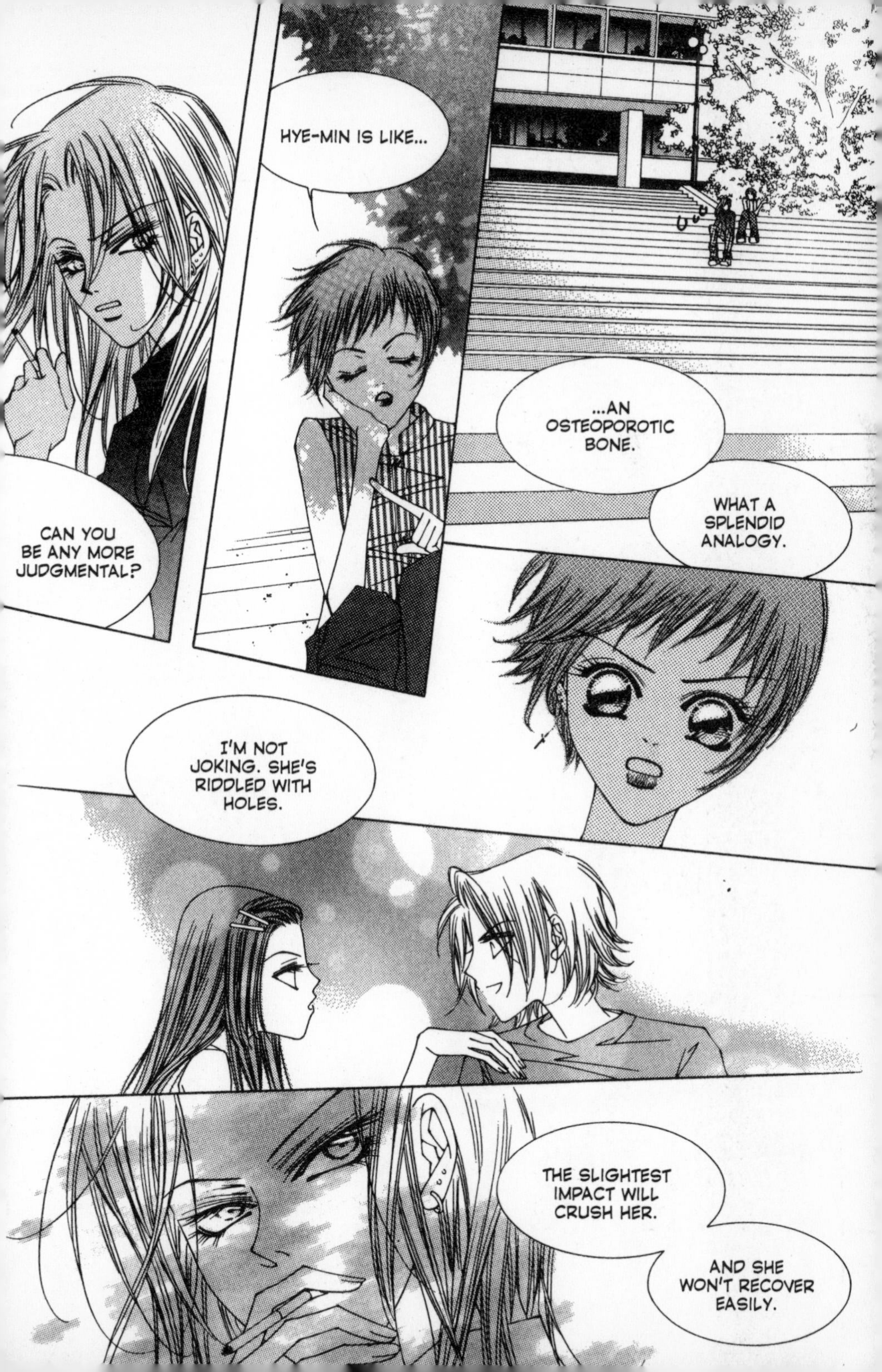
CAN YOU BE ANY MORE JUDGMENTAL?
HYE-MIN IS LIKE...
...AN OSTEOPOROTIC BONE.
WHAT A SPLENDID ANALOGY.
I'M NOT JOKING. SHE'S RIDDLED WITH HOLES.
THE SLIGHTEST IMPACT WILL CRUSH HER.
AND SHE WON'T RECOVER EASILY.

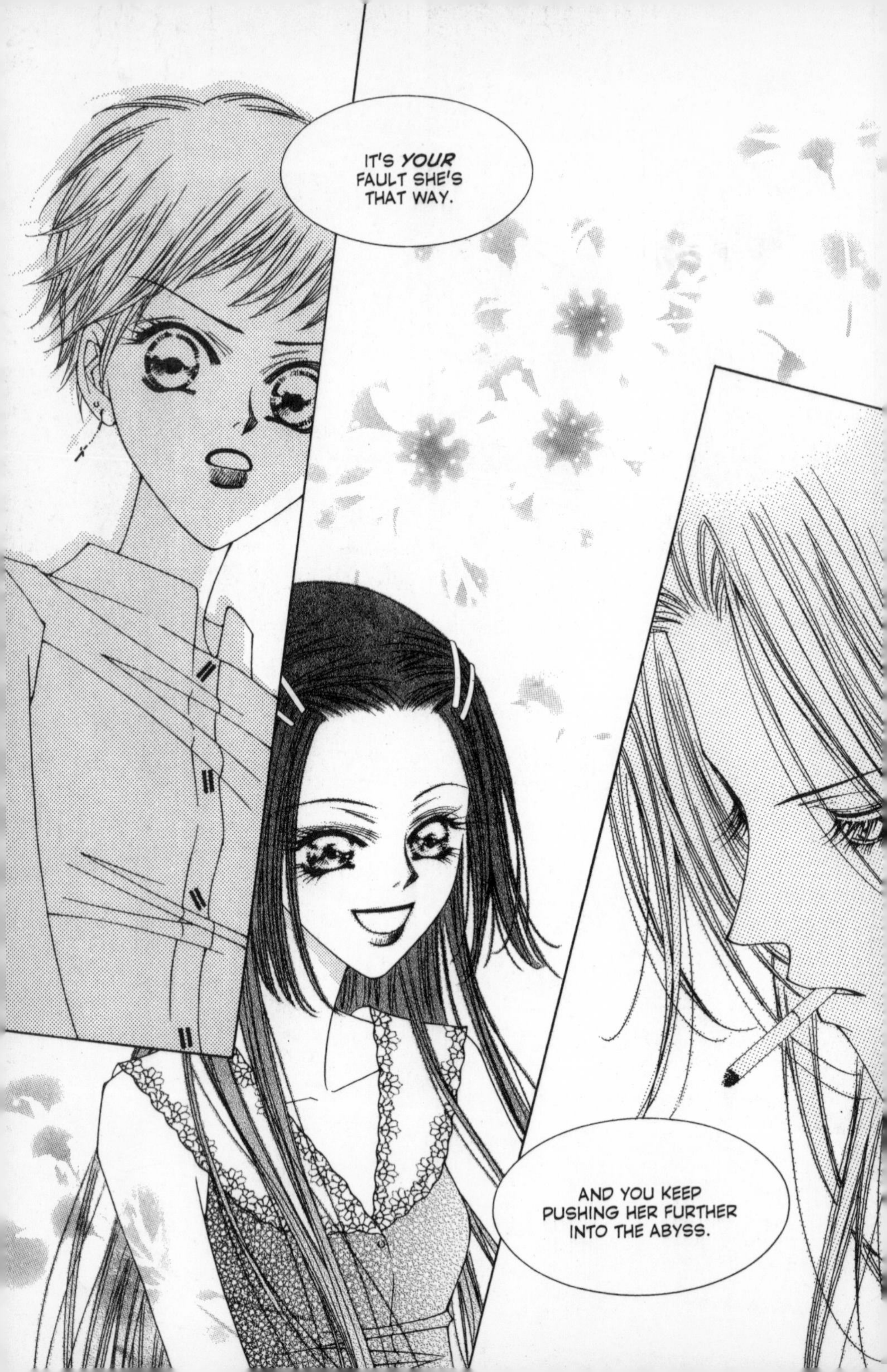
IT'S *YOUR* FAULT SHE'S THAT WAY.
AND YOU KEEP PUSHING HER FURTHER INTO THE ABYSS.

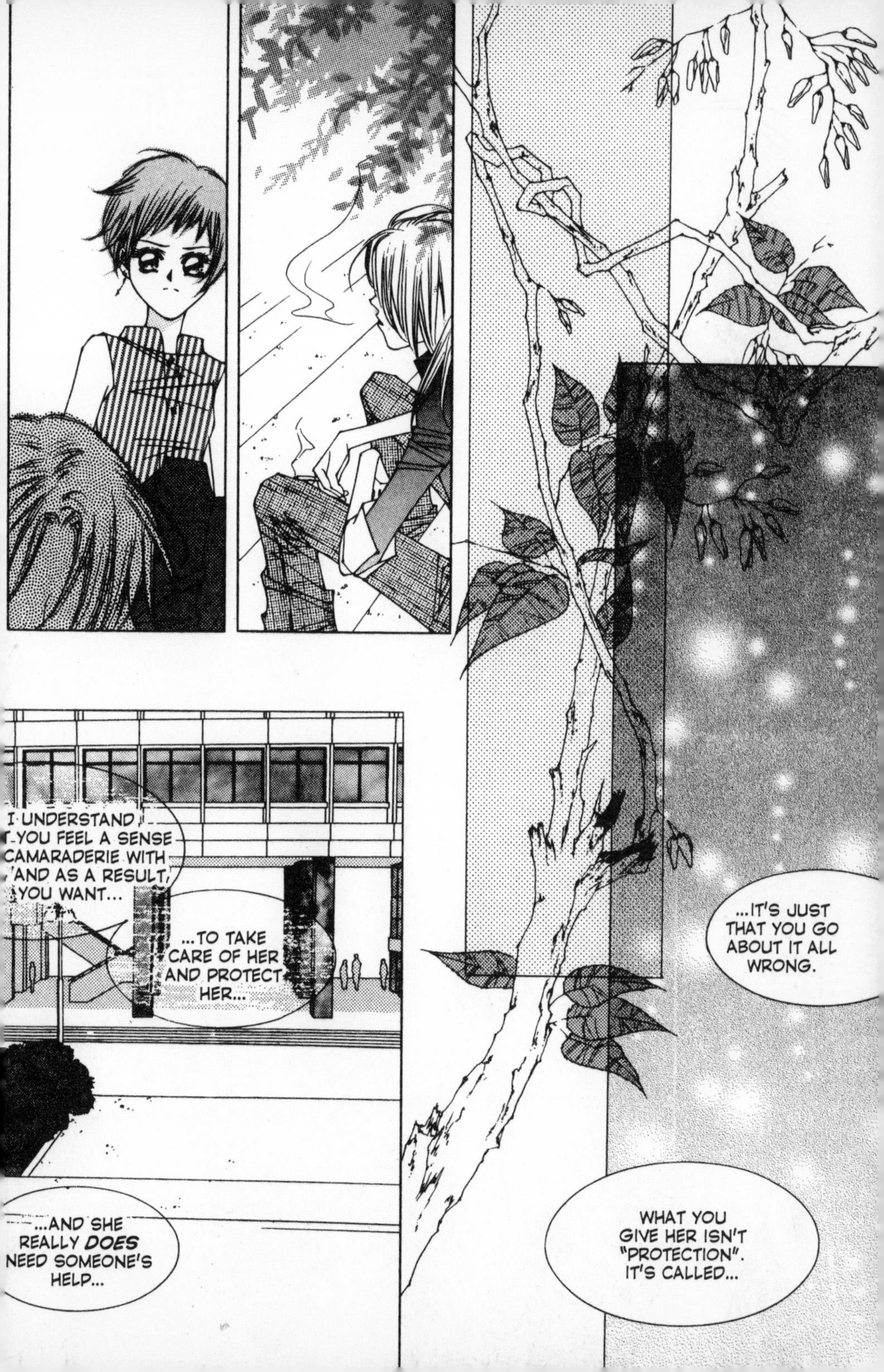
I UNDERSTAND YOU FEEL A SENSE CAMARADERIE WITH AND AS A RESULT, YOU WANT...
...TO TAKE CARE OF HER AND PROTECT HER...
...AND SHE REALLY ***DOES*** NEED SOMEONE'S HELP...
...IT'S JUST THAT YOU GO ABOUT IT ALL WRONG.
WHAT YOU GIVE HER ISN'T "PROTECTION". IT'S CALLED...

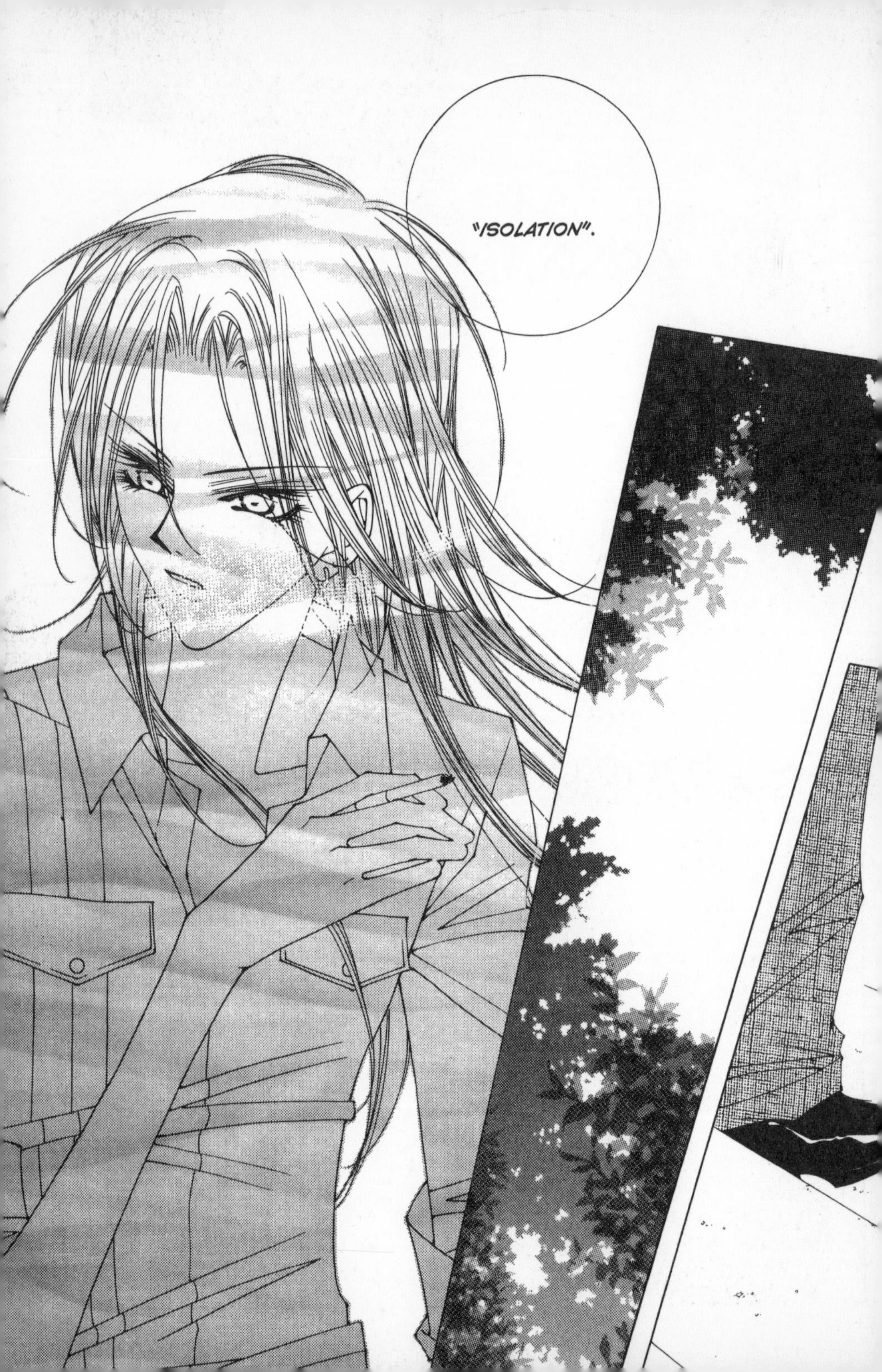
"ISOLATION".

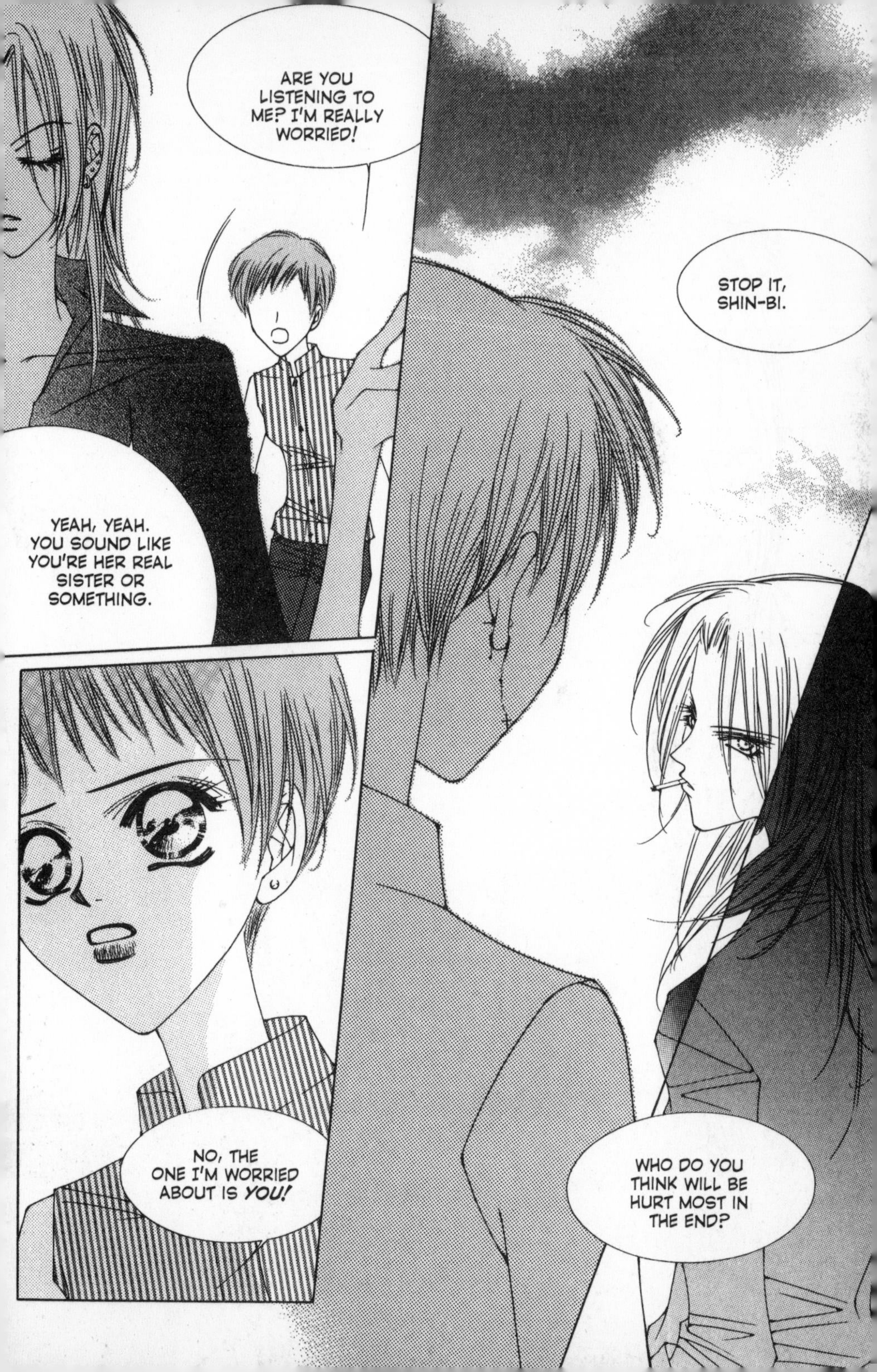
ARE YOU LISTENING TO ME? I'M REALLY WORRIED!
YEAH, YEAH. YOU SOUND LIKE YOU'RE HER REAL SISTER OR SOMETHING.
NO, THE ONE I'M WORRIED ABOUT IS *YOU!*
STOP IT, SHIN-BI.
WHO DO YOU THINK WILL BE HURT MOST IN THE END?

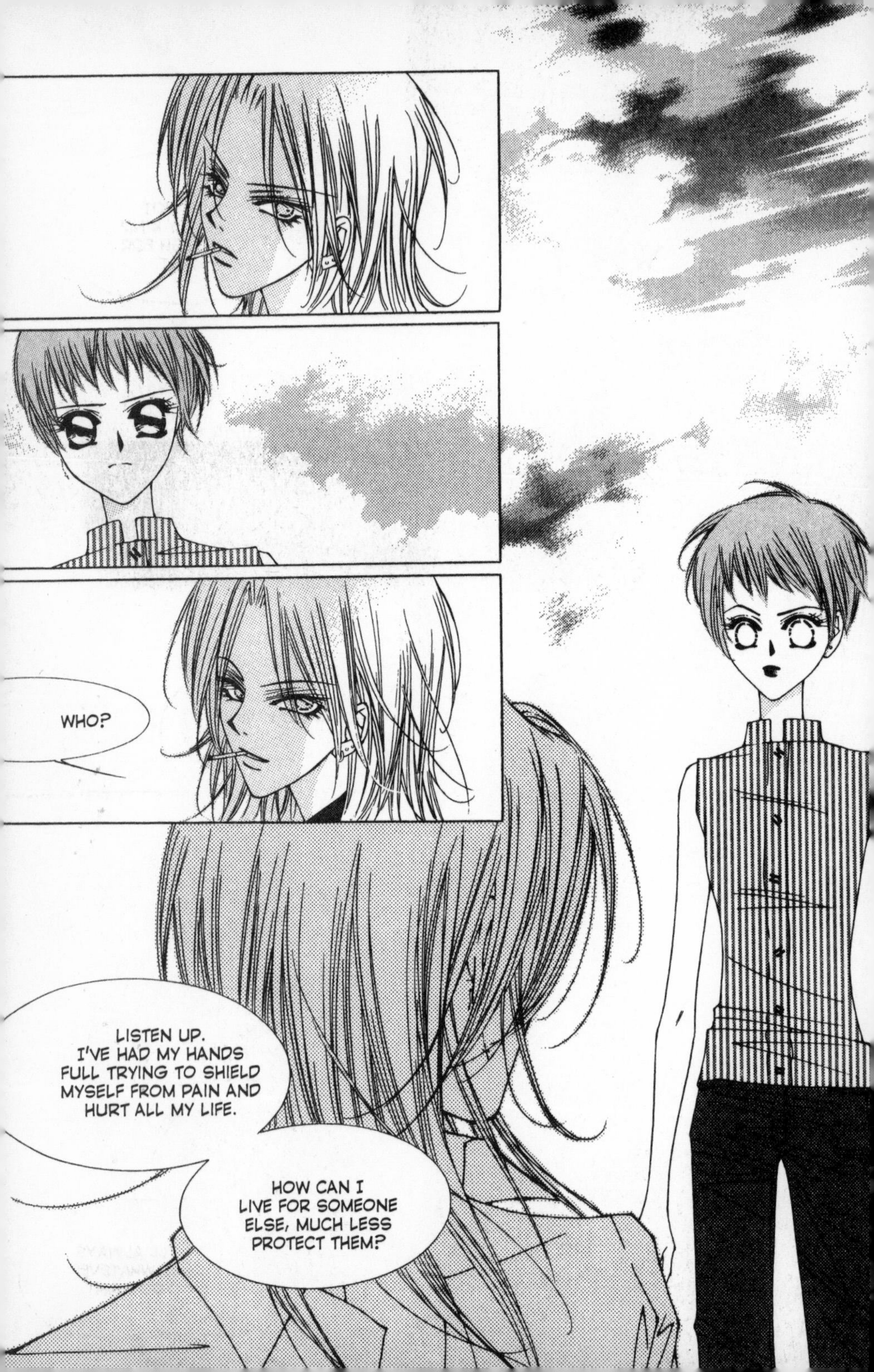
WHO?
LISTEN UP. I'VE HAD MY HANDS FULL TRYING TO SHIELD MYSELF FROM PAIN AND HURT ALL MY LIFE.
HOW CAN I LIVE FOR SOMEONE ELSE, MUCH LESS PROTECT THEM?

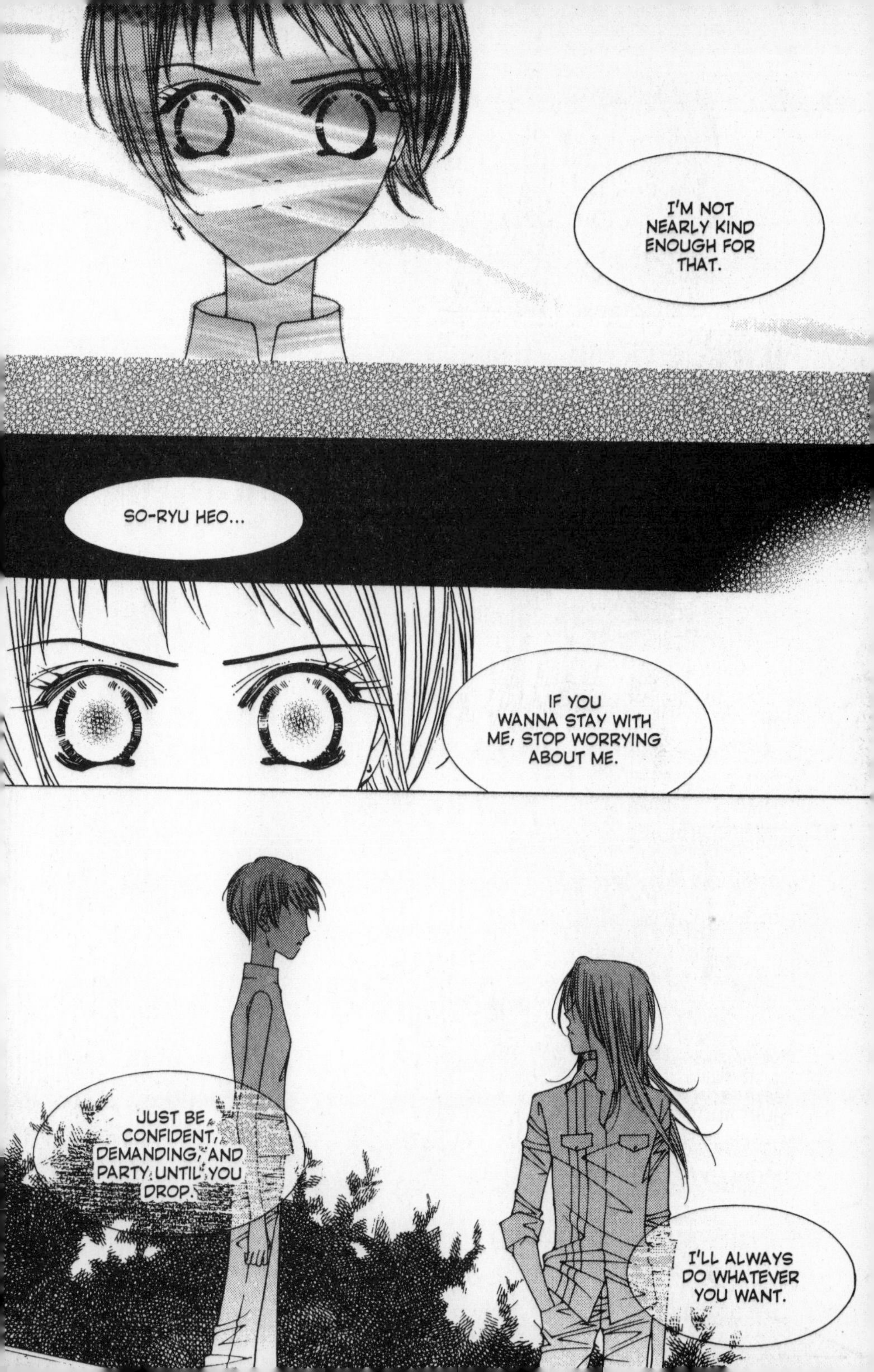
I'M NOT NEARLY KIND ENOUGH FOR THAT.
SO-RYU HEO...
IF YOU WANNA STAY WITH ME, STOP WORRYING ABOUT ME.
I'LL ALWAYS DO WHATEVER YOU WANT.
JUST BE CONFIDENT, DEMANDING, AND PARTY UNTIL YOU DROP.

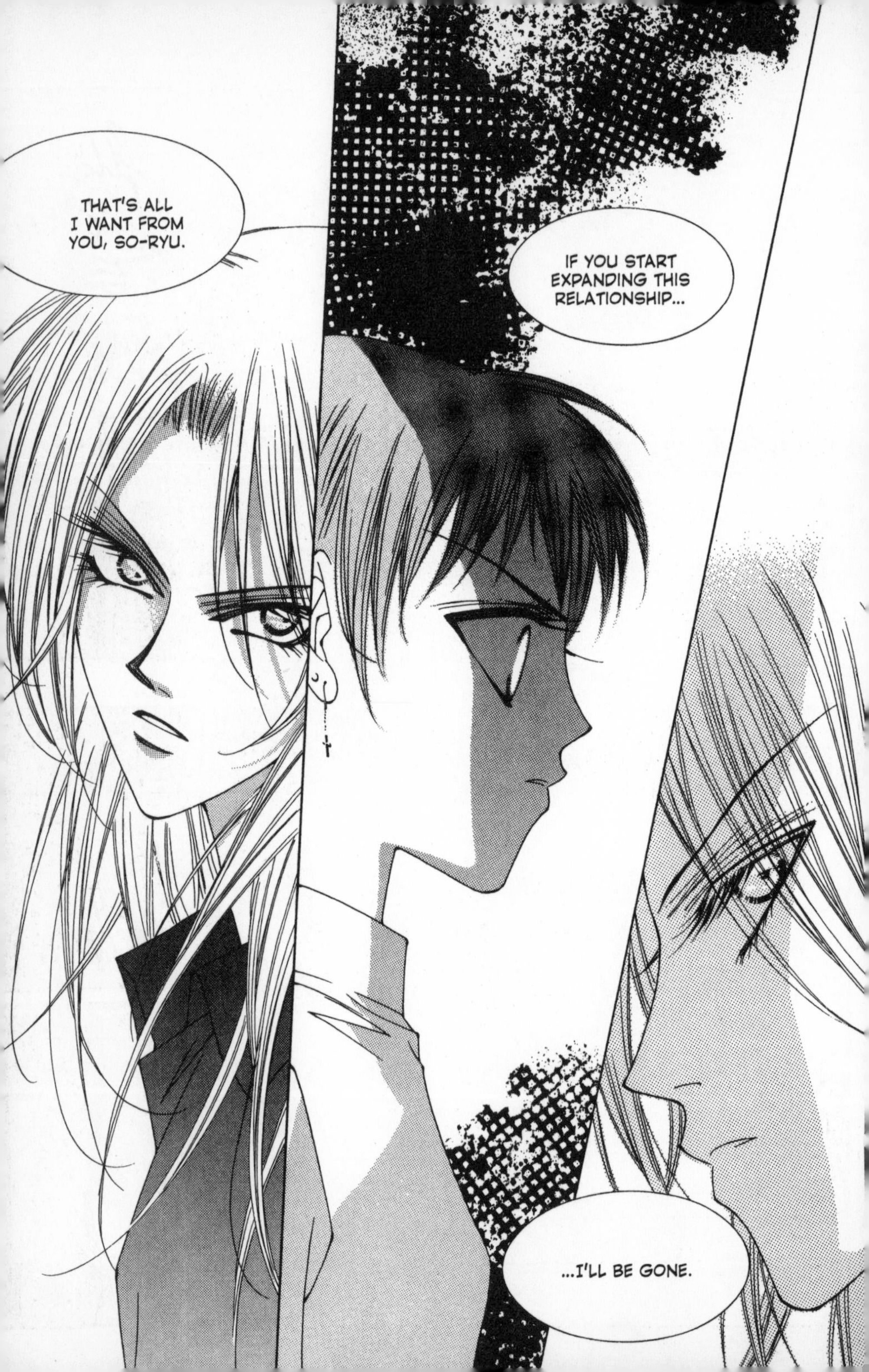
THAT'S ALL I WANT FROM YOU, SO-RYU.
IF YOU START EXPANDING THIS RELATIONSHIP...
...I'LL BE GONE.

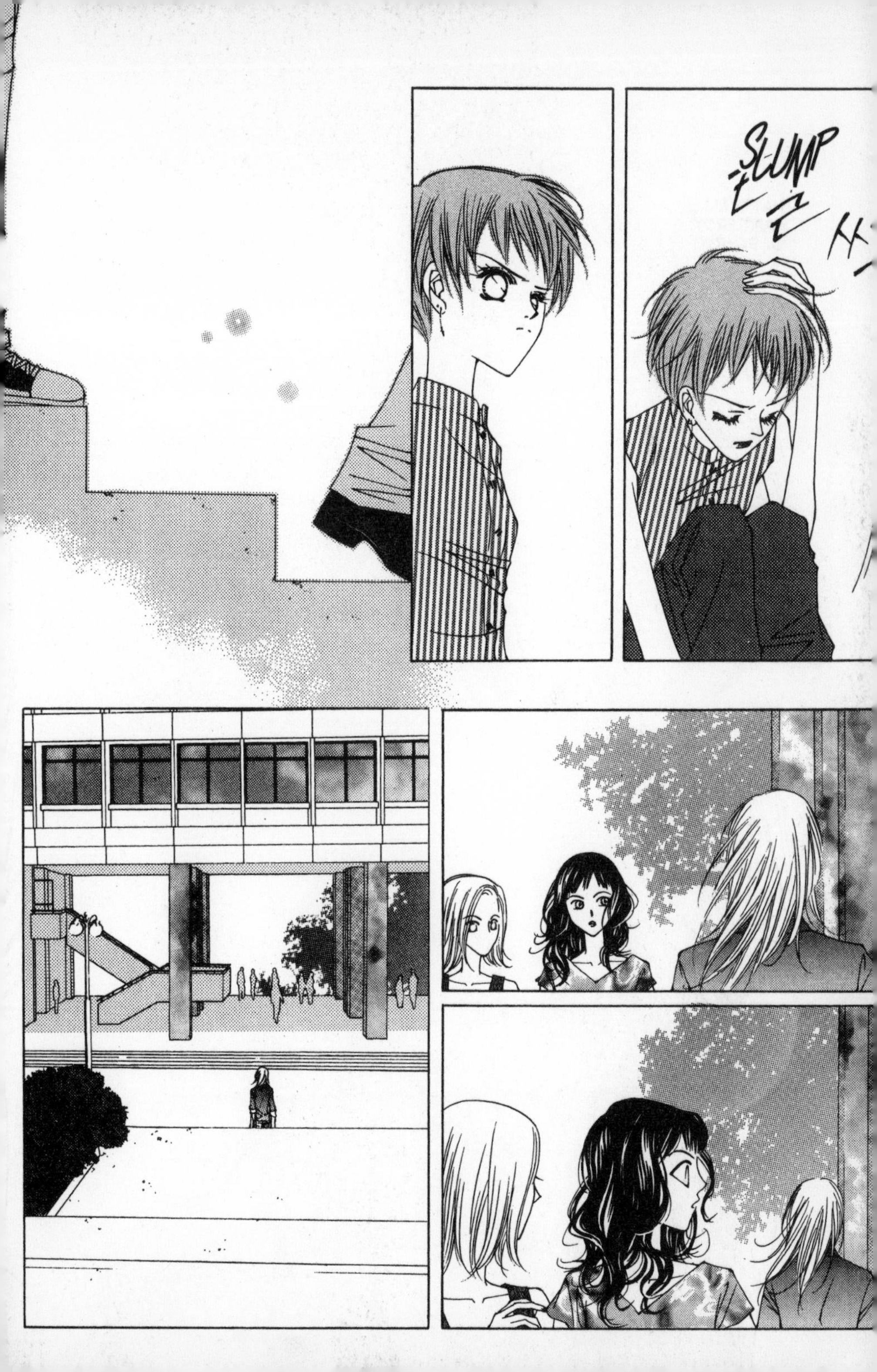
SLUMP

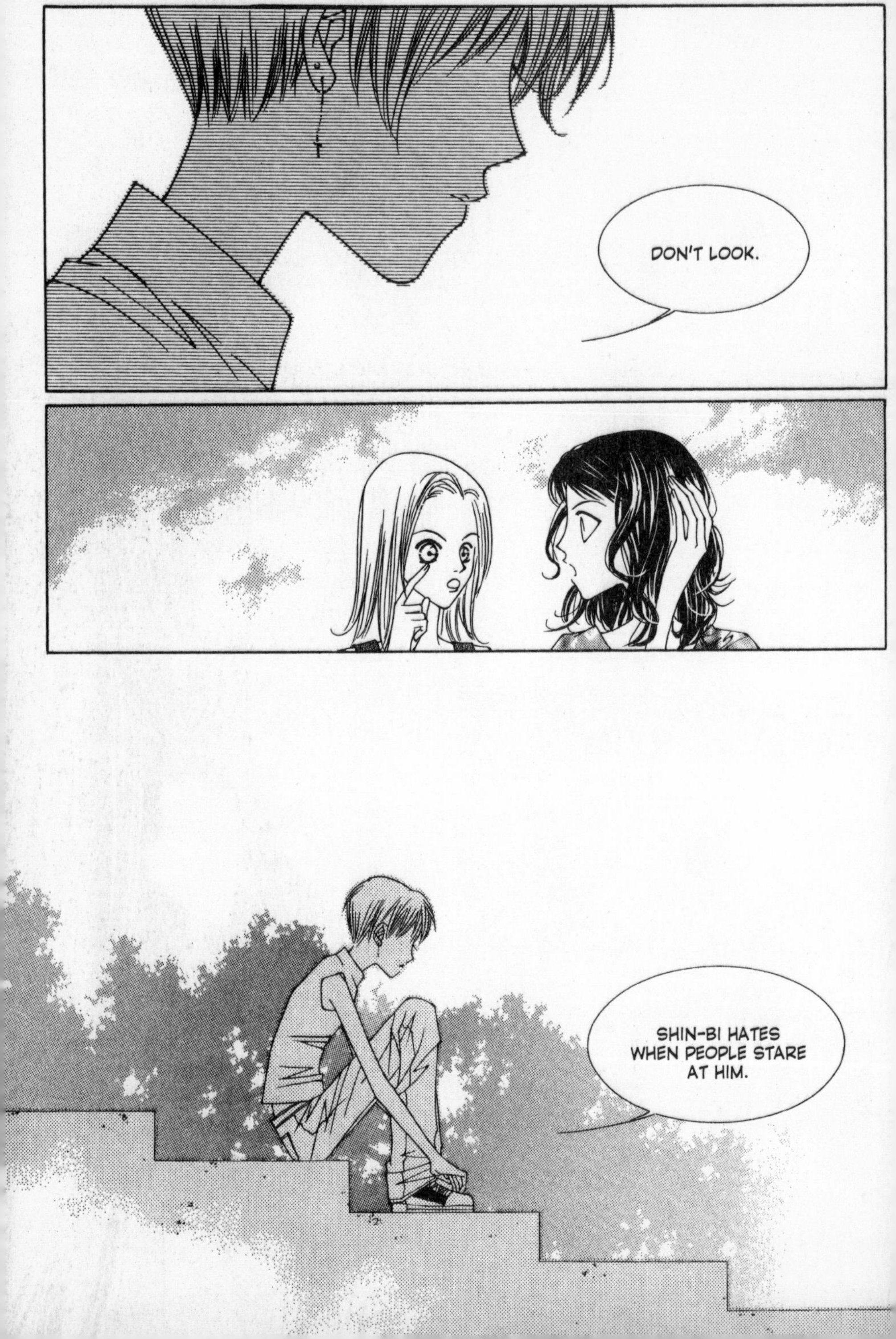
DON'T LOOK.
SHIN-BI HATES WHEN PEOPLE STARE AT HIM.

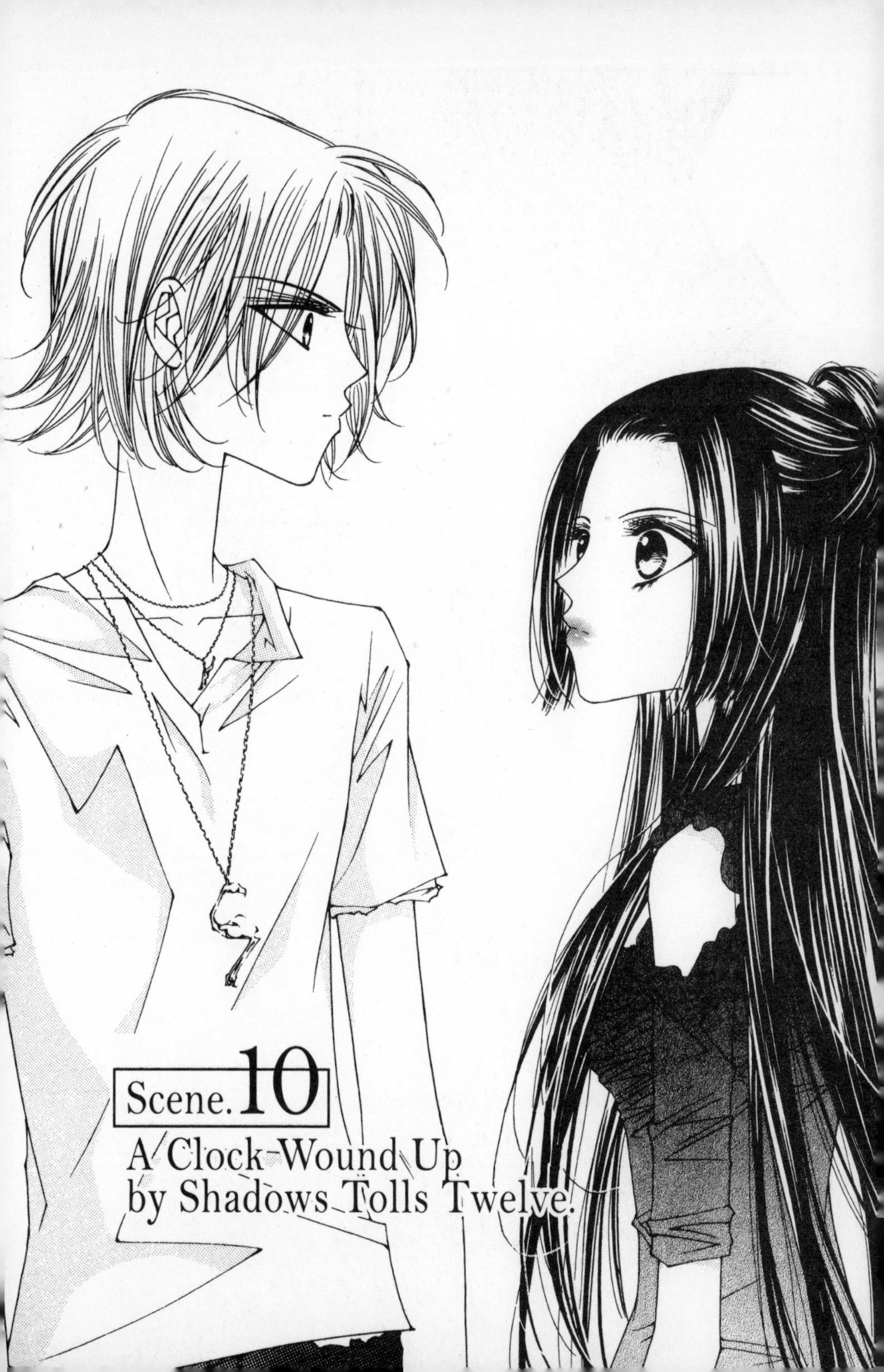
Scene. 10
A Clock Wound Up
by Shadows Tolls Twelve.

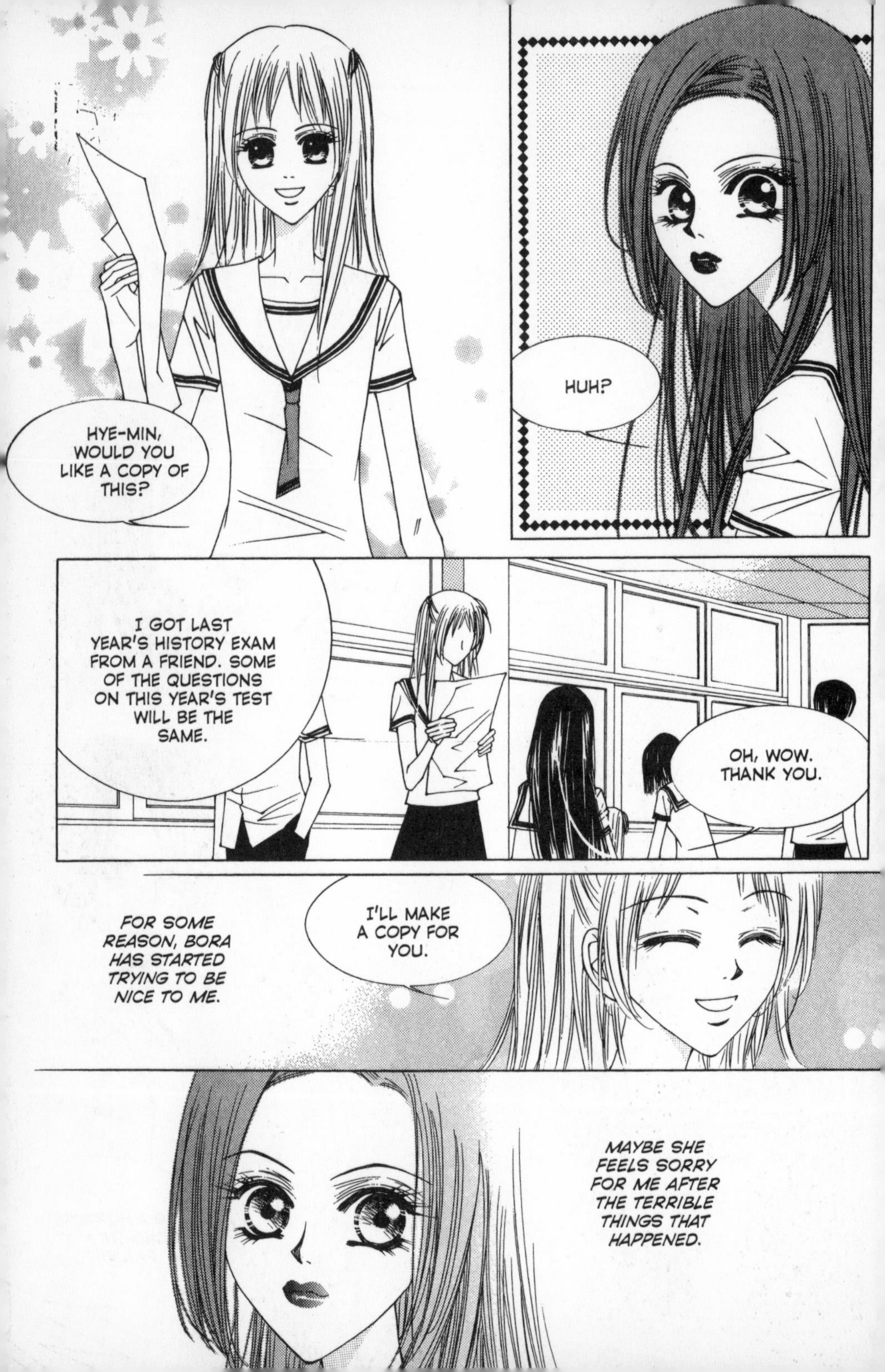
HYE-MIN, WOULD YOU LIKE A COPY OF THIS?
HUH?
I GOT LAST YEAR'S HISTORY EXAM FROM A FRIEND. SOME OF THE QUESTIONS ON THIS YEAR'S TEST WILL BE THE SAME.
OH, WOW. THANK YOU.
FOR SOME REASON, BORA HAS STARTED TRYING TO BE NICE TO ME.
I'LL MAKE A COPY FOR YOU.
MAYBE SHE FEELS SORRY FOR ME AFTER THE TERRIBLE THINGS THAT HAPPENED.

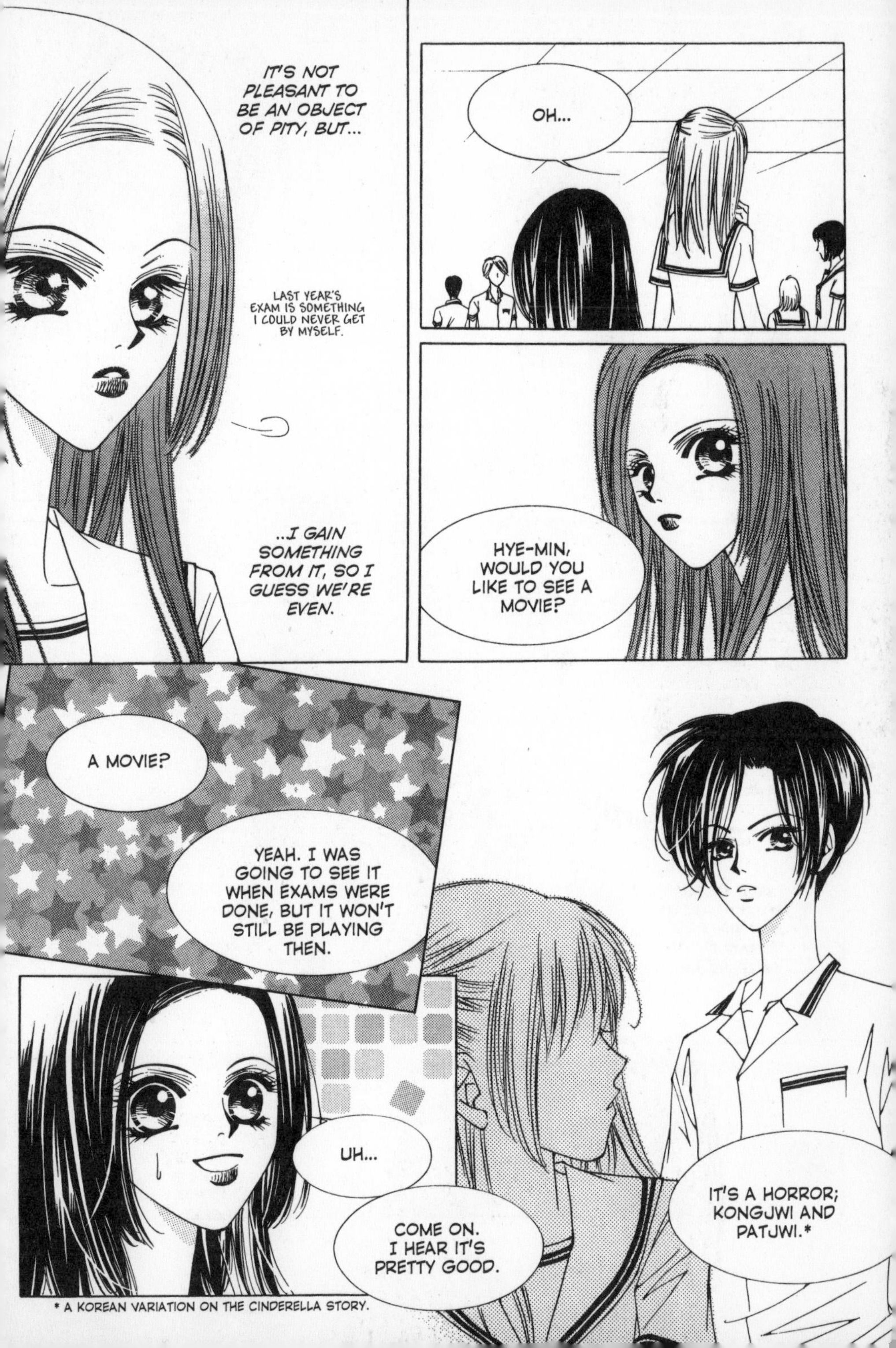
IT'S NOT PLEASANT TO BE AN OBJECT OF PITY, BUT...
LAST YEAR'S EXAM IS SOMETHING I COULD NEVER GET BY MYSELF.
...I GAIN SOMETHING FROM IT, SO I GUESS WE'RE EVEN.
OH...
HYE-MIN, WOULD YOU LIKE TO SEE A MOVIE?
A MOVIE?
YEAH. I WAS GOING TO SEE IT WHEN EXAMS WERE DONE, BUT IT WON'T STILL BE PLAYING THEN.
UH...
COME ON. I HEAR IT'S PRETTY GOOD.
IT'S A HORROR; KONGJWI AND PATJWI.*
* A KOREAN VARIATION ON THE CINDERELLA STORY.

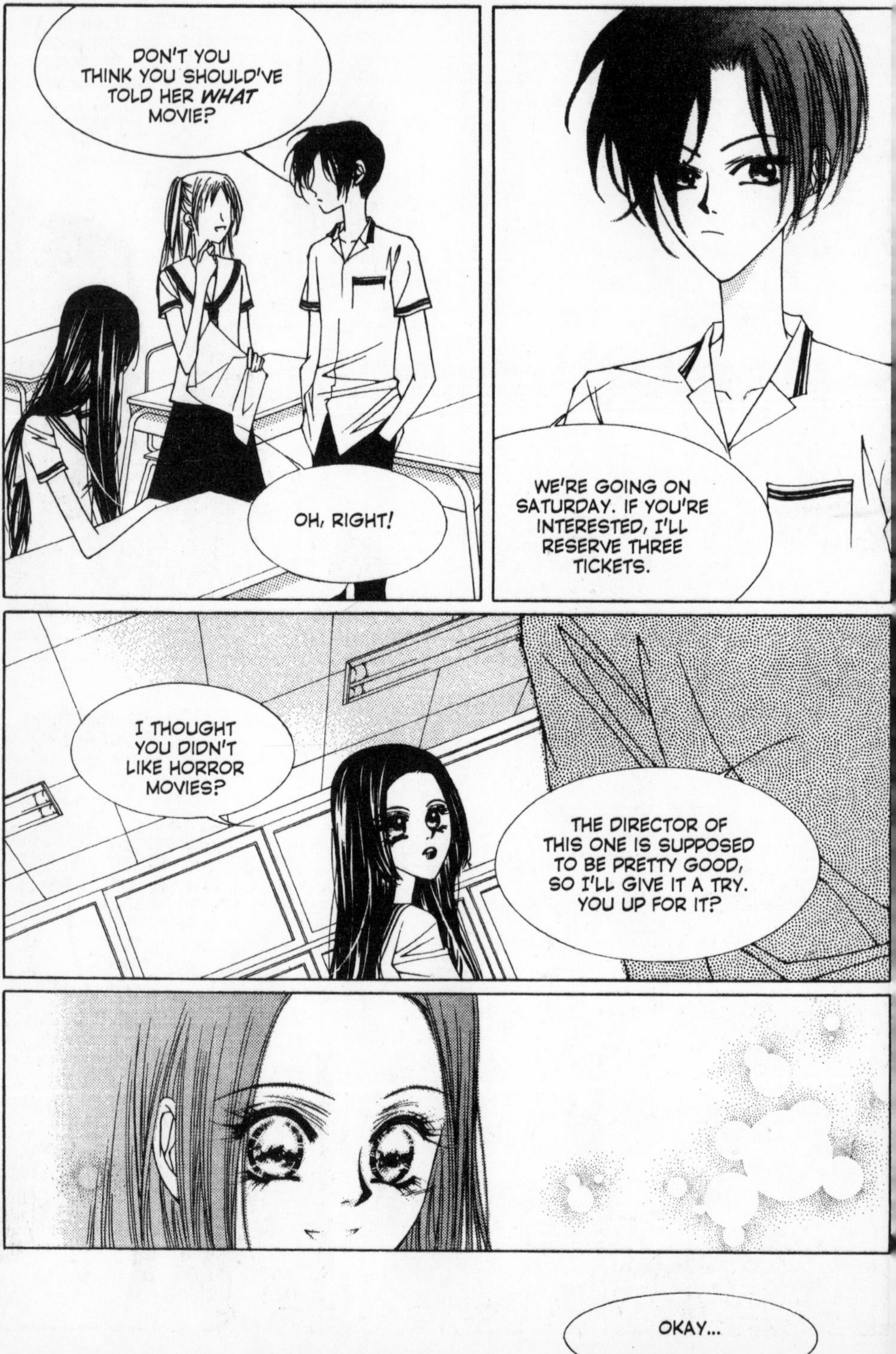
DON'T YOU THINK YOU SHOULD'VE TOLD HER *WHAT* MOVIE?
OH, RIGHT!
WE'RE GOING ON SATURDAY. IF YOU'RE INTERESTED, I'LL RESERVE THREE TICKETS.
I THOUGHT YOU DIDN'T LIKE HORROR MOVIES?
THE DIRECTOR OF THIS ONE IS SUPPOSED TO BE PRETTY GOOD, SO I'LL GIVE IT A TRY. YOU UP FOR IT?
OKAY...

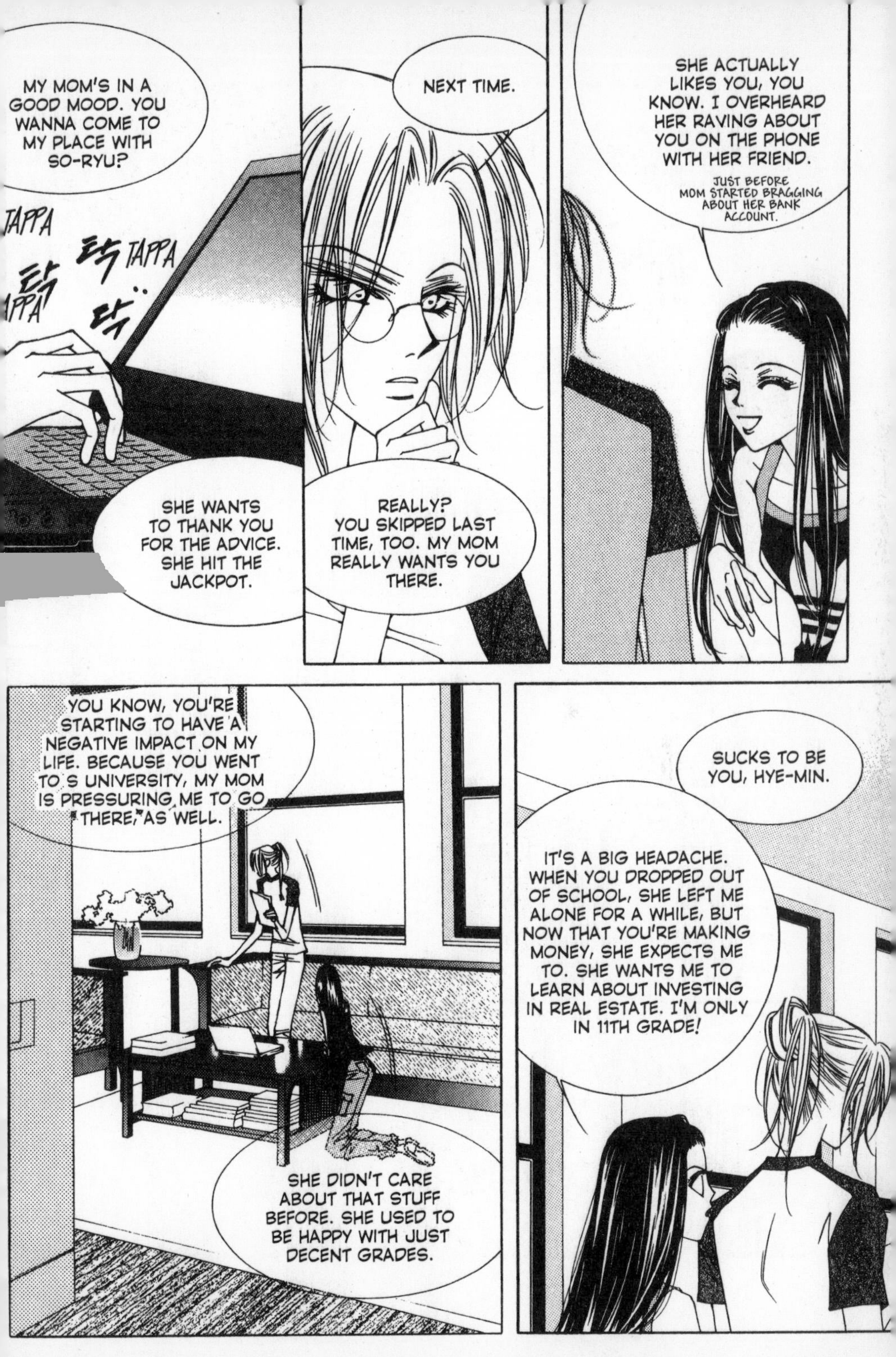
MY MOM'S IN A GOOD MOOD. YOU WANNA COME TO MY PLACE WITH SO-RYU?
TAPPA
탁 TAPPA
탁 TAPPA
닥
SHE WANTS TO THANK YOU FOR THE ADVICE. SHE HIT THE JACKPOT.
NEXT TIME.
REALLY? YOU SKIPPED LAST TIME, TOO. MY MOM REALLY WANTS YOU THERE.
SHE ACTUALLY LIKES YOU, YOU KNOW. I OVERHEARD HER RAVING ABOUT YOU ON THE PHONE WITH HER FRIEND.
JUST BEFORE MOM STARTED BRAGGING ABOUT HER BANK ACCOUNT.
YOU KNOW, YOU'RE STARTING TO HAVE A NEGATIVE IMPACT ON MY LIFE. BECAUSE YOU WENT TO S UNIVERSITY, MY MOM IS PRESSURING ME TO GO THERE, AS WELL.
SHE DIDN'T CARE ABOUT THAT STUFF BEFORE. SHE USED TO BE HAPPY WITH JUST DECENT GRADES.
SUCKS TO BE YOU, HYE-MIN.
IT'S A BIG HEADACHE. WHEN YOU DROPPED OUT OF SCHOOL, SHE LEFT ME ALONE FOR A WHILE, BUT NOW THAT YOU'RE MAKING MONEY, SHE EXPECTS ME TO. SHE WANTS ME TO LEARN ABOUT INVESTING IN REAL ESTATE. I'M ONLY IN 11TH GRADE!

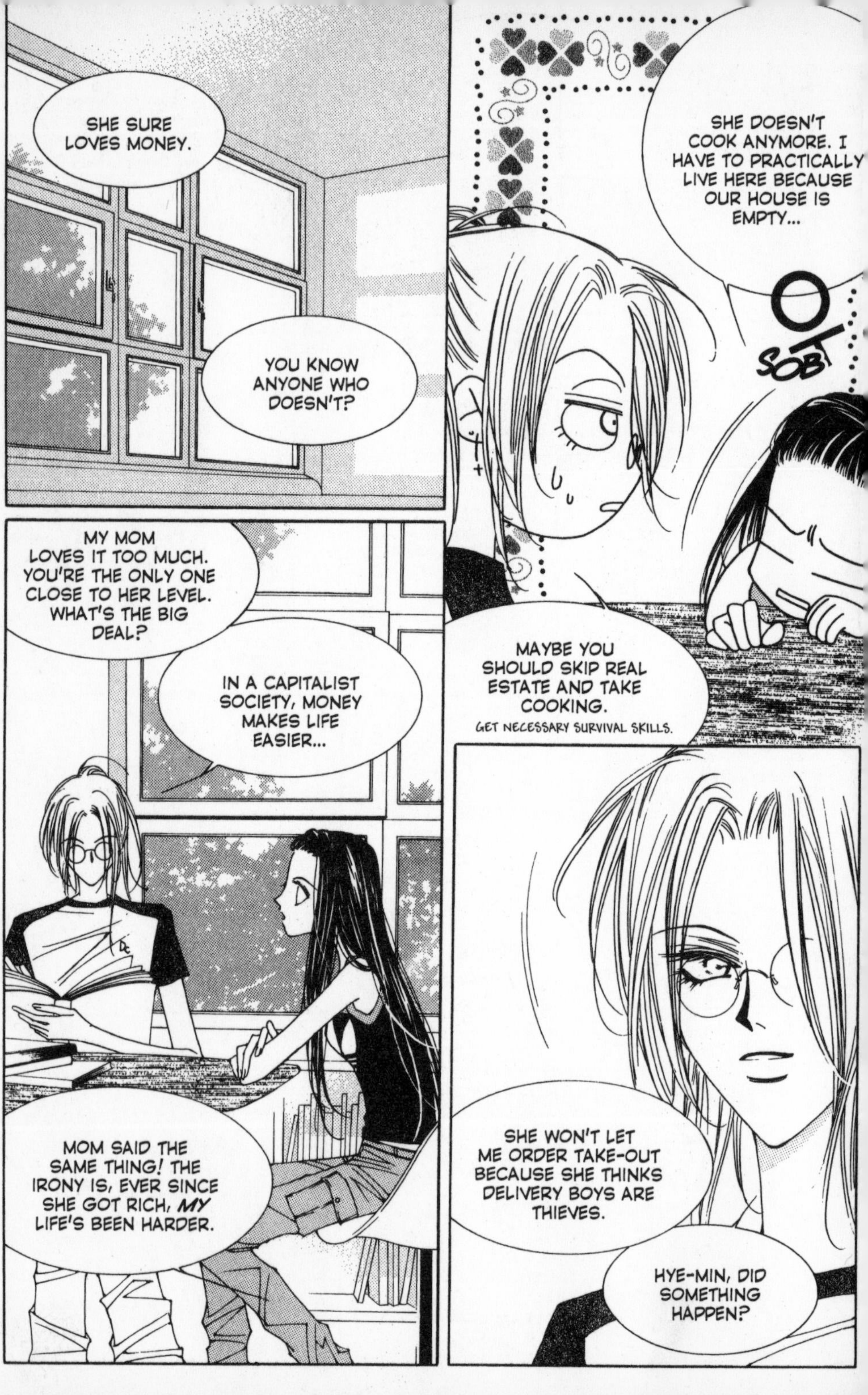
SHE SURE LOVES MONEY.
YOU KNOW ANYONE WHO DOESN'T?
MY MOM LOVES IT TOO MUCH. YOU'RE THE ONLY ONE CLOSE TO HER LEVEL. WHAT'S THE BIG DEAL?
IN A CAPITALIST SOCIETY, MONEY MAKES LIFE EASIER...
MOM SAID THE SAME THING! THE IRONY IS, EVER SINCE SHE GOT RICH, *MY* LIFE'S BEEN HARDER.
SHE DOESN'T COOK ANYMORE. I HAVE TO PRACTICALLY LIVE HERE BECAUSE OUR HOUSE IS EMPTY...
SOB
MAYBE YOU SHOULD SKIP REAL ESTATE AND TAKE COOKING.
GET NECESSARY SURVIVAL SKILLS.
SHE WON'T LET ME ORDER TAKE-OUT BECAUSE SHE THINKS DELIVERY BOYS ARE THIEVES.
HYE-MIN, DID SOMETHING HAPPEN?

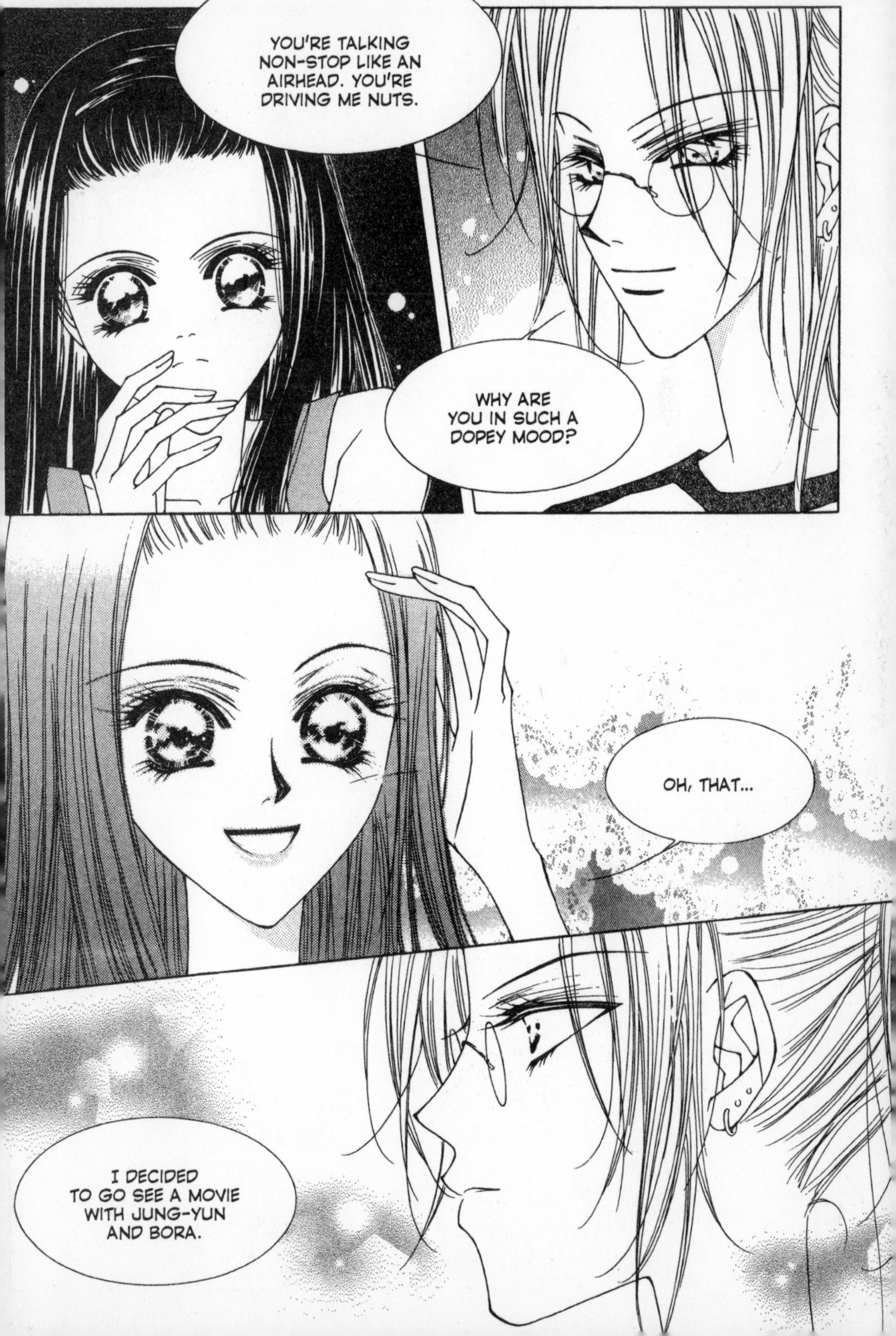
YOU'RE TALKING NON-STOP LIKE AN AIRHEAD. YOU'RE DRIVING ME NUTS.
WHY ARE YOU IN SUCH A DOPEY MOOD?
OH, THAT...
I DECIDED TO GO SEE A MOVIE WITH JUNG-YUN AND BORA.

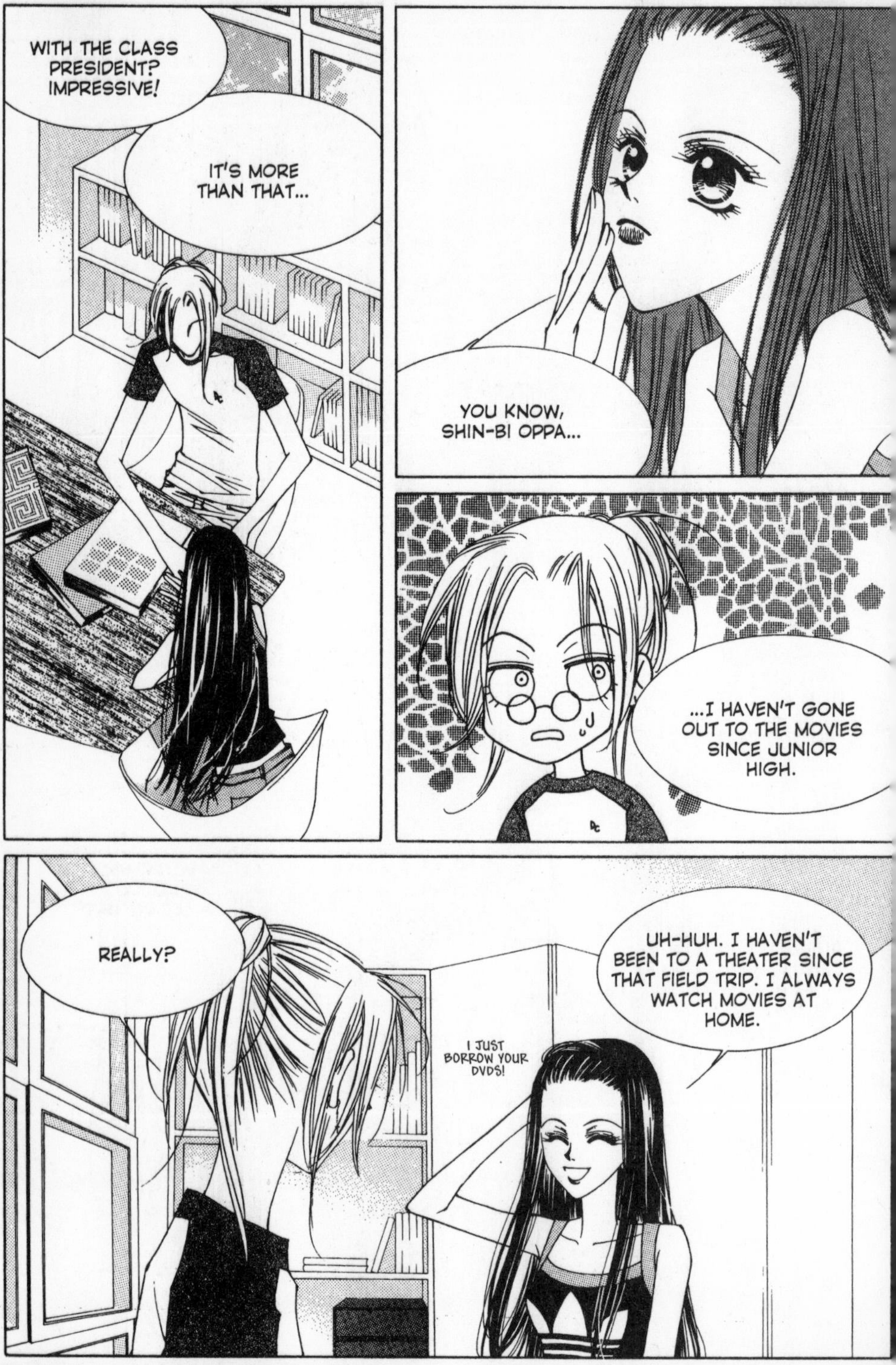
WITH THE CLASS PRESIDENT? IMPRESSIVE!
IT'S MORE THAN THAT...
YOU KNOW, SHIN-BI OPPA...
...I HAVEN'T GONE OUT TO THE MOVIES SINCE JUNIOR HIGH.
REALLY?
UH-HUH. I HAVEN'T BEEN TO A THEATER SINCE THAT FIELD TRIP. I ALWAYS WATCH MOVIES AT HOME.
I JUST BORROW YOUR DVDS!

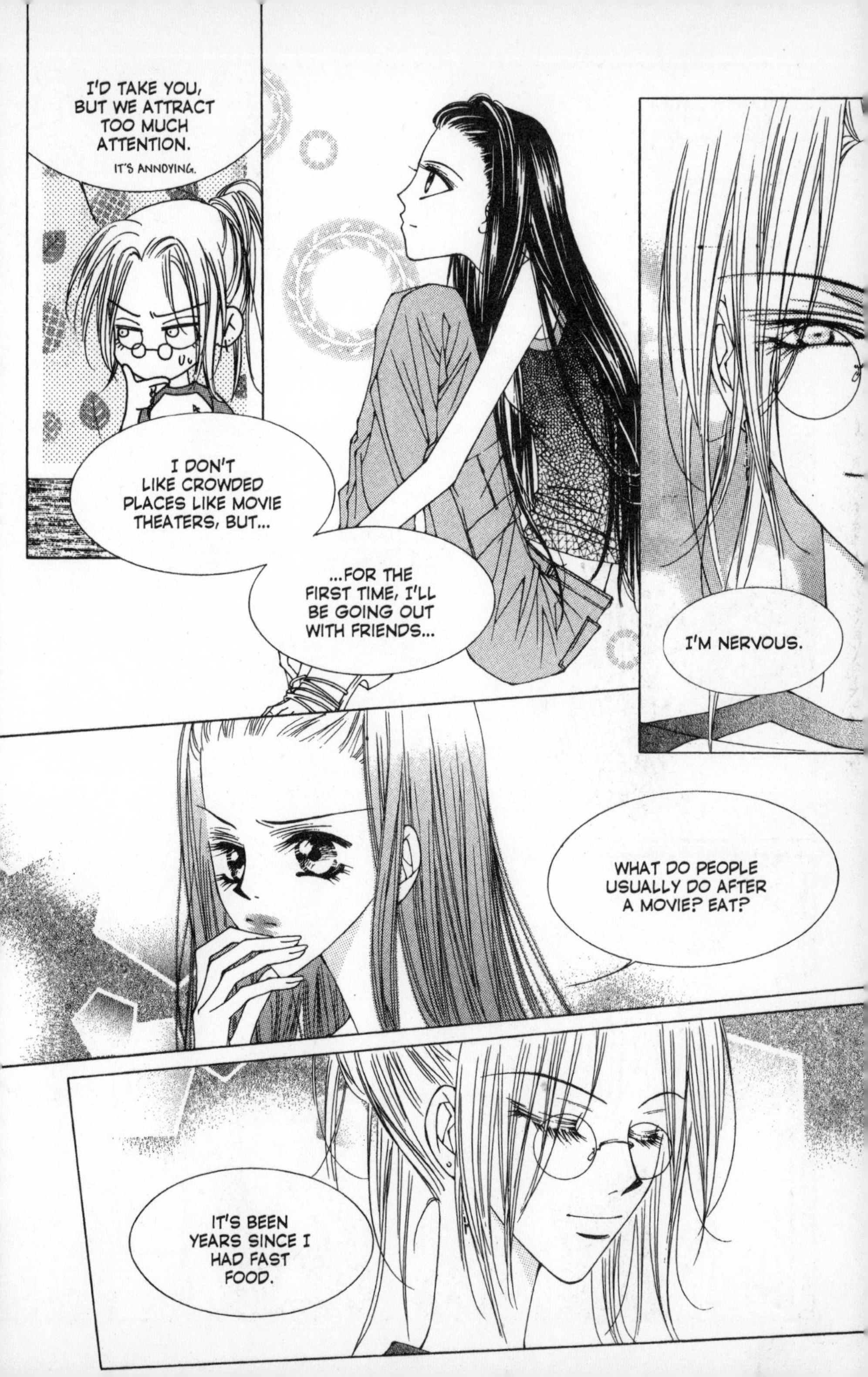
I'D TAKE YOU, BUT WE ATTRACT TOO MUCH ATTENTION.
IT'S ANNOYING.
I DON'T LIKE CROWDED PLACES LIKE MOVIE THEATERS, BUT...
...FOR THE FIRST TIME, I'LL BE GOING OUT WITH FRIENDS...
I'M NERVOUS.
WHAT DO PEOPLE USUALLY DO AFTER A MOVIE? EAT?
IT'S BEEN YEARS SINCE I HAD FAST FOOD.

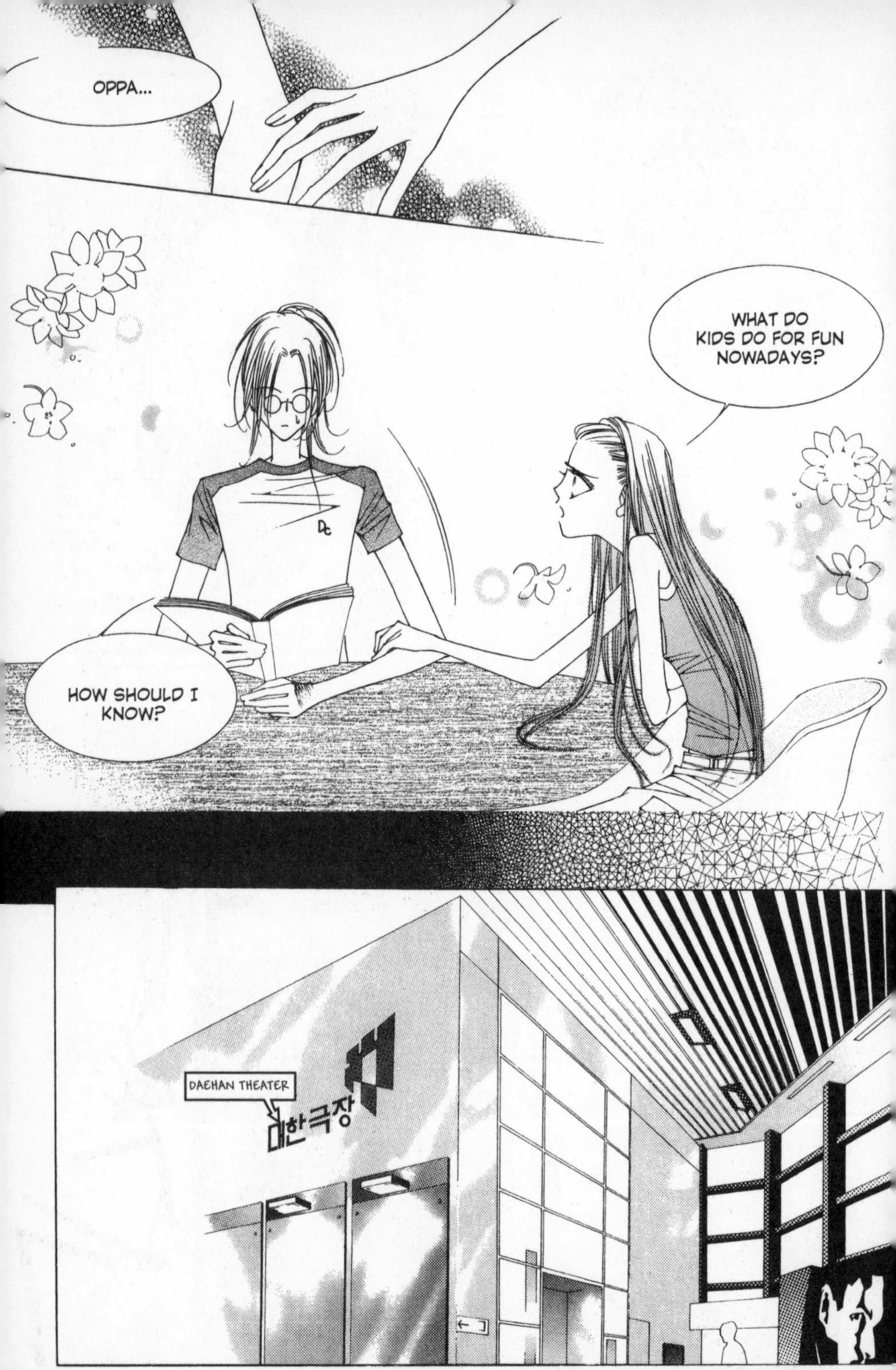
OPPA...
WHAT DO KIDS DO FOR FUN NOWADAYS?
HOW SHOULD I KNOW?
DAEHAN THEATER
대한극장

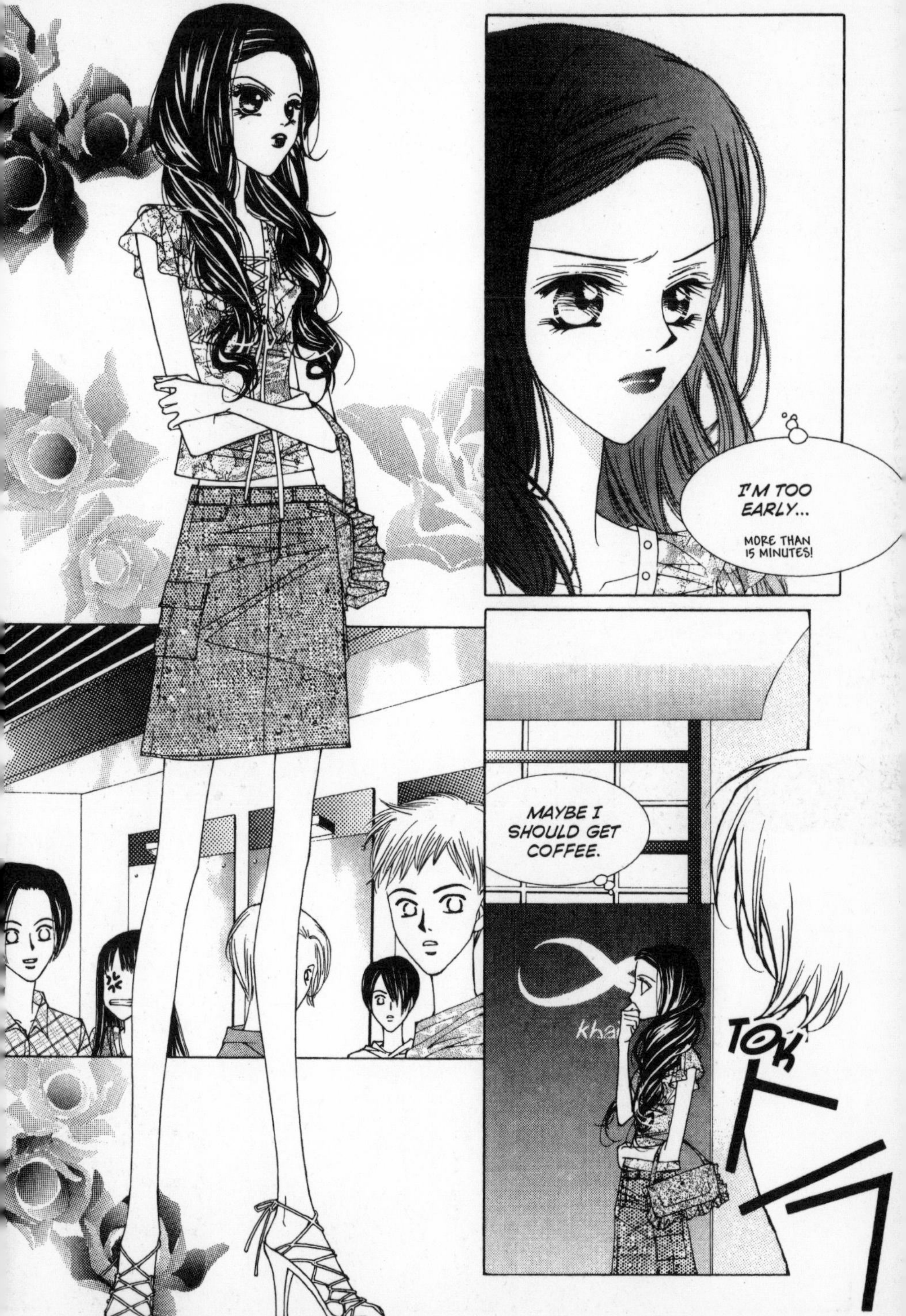
I'M TOO EARLY...
MORE THAN 15 MINUTES!
MAYBE I SHOULD GET COFFEE.
khai
TOK

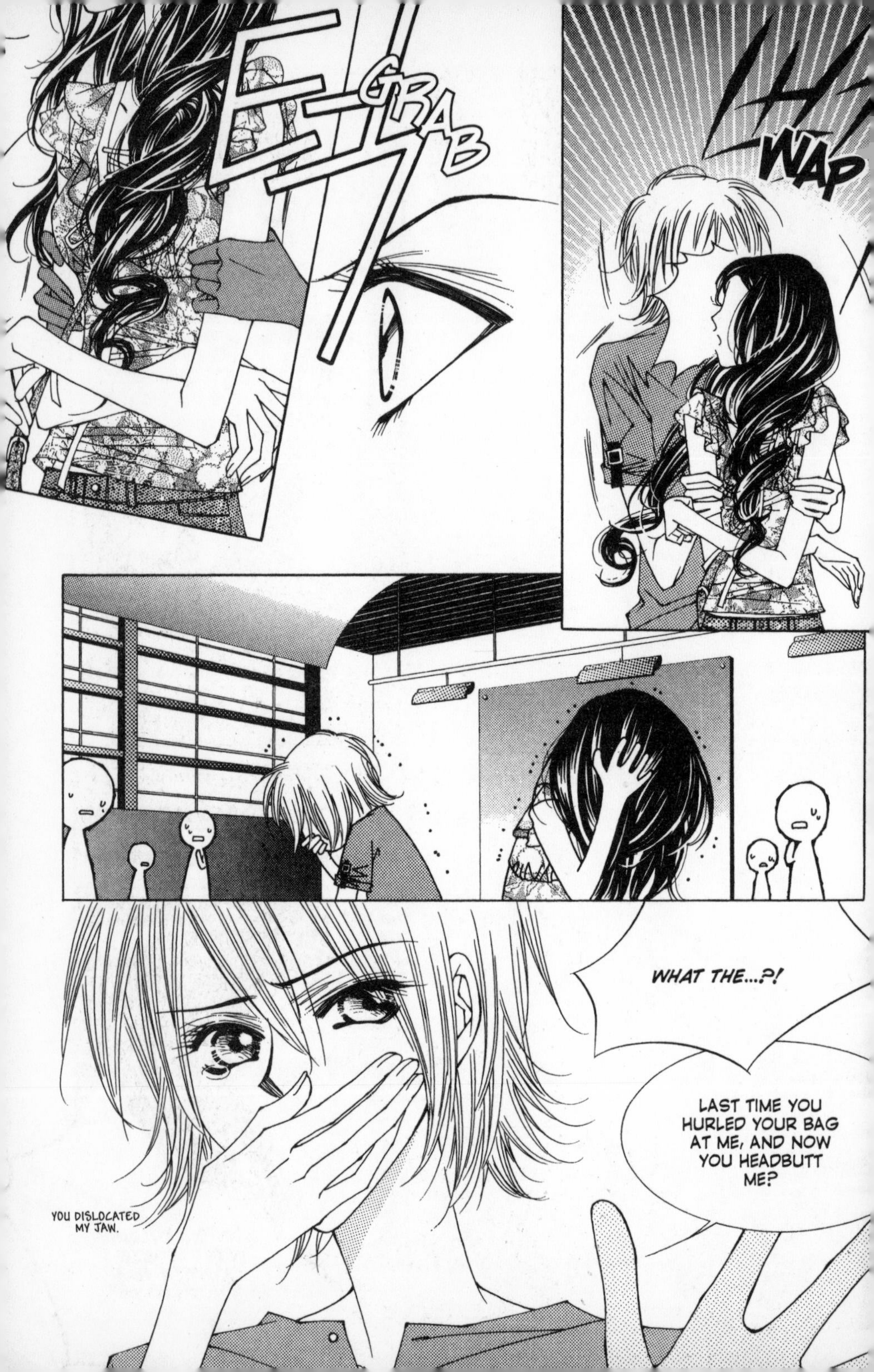
GRAB
WAP
WHAT THE...?!
LAST TIME YOU HURLED YOUR BAG AT ME, AND NOW YOU HEADBUTT ME?
YOU DISLOCATED MY JAW.

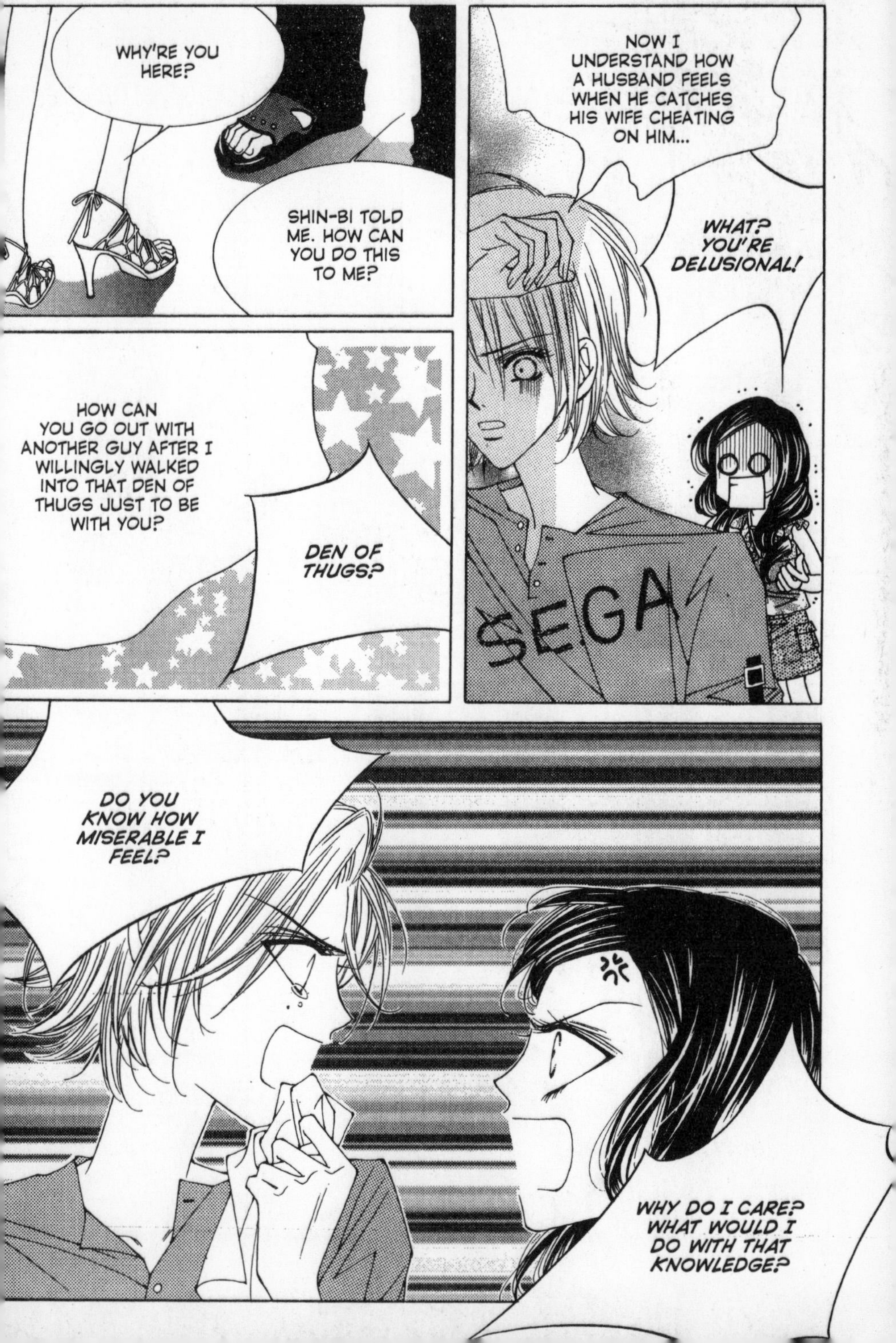
WHY'RE YOU HERE?
SHIN-BI TOLD ME. HOW CAN YOU DO THIS TO ME?
HOW CAN YOU GO OUT WITH ANOTHER GUY AFTER I WILLINGLY WALKED INTO THAT DEN OF THUGS JUST TO BE WITH YOU?
DEN OF THUGS?
NOW I UNDERSTAND HOW A HUSBAND FEELS WHEN HE CATCHES HIS WIFE CHEATING ON HIM...
WHAT? YOU'RE DELUSIONAL!
SEGA
DO YOU KNOW HOW MISERABLE I FEEL?
WHY DO I CARE? WHAT WOULD I DO WITH THAT KNOWLEDGE?

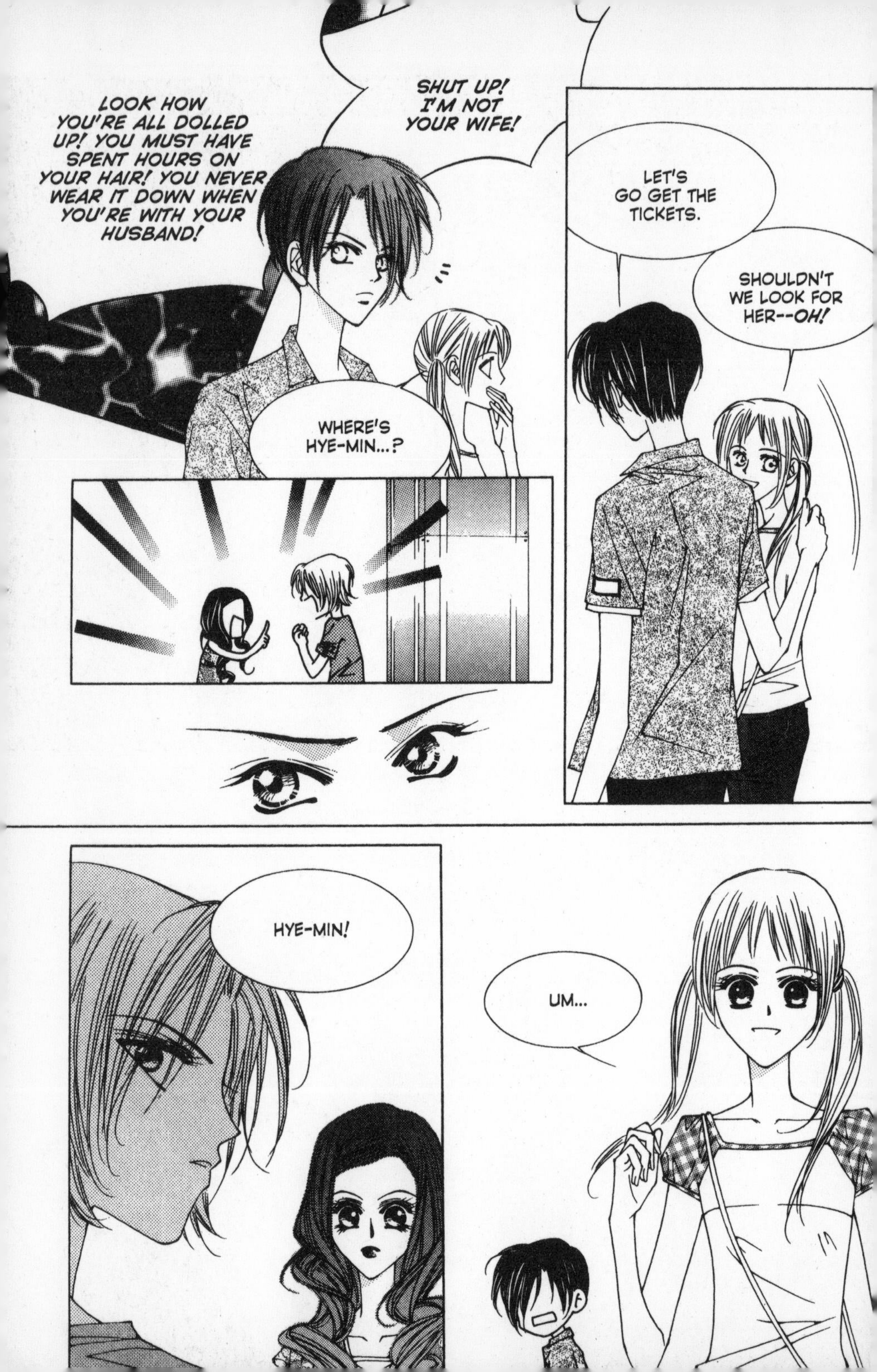
LOOK HOW YOU'RE ALL DOLLED UP! YOU MUST HAVE SPENT HOURS ON YOUR HAIR! YOU NEVER WEAR IT DOWN WHEN YOU'RE WITH YOUR HUSBAND!
SHUT UP! I'M NOT YOUR WIFE!
WHERE'S HYE-MIN...?
LET'S GO GET THE TICKETS.
SHOULDN'T WE LOOK FOR HER--OH!
HYE-MIN!
UM...

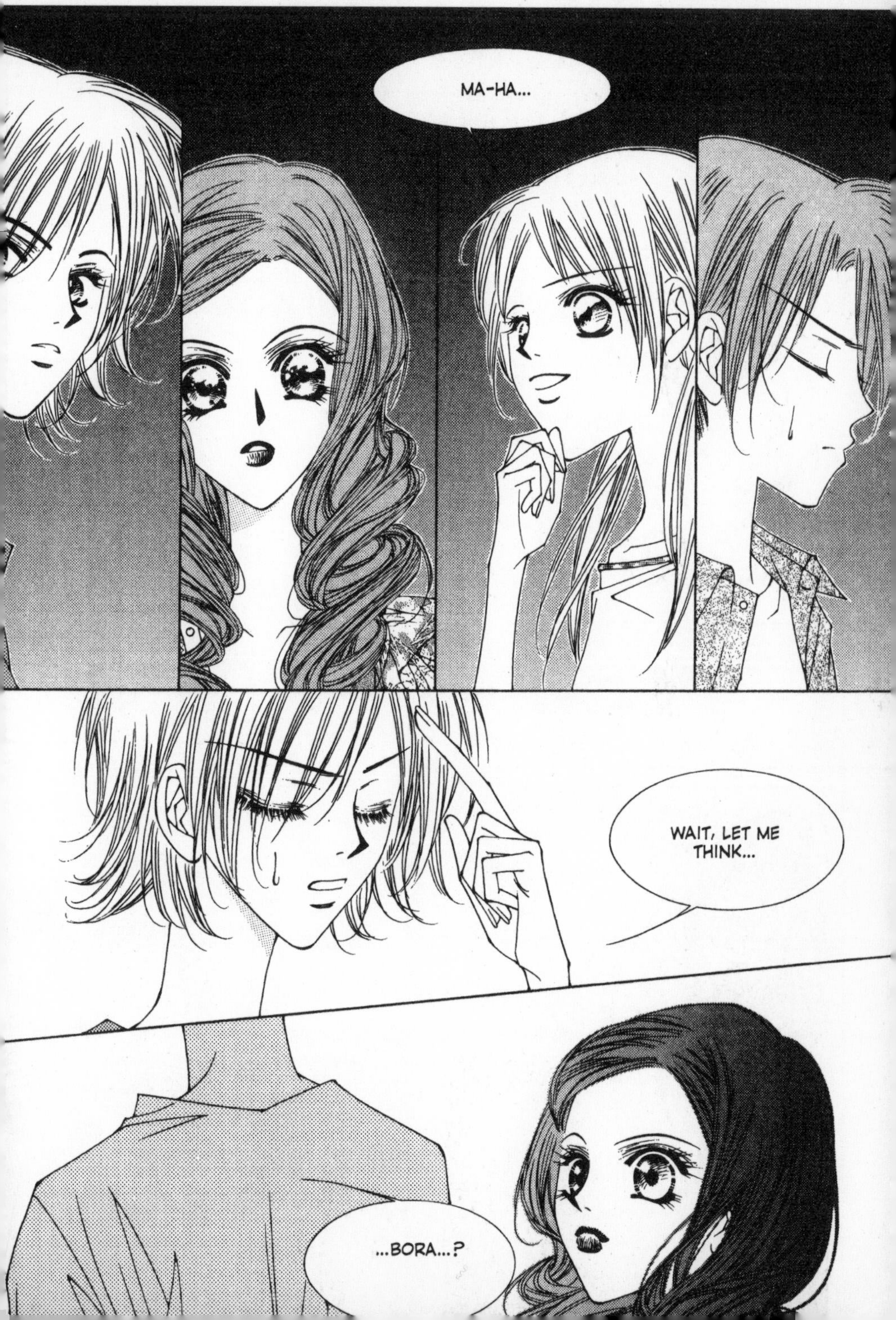
MA-HA...
WAIT, LET ME THINK...
...BORA...?

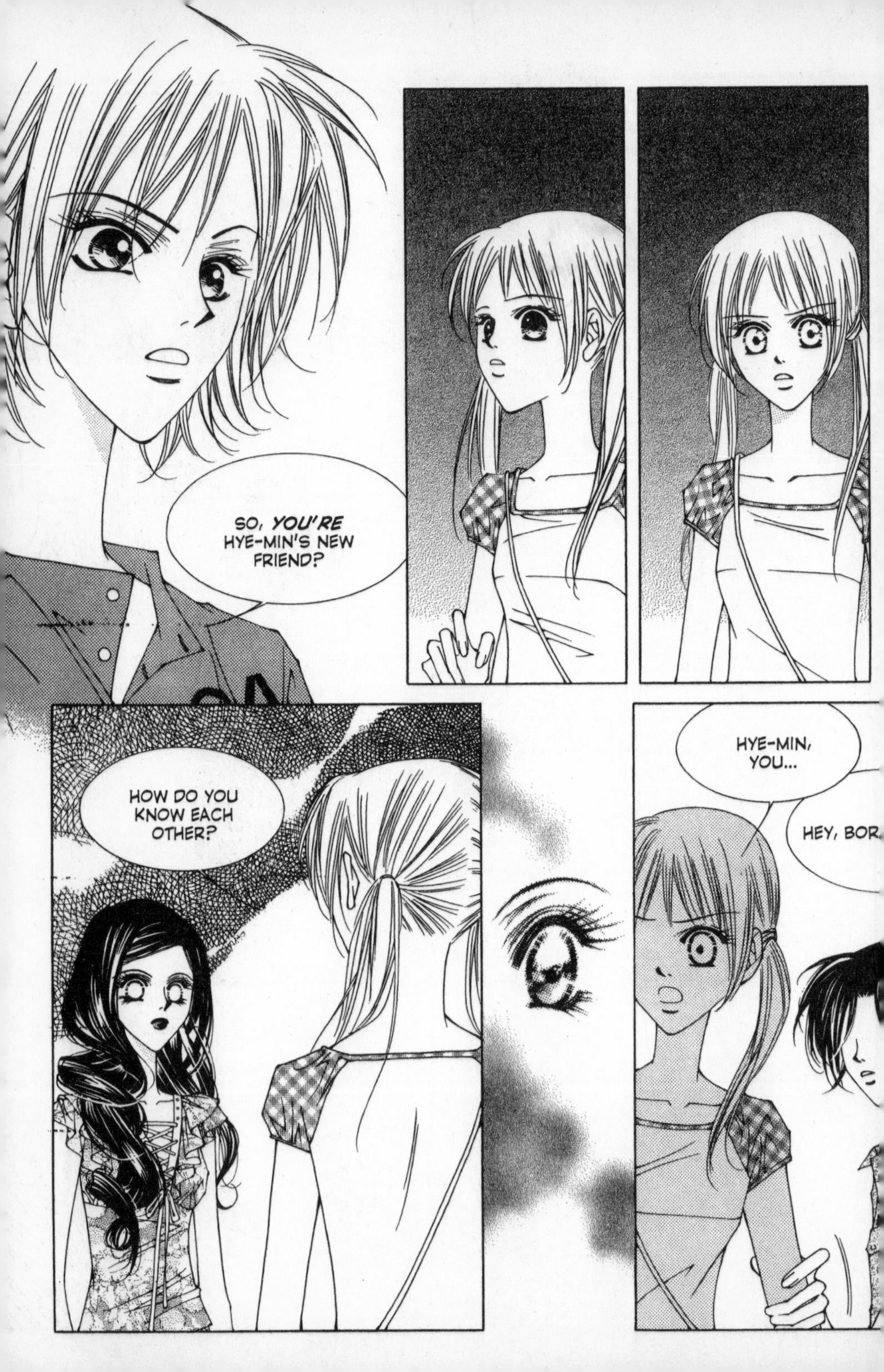
SO, *YOU'RE* HYE-MIN'S NEW FRIEND?
HOW DO YOU KNOW EACH OTHER?
HYE-MIN, YOU...
HEY, BOR

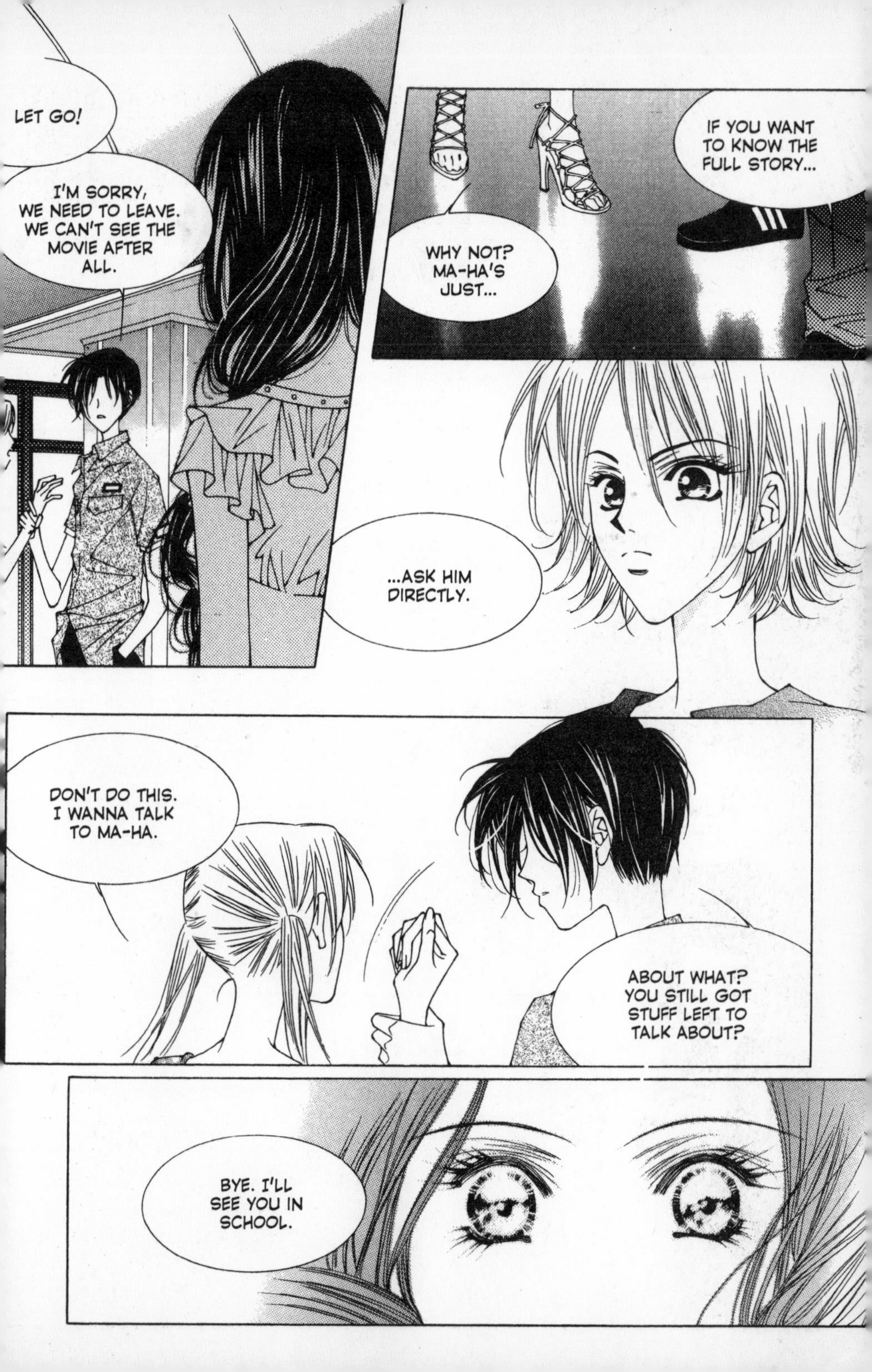
LET GO!
I'M SORRY, WE NEED TO LEAVE. WE CAN'T SEE THE MOVIE AFTER ALL.
WHY NOT? MA-HA'S JUST...
IF YOU WANT TO KNOW THE FULL STORY...
...ASK HIM DIRECTLY.
DON'T DO THIS. I WANNA TALK TO MA-HA.
ABOUT WHAT? YOU STILL GOT STUFF LEFT TO TALK ABOUT?
BYE. I'LL SEE YOU IN SCHOOL.

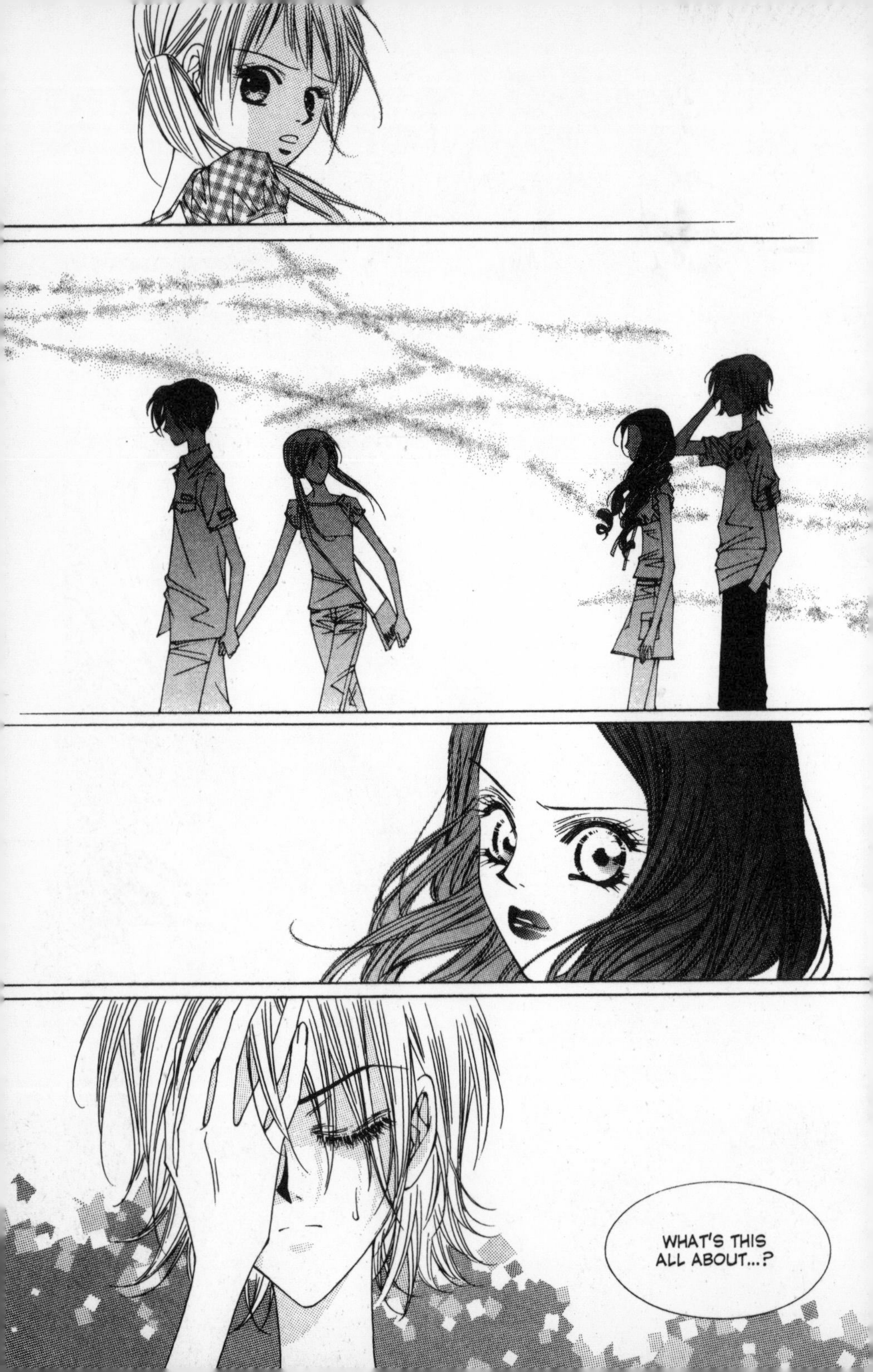
WHAT'S THIS
ALL ABOUT...?

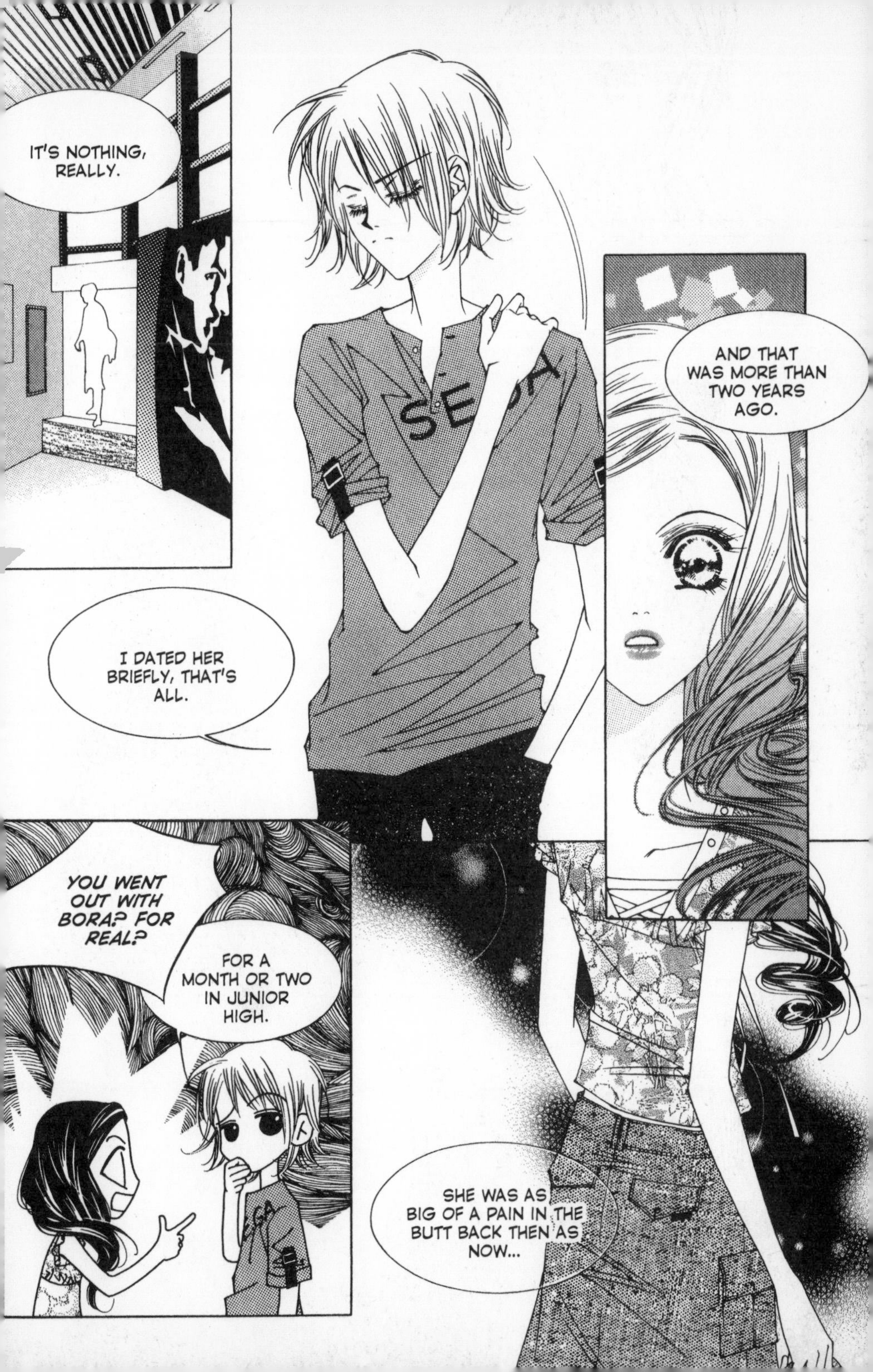
IT'S NOTHING, REALLY.
I DATED HER BRIEFLY, THAT'S ALL.
AND THAT WAS MORE THAN TWO YEARS AGO.
YOU WENT OUT WITH BORA? FOR REAL?
FOR A MONTH OR TWO IN JUNIOR HIGH.
SHE WAS AS BIG OF A PAIN IN THE BUTT BACK THEN AS NOW...

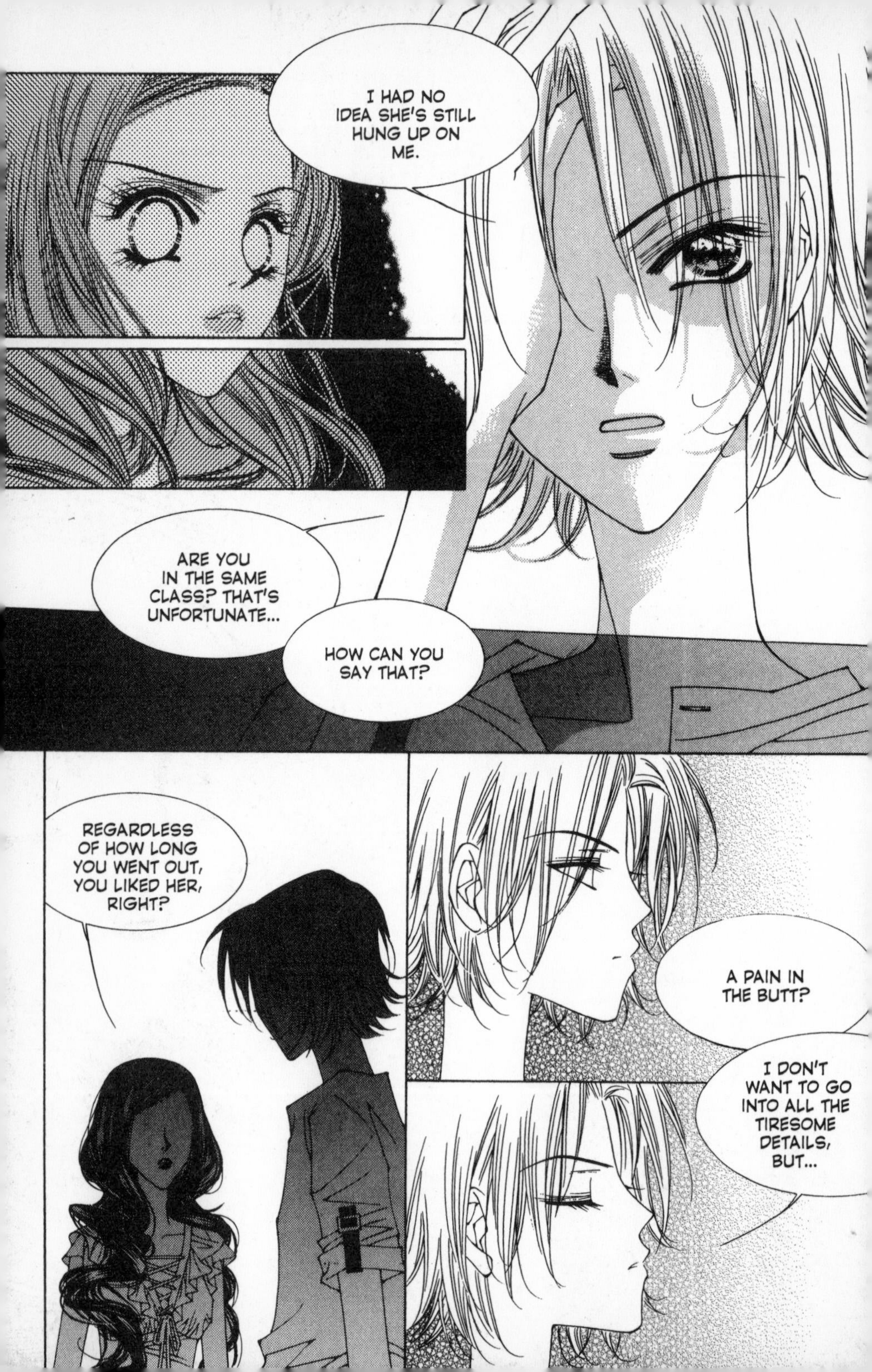
I HAD NO IDEA SHE'S STILL HUNG UP ON ME.
ARE YOU IN THE SAME CLASS? THAT'S UNFORTUNATE...
HOW CAN YOU SAY THAT?
REGARDLESS OF HOW LONG YOU WENT OUT, YOU LIKED HER, RIGHT?
A PAIN IN THE BUTT?
I DON'T WANT TO GO INTO ALL THE TIRESOME DETAILS, BUT...

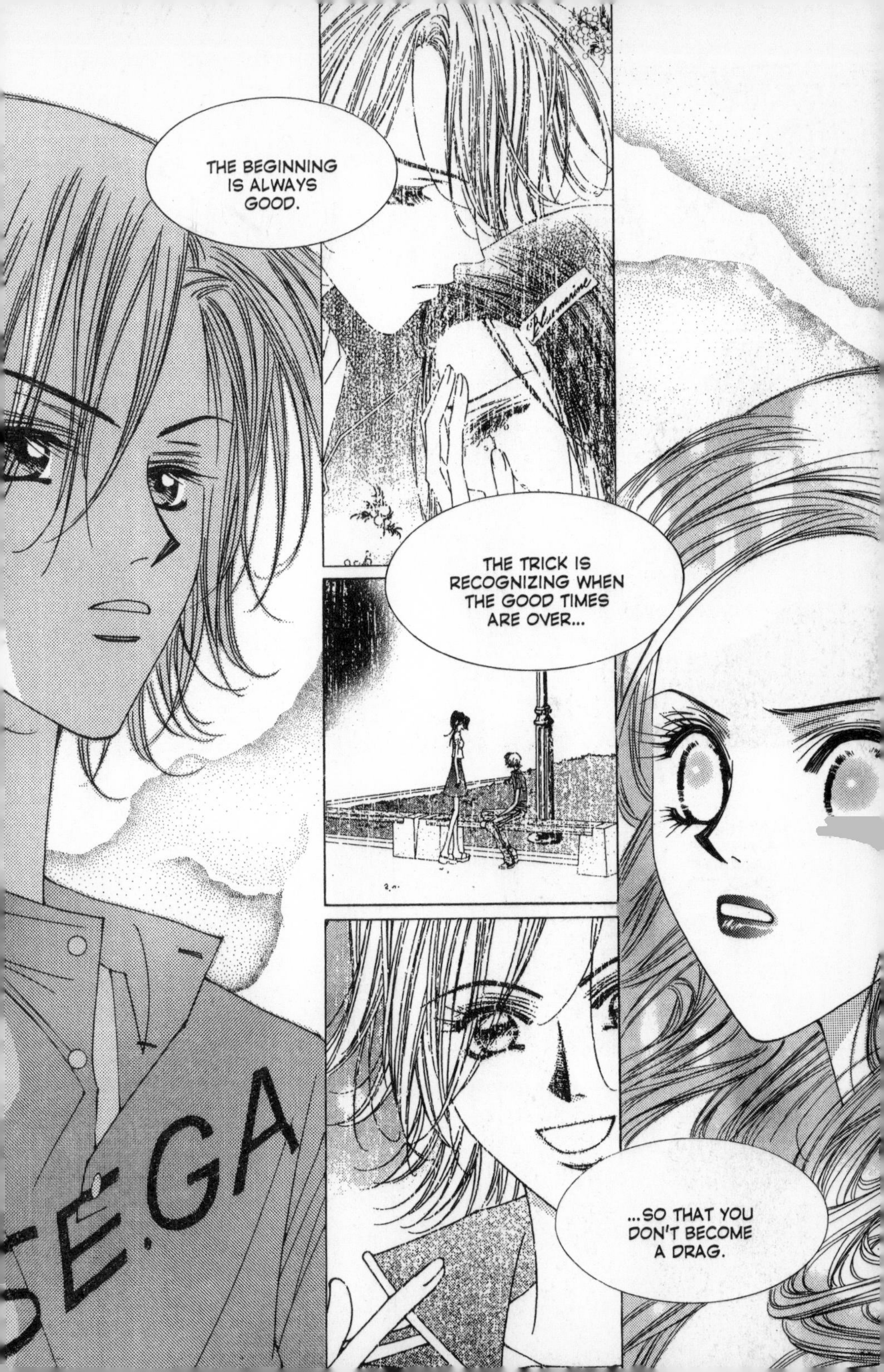
THE BEGINNING IS ALWAYS GOOD.
THE TRICK IS RECOGNIZING WHEN THE GOOD TIMES ARE OVER...
...SO THAT YOU DON'T BECOME A DRAG.
SE.GA

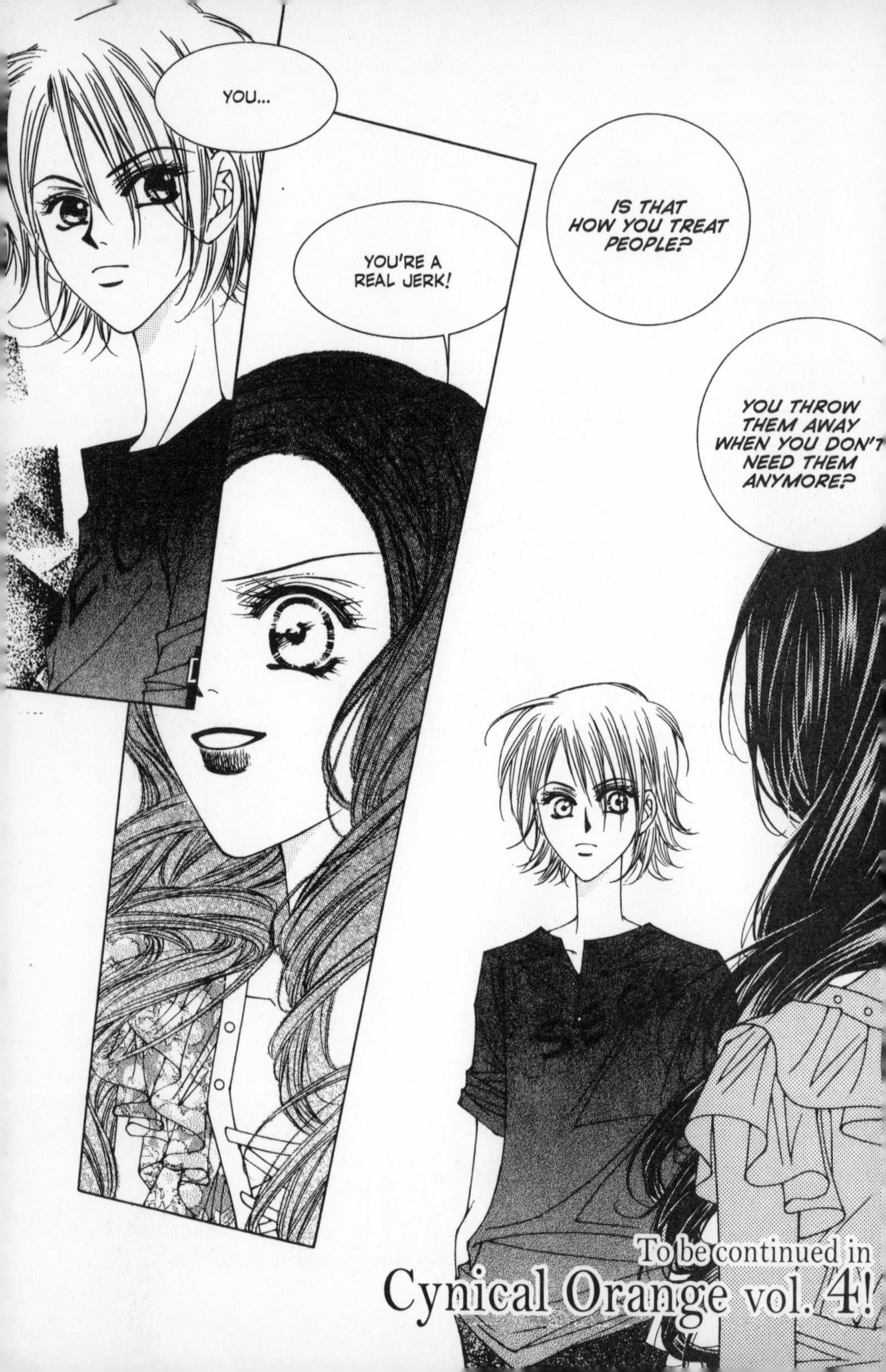
YOU...
YOU'RE A REAL JERK!
IS THAT HOW YOU TREAT PEOPLE?
YOU THROW THEM AWAY WHEN YOU DON'T NEED THEM ANYMORE?
To be continued in
Cynical Orange vol. 4!

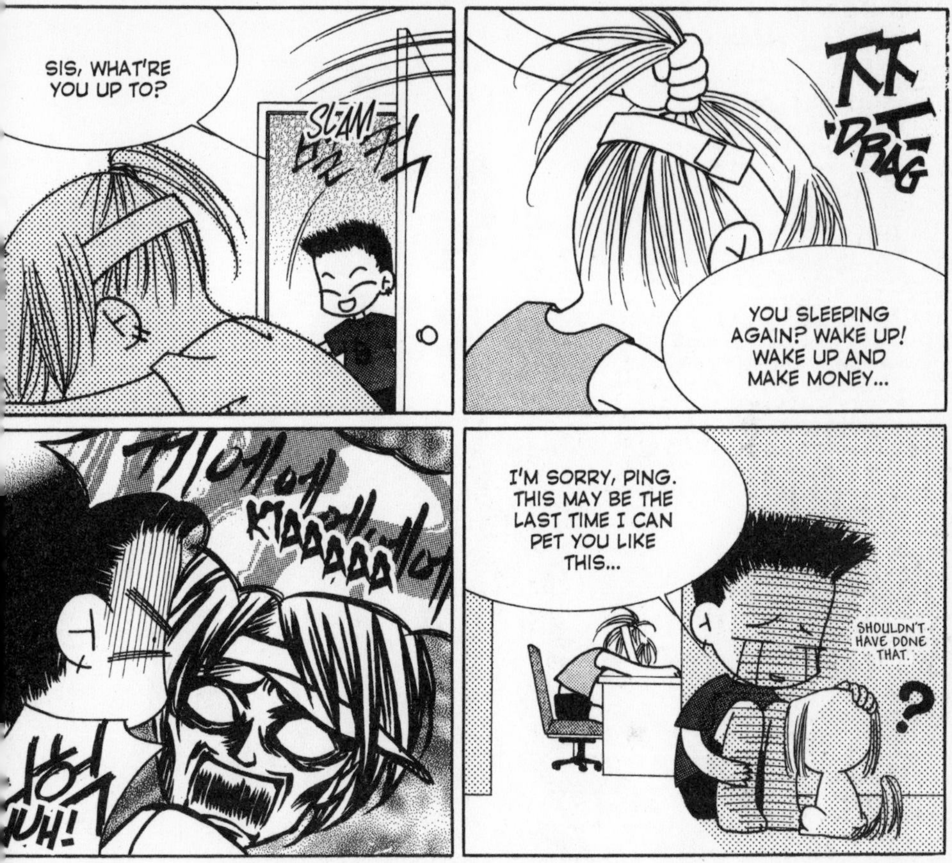
SIS, WHAT'RE YOU UP TO?
SLAM
DRAG
YOU SLEEPING AGAIN? WAKE UP! WAKE UP AND MAKE MONEY...
KYAAAAA
UH!
I'M SORRY, PING. THIS MAY BE THE LAST TIME I CAN PET YOU LIKE THIS...
SHOULDN'T HAVE DONE THAT.
?

=BONUS TRACK=

LET THE SLEEPING DOGS SLEEP!

WOMEN'S CLOTHING DURING T'ANG DYNASTY

ONE OF THE MOST EXTRAVAGANT STYLES IN THE HISTORY OF WOMEN'S WEAR IN CHINA. IN THE ENTIRE HISTORY OF THE COUNTRY, THERE ISN'T A STYLE OF DRESS MORE PROVOCATIVE, MORE LAVISH, OR MORE BOLD THAN THIS ONE. WOMEN SIMPLY DID AWAY WITH THE TOP AND WALKED AROUND WITH A FLOWING JACKET OR A WRAP DRAPED OVER THEIR NAKED SHOULDERS! (T'ANG FASHION, PLEASE COME BACK!) HAIR ORNAMENTS AND ACCESSORIES WERE ALSO HIGHLY DEVELOPED--THE CRAFTSMANSHIP AND THE METICULOUS ATTENTION TO DETAIL WERE EXCEPTIONAL. AH...I'D LOVE TO SEE IT WITH MY OWN EYES! SOMEONE INVENT A TIME MACHINE!

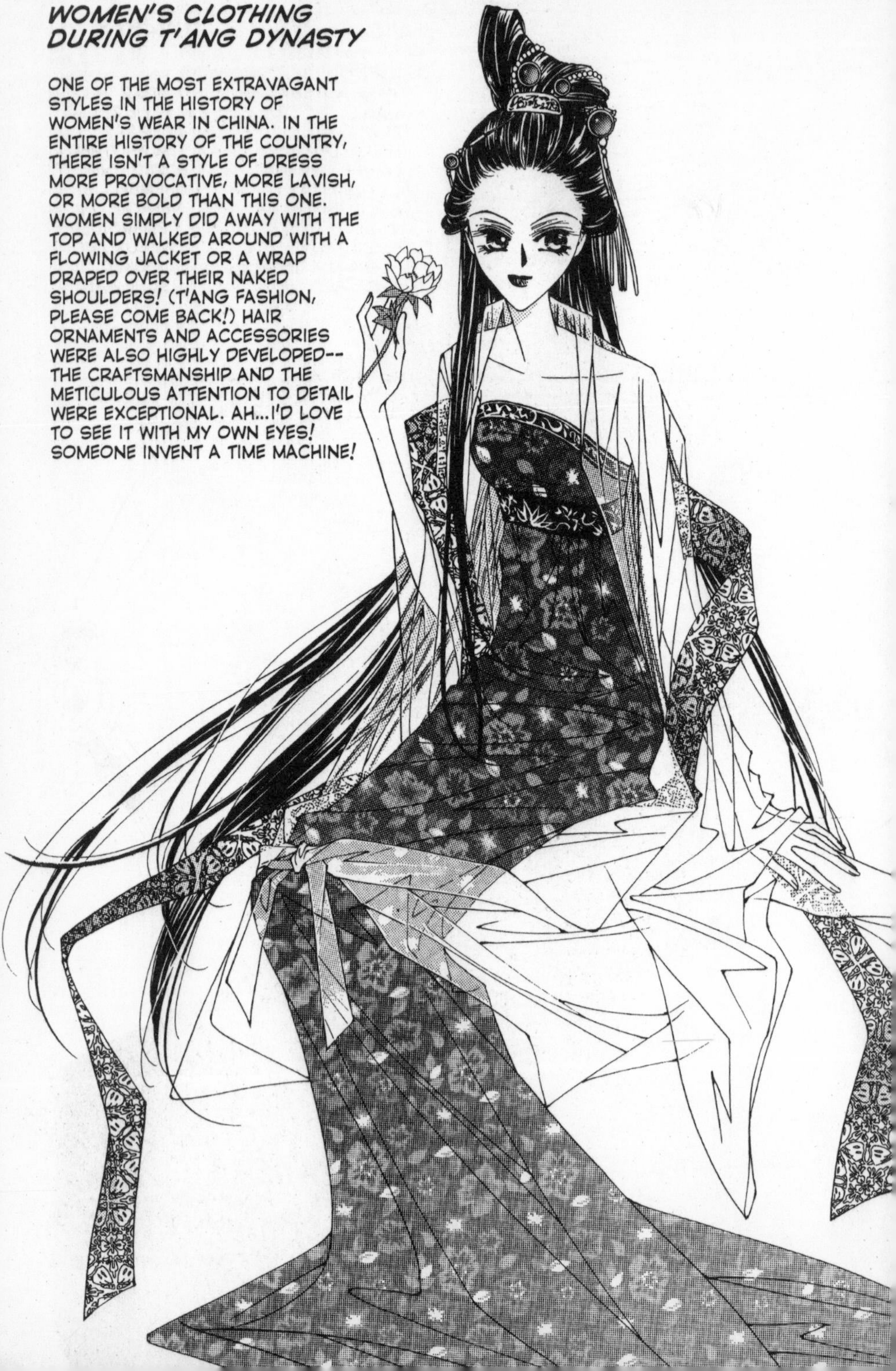

MILITARY UNIFORM DURING T'ANG DYNASTY

ARMORED UNIFORMS WERE AN IMPORTANT PART OF MEN'S WEAR IN CHINA DURING THE ERA. AFTER ALL, WE'RE TALKING ABOUT A COUNTRY THAT ENGAGED IN ONE WAR AFTER ANOTHER. DURING THIS PERIOD, ARMORED UNIFORMS BECAME HIGHLY AESTHETIC, EMBELLISHED WITH GOLD AND SILVER. EVEN THE UNDER GARMENTS WERE LAVISHLY EMBROIDERED. ONE CAN ONLY IMAGINE HOW LUXURIOUS THE WARRIORS MUST HAVE LOOKED...IN A WORD, THEY WERE VERY COOL. I WANT TO SEE IT ALL!!

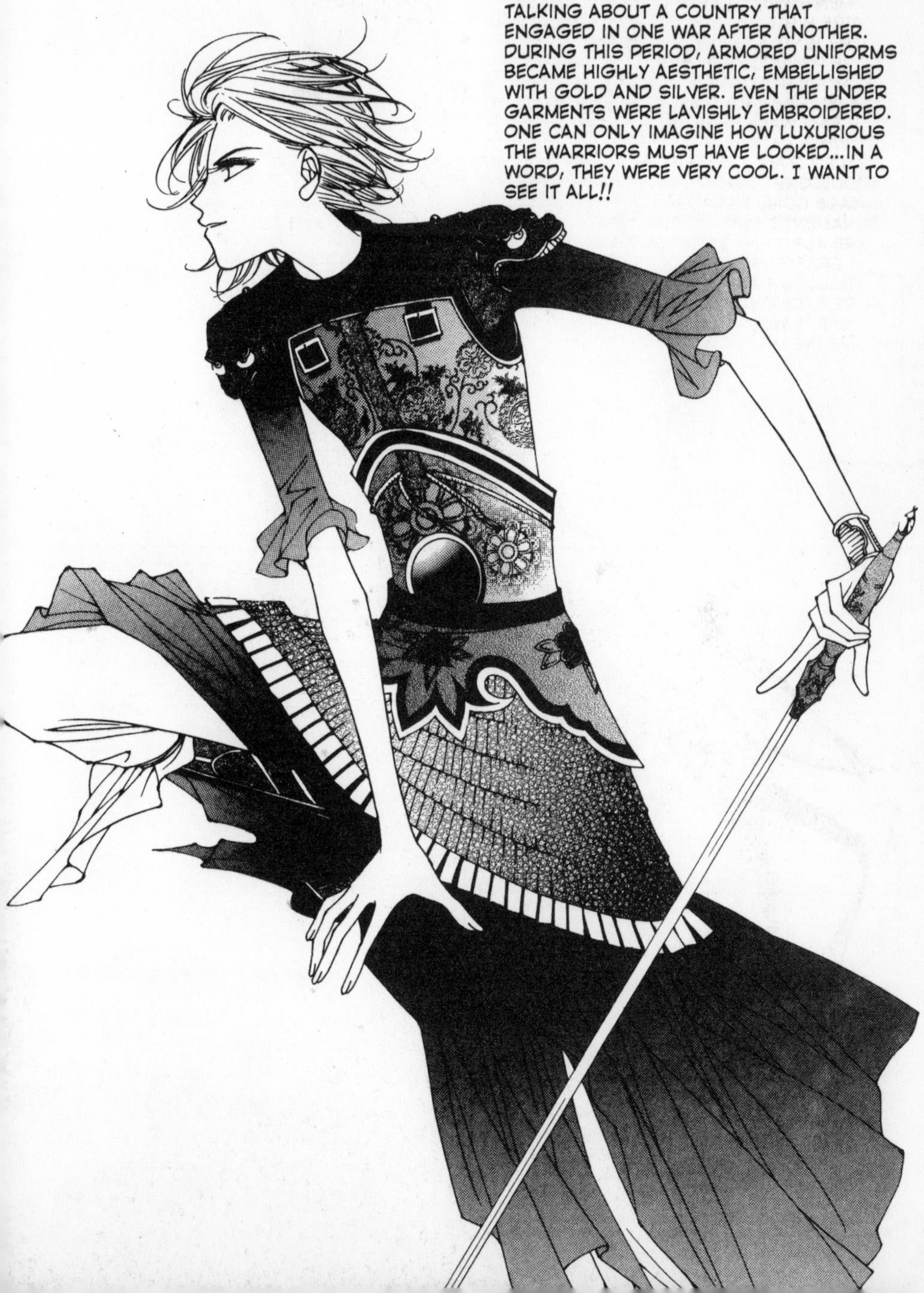

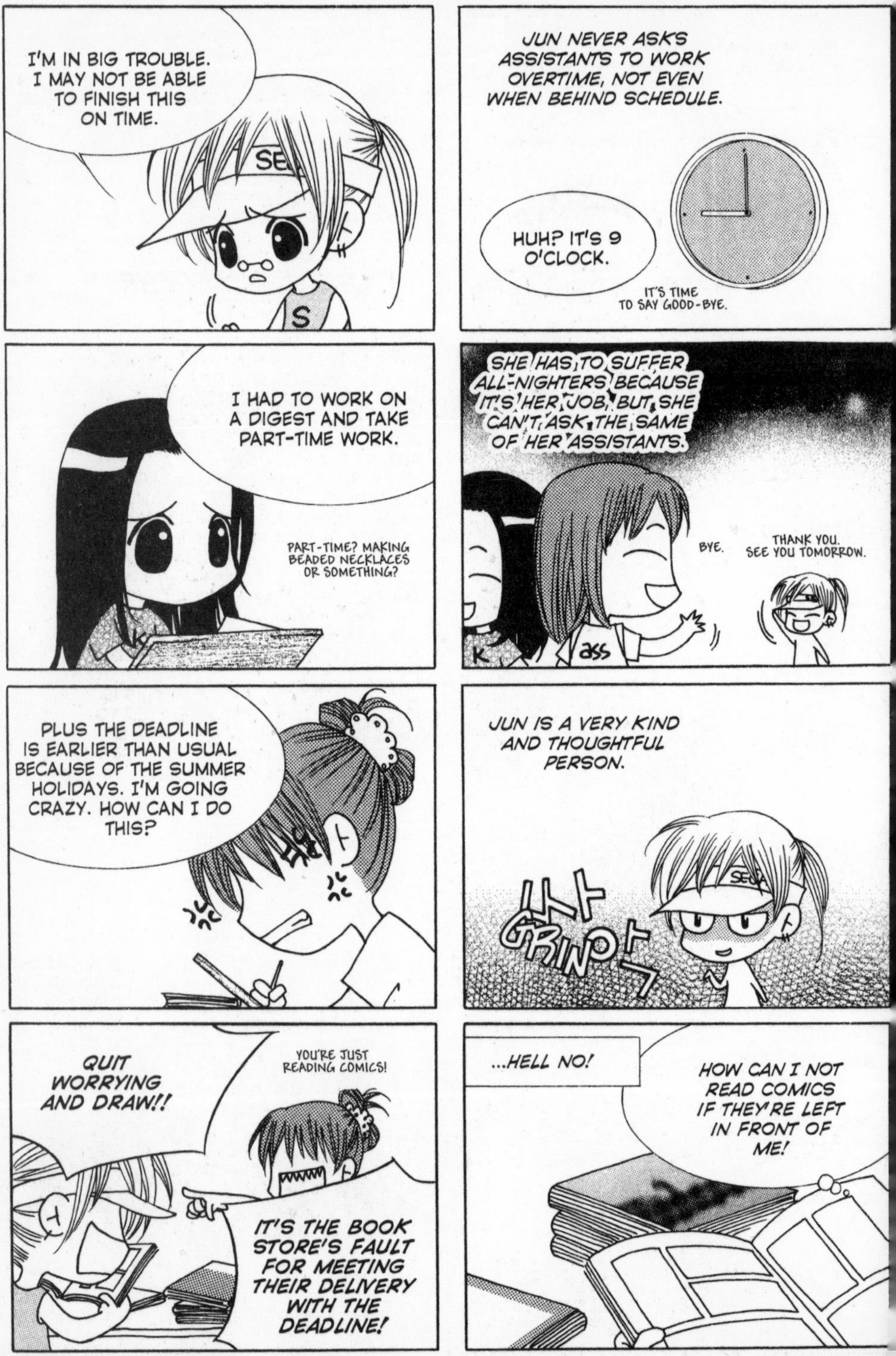
I'M IN BIG TROUBLE. I MAY NOT BE ABLE TO FINISH THIS ON TIME.
JUN NEVER ASKS ASSISTANTS TO WORK OVERTIME, NOT EVEN WHEN BEHIND SCHEDULE.
HUH? IT'S 9 O'CLOCK.
IT'S TIME TO SAY GOOD-BYE.
I HAD TO WORK ON A DIGEST AND TAKE PART-TIME WORK.
PART-TIME? MAKING BEADED NECKLACES OR SOMETHING?
SHE HAS TO SUFFER ALL-NIGHTERS BECAUSE IT'S HER JOB, BUT SHE CAN'T ASK THE SAME OF HER ASSISTANTS.
BYE.
THANK YOU. SEE YOU TOMORROW.
PLUS THE DEADLINE IS EARLIER THAN USUAL BECAUSE OF THE SUMMER HOLIDAYS. I'M GOING CRAZY. HOW CAN I DO THIS?
JUN IS A VERY KIND AND THOUGHTFUL PERSON.
GRIN
QUIT WORRYING AND DRAW!!
YOU'RE JUST READING COMICS!
IT'S THE BOOK STORE'S FAULT FOR MEETING THEIR DELIVERY WITH THE DEADLINE!
...HELL NO!
HOW CAN I NOT READ COMICS IF THEY'RE LEFT IN FRONT OF ME!

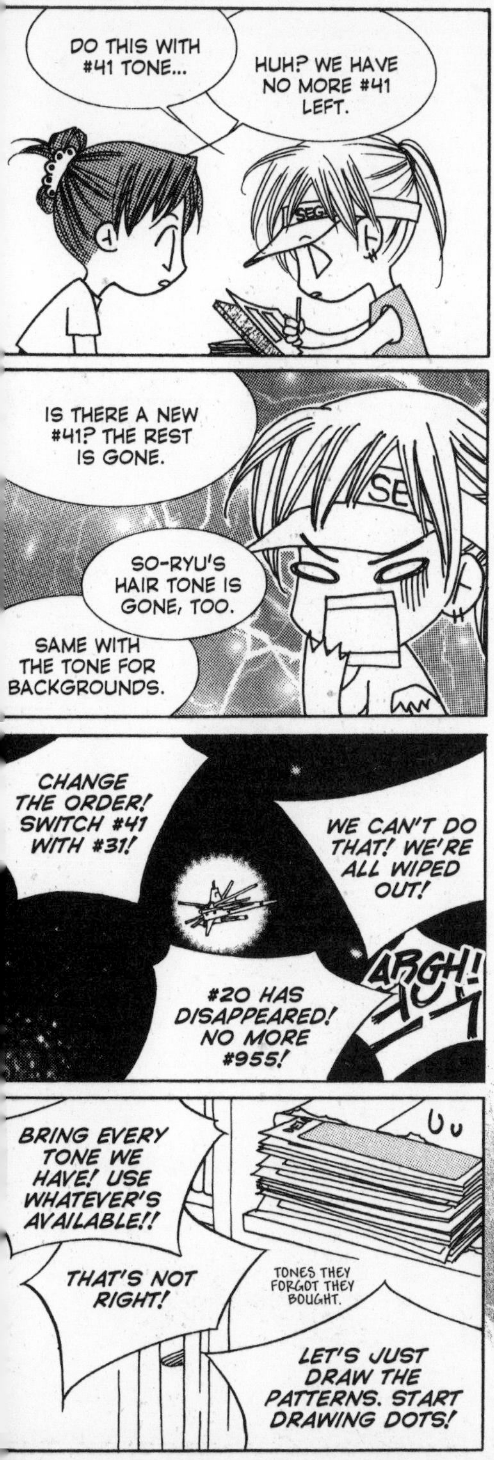
DO THIS WITH #41 TONE...
HUH? WE HAVE NO MORE #41 LEFT.
IS THERE A NEW #41? THE REST IS GONE.
SO-RYU'S HAIR TONE IS GONE, TOO.
SAME WITH THE TONE FOR BACKGROUNDS.
CHANGE THE ORDER! SWITCH #41 WITH #31!
WE CAN'T DO THAT! WE'RE ALL WIPED OUT!
ARGH!
#20 HAS DISAPPEARED! NO MORE #955!
BRING EVERY TONE WE HAVE! USE WHATEVER'S AVAILABLE!!
THAT'S NOT RIGHT!
TONES THEY FORGOT THEY BOUGHT.
LET'S JUST DRAW THE PATTERNS. START DRAWING DOTS!

WORDS FROM THE CREATOR

THIS IS MY 10TH BOOK PUBLISHED. (SO SHOCKING!) I HAVE DRAWN 1800 PAGES WORTH OF MANHWA. (EVEN MORE SHOCKING!) SOMEHOW, PUBLISHING ONE OR TWO DIGESTS CAN BE DONE THROUGH SHEER CHANCE, BUT PUBLISHING OVER TEN BOOKS MEANS YOU'RE DOING SOMETHING RIGHT. IN MY CASE, THIS IS POSSIBLE BECAUSE OF THE READERS WHO BUY MY COLLECTIONS. I THOUGHT SAYING, "OH, THIS IS THE 10TH BOOK." WOULD ONLY BE POSSIBLE IN SOME FANTASY LIFE. THANK YOU SO MUCH TO ALL THE FOLKS WHO HELPED ME ACCOMPLISH MY DREAM. I'LL DO MY BEST TO GET TO WHERE I CAN SAY, "THIS IS MY 20TH BOOK." I'M SO EXCITED TO SEE WHAT MY 20TH WILL BE AND WHAT IT WILL LOOK LIKE. PLEASE KEEP READING MY WORK.

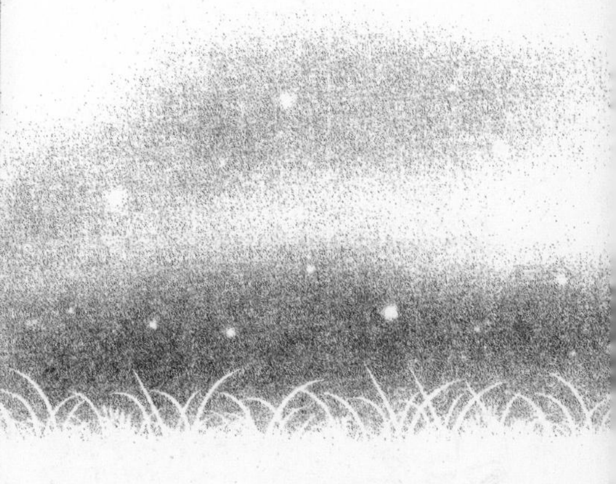

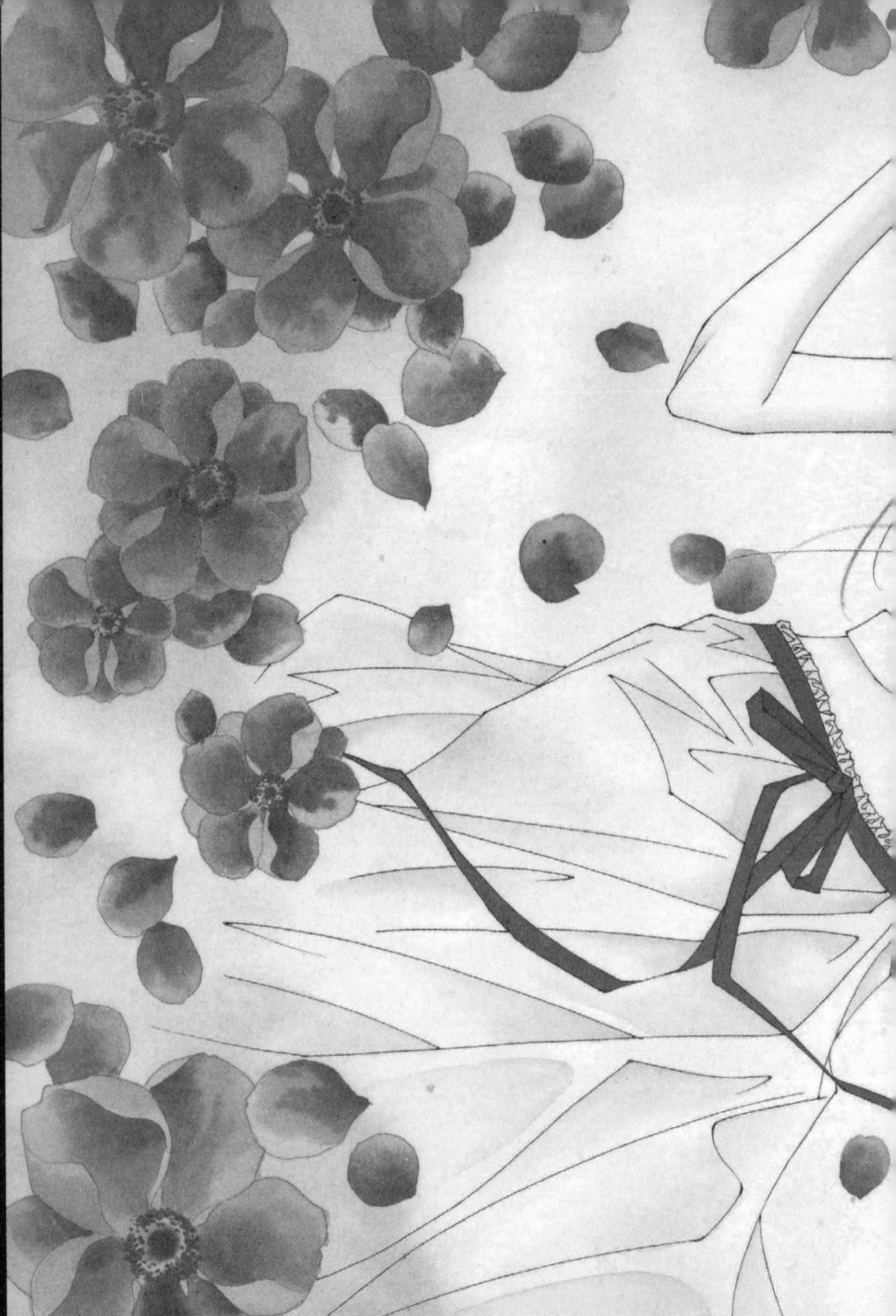

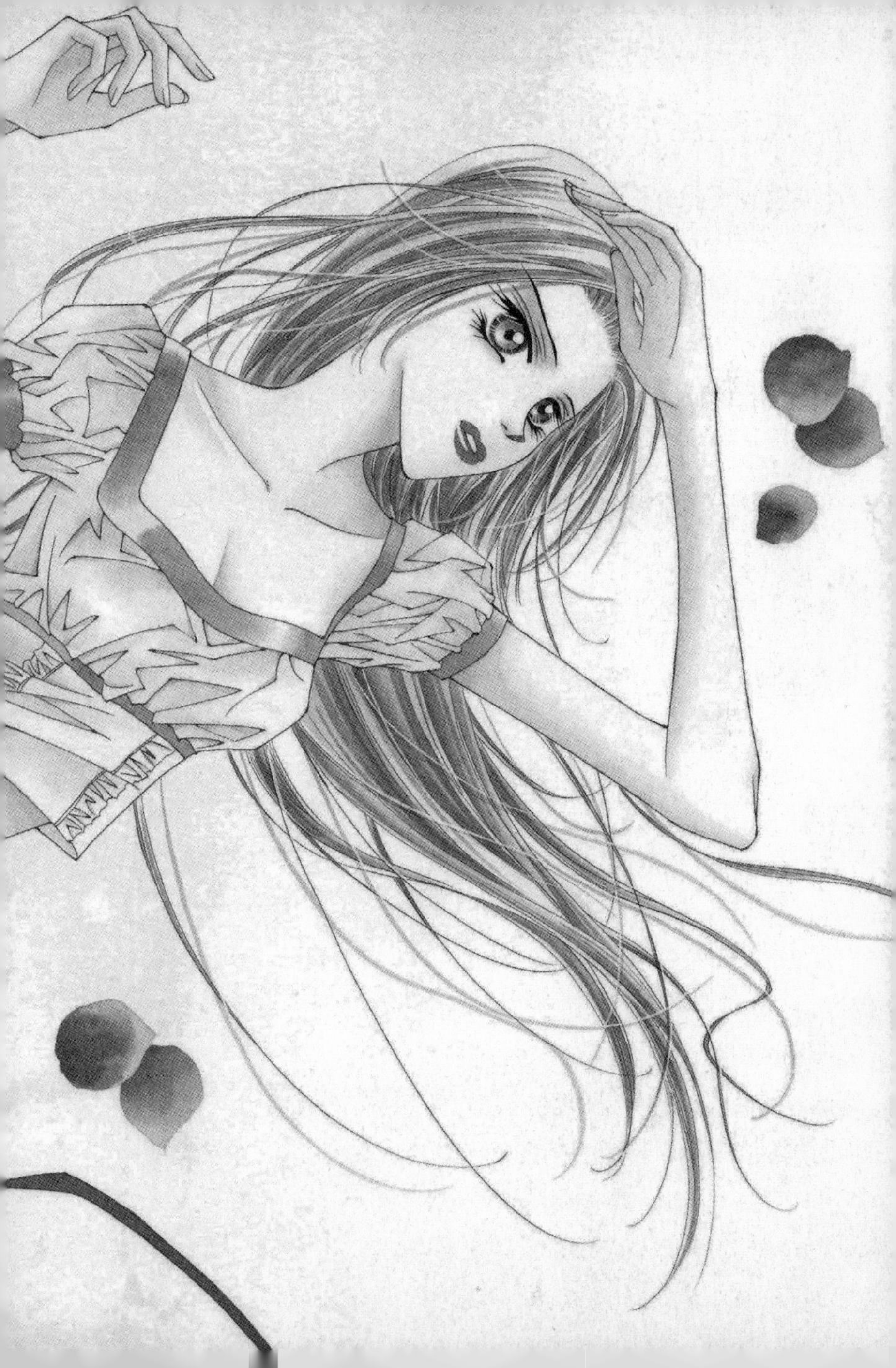

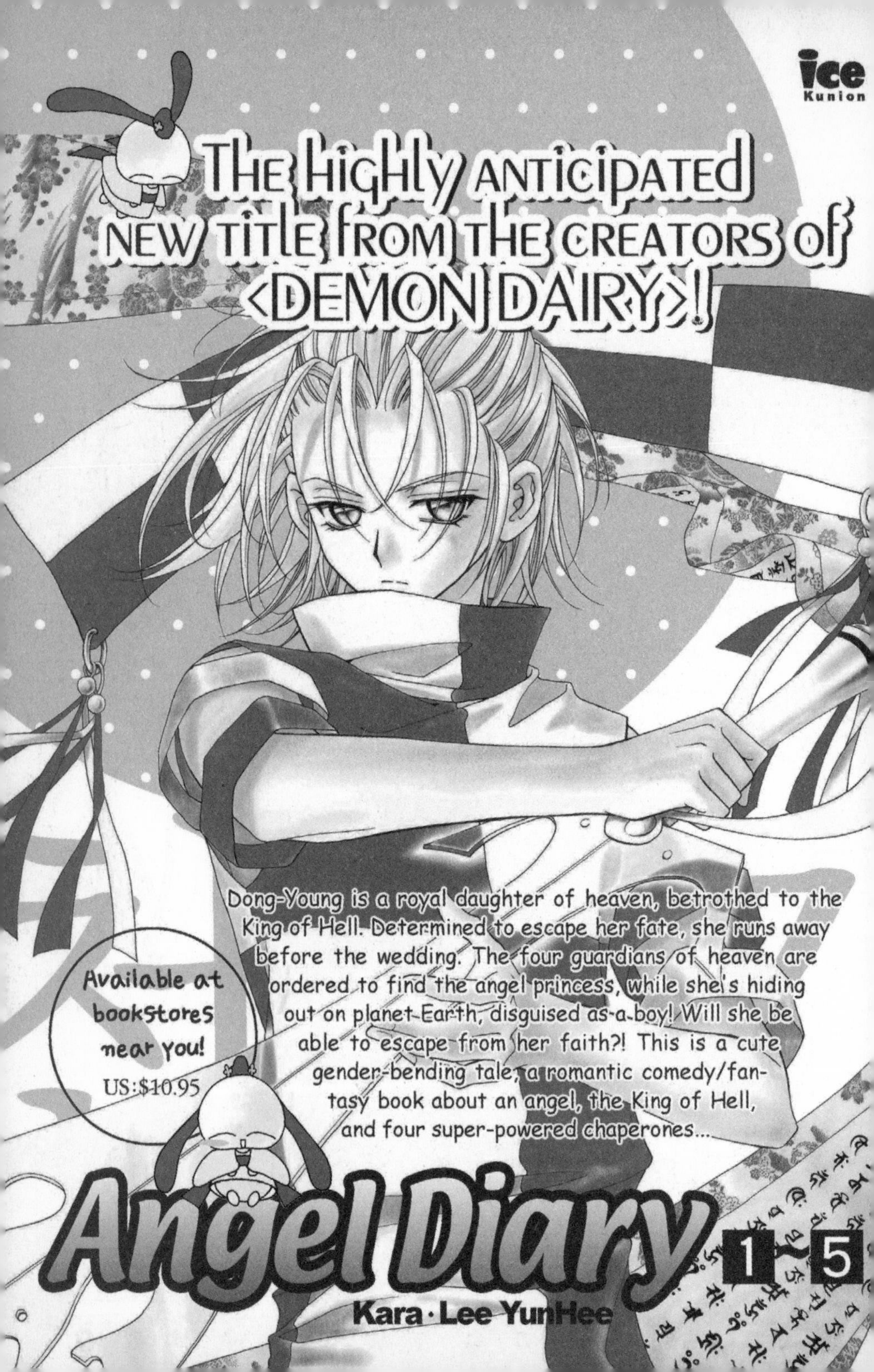
ice
Kunion
The highly anticipated NEW title from the creators of <DEMON DAIRY>!
Dong-Young is a royal daughter of heaven, betrothed to the King of Hell. Determined to escape her fate, she runs away before the wedding. The four guardians of heaven are ordered to find the angel princess, while she's hiding out on planet Earth, disguised as a boy! Will she be able to escape from her faith?! This is a cute gender-bending tale, a romantic comedy/fantasy book about an angel, the King of Hell, and four super-powered chaperones...
Available at bookstores near you!
US:$10.95
Angel Diary 1~5
Kara · Lee YunHee

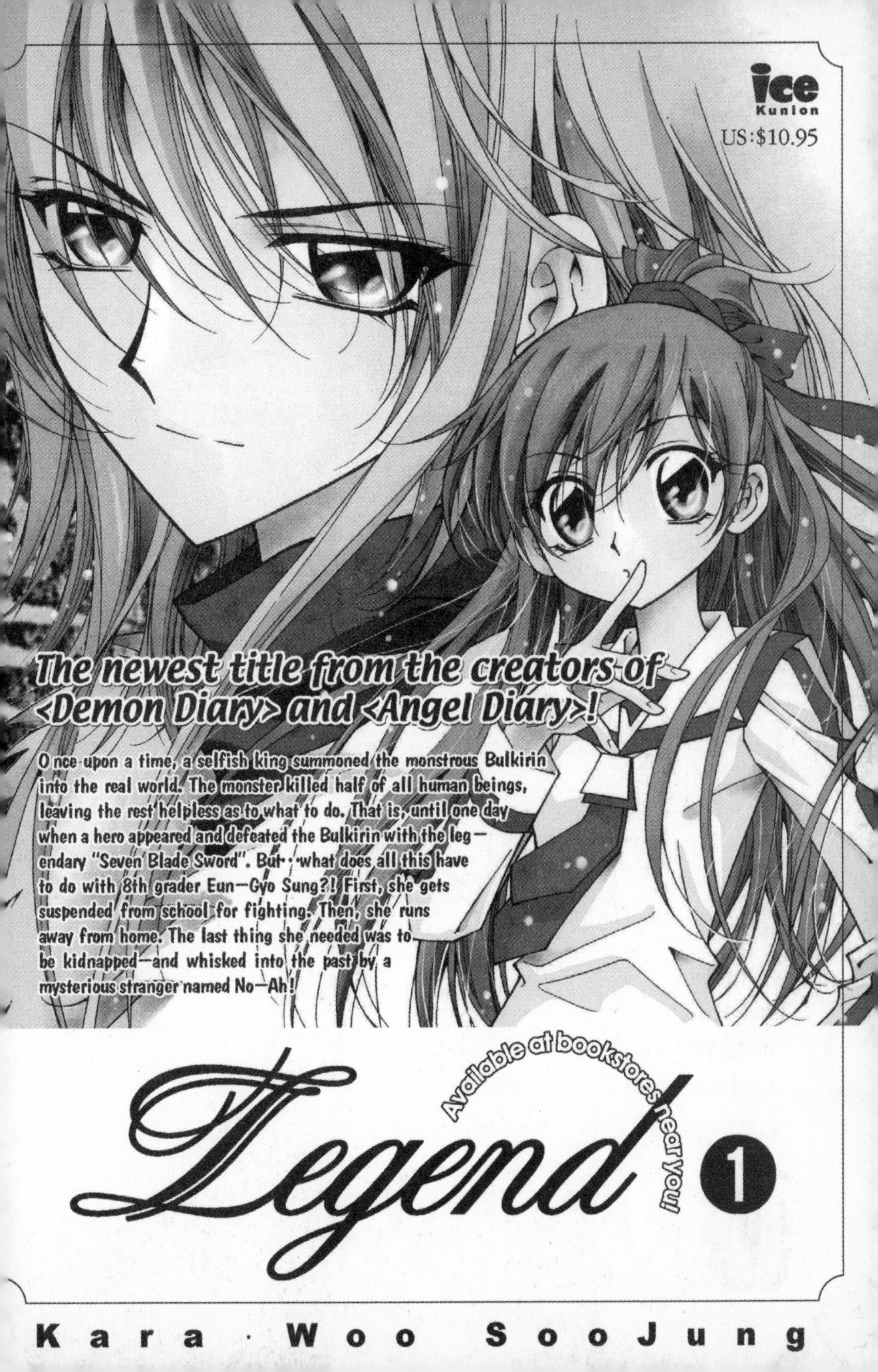
ice Kunion
US:$10.95
The newest title from the creators of <Demon Diary> and <Angel Diary>!
Once upon a time, a selfish king summoned the monstrous Bulkirin into the real world. The monster killed half of all human beings, leaving the rest helpless as to what to do. That is, until one day when a hero appeared and defeated the Bulkirin with the legendary "Seven Blade Sword". But··what does all this have to do with 8th grader Eun-Gyo Sung?! First, she gets suspended from school for fighting. Then, she runs away from home. The last thing she needed was to be kidnapped—and whisked into the past by a mysterious stranger named No-Ah!
Legend 1
Available at bookstores near you!
Kara · Woo SooJung

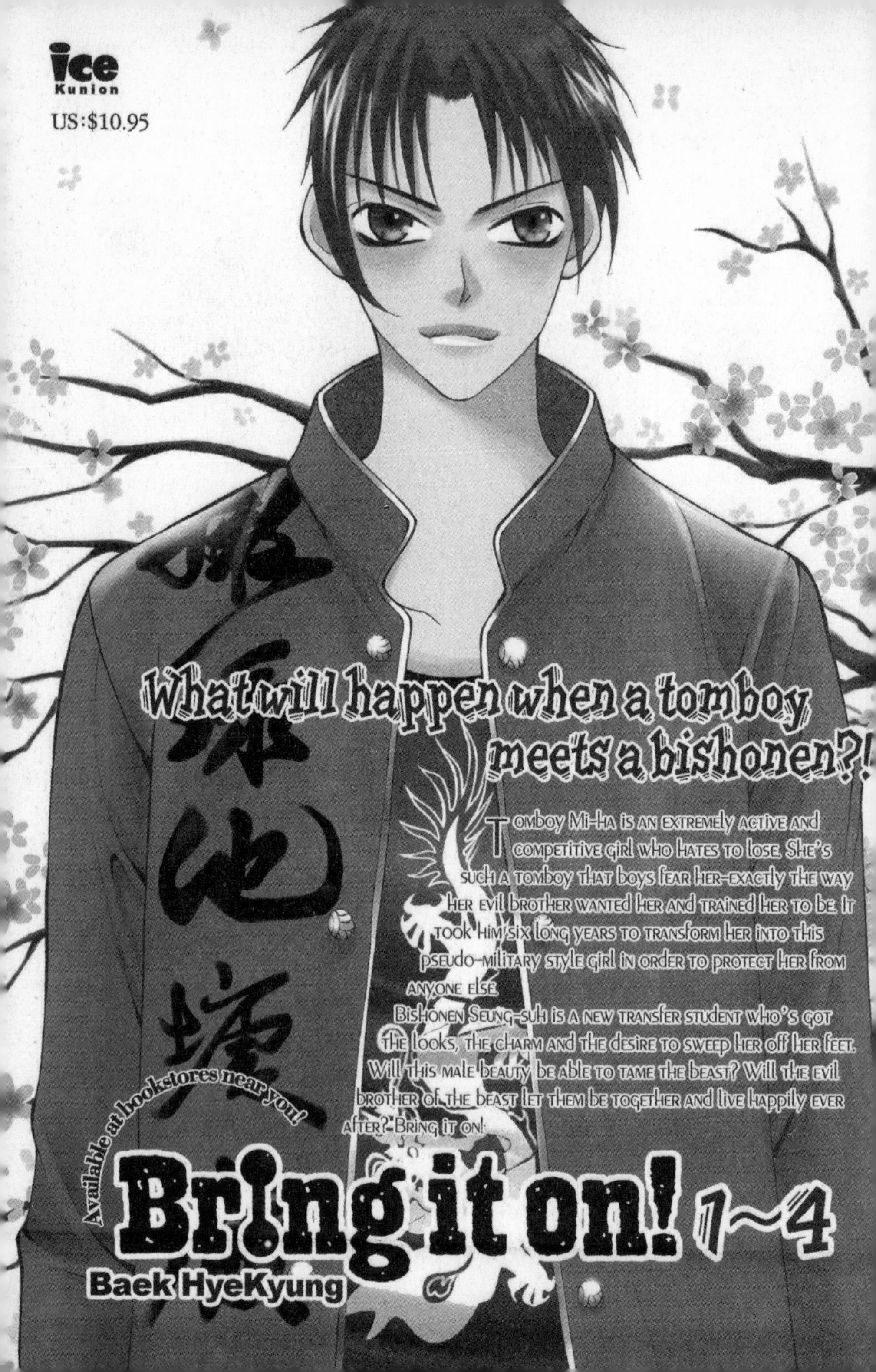
ice
Kunion
US:$10.95
What will happen when a tomboy meets a bishonen?!
Tomboy Mi-ha is an extremely active and competitive girl who hates to lose. She's such a tomboy that boys fear her-exactly the way her evil brother wanted her and trained her to be. It took him six long years to transform her into this pseudo-military style girl in order to protect her from anyone else.
Bishonen Seung-suh is a new transfer student who's got the looks, the charm and the desire to sweep her off her feet. Will this male beauty be able to tame the beast? Will the evil brother of the beast let them be together and live happily ever after? Bring it on!
Available at bookstores near you!
Bring it on! 1~4
Baek HyeKyung

ice
Kunion

US:$10.95

Available at bookstores near you!

CHOCOLAT
1~4

Shin JiSang · Geo

Kum-ji was a little late in getting under the spell of the chart-topping band, DDL. Unable to join the DDL fan club, she almost gives up on meeting her idols, until she develops a cunning plan-to become a member of a rival fan club for the brand-new boy band Yo-I. This way she can act as Yo-I's fan club member and also be together near

How far would you go to meet your favorite boy band?

Yo-I, who always seem to be in the same shows as DDL. Perfect plan...except being a fanatic is a lot more complicated than she expects. Especially when you're actually a fan of someone else. This full-blown love comedy about a fan club will make you laugh, cry, and laugh some more.

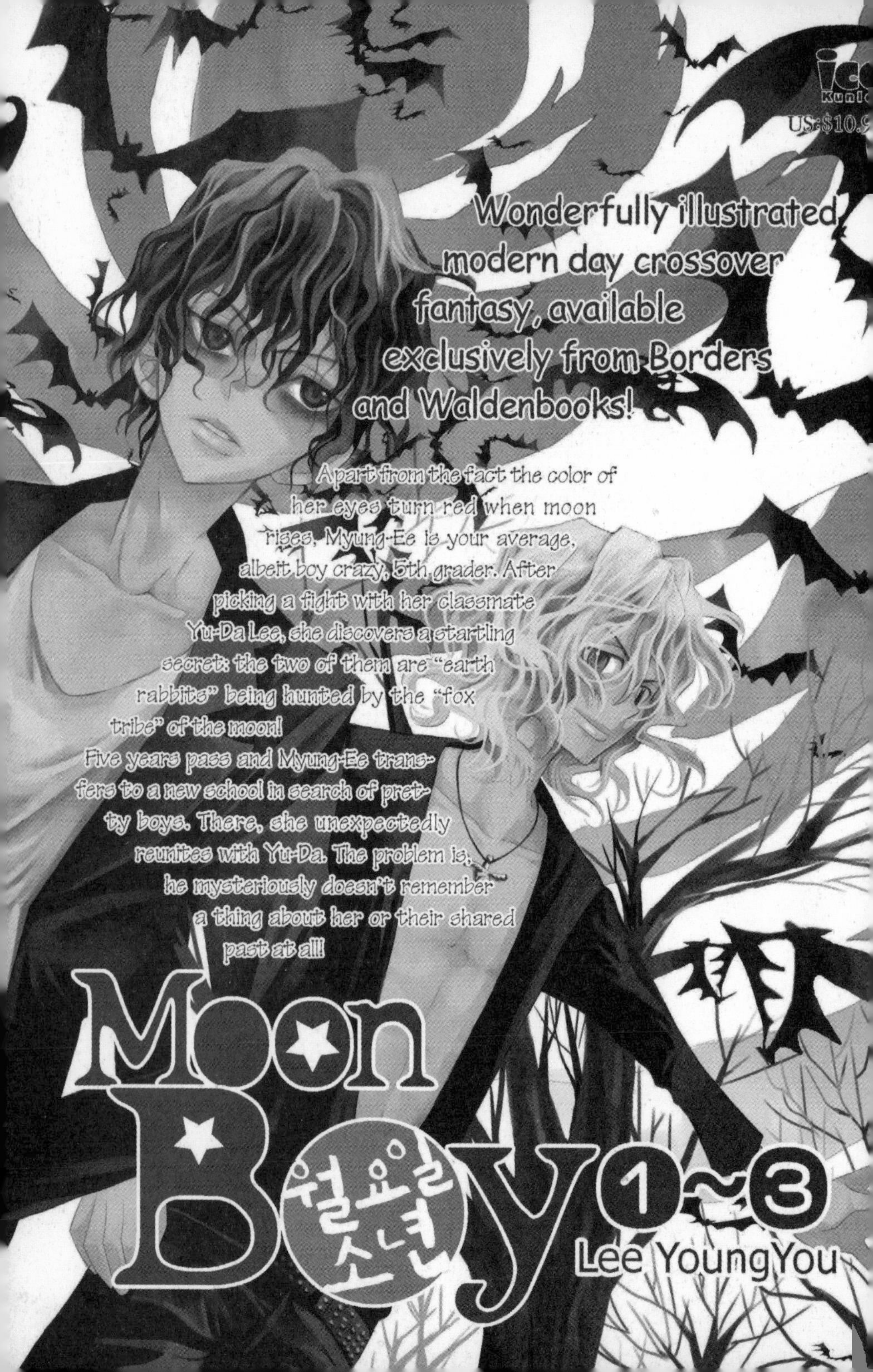
ice Kunio
US:$10.9
Wonderfully illustrated modern day crossover fantasy, available exclusively from Borders and Waldenbooks!
Apart from the fact the color of her eyes turn red when moon rises, Myung-Ee is your average, albeit boy crazy, 5th grader. After picking a fight with her classmate Yu-Da Lee, she discovers a startling secret: the two of them are "earth rabbits" being hunted by the "fox tribe" of the moon!
Five years pass and Myung-Ee transfers to a new school in search of pretty boys. There, she unexpectedly reunites with Yu-Da. The problem is, he mysteriously doesn't remember a thing about her or their shared past at all!
Moon Boy
월요일 소년
1~3
Lee YoungYou

US:$10.95

Sometimes, just being a teenager is hard enough.

Da-Eh, an aspiring manhwa-artist who lives with her father and her little brother, comes across Sun-Nam, a softie whose ultimate goal is simply to become a 'Tough guy'. Whenever these two meet, trouble follows. Meanwhile, Ta-Jun, the hottest guy in town, finds himself drawn to the one girl that his killer smile does not work on-Da-Eh. With their complicated family history hanging on their shoulders, watch how these three teenagers find their way out into the world!

Available at bookstores near you!

HISSING 1~2

Kang EunYoung

Available at bookstores near you!

The Antique Gift Shop 1~3
Lee Eun

Can you feel the souls of the antiques?
Do you believe?

Did you know that an antique possesses a soul of its own? The Antique Gift shop specializes in such items that charm and captivate the buyers that they are destined to belong to. Guided by a mysterious and charismatic shopkeeper, the enchanted relics lead their new owners on a journey into the alternate cosmic universe to their true destinies. Eerily bittersweet and dolefully melancholy, The Antique Gift shop opens up a portal to a world where torn lovers unite, broken friendships are mended, and regrets are resolved. Can you feel the power of the antiques?

Totally new Arabian nights, where Shahrazad is a guy!

US:$10.95

Everyone knows the story of Shahrazad and her wonderful tales in the Arabian Nights. For one thousand and one nights, the stories that she created entertained the mad Sultan and eventually saved her life. In this version, our Shahrazad is a guy who wanted to save his sister from the mad Sultan by disguising himself as a woman. When he puts his life on the line, what kind of strange and wacky stories would he tell? This new twist on one of the greatest classical tales, Arabian Nights, might just keep you awake for another <one thousand and one nights>.

Available at bookstores near you!

One thousand and one nights 1~3

Han SeungHee · Jeon JinSeok

Danbi Original

Cynical Orange vol.3

Story and art by JiUn Yun

Translation SukHee Ryu · HyeYoung Im
English Adaptation Jamie S. Rich
Touch-up and Lettering Terri Delgado · Marshall Dillon
Graphic Design EunKyung Kim

ICE Kunion

English Adaptation Editor HyeYoung Im · J. Torres
Managing Editor Marshall Dillon
Marketing Manager Erik Ko
Assistant Editor SoYeon Kim
Senior Editor JuYoun Lee
Editorial Director DongEun Lee
Managing Director Jackie Lee
Publisher and C.E.O. JaeKook Chun

Published by ICE Kunion
SIGONGSA 2F Yeil Bldg. 1619-4, Seocho-dong, Seocho-gu, Seoul, 137-878, Korea

ISBN : 978-89-527-4494-4

First printing, December 2006
10 9 8 7 6 5 4 3 2 1
Printed in Canada

www.ICEkunion.com/www.koreanmanhwa.com